Blender 3D Cookbook

Build your very own stunning characters in Blender from scratch

Enrico Valenza

PUBLISHING

BIRMINGHAM - MUMBAI

Blender 3D Cookbook

First published: July 2015

Production reference: 1270715

Published by Packt Publishing Ltd.
Livery Place
35 Livery Street
Birmingham B3 2PB, UK.

ISBN 978-1-78398-488-6

www.packtpub.com

Credits

Author

Enrico Valenza

Reviewers

Luo Congyi

Waqas Abdul Majeed

Reynante M. Martinez

Jordan Matelsky

Ian Smithers

Commissioning Editor

Ashwin Nair

Acquisition Editor

Kevin Colaco

Content Development Editor

Rahul Nair

Technical Editor

Taabish Khan

Copy Editors

Ting Baker

Trishya Hajare

Ameesha Smith-Green

Project Coordinator

Judie Jose

Proofreader

Safis Editing

Indexer

Priya Sane

Production Coordinator

Shantanu N. Zagade

Cover Work

Shantanu N. Zagade

About the Author

Enrico Valenza, also known as "EnV" on the Web, is an Italian freelance illustrator, mainly collaborating with publishers such as Mondadori Ragazzi and Giunti as a cover artist for sci-fi and fantasy books.

He graduated from Liceo Artistico Statale in Verona (Italy) and was later a student of illustrator and painter Giorgio Scarato.

When he started to work, computers weren't that much in use among normal people, and he spent the first 15 years of his career doing illustration with traditional media, usually on cardboard; he specialized in the use of the air-graph, a technique particularly esteemed for advertisement work.

When the movie *Jurassic Park* came to theaters, he decided to buy a computer and try this "computer graphic" everyone was talking about. When it comes to the many aspects of CG, he has been totally self-taught; it has been his encounter with the open source philosophy that actually opened a brand new world of possibilities, Blender in particular.

In 2005, he won the Suzanne Award for "Best Animation, Original Idea and Story" with the animation "New Penguoen 2.38."

In 2006, he joined the Orange Team in Amsterdam for the 2 last weeks of production to help in finalizing the shots of the first open source cg animated short movie produced by the Blender Foundation, *Elephants Dream*.

From 2007 to 2008, he has been a lead artist in the Peach Project team for the production of *Big Buck Bunny*, the second Blender Foundation's open movie.

From 2010 to 2011, he has been an art director at CINECA (Bologna, Italy) for the "Museo della Città di Bologna" project, which is the production of a stereoscopic CG-animated documentary made in Blender and which explains the history of the city of Bologna.

Also, being a Blender Certified Trainer, he often collaborates as a cg artist with production studios that have decided to switch their pipeline to open source.

Enrico uses Blender almost on a daily basis for his illustration jobs, rarely to have the illustration rendered straight by the 3D package and more often as a starting point for painting over with other open source applications.

He has conducted several presentations and workshops about Blender and its use in productions.

I would like to say thanks to my family: my father, Giuseppe, and my mother, Licia, for giving me the opportunity to follow what I always thought was my path in life; my wonderful wife, Micaela, and my beautiful daughters, Sara and Elisa, for just being there and encouraging me in the making of this book.

About the Reviewers

Luo Congyi has spent over 4 years on the localization of Blender in China on behalf of Blender as a Blender Foundation Certified Trainer (BFCT), doing such things as translating the training DVD from `http://www.blender.org` and Open Movie Project tutorial series as well as the i18n translation of Blender itself.

Meanwhile, Luo is now maintaining `http://www.blenderget.com` to provide the translated Blender news and tutorials to the whole world as well as the current Open Movie on Gooseberry's blog.

Besides his online work, Luo has written the first and also the best-selling Blender book, *Blender: The Definitive Guide*, *Mechanical Industry Press*, in Chinese, and it is ranked 4.5 on Amazon. Also, he had made some open presentations in several conferences, such as Open Source Technology Conference and HTML5 annual meeting to talk about the Blender.

I would like to appreciate Env's great offer to me; it is my honor to join the review work of this book. Also, I would like to thank my parents and my wife, Li Jie, who supported me during these days.

Waqas Abdul Majeed is a CG Generalist originally from Lahore, Pakistan, but is based in Dubai, UAE. He enrolled in bachelors of animation in 2008 and completed his graduation in 2010. Being an open source technology fan, he started to define his workflow from the commercial tools he widely used to work on his personal or commercial projects on open source and discovered Blender 3D. Ever since, he mostly uses open source technology at work, for freelance and personal projects. He is directing *Luke's Escape - An Animated Short* and has also modeled some environments and props in the film; Luke's Escape was presented at the Blender Conference in Amsterdam in 2013.

He also has a lot of interest in video games; in 2013, he started to explore Unity3D, a well-known game engine, and recently he has been focusing more on the technical side. He works with artists and the programmers, mostly solving problems and finding solutions, but at the same time, he does very much like modeling, texturing, lighting, and rendering. His website is http://waqasmajeed.com and his Twitter handle is @iowaqas.

I am very much thankful to Packt Publishing for giving me the opportunity to review this book; I must say that I've myself learned a lot from this book and I hope the other readers do as well. I also would like to thank my parents, friends, and mentors for always being supportive and believing in what I do.

Reynante M. Martinez is a self-taught computer graphics artist with a variety of backgrounds and skills, including web design, illustration, photography, graphic design, architecture, and other related fields. He has been using Blender (alongside other open source applications) for over 10 years now.

He is currently working as a staff and production artist at Blender Guru. Over the past few years, he has worked as a team leader in several local animation studios, participated in collaborative short films, and also tendered his services as a 3D instructor to several colleges and universities in the Philippines.

I'd like to thank Shipra Chawhan for the patience and tenacity in keeping me updated on things and for this opportunity. I'd also like to extend my gratitude to my fiancée and my family for the utmost support and love.

Jordan Matelsky is a student of neuroscience and computer science at Johns Hopkins University in Baltimore and a co-principal of Medella Medical (http://medellamedical.com), where he seeks to bring beautiful, conscientious designs to the world of medicine and healthcare.

Jordan has been an avid user of Blender since both he and the software were younger and simpler. Now, as an active software developer, he enjoys finding ways to bring music, knowledge, and 3D design to the Internet.

Jordan can be reached at http://jordan.matelsky.com or on Twitter (@j6m8).

I thank my parents, Robin and Paul, for all they have done to nurture my bizarre hobbies and interests. Also, I thank my sister, Loren, who is by far the best sister I have ever had.

Ian Smithers is an experienced software developer specializing in game and web development. In 2002, he started to work at Electronic Arts, which kick-started his career in game development. Over the last 10 years, Ian has acquired a unique set of skills due to his diverse background and experience. Currently, he works as a .NET developer in Melbourne, Australia, but continues to offer a variety of services as a freelance game and app developer. He has most recently completed a VR app using Samsung's Gear VR technology based on Oculus and using Unity. In his spare time, Ian enjoys mathematics and philosophy, and he whittles the hours away on interesting prototypes and catching up on the latest and greatest in video games.

I would like to say thank you to Packt Publishing, especially Judie and Shipra, for their patience and understanding. I would also like to say a huge thank you to my wife, Elain, and of course, our families. I really hope readers enjoy this book; it was a lot of fun to work through.

www.PacktPub.com

Support files, eBooks, discount offers, and more

For support files and downloads related to your book, please visit www.PacktPub.com.

Did you know that Packt offers eBook versions of every book published, with PDF and ePub files available? You can upgrade to the eBook version at www.PacktPub.com and as a print book customer, you are entitled to a discount on the eBook copy. Get in touch with us at service@packtpub.com for more details.

At www.PacktPub.com, you can also read a collection of free technical articles, sign up for a range of free newsletters and receive exclusive discounts and offers on Packt books and eBooks.

https://www2.packtpub.com/books/subscription/packtlib

Do you need instant solutions to your IT questions? PacktLib is Packt's online digital book library. Here, you can search, access, and read Packt's entire library of books.

Why Subscribe?

- Fully searchable across every book published by Packt
- Copy and paste, print, and bookmark content
- On demand and accessible via a web browser

Free Access for Packt account holders

If you have an account with Packt at www.PacktPub.com, you can use this to access PacktLib today and view 9 entirely free books. Simply use your login credentials for immediate access.

Table of Contents

Preface

This cookbook is based on the ultimate 2.7 series of Blender and illustrates the workflow to create from scratch the monster creature Gidiosaurus, a fictional humanoid biped reptilian warrior, almost 2 meters tall, with scaled skin and wearing a sort of simple medieval armor.

So, by the use of recipes in this book, we'll see all the stages that a character's creation workflow usually undergoes in a production pipeline based on the open source software Blender; starting from concept sketches used as reference templates for the modeling and sculpting; going through the re-topology, UDIM unwrapping, rigging, texturing, and shading stages; and finally ending with the lighting, the rendering of a simple walk cycle animation, and also a bit of compositing. You will find quite a lot of stuff in the industry usually solved through the use of different applications, but that can be almost completely tackled just in Blender!

The order of all the stages of such a workflow is mandatory for most of them; for example, all the stages from *Chapter 1, Modeling the Character's Base Mesh*, to *Chapter 4, Re-topology of the High Resolution Sculpted Character's Mesh*, but can also be subjective in others.

In fact, stages such as the rigging and the skinning, the unwrapping of the mesh, the creation of the shaders, and the textures painting are often, at least in my experience, simultaneous or interchangeable. I usually build the rig and make a quick skinning of the mesh to verify that the deformations work correctly and then, if it's the case, I modify the mesh, fix the unwrap, tweak the vertex groups weights, modify the rig, and so on.

That's why in this book, after the unwrapping stage (*Chapter 5, Unwrapping the Low Resolution Mesh*), there are chapters about the rigging, skinning, and animation, and only later there are the chapters about the shaders and the textures creation, which ideally would have been the natural followers. While we are rigging a character, sometimes the need for some modifications in the mesh topology or even in the geometry turns up, usually to allow for better deformation in certain areas; this is the kind of corrections that we prefer to have before the unwrapping and the complex texture painting stages are done.

Because the different stages must be kept separated and explained one by one through recipes, it would be difficult to keep this kind of simultaneity in the cookbook. That's why, in very few cases, you'll find *blank* steps linking to other recipes and some images showing the future effect of the involved processes; for example, in *Chapter 2, Sculpting the Character's Base Mesh*, there are recipes about the different ways to obtain the mesh subdivision that at a certain step link to a later recipe, or in *Chapter 6, Rigging the Low Resolution Mesh*, there are examples of the deformation effects that the rig will have on the already skinned mesh even if the reader hasn't approached the skinning stage yet and so on. If this is the case, it is clarified at the time.

If you are not a total beginner in Blender, you are probably already using your customized version of the User Interface, with your personal preferences as add-ons, modified screens, and whatever else already set in the User Preferences panel.

In this cookbook, by the way, we'll presume to start our workflow with the Factory Settings, which is the basic interface and the preferences situation we have at the very first time we start Blender just after to have downloaded the zip and uncompressed it to some location on our hard drive.

If this the case, in the *Getting ready* section of the recipes, instructions about any required add-on and/or particular settings to be enabled are provided.

In the making of this cookbook, I've used versions of Blender from 2.71 to 2.73a. So, besides the version number that you'll see in the images written in the main header, you can sometimes find a screenshot showing buttons or features not appearing in the other images; such as, for example, for the Node Editor toolbar between versions 2.71 and 2.72, as shown in the following screenshot (only relevant to Cycles):

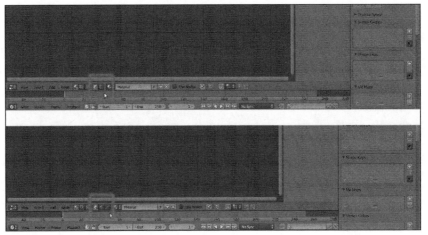

In no case, things like these should be an issue because there aren't many differences in these versions, only improvements, and the provided files have been tested under all of them. Obviously, new features or bug fixes introduced in version 2.73a are not available in the previous ones, so always use the latest official Blender release (also, the new versions 2.74 and 2.75a, although not debated in the cookbook, are OK).

A list of the new features available in the new versions can be found at `http://wiki.blender.org/index.php/Dev:Ref/Release_Notes/2.73`, `http://wiki.blender.org/index.php/Dev:Ref/Release_Notes/2.74`, and `http://wiki.blender.org/index.php/Dev:Ref/Release_Notes/2.75`.

I want to assure you that no Gidiosaurus has been harmed in the making of this cookbook. Moreover, the Gidiosaurus is totally a fictional character and any reference to extinct or still living creatures is totally coincidental and fortuitous. Even more, the name Gidiosaurus (from *Gidio* = Gidio and *saurus* = lizard) is copyrighted; the Gidiosaurus character has been designed, sculpted, and modeled by Enrico Valenza and is released under the Creative Commons license CC BY-NC-ND 4.0 (`http://creativecommons.org/licenses/by-nc-nd/4.0/`). This means that any version of the Gidiosaurus model or the character's textures provided through blend files with this cookbook, besides special distribution permission granted by the author to Packt Publishing for this cookbook, cannot be used for commercial purposes, but only for personal projects and the appropriate credit must always be given anyway.

What this book covers

Chapter 1, Modeling the Character's Base Mesh, explains the different methods to set reference templates in Blender and the use of the Skin modifier to model the character's base mesh.

Chapter 2, Sculpting the Character's Base Mesh, explains how to prepare and sculpt the base mesh.

Chapter 3, Polygonal Modeling of the Character's Accessories, explains the polygonal modeling of the character's accessories and the use of Curves to add detailing.

Chapter 4, Re-topology of the High Resolution Sculpted Character's Mesh, explains how to plan the re-topology through the Grease Pencil and how to use the tools to re-topologize the sculpted mesh.

Chapter 5, Unwrapping the Low Resolution Mesh, explains how to UDIM unwrap the re-topologized mesh.

Chapter 6, Rigging the Low Resolution Mesh, explains the different methods to build the rig in Blender.

Chapter 7, Skinning the Low Resolution Mesh, explains the different methods and tools to skin the character's mesh to the rig.

Chapter 8, Finalizing the Model, explains how to create shape keys, the drivers, the use of the bone's constraints, and the finalizing of the model.

Chapter 9, Animating the Character, explains how to link the asset to be animated from a library, how to proxify it, how to animate a simple walkcycle, and the use of Non Linear Animation.

Chapter 10, Creating the Textures, explains how to paint textures both in Blender Internal and in Cycles, how to make them tileable, and how to bake them.

Chapter 11, Refining the Textures, explains how to bake the details of the sculpted mesh to a normal map, how to create a Vertex Colors map, and the possible use of the Quick Edit tool to paint directly onto the model through an external 2D image editor application.

Chapter 12, Creating the Materials in Cycles, explains the creation of the shaders in Cycles.

Chapter 13, Creating the Materials in Blender Internal, explains the creations of similar shaders in Blender Internal.

Chapter 14, Lighting, Rendering, and a Little Bit of Compositing, explains the setup of the lighting, image based lighting both in Blender Internal and in Cycles, how to render a preview OpenGL playblast, some suggestions to try to avoid fireflies and noise in Cycles, and the compositing of the rendered passes of both the render engines into one single final image.

What you need for this book

The only software strictly needed to put into practice the content of this cookbook is the last official Blender release (from 2.73 to 2.75a). You just have to download it from `http://www.blender.org/download/get-blender`; some Python script may be necessary in some recipes, but for the most part, they should all be included in the Blender package. Eventually, you can quite surely find any missing add-on at `http://wiki.blender.org/index.php/Extensions:2.6/Py/Scripts`.

Any particular texture needed for the exercises in the book is provided as a free download on the Packt Publishing website itself.

Not essential, but handy to have is a 2D image editor, in case you want to adapt your own textures to replace the provided ones; I suggest you try Gimp, an open source image editor that you can download from `http://www.gimp.org`; any other one you prefer is perfect anyway.

Who this book is for

This book is aimed at the professionals that already have good 3D CGI experience with commercial packages and have now decided to try the open source Blender and want to experiment with something more complex than the average tutorials on the web.

However, it's also aimed at the intermediate Blender users who simply want to go some steps further.

It's taken for granted that you already know how to move inside the Blender interface, that you already have 3D modeling knowledge, and also that of basic 3D modeling and rendering concepts, for example, edge-loops, n-gons, or samples.

In any case, it's also possible for a keen beginner to follow this book, by combining it with the manual on the BlenderWiki or preceding it with a basic Blender UI tutorial on the web.

The keyboard/mouse shortcuts for the operations in the recipes are, at least in all the more relevant cases, indicated in brackets.

Sections

In this book, you will find several headings that appear frequently (Getting ready, How to do it, How it works, There's more, and See also).

To give clear instructions on how to complete a recipe, we use these sections as follows:

Getting ready

This section tells you what to expect in the recipe and describes how to set up any software or any preliminary settings required for the recipe.

How to do it...

This section contains the steps required to follow the recipe.

How it works...

This section usually consists of a detailed explanation of what happened in the previous section.

There's more...

This section consists of additional information about the recipe in order to make the reader more knowledgeable about the recipe.

See also

This section provides helpful links to other useful information for the recipe.

Conventions

In this book, you will find a number of text styles that distinguish between different kinds of information. Here are some examples of these styles and an explanation of their meaning.

Code words in text, database table names, folder names, filenames, file extensions, pathnames, dummy URLs, user input, and Twitter handles are shown as follows: "Reopen the `Gidiosaurus_base_mesh.blend` file."

Sequences of operations, such as for example adding nodes to the **Node Editor** or objects in the 3D view, are written as follows: "*Shift + A* | **Texture** | **Voronoi Texture**."

This means that you need to press the *Shift* and the *A* keys at the same time, then move the mouse pointer on the **Texture** item in a pop-up menu and click or select the desired final item.

New terms and **important words** are shown in bold. Words that you see on the screen, for example, in menus or dialog boxes, appear in the text like this: "Under the **Empty** subpanel, click on the **Open** button."

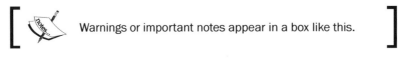

Warnings or important notes appear in a box like this.

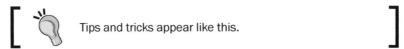

Tips and tricks appear like this.

Reader feedback

Feedback from our readers is always welcome. Let us know what you think about this book—what you liked or disliked. Reader feedback is important for us as it helps us develop titles that you will really get the most out of.

To send us general feedback, simply e-mail feedback@packtpub.com, and mention the book's title in the subject of your message.

If there is a topic that you have expertise in and you are interested in either writing or contributing to a book, see our author guide at www.packtpub.com/authors.

Customer support

Now that you are the proud owner of a Packt book, we have a number of things to help you to get the most from your purchase.

Downloading the example code

You can download the example code files from your account at http://www.packtpub.com for all the Packt Publishing books you have purchased. If you purchased this book elsewhere, you can visit http://www.packtpub.com/support and register to have the files e-mailed directly to you.

Downloading the color images of this book

We also provide you with a PDF file that has color images of the screenshots/diagrams used in this book. The color images will help you better understand the changes in the output. You can download this file from https://www.packtpub.com/sites/default/files/downloads/B00286_Graphics.pdf.

Errata

Although we have taken every care to ensure the accuracy of our content, mistakes do happen. If you find a mistake in one of our books—maybe a mistake in the text or the code—we would be grateful if you could report this to us. By doing so, you can save other readers from frustration and help us improve subsequent versions of this book. If you find any errata, please report them by visiting http://www.packtpub.com/submit-errata, selecting your book, clicking on the **Errata Submission Form** link, and entering the details of your errata. Once your errata are verified, your submission will be accepted and the errata will be uploaded to our website or added to any list of existing errata under the Errata section of that title.

To view the previously submitted errata, go to https://www.packtpub.com/books/content/support and enter the name of the book in the search field. The required information will appear under the **Errata** section.

Piracy

Piracy of copyrighted material on the Internet is an ongoing problem across all media. At Packt, we take the protection of our copyright and licenses very seriously. If you come across any illegal copies of our works in any form on the Internet, please provide us with the location address or website name immediately so that we can pursue a remedy.

Please contact us at copyright@packtpub.com with a link to the suspected pirated material.

We appreciate your help in protecting our authors and our ability to bring you valuable content.

Questions

If you have a problem with any aspect of this book, you can contact us at questions@packtpub.com, and we will do our best to address the problem.

1

Modeling the Character's Base Mesh

In this chapter, we will cover the following recipes:

- ▶ Setting templates with the Images as Planes add-on
- ▶ Setting templates with the Image Empties method
- ▶ Setting templates with the Background Images tool
- ▶ Building the character's base mesh with the Skin modifier

Introduction

In this chapter, we are going to do two things: set up templates to be used as a reference for the modeling, and build up a base mesh for the sculpting of the character.

To set up templates in a Blender scene, we have at least three different methods to choose from: the **Images as Planes** add-on, the **Image Empties** method, and the **Background Images** tool.

A base mesh is usually a very low poly and simple mesh roughly shaped to resemble the final character's look. There are several ways to obtain a base mesh: we can use a ready, freely downloadable mesh to be adjusted to our goals, or we can model it from scratch, one polygon at a time. What's quite important is that it should be made from all quad faces.

To build the base mesh for our character, we are going to use one of the more handy and useful modifiers added to Blender: the **Skin** modifier. However, first, let us add our templates.

Setting templates with the Images as Planes add-on

In this recipe, we'll set the character's templates by using the **Images as Planes** add-on.

Getting ready

The first thing to do is to be sure that all the required add-ons are enabled in the preferences; in this first recipe, we need the **Images as Planes** and **Copy Attributes Menu** add-ons. When starting Blender with the factory settings, they appear gray in the **User Preferences** panel's **Add-ons** list, meaning that they are not enabled yet. So, we'll do the following:

1. Call the **User Preferences** panel (*Ctrl + Alt + U*) and go to the **Add-ons** tab.

2. Under the **Categories** item on the left-hand side of the panel, click on **3D View**.

3. Check the empty little checkbox on the right-hand side of the **3D View: Copy Attributes Menu** add-on to enable it.

4. Go back to the **Categories** item on the left-hand side of the panel and click on **Import-Export**.

5. Scroll down the add-ons list to the right-hand side to find the **Import-Export: Import Images as Planes** add-on (usually, towards the middle of the long list).

6. Enable it, and then click on the **Save User Settings** button to the left-bottom of the panel and close it.

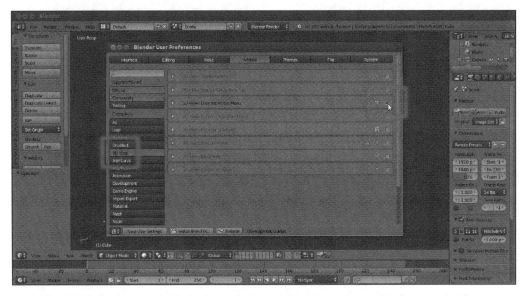

The User Preferences panel with the Categories list and the Addons tab to enable the several add-ons

There are still a few things we should do to prepare the 3D scene and make our life easier:

7. Delete the already selected **Cube** primitive.

8. Select the **Lamp** and the **Camera** and move them on to a different layer; I usually have them on the **sixth** layer (*M* key), in order to keep free and empty both the first and second rows of the left layer's block.

9. The **Outliner** can be found in the top-right corner of the default workspace. It shows a list view of the scene. Set **Display Mode** of the **Outliner** to **Visible Layers**.

10. Lastly, save the file as `Gidiosaurus_base_mesh.blend`.

How to do it...

Although not strictly necessary, it would be better to have the three (at least in the case of a biped character, the **Front**, **Side**, and **Back** view) templates as separated images. This will allow us to load a specific one for each view, if necessary. Also, to facilitate the process, all these images should be the same height in pixels.

In our case, the required three views are provided for you in the files that accompany this book. You will find them in the `templates` folder. The **Import Images as Planes** add-on will take care of loading them into the scene:

1. Left-click on **File | Import | Images as Planes** in the top-left menu on the main header of the Blender UI.

2. On the page that just opened, go to the **Material Settings** column on the left-hand side (under the **Import Images as Planes** options) and enable the **Shadeless** item. Then, browse to the location where you placed your `templates` folder and load the `gidiosaurus_front.png` image:

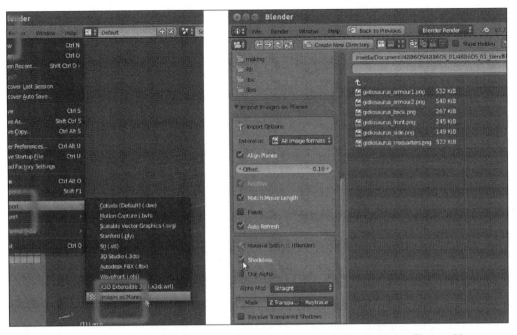

The Import pop-up menu and the material settings subpanel of the Import Images as Planes add-on

3. Rotate 90 degrees on the *x* axis (*R* | *X* | **90** | *Enter*) of the **Plane** that just appeared at the center of the scene (at the **3D Cursor** location, actually; to reset the position of the **3D Cursor** at the center of the scene, press the *Shift + C* keys).

4. Press *N* to call the **Properties** sidepanel on the right-hand side of the active 3D window, and then go to the **Shading** subpanel and enable the **Textured Solid** item.

5.   Press *1* on the numpad to go to the **Front** view:

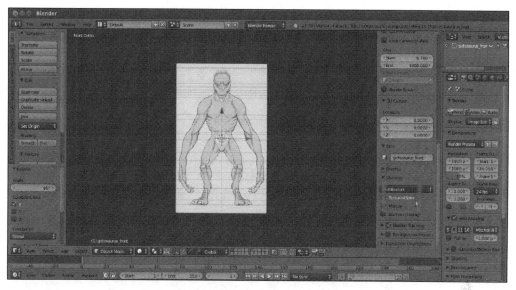

The imported plane with the relative UV-mapped image

Now, we know that our **Gidiosaurus** is a **2.5** meters tall beast. So, assuming that **1 Blender Unit** is equal to **1 meter**, we must scale the plane to make the character's front template **two and a half Blender Units** tall (Note that it is not the plane that must be 2.5 units tall, it's the character's shape inside the plane).

6.   Add an **Empty** to the scene (*Shift + A* | **Empty** | **Plain Axes**).

7.   Duplicate it and move it **2.5** units up on the *z* axis (*Shift + D* | *Z* | **2.5** | *Enter*).

8.   Go to the **Outliner** and click on the arrows on the side of the names of the two **Empties (Empty** and **Empty.001**), in order to make them gray and the **Empties** not selectable.

9.   Select the **Plane** and move it to align the bottom (feet) guideline to the horizontal arm of the first **Empty** (you actually have to move it on the *z* axis by **0.4470**, but note that by pressing the *Ctrl* key, you can restrict movements to the grid and with *Ctrl + Shift*, you can have even finer control).

10. Be sure that the **3D Cursor** is at the object origin, and press the period key to switch *Pivot center for rotation/scaling* to the **3D Cursor**.

11. Press S to scale the **Plane** bigger and align the top-head guideline to the horizontal arm of the second **Empty** (you have to scale it to a value of **2.8300**):

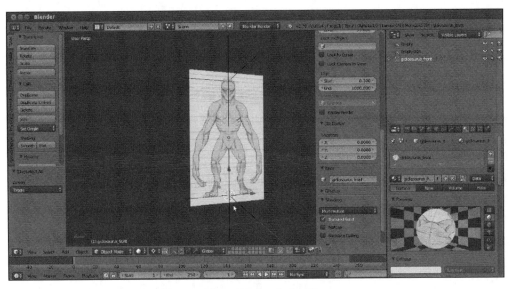

The properly scaled plane in the 3D scene

12. Left-click again on **File | Import | Images as Planes** in the top-left menu on the main header of the Blender UI.

13. Browse to the location where you placed your `templates` folder and this time load the `gidiosaurus_side.png` image.

14. *Shift* + right-click on the first **Plane** (`gidiosaurus_front.png`) to select it and make it the active one. Then, press *Ctrl + C* and from the **Copy Attributes** pop-up menu, select **Copy Location**.

15. Press *Ctrl + C* again and this time select **Copy Rotation**; press *Ctrl + C* one more time and select **Copy Scale**.

16. Right-click to select the second **Plane** (`gidiosaurus_side.png`) in the 3D view, or click on its name in the **Outliner**, and rotate it 90 degrees on the z axis (*R | Z |* **90** *| Enter*).

17. Optionally, you can move the second **Plane** to the second layer (*M |* second button on the **Move to Layer** panel).

18. Again, left-click on **File | Import | Images as Planes**, browse to the `templates` folder, and load the `gidiosaurus_back.png` image.

19. Repeat from step 12 to step 15 and move the third **Plane** on a different layer.

20. Save the file.

How it works...

We used a Python script, which is an add-on, to import planes into our scene that are automatically UV-mapped with the selected image, and inherit the images' height/width aspect ratio.

To have the textures/templates clearly visible from any angle in the 3D view, we have enabled the **Shadeless** option for the **Planes** materials; we did this directly in the importer preferences. We can also set each material to shadeless later in the **Material** window.

We then used another add-on to copy the attributes from a selected object, in order to quickly match common parameters such as location, scale, and rotation:

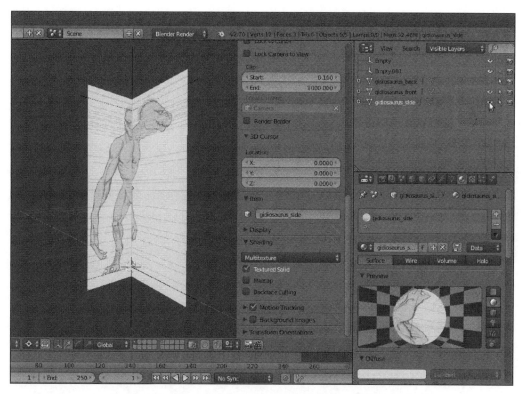

The template planes aligned to the x and y axis (Front and Side views)

The imported **Planes** can be placed on different layers for practicality; they can also be on a single layer and their visibility can be toggled on and off by clicking on the eye icon in the **Outliner**.

Setting templates with the Image Empties method

In this recipe, we'll set the character's templates by using **Image Empties**.

Getting ready

For this and the following recipes, there is no need for any particular preparations. Anyway, it is handy to prepare the two **Empties** to have markers in the 3D view for the **2.5** meters height of the character; so we'll do the following:

1. Start a brand new Blender session and delete the already selected **Cube** primitive.

2. Select the **Lamp** and **Camera** and move them on a different layer; I usually have them on the **sixth** layer, in order to keep free and empty both the first and second rows of the left layer's block.

3. Add an **Empty** to the scene (*Shift + A* | **Empty** | **Plain Axes**).

4. Duplicate it and move it **2.5** units up on the z axis (*Shift + D* | *Z* | **2.5** | *Enter*).

5. Go to the **Outliner** and click on the arrows on the side of the names of the two **Empties** (**Empty** and **Empty.001**), in order to make them gray and the **Empties** not selectable.

6. Save the file as Gidiosaurus_base_mesh.blend.

How to do it...

So, now we are going to place the first **Image Empty** in the scene:

1. Add an **Empty** to the scene (*Shift + A* | **Empty** | **Image**; it's the last item in the list).

2. Go to the **Object Data** window in the main **Properties** panel on the right-hand side of the Blender UI; under the **Empty** subpanel, click on the **Open** button.

3. Browse to the templates folder and load the gidiosaurus_front.png image.

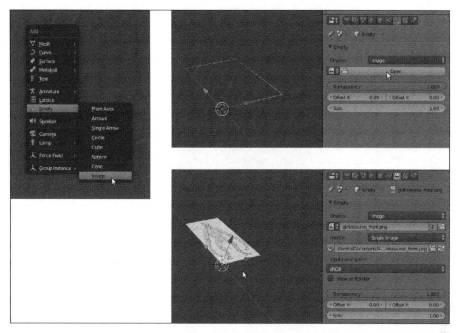

The Add pop-up menu and the Image Empty added to the 3D scene, with the settings to load and set the image

4. Set the **Offset X** value to **-0.50** and **Offset Y** to **-0.05**. Set the **Size** value to **2.830**:

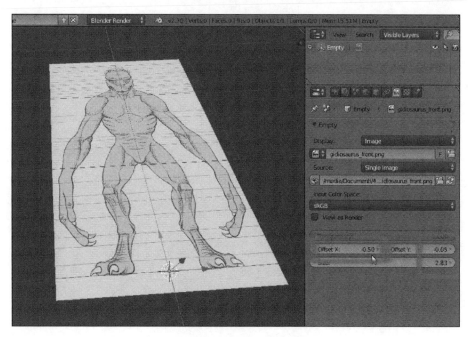

The Offset and Size settings

5. Rotate the **Empty** 90 degrees on the x axis (*R* | *X* | **90** | *Enter*).

6. Go to the **Outliner** and rename it `Empty_gidiosaurus_front`.

7. Duplicate it (*Shift + D*), rotate it 90 degrees on the z axis, and in the **Outliner**, rename it as `Empty_gidiosaurus_side`.

8. In the **Empty** subpanel under the **Object Data** window, click on the little icon (showing **3** users for that data block) on the right-hand side of the image name under **Display**, in order to make it a single user. Then, click on the little folder icon on the right-hand side of the image path to go inside the `templates` folder again, and load the `gidiosaurus_side.png` image.

9. Reselect **Empty_gidiosaurus_front** and press *Shift + D* to duplicate it.

10. Go to the **Empty** subpanel under the **Object Data** window, click on the little icon (showing **3** users for that datablock) on the right-hand side of the image name under **Display**, in order to make it a single user. Then, click on the little folder icon on the right-hand side of the image path to go inside the `templates` folder again, and this time load the `gidiosaurus_back.png` image.

11. Go to the **Outliner** and rename it `Empty_gidiosaurus_back`.

How it works...

We have used one of the most underrated (well, in my opinion) tools in Blender: **Empties,** which can show images! Compared to the **Images as Planes** add-on, this has some advantages: these are not 3D geometry and the images are also visible in the 3D view without the **Textured Solid** option enabled (under **Shading**) and in **Wireframe** mode.

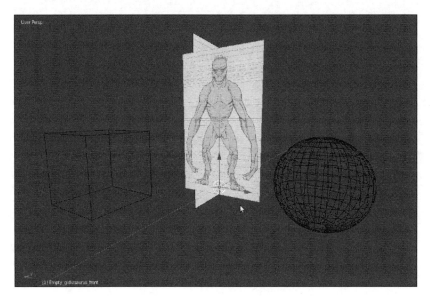

The Image Empties appear as textured also in Wireframe viewport shading mode

Exactly, as for the imported **Planes** of the former recipe, the visibility in the 3D view of the **Image Empties** can be toggled on and off by clicking on the eye icon in the **Outliner**.

Setting templates with the Background Images tool

In this recipe, we'll set the character's templates by using the **Background Images** tool.

Getting ready

As in the former recipe, no need for any particular preparations; just carry out the preparatory steps as mentioned in the *Getting ready* section of the previous recipe.

How to do it...

So let's start by adding the templates as background images; that is, as reference images only visible in the background in **Ortho** view mode and, differently from the previous recipes, not as 3D objects actually present in the middle of the scene:

1. Press *1* on the numpad to switch to the orthographic **Front** view and press *Alt + Home* to center the view on the **3D Cursor**.

2. If not already present, press *N* to bring up the **Properties** sidepanel to the right-hand side of the 3D window; scroll down to reach the **Background Images** subpanel and enable it with the checkbox. Then click on the little arrow to expand it.

3. Click on the **Add Image** button; in the new option panel that appears, click on the **Open** button and browse to the `templates` folder to load the `gidiosaurus_front.png` image.

4. Click on the little window to the side of the **Axis** item and switch from **All Views** to **Front**, and then set the **Opacity** slider to **1.000**.

5. Increase the **Y** offset value to make the bottom/feet guideline of the reference image aligned to the horizontal arm of the first **Empty** (you have to set it to **0.780**).

6. Scale **Size** smaller, using both the **Empties** that we set as references for the **2.5** meters height of the creature (you actually have to set the **Scale** value to **0.875**).

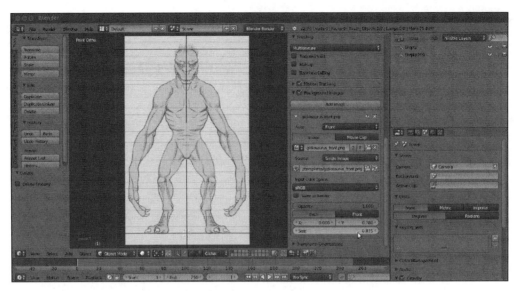

The background image scaled and positioned through the settings in the N sidepanel

7. Click on the little white arrow on the top-left side of the `gidiosaurus_front.png` subwindow to collapse it.

8. Click on the **Add Image** button again; then, in the new option panel, click on the **Open** button, browse to the `templates` folder, and load the `gidiosaurus_side.png` image. Then, set the **Axis** item to **Right**, **Opacity** to **1.000**, **Scale** to **0.875**, and **Y** to **0.780**.

9. Repeat the operation for the `gidiosaurus_back.png` image, set **Axis** to **Back**, and so on.

Press *3* on the numpad to switch to the **Side** view, *1* to switch to the **Front** view, and *Ctrl + 1* to switch to the **Back** view, but remember that you must be in the **Ortho** mode (*5* key on the numpad) to see the background templates:

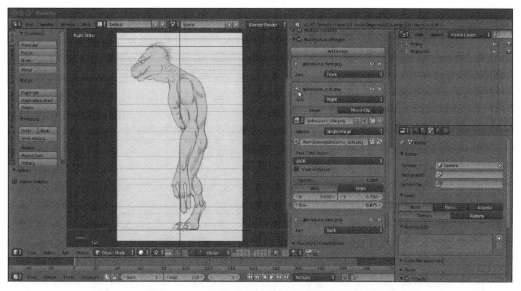

The N sidepanel settings to assign the background image to a view

Building the character's base mesh with the Skin modifier

In the previous recipes, we saw three different ways to set up the template images; just remember that one method doesn't exclude the others, so in my opinion, the best setup you can have is: **Image Empties** on one layer (visibility toggled using the eye icons in the **Outliner**) together with **Background Images**. This way you can not only have templates visible in the three orthographic views, but also in the perspective view (and this can sometimes be really handy).

However, whatever the method you choose, now it's time to start to build the character's base mesh. To do this, we are going to use the **Skin** modifier.

Getting ready

First, let's prepare the scene:

1. In case it's needed, reopen the `Gidiosaurus_base_mesh.blend` file.

2. Click on an empty scene layer to activate it; for example, the **11th**.

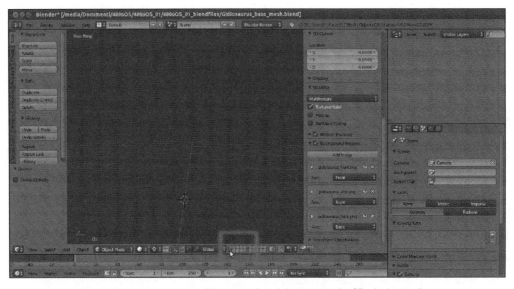

The starting empty scene and the scene layer's buttons on the 3D window toolbar

3. Be sure that the **3D Cursor** is at the center of the scene (*Shift + C*).

4. Add a **Plane** (press *Shift + A* and go to **Mesh | Plane**). If you are working with the **Factory Settings**, you must now press *Tab* to go in to **Edit Mode**, and then *Shift + right-click* to deselect just one vertex.

5. Press *X* and delete the three vertices that are still selected.

6. Right-click to select the remaining vertex and put it at the cursor location in the center of the scene (*Shift + S*, and then select **Selection to Cursor**).

7. Go to the **Object Modifiers** window on the main **Properties** panel, to the right-hand side, and assign a **Skin** modifier; a cube appears around the vertex. Uncheck **X** under **Symmetry Axes** in the modifier's panel:

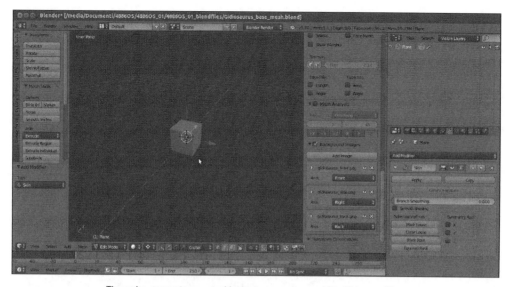

The cube geometry created by just one vertex and the Skin modifier

8. Assign a **Mirror** modifier and check **Clipping**.

9. Assign a **Subdivision Surface** modifier and check **Optimal Display**.

10. Go to the toolbar of the 3D view to click on the *Limit selection to visible* icon and disable it; the icon appears only in **Edit Mode** and in all the viewport shading modes, except for **Wireframe** and **Bounding Box**, and has the appearance of a cube with the vertices selected:

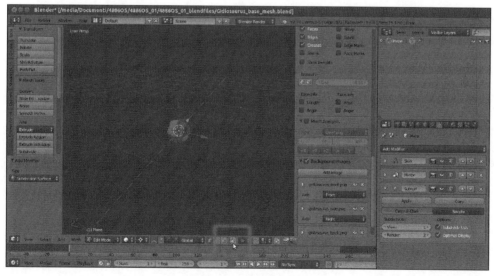

The "Limit selection to visible" button on the 3D viewport toolbar and the cube geometry subdivided through the Subdivision Surface modifier

11. Press *3* on the numpad to go in the **Side** view:

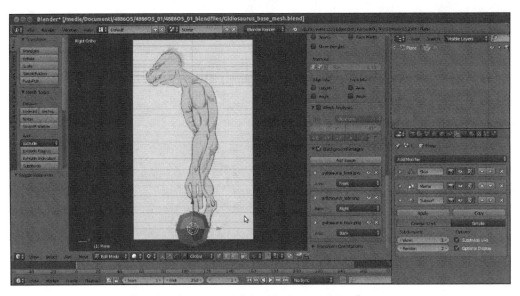

The created geometry and the side-view template reference

How to do it...

We are now going to move and extrude the vertex according to our template images, working as guides, and therefore generating a 3D geometry (thanks to the **Skin** modifier):

1. Press *G* and move the vertex to the pelvis area. Then, press *Ctrl + A* and move the mouse cursor towards the vertex to lower the weight/influence of the vertex itself on the generated mesh; scaling it smaller to fit the hip size showing on the template:

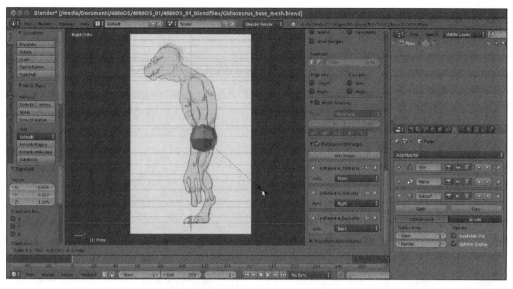

Moving the geometry to the character's pelvis area

2. Press *E* and extrude the vertex by moving it up on the *z* axis; place it at the bottom of the rib cage.

3. Go on extruding the vertex by following the lateral shape of the character in the template. Don't be worried about the volumes; for the moment, just build a *stick-figure* going up the torso:

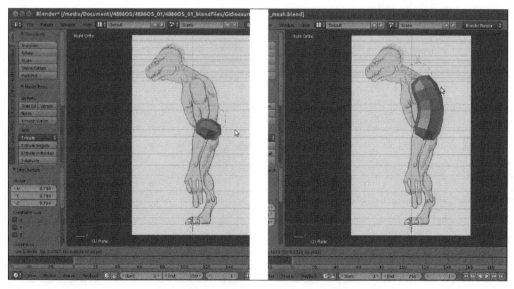

Extruding the vertices to create a new geometry

4. Proceed to the neck and stop at the attachment of the head location.

5. Select the last two vertices you extruded; press *Ctrl + A* and move the mouse cursor towards them to scale down their influence in order to provide a slim-looking neck:

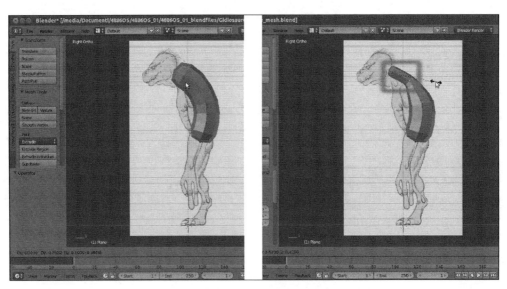

Scaling down the influence of the vertices

6. Press *1* on the numpad to switch to the **Front** view, and then select the bottom vertex and extrude it down to cover the base of the creature's pelvis. Press *Ctrl + A | X* to scale it only on the *x* axis:

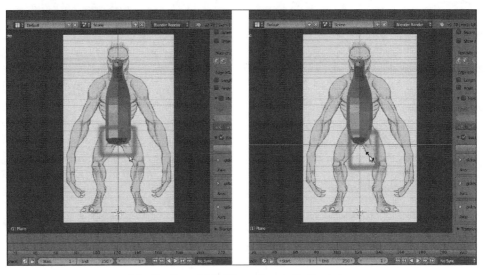

Adjusting the weight of the vertices in the Front view

7. Go to the **Mirror** modifier and uncheck the **Clipping** item.

8. Select the middle thorax vertex and extrude it to the right-hand side to build the shoulder. Press *Ctrl + A* to scale it smaller:

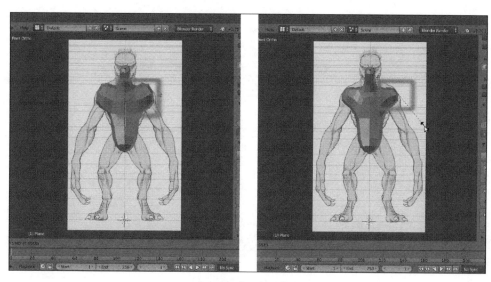

Creating the shoulders

9. Extrude the shoulder vertex, following the arm shape, and stop at the wrist; select the just-extruded arms' vertices and use *Ctrl + A* to scale them smaller.

10. Reselect the shoulder vertex, and use *Shift + V* to slide it along the shoulder's edge in order to adjust the location and fix the area shape:

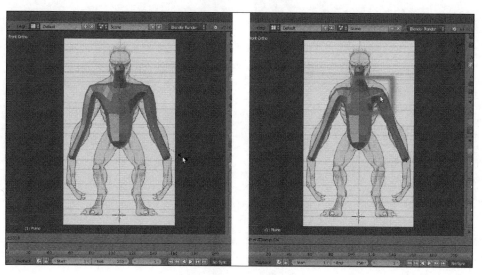

Creating the arms

11. Select the middle thorax vertex we extruded the shoulder from and go to the **Skin** modifier; click on the **Mark Loose** button:

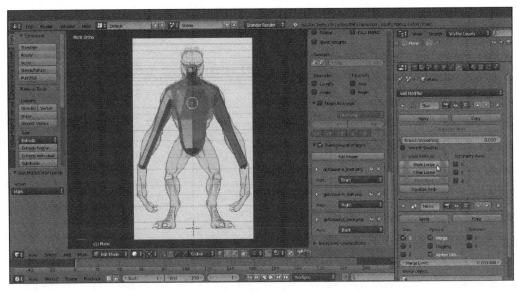

Making a more natural transition from the thorax to the arms

12. Select the second vertex from the bottom and extrude it to the right-hand side to build the hip, and then extrude again and stop at the knee. Use *Ctrl + A* on the vertex to make it smaller:

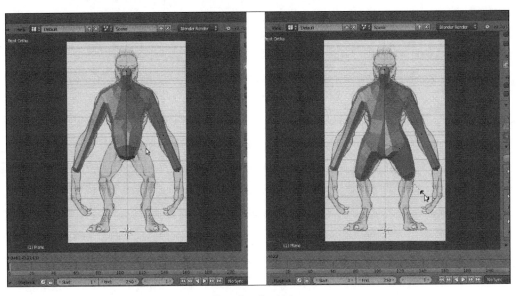

Extruding the thighs

13. Go on extruding the vertex to build the leg. Then, select the wrist vertex and extrude it to build the hand:

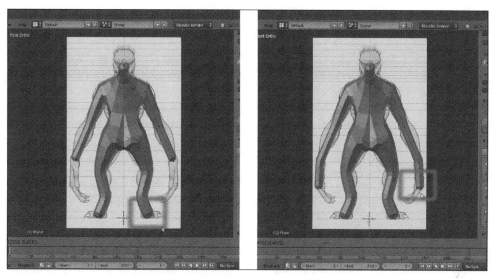

Extruding to complete the leg

14. Press *3* to go to the **Side** view.

15. Individually, select the vertices of the knee, ankle, and foot, and move them to be aligned with the character's posture (you can use the widget for this and, if needed, you can press *Z* to go in to **Wireframe** viewport shading mode); do the same with the vertices of the arm:

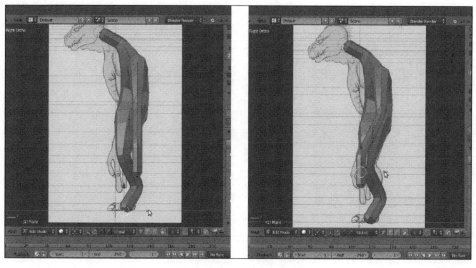

Adjusting the arm's position

16. Select the vertices of the shoulder and elbow, and move them forward according to the template position; do the same with the vertices of the neck and waist:

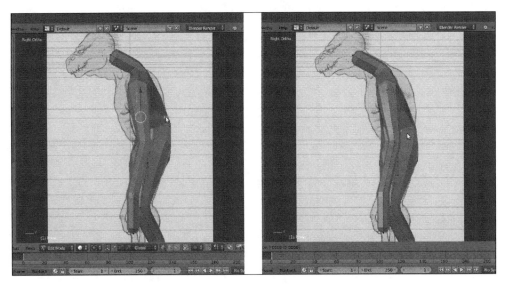

Adjusting the position of the shoulders, thorax, and neck

17. Select the vertex connecting the shoulder to the thorax and use *Shift + V* to slide it upwards, in order to make room for more vertices in the chest area. Use *Shift* to select the vertex at the bottom of the rib cage and press *W*; in the **Specials** pop-up menu, select **Subdivide** and, right after the subdivision, in the option panel at the bottom-left of the Blender UI, set **Number of Cuts** to **2**:

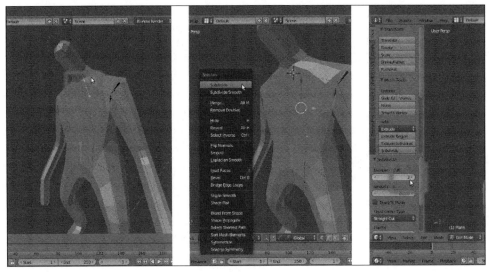

Subdividing an edge

18. In the **Side** view, select the upper one of the new vertices and use *Ctrl + A* to scale it bigger. Adjust the position and scale of the vertices around that area (neck and shoulder) to obtain, as much as possible, a shape that is more regular and similar to the template. However, don't worry too much about a perfect correspondence, it can be adjusted later:

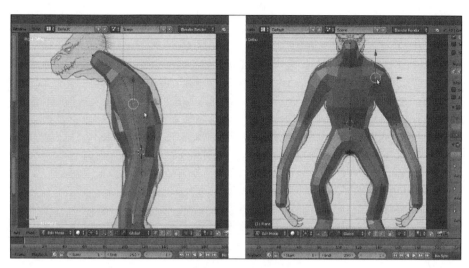

Refining the shoulder's shape

19. Extrude the bulk of the head. Select the last hand vertex and scale it smaller. Then, select the upper hand vertex and extrude two more fingers (scale their influence smaller and adjust their position to obtain a more regular and ordinate flow of the polygons in the generated geometry):

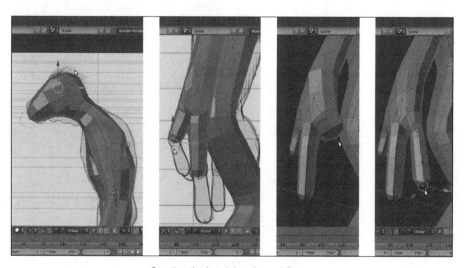

Creating the head, hands, and fingers

20. As always, following the templates as reference, extrude again to complete the fingers; use all the templates to check the accuracy of the proportions and positions, and the **Front**, **Side**, and **Back** views too:

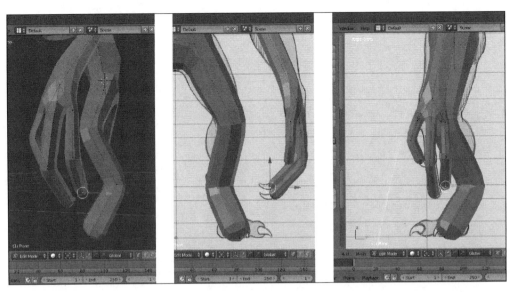

Adjusting the position of the fingers according to the templates

21. Do the same thing for the foot, and we are almost done with the major part of the mesh:

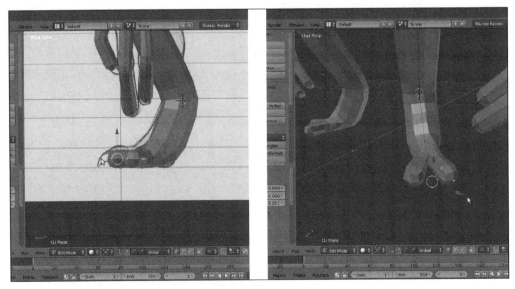

Creating the feet toes

Now, it's only a matter of refining, as much as possible, the mesh's parts to resemble best the final shape of the character. Let's try with the arm first:

22. Select the two extreme vertices of the forearm and press *W* | **Subdivide** | **2** (in the bottom **Tool** panel) to add **2** vertices in the middle. Then, use *Ctrl + A* to scale and move them outward to curve the forearm a little bit. Do the same for the thigh by slightly moving the vertices outward and backward:

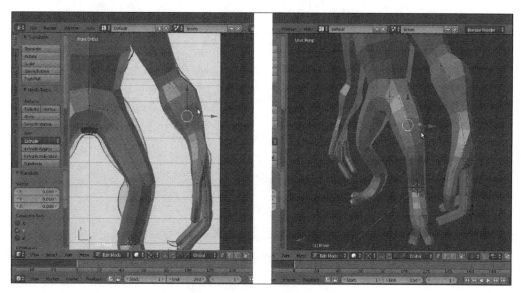

Refining the shape of arms and legs

23. Repeat the same procedure with the upper arm, shin, foot, and fingers; any part where it's possible, but don't go crazy about it. The goal of such a technique is just to quickly obtain a mesh that is good enough to be used as a starting point for the sculpting, and not an already finished model:

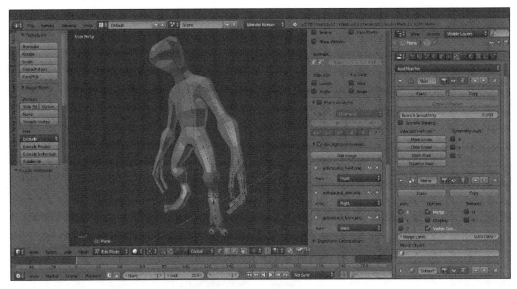

The completed base mesh

24. Press *Tab* to go out of the **Edit Mode**; go to the **Outliner** and rename the base mesh as `Gidiosaurus`. Then, save the file.

How it works...

The **Skin** modifier is a quick and simple way to build almost any shape; its use is very simple: first, you extrude vertices (actually, it would be enough to add vertices; it's not mandatory to extrude them, but certainly it's more handy than using *Ctrl* + left-click to add them at several locations), and then using the *Ctrl* + *A* shortcut, you scale smaller or bigger the influence that these vertices have on the 3D geometry generated on the fly.

If you have already tried it, you must have seen that the more the complexity of the mesh grows, the more the generated geometry starts to become a little unstable, often resulting in intersecting and overlapping faces. Sometimes this seems unavoidable, but in any case it is not a big issue and can be easily fixed through a little bit of editing. We'll see this in the next chapter.

2
Sculpting the Character's Base Mesh

In this chapter, we will cover the following recipes:

- ▸ Using the Skin modifier's Armature option
- ▸ Editing the mesh
- ▸ Preparing the base mesh for sculpting
- ▸ Using the Multiresolution modifier and the Dynamic topology feature
- ▸ Sculpting the character's base mesh

Introduction

In the previous chapter, we built the base mesh by using the **Skin** modifier and on the base of the reference templates; in this chapter, we are going to prepare this basic mesh for the sculpting, by editing it and cleaning up any *mistakes* the **Skin** modifier may have made (usually, overlapping and triangular faces, missing edge loops, and so on).

Using the Skin modifier's Armature option

The **Skin** modifier has an option to create an **Armature** on the fly to pose the **generated mesh**. This **Armature** can just be useful in cases where you want to modify the position of a part of the generated mesh.

Note that using the generated **Armature** to pose the base mesh, in our case, is not necessary, and therefore this recipe is treated here only as *an example* and it won't affect the following recipes in the chapter.

Getting ready

So, let's suppose that we want the **arms** to be posed more horizontally and widely spread:

1. If this is the case, reopen the `Gidiosaurus_base_mesh.blend` file and save it with a different name (something like `Gidiosaurus_Skin_Armature.blend`).

2. Select the **Gidiosaurus** mesh and press *Tab* to go into **Edit Mode**; then, select the central pelvis vertex.

3. Go to the **Object Modifiers** window under the main **Properties** panel to the right-hand side of the screen and then to the **Skin** modifier subpanel; click on the **Mark Root** button:

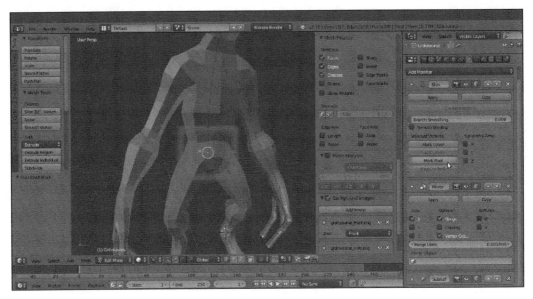

The root vertex

4. Press *Tab* again to exit **Edit Mode**.

How to do it...

Creating the rig (that is the skeleton **Armature** made by bones and used to deform, and therefore, animate a mesh) for our character's base mesh is really simple:

1. Again, in the **Skin** modifier subpanel, click on the **Create Armature** button. The **Armature** is created instantly and an **Armature** modifier is automatically assigned to the mesh; in the modifier stack, move it to the top so that it is above the **Mirror** modifier and our posed half-mesh will be correctly mirrored:

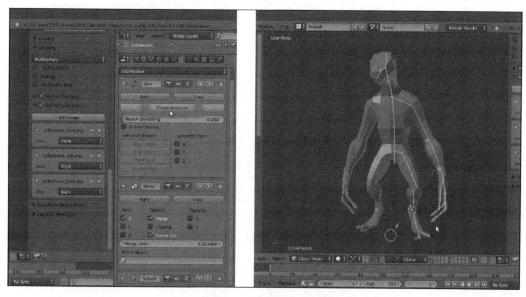

The Armature created by the Skin modifier

2. Press *Ctrl + Tab* to enter **Pose Mode** for the already selected **Armature** and then select the upper bone of the **arm**.

3. In the toolbar of the 3D viewport, find the widget manipulators panel, click on the rotation **Transformation manipulators** (the third icon from the left), and set **Transform Orientation** to **Normal**.

4. By using the rotate widget, rotate the selected bone and consequently the arm (be careful that, as already mentioned, the newly created **Armature** modifier is at the top of the modifier stack, otherwise the rotation will not correctly deform the mirrored mesh):

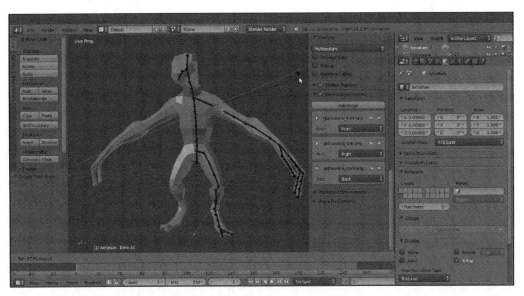

Rotating the arms through the Armature

5. Exit **Pose Mode** and reselect the **Gidiosaurus** mesh.

6. Go to the **Skin** modifier subpanel under the **Object Modifiers** window; click on the **Apply** button to apply the modifier.

7. Go to the **Armature** modifier and click on the **Apply** button to also apply the rig transformations.

8. At this point, we can also select the **Armature** object and delete it (*X* key).

How it works...

By clicking on the **Create Armature** button, the **Skin** modifier creates a bone for each edge connecting the extruded vertices, it adds an **Armature** modifier to the generated base mesh, and automatically assigns vertex groups to the base mesh and skins them with the corresponding bones.

The bones of this **Armature** work in **Forward Kinematics**, which means they are chained following the **child/parent** relation, with the first (**parent**) bone created at the **Root** location we had set at step 3 of the *Getting ready* section.

There's more...

Note that the bones of the **Armature** can be used not only to rotate limbs, but also to scale bigger or smaller parts of the mesh, in order to further tweak the shape of the base mesh.

See also

- ▸ http://www.blender.org/manual/modifiers/generate/skin.html
- ▸ http://www.blender.org/manual/rigging/posing/editing.html#effects-of-bones-relationships

Editing the mesh

Once we have applied the **Skin** and **Armature** modifiers, we are left with an almost ready-to-use base mesh; what we need to do now is clean the possibly overlapping faces and whatever other mistakes were made by the **Skin** modifier.

Be careful not to be confused by the previous recipe, which was meant only as a possible example; we didn't actually use the **Skin** modifier's **Armature** to change the pose of the base mesh.

Getting ready

Let's prepare the mesh and the view:

1. Go to the **Object Modifiers** window under the main **Properties** panel and then to the **Mirror** modifier subpanel and click on the little **X** icon to the right in order to delete the modifier; you are left with half of the mesh (actually the half that is really generated by the **Skin** modifier; the other side was *simulated* by the **Mirror** modifier):

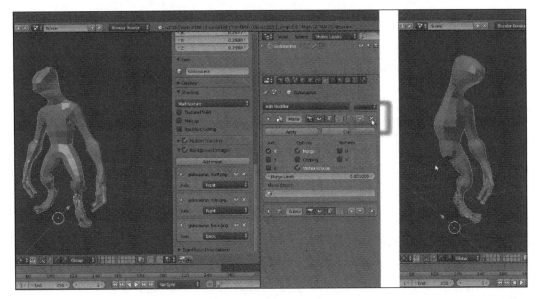

Deleting the Mirror modifier

2. Press *Tab* to go into **Edit Mode**, *7* on the numpad to go into **Top** view, and *Z* to go into the **Wireframe** viewport shading mode.

How to do it...

1. Press *Ctrl + R* to add an edge-loop to the middle of the mesh; don't move the mouse, and left-click a second time to confirm that you want it at **0.0000** location:

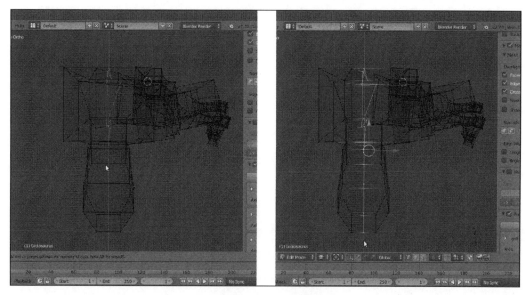

Adding a central edge-loop

Sometimes, depending on the topology created by the **Skin** modifier, you may not be able to make a single clean loop cut by the *Ctrl + R* key shortcut. In this case, still in **Edit Mode**, you can press the *K* key to call the **Knife Tool**, left-click on the mesh to place the cuts, and press *Enter* to confirm (press *Shift + K* if you want only the newly created edge-loops selected after pressing *Enter*). This way, you can create several loop cuts, connect them together and, if necessary, move and/or scale them to the middle along the *x* axis.

In fact, you can do the following:

2. Go out of **Edit Mode** and press *Shift + S*; in the **Snap** pop-up menu, select **Cursor to Selected** (to center the cursor at the middle of the mesh).

3. Press the period (.) key to switch **Pivot Point** to **3D Cursor** and then press *Tab* to go again into **Edit Mode**.

4. With the middle edge-loop already selected, press S | X | 0 | *Enter* to scale all its vertices to the **3D Cursor** position along the x axis and align them at the perfect center:

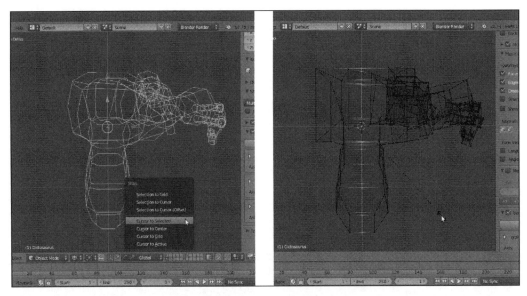

Scaling the central edge-loop vertices along the x axis

5. Press *A* to deselect all the vertices and then press *B* and box-select the vertices on the left-hand side of the screen (actually the mesh's right-side vertices):

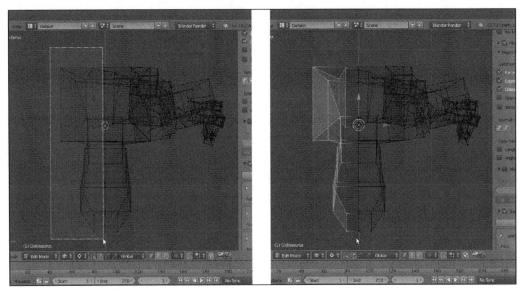

Box-selecting the left vertices

6. Press *X* and, in the **Delete** pop-up menu, select the **Vertices** item to delete them:

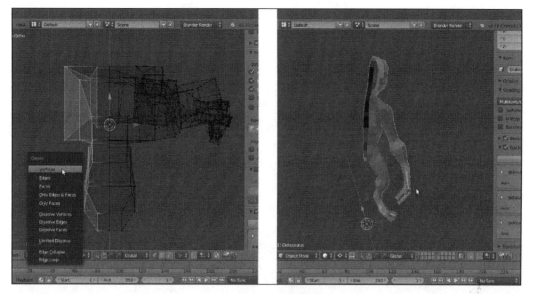

Deleting the left vertices

7. Go out of **Edit Mode** and, in the **Object Modifiers** window, assign a new **Mirror** modifier (check **Clipping**) to the mesh; move it before the **Subdivision Surface** modifier in the stack.

8. If needed, this is the point where you can manually edit the mesh by converting triangle faces to quads (select two consecutive triangular faces and press *Alt + J*), creating, closing, or moving edge-loops (by using the **Knife Tool**, for example, around the arms and legs attachments to the body), and so on.

9. Save the file as `Gidiosaurus_base_mesh.blend`.

Well, in our case, everything went right with the **Skin** modifier, so there is no need for any big editing of the mesh! In effect, it was enough to delete the first **Mirror** modifier (that we actually used mostly for visual feedback) to get rid of all the overlapping faces and obtain a clean base mesh:

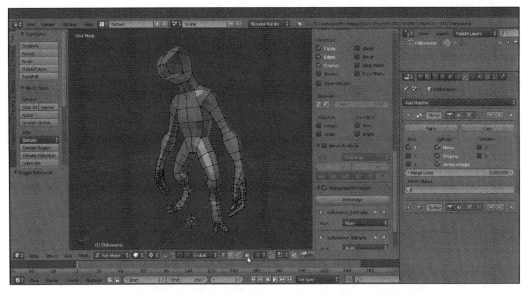

The "clean" mesh with new Mirror and Subdivision Surface modifiers

In the preceding screenshot, the base mesh geometry is showing with a level **1** of subdivision; in **Edit Mode**, it is still possible to see the low-level cage (that is, the *real* geometry of the mesh) as wireframe.

There are a couple of triangular faces (that, if possible, we should always try to avoid; quads faces work better for the sculpting) near the shoulders and on the feet, but we'll fix these automatically later, because before we start with the sculpting process, we will also apply the **Subdivision Surface** modifier.

How it works...

To obtain a clean half-body mesh, we had to delete the first **Mirror** modifier and the vertices of the right half of the mesh; to do this, we had also added a middle edge loop. So, we obtained a perfect left-half mesh and therefore we assigned again a **Mirror** modifier to restore the missing half of the body.

Preparing the base mesh for sculpting

Once we have our base mesh completed, it's time to prepare it for the sculpting.

Getting ready

Open the `Gidiosaurus_base_mesh.blend` file and be sure to be out of **Edit Mode**, and therefore in **Object Mode**.

How to do it...

1. Select the character's mesh and go to the **Object Modifiers** window under the main **Properties** panel to the right.

2. Go to the **Mirror** modifier panel and click on the **Apply** button.

3. If this is the case, expand the **Subdivision Surface** modifier panel, be sure that the **View** level is at **1**, and click on the **Apply** button.

4. Press *Tab* to go into **Edit Mode** and, if necessary, select all the vertices by pressing *A*; then, press *Ctrl + N* to recalculate the normals and exit **Edit Mode**.

5. Go to the **Properties** sidepanel on the right-hand side of the 3D view (or press the *N* key to make it appear) and under the **View** subpanel, change the **Lens** angle to **60.000** (more natural looking than **35.000**, which is set by default).

6. Under the **Display** subpanel, check the **Only Render** item:

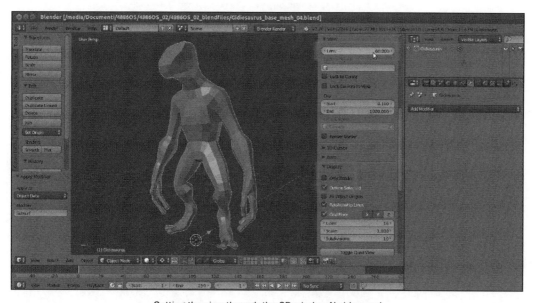

Setting the view through the 3D window N sidepanel

7. Go to the **Shading** subpanel on the sidepanel on the right-hand side of the 3D viewport and check the **Matcap** item.

8. Left-click on the preview window that just appeared and, from the pop-up panel, select the red colored brick material, the one that looks like ZBrush material; obviously, you can choose a different one if you prefer, but in my experience, this is the one that gives the best visual feedback in the 3D view:

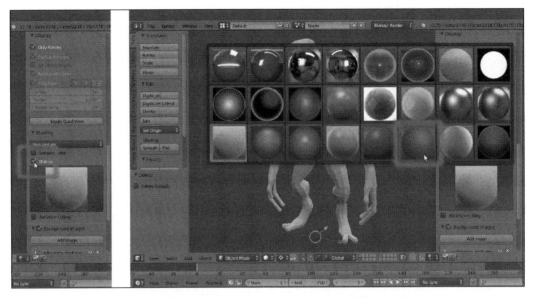

The available matcaps menu and the selected Zbrush-like matcap

9. Put the mouse cursor inside the active 3D window and press *Ctrl* + Spacebar to disable the widget:

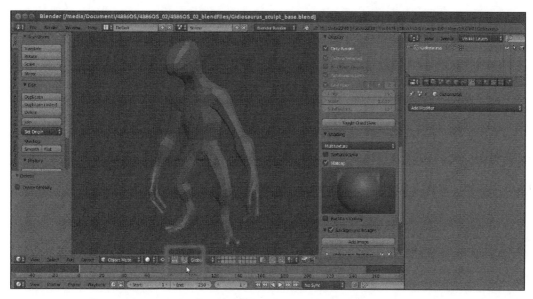

The matcap assigned to the mesh and the widget button in the 3D window toolbar

10. Press *N* to get rid of the **Properties** 3D window sidepanel.

11. Save the file as `Gidiosaurus_Sculpt_base.blend`.

How it works...

By checking the **Only Render** item in the **Display** subpanel under the **Properties** 3D window sidepanel, all the possible disturbing elements that cannot be rendered (such as the **Grid Floor**, **Empties**, **Lamps**, and so on) are hidden, in order to give a clean 3D viewport ready for sculpting.

Note that with this option enabled, sadly, the **Image Empties** we set in the previous chapter to work as templates for references are not visible—instead, the templates we had set as **Background Images** are perfectly visible in the **3** orthographic views.

Matcaps can in some cases slow the performance of your computer, depending on the hardware; in any case, **Matcaps** is a very useful feature, especially for sculpting, as you can see the mesh shape easily.

Changing the **Lens** angle from **35.000** to **60.000** makes the perspective view look more similar to the natural human field of view.

Using the Multiresolution modifier and the Dynamic topology feature

To be sculpted, a mesh needs a big enough amount of vertices to allow the adding of details; in short, we now need a way to add (a lot of!) geometry to our simple base mesh.

Besides the usual subdividing operation in **Edit Mode** (press *Tab*, then *A* to select all the vertices, then press *W* to call the **Specials** menu, click on **Subdivide**, and then set the **Number of Cuts** value in the last operation subpanel at the bottom of the **Tool Shelf**) and the **Subdivision Surface** modifier, in Blender, there are two other ways to increase the amount of vertices: one is by assigning a **Multiresolution** modifier to the mesh (a nondestructive way) and the other is by using the **Dynamic topology** feature. We are going to see both of them.

Getting ready

As usual, let's start from the last `.blend` file we saved: in this case, `Gidiosaurus_Sculpt_base.blend`.

How to do it...

Let's start with the **Multiresolution** modifier method:

1. First of all, save the file as `Gidiosaurus_Multires.blend`.
2. Select the base mesh and go to the **Object Modifiers** window under the main **Properties** panel on the right-hand side of the screen; assign a **Multiresolution** modifier.
3. Click on the **Subdivide** (*Add a new level of subdivision*) button **3** times; the mesh has now reached **143,234** vertices and **143,232** faces.
4. Check the **Optimal Display** item in the modifier panel:

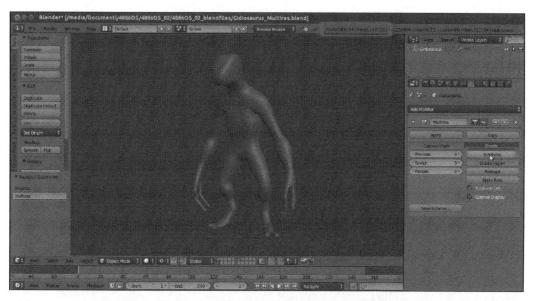

The mesh with a Multiresolution modifier assigned at level 3 of subdivision

5. On the toolbar of the 3D window, click on the mode button to go into **Sculpt Mode**.

6. On the **Tools** tab on the left-hand side of the screen (if necessary, press the *T* key to make the **Tool Shelf** containing the tabs appear), go to the **Symmetry\Lock** subpanel and click on the **X** button under the **Mirror** item.

7. Click on the **Options** tab and, under the **Options** subpanel, uncheck the **Size** item under **Unified Settings**.

8. Start to sculpt.

   At this point, to proceed with the sculpting, you should jump to the next recipe, *Sculpting the character's base mesh*; instead, let's suppose that we have already sculpted our base mesh, so let's move ahead:

9. Exit **Sculpt Mode**.

10. Save the file.

Now, let's see the quick and easy preparation necessary to use the **Dynamic topology** feature for sculpting:

1. Reload the `Gidiosaurus_Sculpt_base.blend` blend file.

2. Then, save it as `Gidiosaurus_Dynatopo.blend`.

3. On the toolbar of the 3D window, select **Sculpt Mode**.

4. On the **Tools** tab on the left-hand side of the screen (press the *T* key to make the **Tool Shelf** containing the tabs appear), go to the **Topology** subpanel and click on the **Enable Dyntopo** button; a popup appears to inform you that the **Dynamic topology** feature doesn't preserve any already existing **Vertex Color**, **UV layer**, or other custom data (only if the mesh has them). Then click on the popup to confirm and go on.

5. Change the **Detail Size** value to **15/20** pixels.

6. Go to the **Symmetry\Lock** subpanel and click on the **X** option under the **Mirror** item:

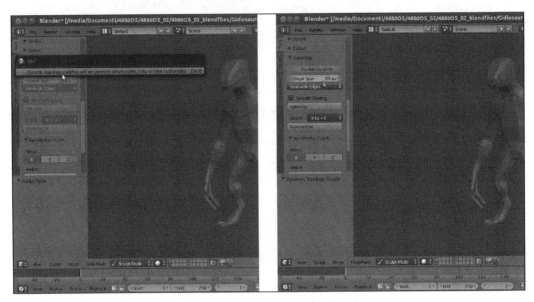

The dynamic topology tool warning and the settings

7. Start to sculpt.

Again, here you can jump to the next recipe, *Sculpting the character's base mesh*; in any case, remember to save the file.

How it works...

The **Multiresolution** modifier increasingly subdivides the mesh at each level by adding vertices; we have seen that from **2,240** starting vertices of the base mesh, we have reached **143,234** vertices at level **3**, and clearly this allows for the sculpting of details and different shapes. The vertices added by the modifier are *virtual*, exactly as the vertices added by the **Subdivision Surface** modifier are; the difference is that the vertices added by the latter are not editable (unless you apply the modifier, but this would be counterproductive), while it's possible to edit (normally through the sculpting) the vertices at each level of subdivision of a **Multiresolution** modifier. Moreover, it's always possible to go back by lowering the levels of subdivision, and the sculpted details will be stored and shown only in the higher levels; this means that the **Multiresolution** method is a nondestructive one and we can, for example, rig the mesh at level **0** and render it at the highest/sculpted level.

The **Dynamic topology** setting is different from the **Multiresolution** modifier because it allows you to sculpt the mesh without the need to heavily subdivide it first, that is, the mesh gets subdivided on the fly *only where needed*, according to the workflow of the brushes and settings, resulting in a much lower vertex count for the final mesh in the end.

As you can see in the screenshots (and in the `.blend` files provided with this cookbook), starting to sculpt the character with the **Multiresolution** modifier or the **Dynamic topology** is quite different. In the end, the process of sculpting is basically the same, but in the first case, you have an already smoothed-looking mesh where you must add or carve features; in the second case, the low resolution base mesh doesn't change its raw look at all until a part gets sculpted and therefore subdivided and modified, that is, all the corners and edges must first be softened, in order to round an otherwise harsh shape.

Sculpting the character's base mesh

Whatever the method you are going to use, it's now time to start with the effective sculpting process.

However, first, a disclaimer: in this recipe, I'm not going to teach you *how to sculpt,* nor is this an anatomy lesson of any kind. For these things, a book itself wouldn't be enough. I'm just going to demonstrate the use of the Blender sculpting tools, showing what brush I used for the different tasks, the sculpting workflow following the reference templates, and some of the more frequently used shortcut keys.

Getting ready

In this recipe, we'll use the **Dynamic topology** method. If you haven't followed the instructions of the previous recipe, just follow the steps from 12 to 17; otherwise, just open the `Gidiosaurus_Dynatopo.blend` file that is provided.

How to do it...

As usual, it's a good habit to save the file with the proper name as the first thing; in this case, save it as `Gidiosaurus_Dynatopo_Sculpt.blend`.

If you are going to use a graphic tablet to sculpt, remember to enable the tablet pressure sensitivity for both size and strength; in any case, it is better to set the respective sliders to values lower than **100 percent**; I usually set the size slider around **30/35** and the strength slider to **0.500**, but this is subjective:

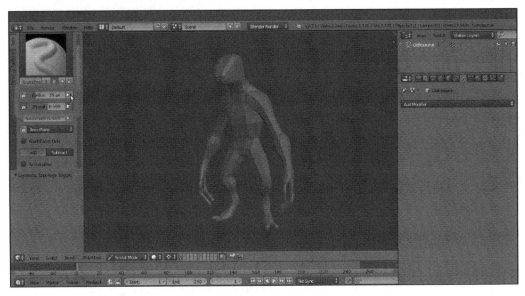

The tablet pressure sensitivity buttons for the size and the strength

1. If you haven't already, go into **Sculpt Mode** and enable the **Dynamic topology** feature by clicking on the **Enable Dyntopo** button in the subpanel with the same name under the **Tool Shelf** panel or by directly pressing *Ctrl + D*.

2. Set the **Detail Size** value to **15**, either by using the slider under the **Enable Dyntopo** button or by pressing *Shift + D* and then moving the mouse to scale it bigger or smaller:

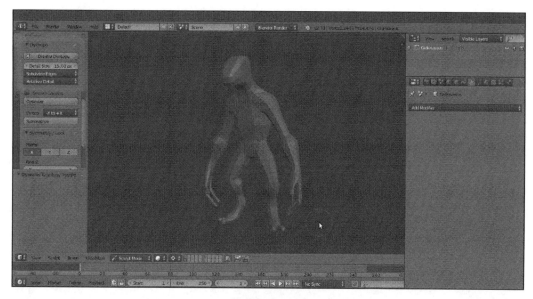

Starting to sculpt

3. Click on the **Brush** selection image (*Brush datablock for storing brush settings for painting and sculpting*) at the top of the **Tools** tab under the **Tool Shelf** panel, and, from the pop-up menu, select the **Scrape/Peaks** brush (otherwise press the *Shift + 3* key shortcut):

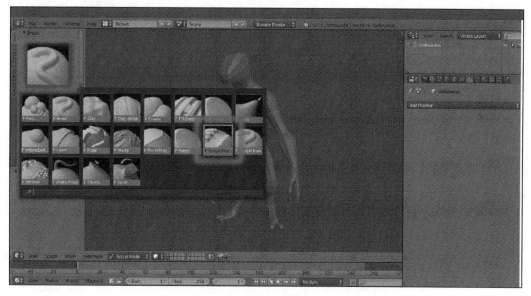

Selecting the Scrape/Peaks brush in the sculpt brushes menu

4. Start to scrape all the edges and soften the corners to obtain a smooth rounded surface:

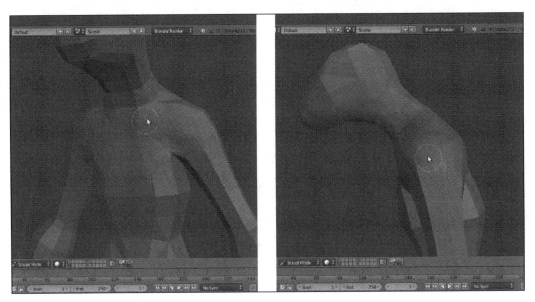

Softening the edges of the mesh

5. Change the brush; select the **Grab** brush (*G* key) and press *3* in the numpad to go into **Side** view; press the *F* key and move the mouse cursor to scale the brush, in this case, to scale it much bigger, around **120** pixels (*Shift + F* is to change the strength of a brush, instead).

6. Using the **Background Image** showing in the orthographic view (the *5* key in the numpad), grab the **spine** and **chest** areas of the mesh and move them to fit the shape of the template:

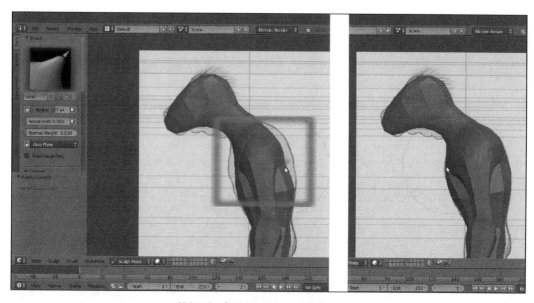

Using the Grab brush to modify the mesh

7. Do the same for the other parts of the mesh that don't fit yet, and do it also in **Front** view (*1* key in the numpad) and **Back** view (*Shift + 1* in the numpad).

8. Select the **Scrape/Peaks** brush again (*Shift + 3* keys) and keep on softening the mesh until almost every part gets rounded and more organic-looking; you can also use the **Smooth** (*S* key) brush to further soften the mesh:

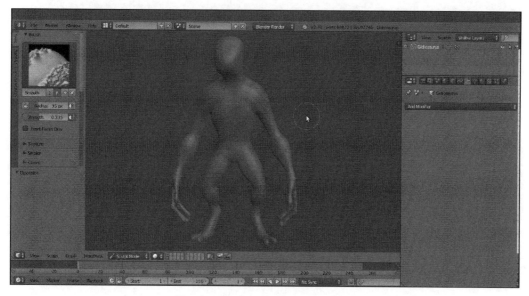

The character is starting to take a shape

9. Open a new window, switch **Editor Type** to **UV/Image Editor** and click on the **Open** button in the toolbar; browse to the `templates` folder and select the `gidiosaurus_trequarters.png` image. Then, click on the little pin icon on the right-hand side of the image name on the window toolbar (*Display current image regardless of object selection*).

10. Select the **Crease** brush (*4* key); using it as a chisel and following the loaded image as a reference, start to outline the character's more important features on the mesh, *drawing* the character's anatomy:

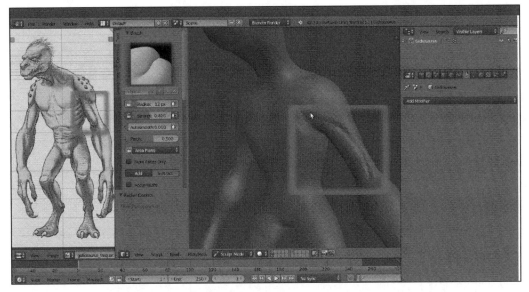

Using the Crease brush as a chisel

11. By pressing *Ctrl* while sculpting, we can temporarily reverse the effect of the brush; so, for example, the **Crease** brush, which usually carves lines in the mesh, can sculpt ridges and spike protrusions. We can use this to add details to the **elbow bones** and **knees** on the fly.

12. By pressing the *Shift* key while sculpting instead, we can temporarily switch whatever brush we are using with the **Smooth** brush, in order to instantly soften any newly added detail or feature.

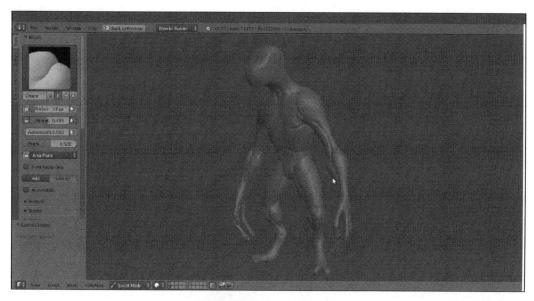

Outlining the major body features

13. When finished with the **body**, exchange the brush for the **Clay Strips** brush (*3* key),
start to add stuff (the **nose**, **eyebrows**, and so on), and outline the features of the
head. Again, press *Ctrl* to subtract clay (for the **eye sockets**, for instance) and *Shift*
to soften.

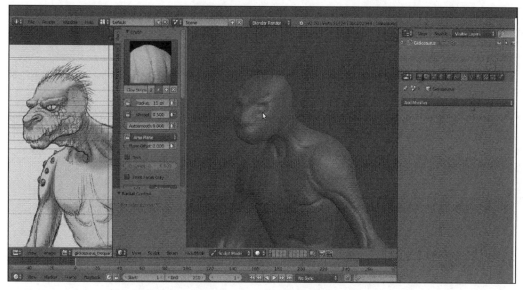

Using the Clay Strips brush to add details and/or carve stuff

14. Always use the templates to check for the proportions and positions of the character's features. Also, use **Wireframe** mode if necessary, by going into **Ortho** view and comparing the sculpted mesh outline with the background template image; use the **Grab** brush to quickly move and shape proportionate features in the right places:

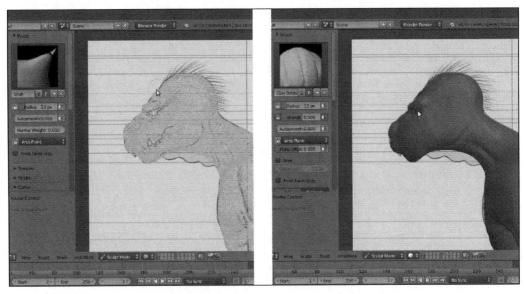

Temporarily switching to the Wireframe viewport shading mode to check the proportions in Side view

15. Using the **Clay Strips** (*3* key), **Smooth** (S key), **SculptDraw** (*Shift + 4* key), **Crease** (*4* key), and **Pinch** (*Shift + 2* key) brushes, build the **head** of the creature and define as many details as possible such as the **eyebrows**, **mouth rim**, **nostrils**, and **eye sockets**; experiment with all the different brushes:

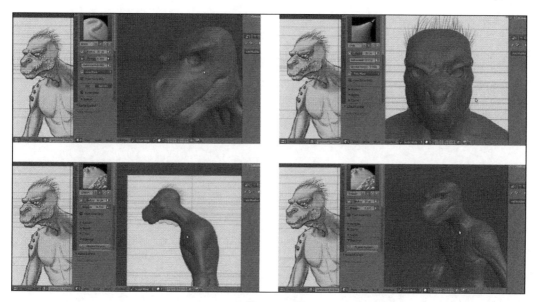

Detailing the head

16. Go out of **Sculpt Mode** and press *N* to make the **Properties** 3D window sidepanel appear; uncheck the **Only Render** item under the **Display** subpanel.

17. Press *Shift + A* and add a **UV Sphere** to the scene. Go into **Edit Mode**, if you haven't done so already, select all the vertices and rotate them **90** degrees on the x axis; then, scale them to **0.1000**. Finally, scale them again to **0.3600**.

18. Exit **Edit Mode** and move the **UV Sphere** to fit inside the **left eye socket** location.

19. Select the character's mesh and press *Shift + S*; then, in the **Snap** pop-up menu, choose **Cursor to Selected**. Select the **UV Sphere** and go to the **Tools** tab under the **Tool Shelf**; click on the **Set Origin** button and choose **Origin to 3D Cursor**. This way we have set the origin of the **UV Sphere** object at the same place as the character's mesh, while the **UV Sphere** mesh itself is located inside the **left eye socket**.

20. Go to the **Object Modifiers** window under the main **Properties** panel and assign a **Mirror** modifier to it.

21. Go to the **Outliner**, press *Ctrl* + left-click on the **UV Sphere** item, and rename it **Eyes**:

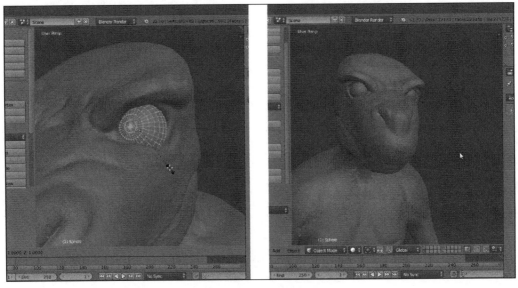

Positioning the eye spheres

22. Press *Shift* + *A* and add a **Cube** primitive. Go into **Edit Mode** and scale it a lot smaller; use the side template as a reference to modify by scaling, extruding, and tweaking the scaled **Cube's** vertices in order to build a low resolution **fang**. Go out of **Edit Mode** and go to the **Object Modifiers** window to assign a **Subdivision Surface** modifier.

23. Duplicate the **fang** and, as always, following the side and front templates as a guide, build all the necessary **teeth** for the **Gidiosaurus**.

24. Select all of them and press *Ctrl* + *J* to join them into one single object; press *Ctrl* + *A* to apply **Rotation & Scale**; then, do the same as in steps 19 and 20.

25. Go to the **Outliner** and rename the new object **Fangs**.

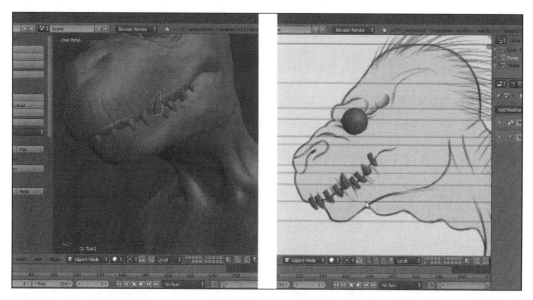

Making the teeth

26. Add a new **Cube** and repeat the process to model the **talons** of the **hands** and **feet**:

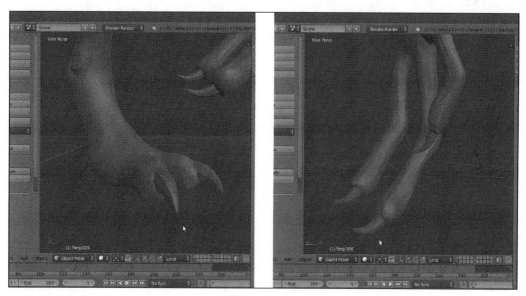

Making the talons

Note that the **Eyes**, **Fangs**, and **Talons** objects are not going to be sculpted, and therefore they are kept as separate objects. Later, we'll start to retopologize the sculpted body of the creature, while the **eyes** will be modeled and detailed in the traditional polygonal way; **fangs** and **talons** are good enough as they are.

27. Reselect the **Gidiosaurus** object and go back into **Sculpt Mode** to keep on refining the creature's shape more and more; don't be afraid to exaggerate the features, we can always smooth them later.

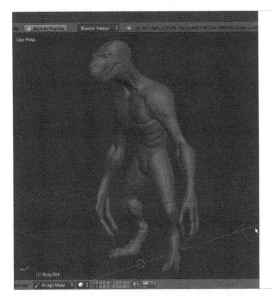 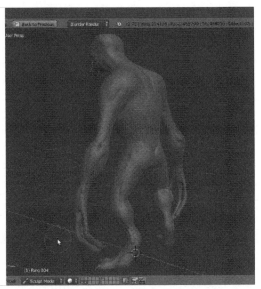

The almost completed sculpted mesh

28. Adjust the shape of the **eyebrows** to perfectly fit the **Eyes** object; then, work more on the **mouth rim** to accommodate the **fangs**.

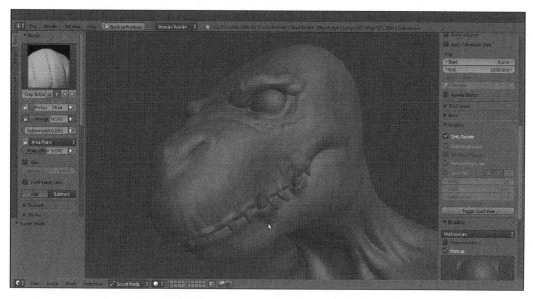

Refining the eyebrows and the mouth rim

29. When you think you have arrived at a good enough point, just go out of **Sculpt Mode** and *remember to save the file!*

Just a quick note: we don't actually need to go out of **Sculpt Mode** to save the file, it's possible to save it periodically (press *Ctrl + S* or *Ctrl + W* to save the file over itself, and *Ctrl + Shift + S* to *save as*) without needing to exit the sculpting session each time.

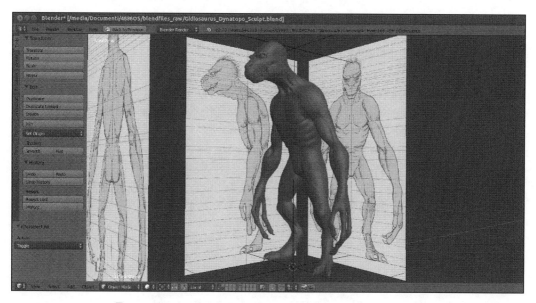

The completed sculpted mesh compared with the reference templates

So, here we are; the character's sculpting is basically done. We can work on it a lot more, tweaking the shapes further and adding details such as **scales**, **wrinkles**, and **veins**, but for this exercise's sake (and for this recipe), this is enough.

There's more...

A nice aspect of the **Dynamic topology** feature is the possibility to actually join different objects into a single mesh; for example, with our **Gidiosaurus**, we can join the **teeth** and the **talons** to the sculpted base mesh and then keep on sculpting the resulting object as a whole.

Actually, there are two ways to do this: simply by joining the objects and by the **Boolean** modifier.

To join the objects in the usual way, we can do the following:

1. Go out of **Sculpt Mode**.
2. Select the first object (that is, the **teeth**), press *Shift* + select the second object (the **talons**), and lastly press *Shift* + select the sculpted base mesh so that it's the active object (the final composited object will retain the active object's characteristics).
3. Press *Ctrl* + *J* and it is done!

This is the way you join objects in Blender in general, and it can actually work quite well. There is only one problem: there will always be a visible seam between the different objects, and although in the case of **teeth** or **talons** this will not be a problem, in other cases it should be avoided. Let's say you are working on a separated **head** and later you want to join it to a **body**; in this case, you don't want a visible seam between the **head** and **neck**, obviously!

So, the option is to use the **Boolean** modifier:

1. Go out of **Sculpt Mode**.
2. Select the character's base mesh and go to the **Object Modifiers** window under the main **Properties** panel; assign a **Boolean** modifier.
3. Click on the **Object** field of the modifier to select the object you want to join (let's say, the **Talons** object) and then click on the **Operation** button to the left to select **Union**.
4. Click on the **Apply** button to apply the modifier.
5. Hide, move onto a different layer, or delete the original object you joined (the **talons**).

Unlike the previous method, with Booleans, it will be possible to sculpt and smooth the joining of the different objects without leaving visible seams.

3
Polygonal Modeling of the Character's Accessories

In this chapter, we will cover the following recipes:

- ▶ Preparing the scene for polygonal modeling
- ▶ Modeling the eye
- ▶ Modeling the armor plates
- ▶ Using the Mesh to Curve technique to add details

Introduction

In the previous two chapters, we did the following:

- ▶ Quickly modeled a simple base mesh, as close as possible to the shape of the reference templates
- ▶ Sculpted this base mesh, refining the shapes and adding details to some extent

We have also quickly modeled very simple teeth and talons, and placed bare UV Spheres as placeholders for the eyes.

It's now time to start some polygonal modeling to complete the eyes, but especially to build the armor that our character is wearing.

Preparing the scene for polygonal modeling

Coming from a sculpting session, our .blend file must first be prepared for the polygonal modeling, verifying that the required add-ons are enabled and all the character's parts are easily visible and recognizable; for this, even though the topic of **Materials** is complex and there will be an entire chapter dedicated to it later in this book, we are going to assign basic materials to these parts so that they have different colors in the 3D viewport.

Getting ready

First, we are going to look for the **LoopTools** add-on, an incredibly useful script by Bartius Crouch that extends the Blender modeling capabilities (and that also has other functionalities, as we'll see in the next chapter about retopology); this add-on is provided with the official Blender release, but still must be enabled. To do this, follow these steps:

1. Start Blender and call the **Blender User Preferences** panel (*Ctrl + Alt + U*); go to the **Addons** tab.

2. Under the **Categories** item on the left-hand side of the panel, click on **Mesh**.

3. Check the empty little checkbox on the right-hand side of the **Mesh: LoopTools** add-on to enable it.

4. Click on the **Save User Settings** button at the bottom-left of the panel to save your preferences and close the panel:

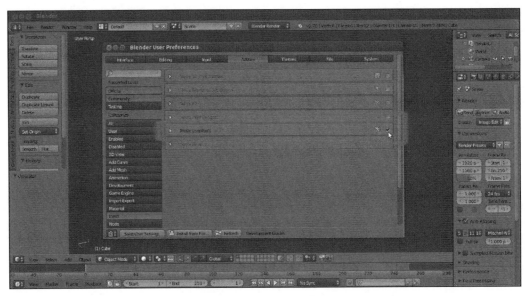

The Blender User Preferences panel

5. Open the Gidiosaurus_Dynatopo_Sculpt.blend file.

How to do it...

Now, we can start with the scene setup:

1. Click on the **11th** scene layer button (the first one in the second row of the first-left layer block of **Visible Layers** in the toolbar of the 3D window) to make it the only one visible (or else, just put the mouse pointer on the 3D viewport and press the *Alt + 11* keys; the *Alt* button is to allow for double digits).

2. Press *Shift* + left-click on the **13th** button to multiactivate it (or use the *Shift + Alt + 13* shortcut).

3. Go to the **Outliner** and click on the little grayed arrow icons on the side of the **Eyes**, **Fangs** and **Talons** items to make them selectable again.

4. If not already present, show the **Properties** 3D window sidepanel (*N* key) and go to the **Shading** subpanel; uncheck the **Matcap** item:

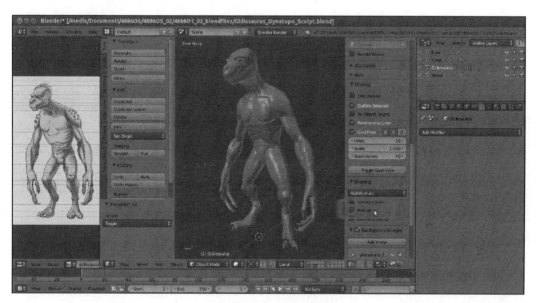

Disabling the Matcap item

5. Select the **Gidiosaurus** mesh; go to the **Material** window under the main **Properties** panel to the right and click on the **New** button to assign a material (note that, at least at the moment, we are using the default **Blender Internal** engine); click on the **Diffuse** button and change the color to **RGB 0.604, 0.800, 0.306** (a greenish hue, but in this case you can obviously choose any color you wish). Double left-click on the material name inside the data block slot to rename it as Body.

6. Select the **Eyes** object and again in the **Material** window under the main **Properties** panel to the right, click on the **New** button to assign a new material; click on the **Diffuse** button and this time change the color to **RGB 0.800, 0.466, 0.000**. Rename the material as `Eyes`.

7. Select the **Fangs** object and repeat the process; change the diffuse color to **RGB 0.800, 0.697, 0.415**. Rename the material as `Enamel`.

8. Select the **Talons** object and go to the **Material** window under the **Properties** panel to the right; click on the little arrows on the left-side of the **New** button and from the pop-up menu, select the `Enamel` material:

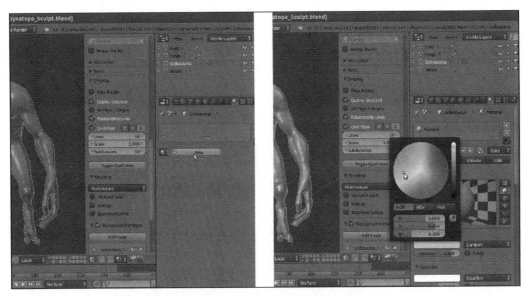

Assigning a material and choosing a color

9. Go to the **UV/Image_Editor** window on the left-hand side of the screen and press *Shift* + left-click on the **X** icon on the right-hand side of the data block name to get rid of the `gidiosaurus_trequarters.png` image. Then, click on the **Open** button, browse to the `templates` folder, and load the `gidiosaurus_armor1.png` image.

10. Save the file as `Gidiosaurus_modeling.blend`.

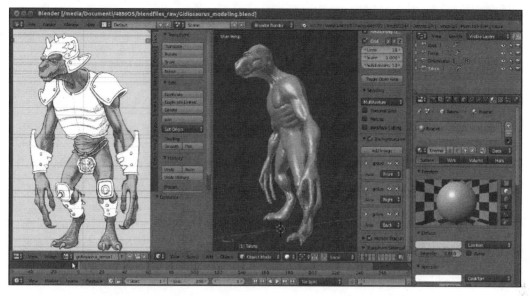

The armoured character's image loaded in the UV/Image Editor for reference

How it works...

We have deselected the **Matcap** view, assigning also differently colored basic materials to the four parts making up the character's mesh (**body, eyes, fangs**, and **talons**) to have a clearer way of differentiating the different pieces of the mesh. Then, we have replaced the template we used as reference for the sculpting of the **Gidiosaurus** body with a new one showing the armor as well (in the `templates` folder there are actually two slightly different versions of the armor; we chose the first one).

We have also activated the **13th** scene layer to be ready for the modeling of the **armor** (in the **11th** we have the character's mesh and in the **12th** we have the **fangs, talons**, and **eyes**).

Note that, in this cookbook, I will always specify scene layers to indicate the **20** 3D layers accessible from the buttons on the viewport toolbar and distinguish them from other types of layer systems present in Blender, such as for the **bones** or the **Grease Pencil** tool and so on.

Modeling the eye

It's now time to start to define the creature's **eyes**. We already had **UV Sphere** placeholders, but we're going to refine this mesh to deliver a more convincing eye. By the way, keep in mind that a good portion of the expressiveness of the eye will be due to the use of appropriate textures; for more information, see *Chapter 12, Creating the Materials in Cycles,* and *Chapter 13, Creating the Materials in Blender Internal*.

Getting ready

Following the previous recipe, there is nothing particular to be prepared before starting, except for the following:

1. Go to the **Properties** 3D view sidepanel (*N* key if not already present) and uncheck the **Background Images** item.

2. Press *3* on the numpad to go in **Side** view and zoom to the **UV Sphere** location, by pressing *Shift + B* and drawing a box around the point you want to zoom at; as you release the mouse button, the selected area will be zoomed in;

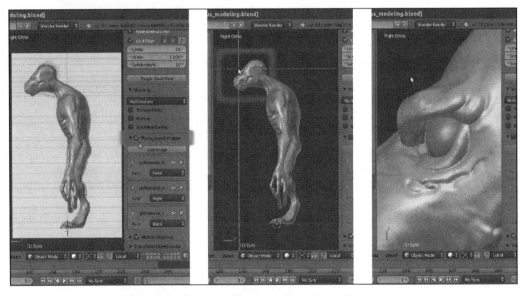

Disabling the background images and zooming to the eyes area

3. Go to the **Outliner** and click on the eye icon on the right-hand side of the **Gidiosaurus** item to hide it; or else, select the mesh in the 3D viewport and press the *H* key. Alternatively, you can also press the slash (*/*) key in the numpad to go in **Local** view, a particular view mode where only the selected objects are still visible (press the slash (*/*) again to go back to the normal view mode).

How to do it...

Without further ado, let us begin to build the eye:

1. Press *Z* to go in the **Wireframe** viewport shading mode.

2. In the **Outliner**, select the **Eyes** item (or else, if you wish, in the 3D viewport, select the **UV Sphere** object) and rename it as **Cornea**.

3. Press *Shift + D* and then immediately press the *Esc* key or right-click to cancel the *Grab/Translate* function, obtaining a duplicated object that now shows as **Cornea.001**; in the **Outliner**, rename the new object as **Eyeball**.

4. Press *Tab* to go in **Edit** Mode; if necessary, press *A* to select all the vertices and scale them to **0.990** (*S | .99 | Enter*).

5. Press *A* to deselect all the vertices. Then, box-select (*B* key) the pole vertex and the first row of vertices at the left-side pole (that is, in total **33** vertices); press *X* to delete them:

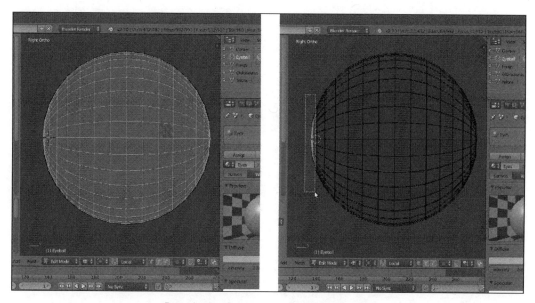

Box-selecting the vertices at the UV Sphere pole

6. Reselect all the remaining vertices; then, press the period (.) key on the numpad to center the view on the selection.

7. Go to the **Outliner** and click on the eye icon on the left-hand side of the **Cornea** item to hide it.

8. Rotate the view to align it with the hole in the **UV Sphere** and, if necessary, press the 5 key on the numpad to go in **Ortho** mode.

9. Press *Z* to go in the **Solid** viewport shading mode and press *A* to deselect everything.

10. Select the first row of vertices around the hole (*Alt* + right-click on the edge-loop). Press *E* to extrude them and then *S* to scale them; keep *Ctrl* + *Shift* pressed and scale to **0.9500** (or else, press S | .95 | Enter).

11. Press *E* and *S* again to extrude and scale the vertices to **0.500**.

12. Press *F* to fill the selection and *Alt* + *P* to poke the created N-gon face (that is, to automatically subdivide the single N-gon face into triangular faces connected to a central vertex).

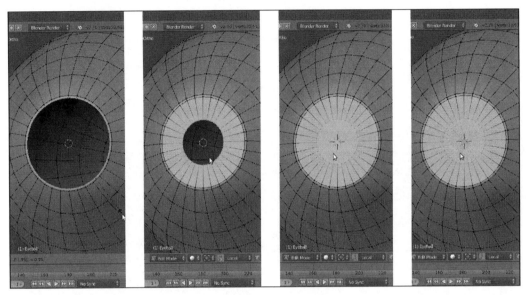

Extruding and closing the eye

13. Press *1* on the numpad to go in **Front** view. Scale the selected vertices to **0.500** on the *x* axis (*S | X | .5 | Enter*).

14. Press *Ctrl + R* and add an edge-loop outside of the iris; keep *Ctrl* pressed and move the mouse to edge-slide it to **-0.900**.

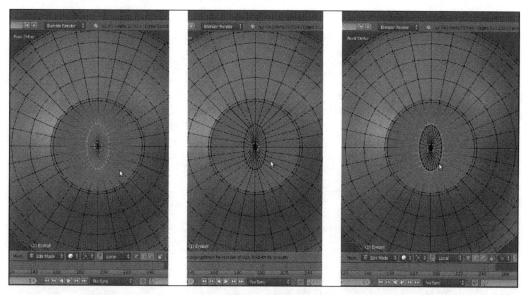

Making the pupil

15. In the toolbar of the 3D window, enable the **PET** (the **Proportional Editing** tool); set it to **Connected** and the **Proportional Editing Falloff** option to **Sphere**.

16. Enable the widget, set it to *Translate* (the second icon from the left, the one with the arrow), set **Transform Orientation** to **Global,** and select the central vertex of the pole. By using the widget, move it on the *y* (green) axis to **0.0030** (click on the green arrow and hold *Shift* for a finer control as you move the mouse on the *y* axis), while with the middle mouse wheel, set the **Proportional size** value of the **PET** to a quite small radius, or **0.01** to be precise:

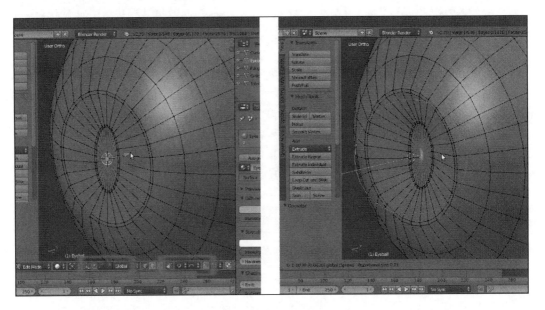

Creating the iris concave shape

17. Press *Ctrl* and the + key on the numpad **3** times, in order to grow the selection starting from the single selected vertex at the center of the iris.

18. Go to the **Material** window, create a new material, and rename it as `Iris`; change its diffuse color to something like **RGB 0.061, 0.025, 0.028** and then click on the **Assign** button:

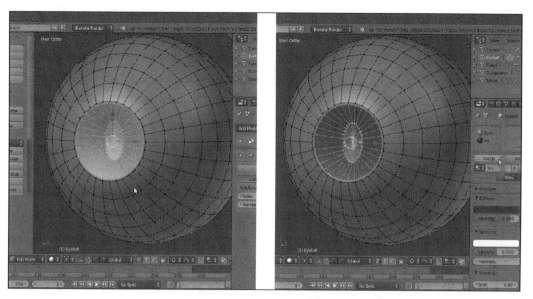

Assigning a material to the iris

19. Press *Ctrl* and the - key on the numpad just **1** time, in order to reduce the selection to the pupil. Go to the **Material** window, create a new material, and rename it as `Pupil`; change its diffuse color to plain black and then click on the **Assign** button.

20. Press *Tab* to go out of **Edit Mode**.

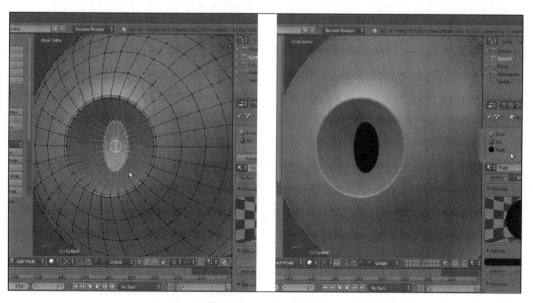

The almost completed eye

21. Go to the **Object Modifiers** window under the main **Properties** panel on the right-hand side of the UI and assign a **Subdivision Surface** modifier; check the **Optimal Display** item.

22. In the **Outliner**, unhide the **Cornea** object and assign a **Subdivision Surface** modifier as well; check the **Optimal Display** item and then hide it again (you can also use the *H* and *Alt + H* keys to do this).

23. Select the **Eyeball** object and go to the **Material** window; select the `Pupil` material and go to the **Specular** subpanel to set the **Intensity** value to **0.000**. Set the **Specular Shader Model** option of both the `Eyes` and `Iris` materials to **WardIso** and the **Slope** value to **0.070**. Set the `Iris` material's **Emit** value (under the **Shading** subpanel) to **0.050**.

24. In the **Outliner**, select the **Cornea** object and in the **Material** window, click on the little icon reporting **2** on the right-hand side of the material name (it's the display of the number of users for that material). The name `Eyes` automatically changes to `Eyes.001`: rename it `Cornea`; then, go to the **Transparency** subpanel and enable it. Set the **Fresnel** value to **1.400** and the **Blend** factor to **2.000**. Go to the **Options** subpanel further down and uncheck the **Traceable** item.

25. Unhide the **Gidiosaurus** mesh (*Alt + H*) and enable the **6th** scene layer (the one with the **Camera** and the **Lamp**). Select the **Lamp** and in the **Object Data** window, change the type to **Sun** and then rotate it to: **X = 55.788948°, Y = 16.162031°**, and **Z = 19.84318°**; you can press *N* and then type these values in the slots of the **Rotation** panel at the top of the **Properties** 3D window sidepanel.

26. Press *N* to hide again the **Properties** 3D window sidepanel and in the toolbar of the 3D window, go to the **Viewport Shading** button and select **Rendered** (or directly press the *Shift + Z* shortcut) to have a nice preview of the effect:

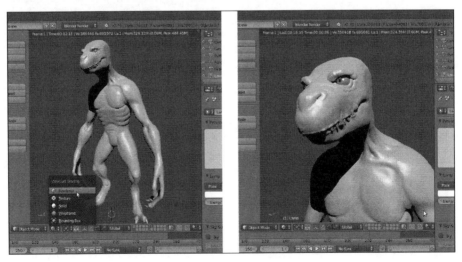

The Rendered preview of our character so far

27. Save the file.

How it works...

Actually, the **eyes** of the character are composed of two distinct objects: the **Eyeball** and the **Cornea** object.

The **Cornea** object is the transparent layer covering the **Eyeball** object, and by clicking on the eye icon in the **Outliner**, it has been made invisible in the 3D viewport but still renderable. With the **Cornea** object visible in the 3D views, **irises** and **pupils** would have been hidden behind, making the work of animating the **eyes** quite hard; animators always need to know what the character is looking at.

Both the **Cornea** and **Eyeball** objects, at the moment, are mirrored to the right by the **Mirror** modifier; this will be changed when we skin the mesh to the **Armature**.

If you can't find the **Rendered** view in the **Viewport Shading** mode button on the 3D viewport's toolbar, you may want to make sure you have the latest version of Blender; only versions after **2.6** have this feature for the Blender Render engine.

Modeling the armor plates

In the previous recipe, we modeled the character's **eye** and we had already modeled the **teeth** in *Chapter 2, Sculpting the Character's Base Mesh*, because we needed them, at that moment, to go on with the sculpting; they had been made with simple **Cube** primitives quickly scaled and tweaked in **Edit Mode**.

It is now time to model the **armor** for our warrior. Let's begin by creating the hard metal plates. We are going to use an approach similar to the modeling of the **fangs**, which is by starting with a **Cube** primitive and subdividing it to have more geometry to be edited in the proper shape, and we'll also use the **LoopTools** add-on to simplify some processes.

Getting ready

We will carry on with the `Gidiosaurus_modeling.blend` file:

1. Press *3* on the numpad to go in **Side** view.

2. By scrolling the middle mouse wheel, zoom back to frame the **Gidiosaurus** mesh in the 3D window.

3. In the **Outliner**, click on the arrow icon on the right-hand side of the **Gidiosaurus** item to make it unselectable.

How to do it...

Now, we can start to build the **armor**; let's go with the **chest** piece:

1. Note that the **3D Cursor** is in the middle of the scene, at the character's pivot location (*Shift + S | Cursor to Selected* or also *Cursor to Active*, just in case).

2. Press *O* to disable the **Proportional Editing** tool; go to the 3D viewport toolbar to verify that the tool button is grayed.

3. Press *Shift + A* and add a **Cube** primitive to the scene.

4. Press *Tab* to go in **Edit Mode** and scale all the vertices to **0.500** (or press *S | .5 | Enter*).

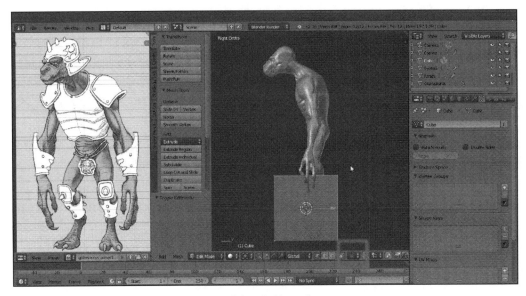

Adding the Cube primitive to the scene

5. Press *Ctrl + R* to add a loop along the *y* axis and then left-click twice to confirm it at the middle of the object:

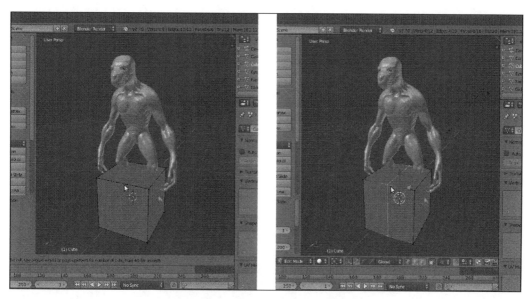

Adding a central vertical edge-loop to the Cube

6. Select the right-side vertices of the **Cube** and delete them; then, assign a **Mirror** modifier and check the **Clipping** item:

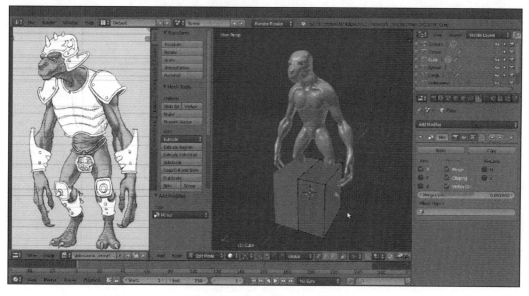

The Cube with the Mirror modifier

7. Go again in **Side** view and press *Z* to go in the **Wireframe** viewport shading mode; select all the vertices and move them upward.

8. Rotate the vertices to reflect the angle of the character's **chest**.

9. Select the upper vertices and scale and rotate them to fit the creature's **neck** area.

10. Select the bottom vertices and scale and rotate them to fit the base of the **chest**:

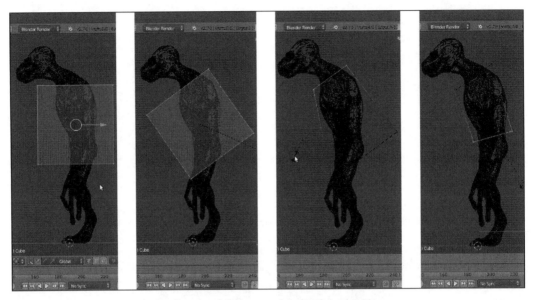

Starting to model the armor from the Cube primitive

11. Press *Ctrl + R* to add a new horizontal edge-loop at the middle of the **Cube**; scale it bigger to fit the shape of the creature's **chest**.

12. While still in **Side** view, grab and move the vertices to conform them to the **chest** shape.

13. Press *1* to go in **Front** view and again move the vertices to adjust them consistently to the character's **chest** shape:

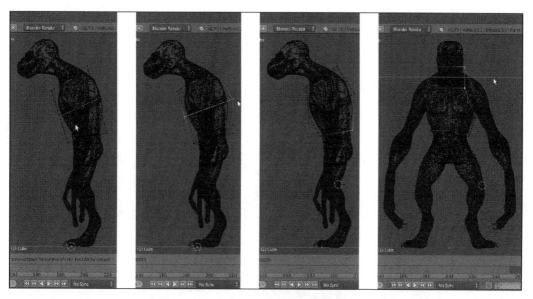

Adding more geometry and shape to the Cube

14. Select the **2** middle outer vertices and move them down, in order to place the edge connecting them just below the character's **armpit**.

15. Press *Ctrl + R* to add a loop along the *x* axis; click twice to confirm it at the middle of the lateral side:

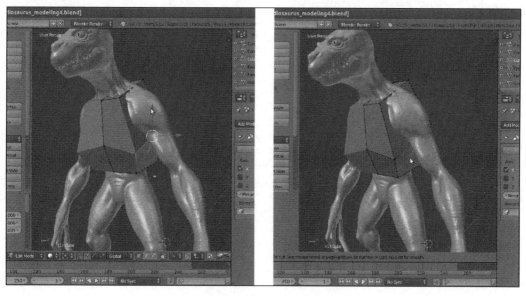

Adding more geometry again

16. Press the slash key (/) on the numpad to go in **Local** view with the selected object (in this case, even if still in **Edit Mode**, it is the **Cube**) and select the upper outer edge-loop.

17. Go to the **Tool Shelf** panel and scroll down the **Tools** tab to find the **LoopTools** subpanel (the **LoopTools** items are available also in the **Specials** menu that we can call by pressing the *W* key in **Edit Mode**); click on the **Circle** button to make the selection on a circular path:

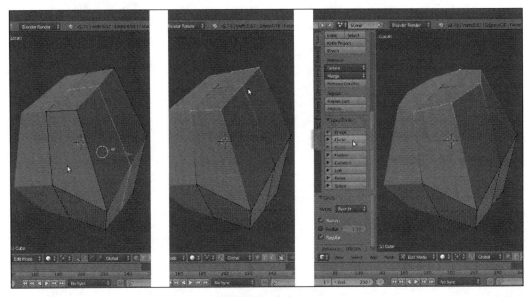

Using the LoopTools add-on

18. Do the same also with the middle and the bottom edge-loop; then, select the central upper and bottom pole's vertices and delete them:

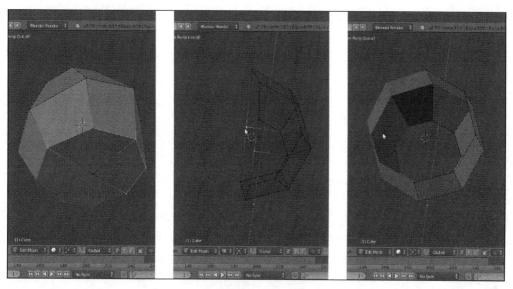

Going on with the modeling

19. Press the slash key (/) on the numpad to go out of **Local** view.

20. Press *Tab* to go out of **Edit Mode** and go to the **Object Modifiers** window under the main **Properties** panel; click on the **Apply** button to apply the **Mirror** modifier.

21. Go back in **Edit Mode** and press *Ctrl + R* to add a horizontal edge-loop to the upper half of the mesh.

22. Scale the new edge-loop to **1.100**:

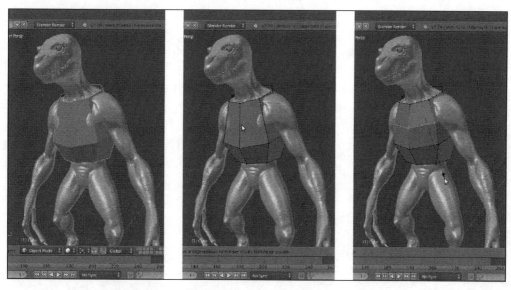

Adapting the shape of the armor to the chest by adding more geometry as edge-loops

23. Add a new horizontal edge-loop also to the lower half of the mesh.

24. Select the middle edge-loop and scale it smaller on the x axis, to **0.900**.

25. Select the bottom edge-loop and scale it smaller on the x axis as well.

26. Select the last edge-loop and repeat the operation.

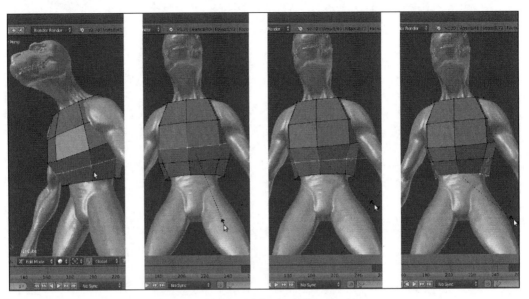

Going on with the modeling by adding edge-loops

27. Press 3 on the numpad to go in **Side** view and Z to go in the **Wireframe** viewport shading mode.

28. If not already, enable the widget in the toolbar of the 3D window; set the **Transformation manipulators** to **scaling** (the last icon to the right) and the **Transform Orientation** option to **Normal**.

29. Select all the vertices and by moving the green scaling manipulator of the widget, scale smaller all the edge-loops on the normal y axis; small enough to almost reach the character's **back** and **chest** surfaces.

30. Deselect everything and then select the middle edge-loop (press *Alt* + right-click); scale it again by using the widget to get close to the **torso** shape:

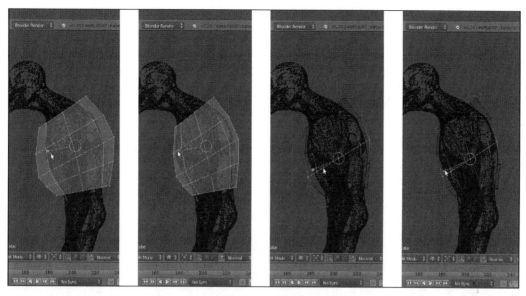

Adjusting the chest armor depth

31. Do the same with the other edge-loops by selecting them individually, rotating and scaling them, and also by moving the vertices.

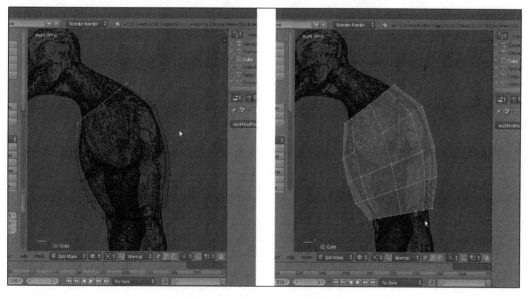

Refining the lateral profile of the armor

32. Press the slash (/) key on the numpad to go again in **Local** view.

33. Select the right-side vertices of the **Cube** and delete them.

34. Go to the **Object Modifiers** panel and assign a new **Mirror** modifier; as usual, check the **Clipping** item.

35. Select the central vertex on the upper-side part and delete it.

36. Select the resulting loop of edges around the resulting hole (you can press *Alt* + right-click and then *Shift* + right-click to add the remaining unselected top vertex to the selection; it doesn't get selected with the edge-loop because there are no faces connecting it to the other vertices, but only edges).

37. Press *E* and then *S* to extrude new faces and scale them (about **0.600**).

38. Select the new edge-loop and go to the **LoopTools** panel under the **Tools** tab of the **Tool Shelf** panel; click on the **Circle** button to make it rounded:

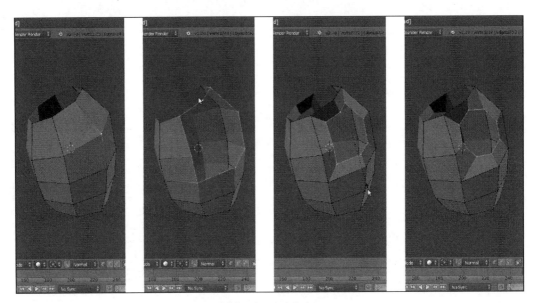

Adding the arm's holes

39. Go in **Front** view and move the edge-loop outward.

40. Go out of **Edit Mode** and press the slash (/) key on the numpad to go out of **Local** view.

41. Press *1* on the numpad to go again in **Front** view. Go to the **Object Modifiers** panel and assign a **Shrinkwrap** modifier to the **Cube**; check the **Keep Above Surface** item and in the **Target** field, select the **Gidiosaurus** name:

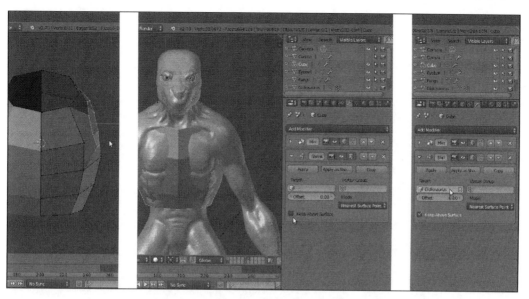

Assigning the Shrinkwrap modifier to the chest armor

42. Set the **Offset** value to **0.05**.

43. Move the **Shrinkwrap** modifier to the top of the modifier stack and click on the **Apply** button.

44. Go in **Edit Mode** and select the **shoulder** edge-loop; go to the **LoopTools** panel and click on the **Flatten** button:

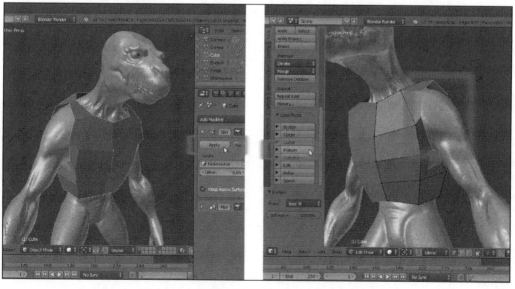

Refining the modeling through the LoopTools add-on

45. Fix, below the **armpit**, the lateral vertices that are curved inwards, by using the *Alt* + *S* shortcut to move them outward along their normal, the **3D Cursor** and the **Snap** pop-up menu (*Shift* + *S*) to place them midway from other vertices, and the *Shift* + *V* shortcut to slide them along the edges:

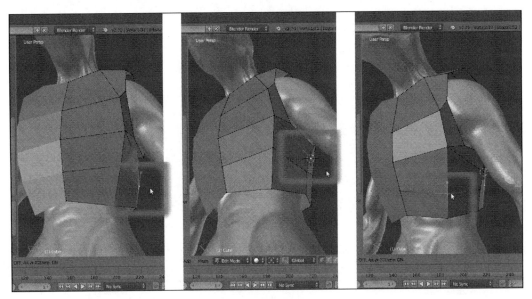

Tweaking vertices

46. Press the *K* key to activate the **Knife Topology Tool**; by keeping the *Ctrl* key pressed to constrain the cuts to the middle of the edges, cut a new edge-loop as shown in the following screenshot (each time, press *Enter* to confirm the cut and then pass to the following one):

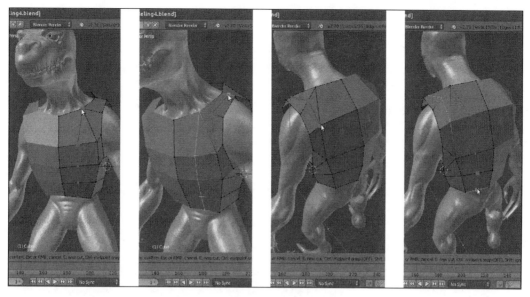

Using the Knife tool

47. Press *Alt* + *J* to join the already selected triangular faces into quads:

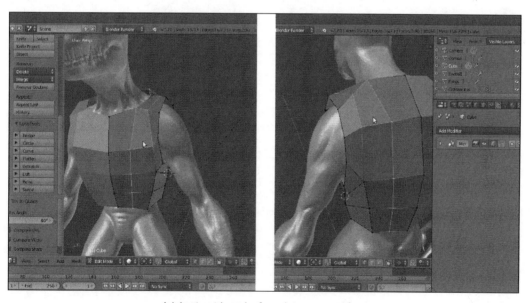

Joining two triangular faces into one quad face

48. Select all the vertices and press *Ctrl + N* to recalculate the normals.

49. Deselect all the vertices and go to the **Object Modifiers** window; assign a **Subdivision Surface** modifier, set the **Subdivisions** level for **View** to **2**, and check the **Optimal Display** item. Click on the *Adjust edit cage to modifier result* icon, the last one to the right with the editing triangle, in order to see the effect of the modifier in **Edit Mode**.

50. Go out of **Edit Mode** and then go to the **Tools** tab under the **Tool Shelf**; under the **Edit** subpanel, select the **Smooth** shading.

51. Go back in **Edit Mode** and select the vertices (in our case, mainly on the side and back) corresponding to areas where the sculpted mesh is overlapping the **armor**. Press *Alt + S* to scale their position along their normals and so fix the overlapping; then, select the upper vertices of the **shoulder** and move them closer to the character's **shoulder** surface:

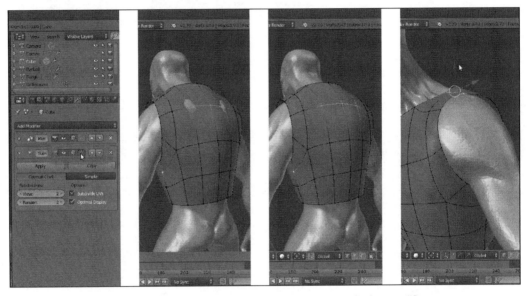

Tweaking vertices with the visible cage of the Subdivision Surface modifier

52. Repeat the operations of the previous step on all the vertices that need it; select the vertices on the **belly** and press *Shift + V* to move them upward, but along the edges to model the arc shape at the bottom of the **plate**:

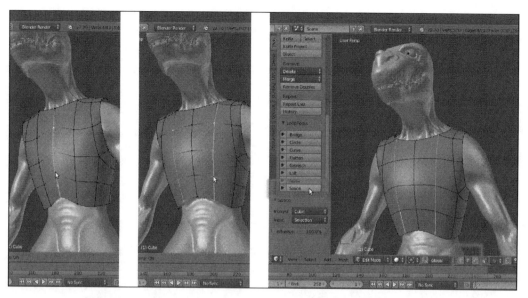

Sliding the vertices and adjusting the polygonal flow through the LoopTools add-on

53. Select the edges of the front and back and click on the **Space** button in the **LoopTools** add-on panel; if needed, tweak the value of the **Influence** slider at the bottom of the **Tools** tab to set the amount for the operation.

54. Add edge-loops at the bottom of the **armor** and at the **shoulder** opening to create a rim; extrude the **neck** opening upwards to create a kind of short collar:

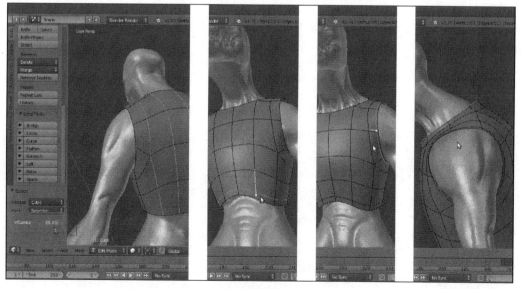

Extruding geometry

55. Add edge-loops on the front of the **chest** plate as shown in the following screenshot (*Ctrl + R* and then slide it to **0.500**) and then select the front vertices of the alternate edge-loops and in **Side** view, move them forward.

56. Select the last bottom edge-loop and scale it bigger (to **1.100**):

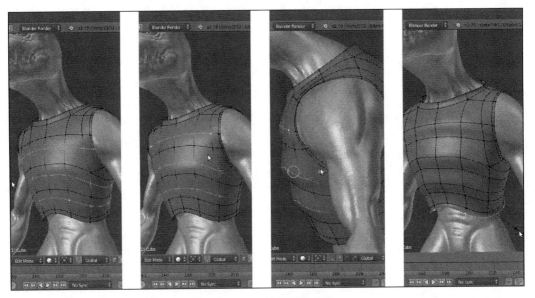

Adding edge-loops to add detailing to the armor

57. Move the front vertices of the **breast** and **belly** downward, using the image loaded in **UV/Image Editor** as reference. Add more edge-loops to add definition to the front of the **chest** plate (in the following screenshot, the three added edge-loops are selected at the same time only to highlight them; in Blender, they must be added one at a time). Then, smooth the resulting oddly spaced back vertices by using the **Space** button of the **LoopTools** add-on:

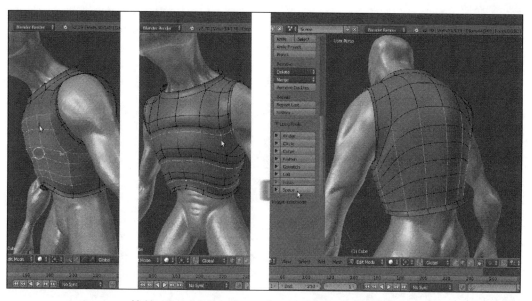

Making the edges' length even through the LoopTools add-on

58. In the **Outliner**, rename the **Cube** item as **Breastplate** (by either double-left-clicking or by pressing *Ctrl* + left-click on the item).

59. Then, go to the **Material** window under the main **Properties** panel and assign a new material to the **Breastplate** object; rename the material as Armor_dark. Set the diffuse color to **RGB 0.605, 0.596, 0.686** and the **Diffuse Shader Model** option to **Oren-Nayar**; set the specular color to **RGB 0.599, 0.857, 1.000** and the **Specular Shader Model** option to **WardIso**; set the **Intensity** value to **0.164** and the **Slope** value to **0.100**. Under the **Shading** subpanel, check the **Cubic Interpolation** item.

60. Go to the **Object Modifiers** window and assign a **Solidify** modifier; move it up in the stack, before the **Subdivision Surface** modifier. Set the **Thickness** value to **0.0150** and check the **Even Thickness** item.

61. Set **Viewport Shading** to **Rendered** to have a quick preview (be sure to have the proper scene layers activated, that is, the **6th** for the lighting and the **11th** and **13th** for the **character** and **armor**). Then, go to the **World** window under the main **Properties** panel and activate the **Indirect Lighting** tab; then, click on the **Approximate** button under the **Gather** subpanel. For the moment, leave the rest as it is:

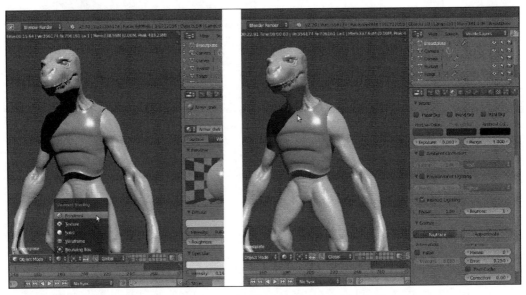

The Rendered result so far, with some World Lighting setting

62. Save the file.

How it works...

This is the usual polygonal modeling process that is common to most aspects of 3D packages. Starting from a **Cube** primitive, we moved and arranged the vertices to model the **chest** armor plate, extruding and also adding new edge-loops by using the **Knife Topology Tool** and the *Ctrl + R* shortcut.

We used the **Mirror** modifier to work only on half of the mesh and to have the other half automatically updated. In some cases, we had to temporarily apply the **Mirror** modifier to better scale the edges as complete circles (otherwise, they would have been half circles with odd scaling pivot points); then, we had to delete the vertices from one side and assign the **Mirror** modifier again.

At a certain point, as the **armor's** shape got more defined, we started to tweak the vertices in **Edit Mode**, but with the **Subdivision Surface** modifier applied to the editing cage in order to have the right feedback while conforming the **armor's** shape to the **character's** shape.

We also used a few of the options available in the **LoopTools** add-on that has been revealed to be an incredibly handy aid in the modeling process.

See also

▸ https://sites.google.com/site/bartiuscrouch/looptools

▸ http://www.blender.org/manual/modeling/index.html

Using the Mesh to Curve technique to add details

In the previous recipe, we modeled the basic bulk of the **Breastplate**. We are now going to see a simple but effective technique to add detailing to the borders of the **armor** plate.

How to do it...

Assuming we have gone out of **Edit Mode** and then saved the file, reopen the Gidiosaurus_ modeling.blend file and proceed with the following:

1. Go back in **Edit Mode** and select the edge-loop around the **neck** (*Alt* + right-click), the edge-loop around the **shoulder** hole (*Alt* + *Shift* + right-click), and the last one at the base of the **Breastplate** (*Alt* + *Shift* + right-click again).

2. Press *Shift* + *D* and soon after, the right-mouse button to duplicate without moving them; press *P* to separate them (in the **Separate** pop-up menu, choose the **Selection** item):

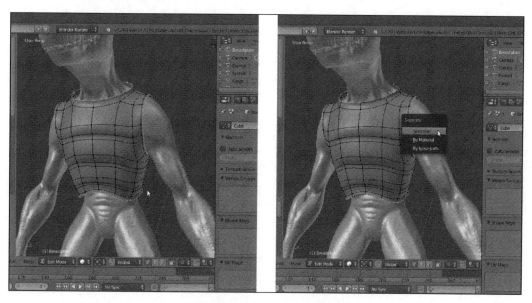

Separating geometry by selection

3. Go out of **Edit Mode** to select the **Breastplate.001** object (the duplicated edge-loops).

4. Press *Alt + C* and in the **Convert to** pop-up menu, select the first item: **Curve from Mesh/Text**.

5. The mesh edge-loops actually get converted into **Curve** objects, as you can see in the **Object Data** window under the main **Properties** panel on the right-hand side of the UI:

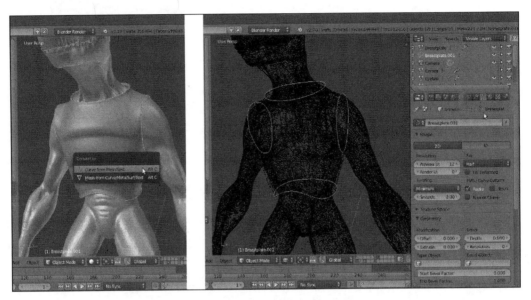

Converting the geometry in Curves

6. In the **Object Data** window, under the **Geometry** tab, set the **Extrude** value to **0.002** and the **Depth** value to **0.010**; then, under the **Shape** tab, set the **Fill** mode to **Full**:

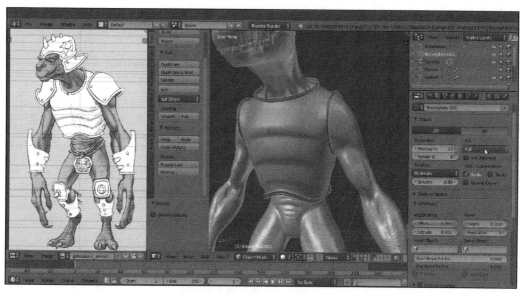

"Modeling" the Curves by the settings

7. Press *Alt* + *C* and this time, in the **Convert to** pop-up menu, select the second item: **Mesh from Curve/Meta/Surf/Text**.

8. Press *Tab* to go in **Edit Mode**, press *A* to select all the vertices, and in the **Mesh Tools** tab under the **Tools** tab in the **Tool Shelf** panel, click on the **Remove Doubles** button (note that in the top main header, a message appears: **Removed 2240 vertices**; so always remember to remove the doubles after a conversion!).

9. Go out of **Edit Mode** and click on the **Smooth** button in the **Edit** subpanel; in the **Outliner**, rename it as **Breastplate_decorations**.

10. Assign a **Subdivision Surface** modifier, with the **Subdivision** level as **2** and **Optimal Display** enabled.

11. Go to the **Material** window and assign a new material; rename it as `Armor_light` and copy all the settings and options from the `Armor_dark` material, except for the diffuse and the specular colors—set them to **RGB 1.000** (pure white; a faster way is to assign the `Armor_dark` material, make it a single user, change the colors to white, and rename the material as `Armor_light`).

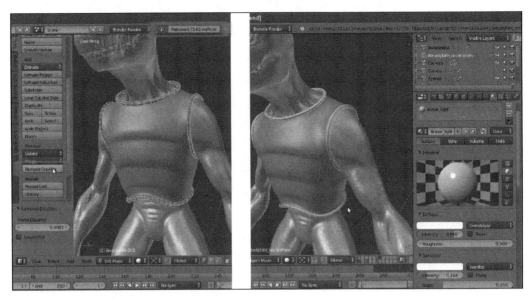

Assigning a new material

12. As always, remember to save the file.

How it works...

Even if at first sight this seems a complex process, actually it's one of the easiest and fastest ways to model a mesh. We have just duplicated the edge-loops that are located where we had the intention of adding the modeled borders. With a simple shortcut, we have converted them to a **curve** object that can be beveled both by other curve objects or simply by values to be inserted in the fields under the **Geometry** tab. Then, once we obtained the shape we wanted, we converted the curve back to a mesh object.

We could have kept the armor decorations as **curves**, but by converting them to meshes, we have the opportunity to unwrap them for the mapping of the textures according to the rest of the **armor**.

Note that the **Preview U** value under the **Resolution** item in the **Shape** subpanel for the **curve** objects should be kept low if you don't want a resulting mesh with a lot of vertices; you can set it quite lower than the default **12**. Just experiment before the final conversion, while keeping in mind that once converted to mesh, the **decorations** will probably be smoothed by a **Subdivision Surface** modifier with the rest of the **armor**; in any case, the obtained **decorations** mesh can also be simplified at a successive stage.

In this chapter, we saw the process that can be used to model the **armor** meshes. We will not demonstrate the rest of the **armor** modeling, as the same techniques can be used over again. However, feel free to model the rest of the **armor** on your own or have a look at the provided `Gidiosaurus_modeling_02.blend` file:

The completed armor as it appears in the rendering

4
Re-topology of the High Resolution Sculpted Character's Mesh

In this chapter, we will cover the following recipes:

- ▶ Using the Grease Pencil tool to plan the edge-loops flow
- ▶ Using the Snap tool to re-topologize the mesh
- ▶ Using the Shrinkwrap modifier to re-topologize the mesh
- ▶ Using the LoopTools add-on to re-topologize the mesh
- ▶ Concluding the re-topologized mesh

Introduction

The re-topology of a mesh, as the name itself explains, is simply the reconstruction of that mesh with a different topology; usually, the re-topology is used to obtain a low resolution mesh from a high resolution one.

In our case, this is obviously needed because we are later going to rig and animate our **Gidiosaurus**, and these tasks would be almost impossible with a mesh as dense as the high resolution sculpted one; we not only need to reconstruct the shape of the mesh with a lower number of vertices, but also with the edge-loops properly placed and flowing for the best render and deformation of the character's features.

In Blender, we have several tools to accomplish this task, both hardcoded into the software or as add-ons to be enabled, and in this chapter, we are going to see them.

Using the Grease Pencil tool to plan the edge-loops flow

It would be perfectly possible to start immediately to re-topologize the high resolution mesh, at least for an expert modeler; by the way, it's usually a good practice to have a guide to be followed in the process, to solve a priori any issue (or at least most of them) that we would come across.

So, let's start this chapter by planning what the right topology can be for a low resolution mesh of our **Gidiosaurus** character; we are going to use the **Grease Pencil** tool to draw the paths of the edge-loops and polygons flow, straight onto the sculpted mesh.

Getting ready

First, let's prepare the screen:

1. Open the `Gidiosaurus_modeling_02.blend` file.

2. Go to the **UV/Image Editor** window to the left and *Shift* + left-click on the **X** icon on the toolbar to get rid of the template image (to be more technically precise, to unlink the template image data block; the *Shift* key is to set the users to **0** and definitely eliminate the image from the file).

3. Put the mouse pointer on the border between the two windows and right-click; in the little **Area Options** pop-up panel, left-click on the **Join Area** item and then slightly move the mouse pointer to the left and left-click again, to join the two windows and obtain a single big 3D viewport window:

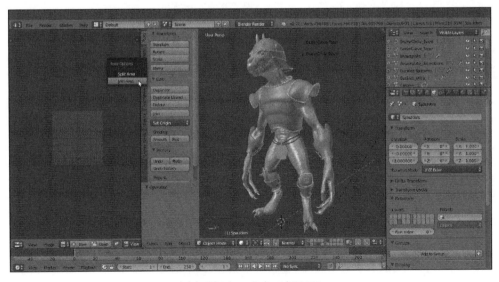

Joining the two windows into one

4. Click on the **11th** scene layer button to show only the sculpted **Gidiosaurus** mesh and parts such as the **teeth**, **eyes**, and so on.

5. Go to the **Outliner** and click on the icons showing an eye image placed to the right side of the **Eyeballs**, **Fangs**, and **Talons** items to hide them.

6. Press the *N* key to make the **Properties** 3D view sidepanel appear to the right of the 3D window and scroll it to find the **Grease Pencil** subpanel (already enabled by default); go to the **Tool Shelf** panel to the left of the 3D window and click on the **Grease Pencil** tab:

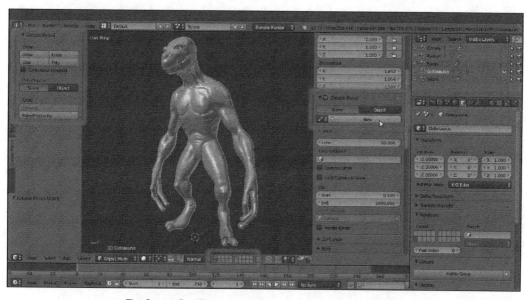

The Grease Pencil panels and the screen layout in current state

7. Check to enable the **Continuous Drawing** item just below the four buttons at the top of the **Grease Pencil** tab on the **Tool Shelf**.

8. Go to the **Grease Pencil** subpanel under the **Properties** 3D view sidepanel to the right and click on the **New** button; then, click on the **+** icon button to the left side to add a new **Grease Pencil** layer, which is by default labeled **GP_Layer**; set the **Stroke** color to **RGB 1.000, 0.000, 0.350** and **Thickness** of the strokes to **4** pixels.

9. Double-click on the **GP_Layer** name to rename it as **Head**.

10. Go to the **Tool Shelf** and, under **Stroke Placement**, click on the **Surface** button:

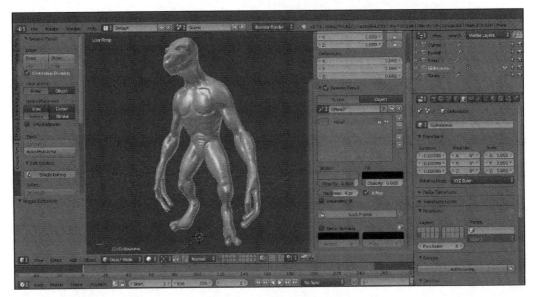

Starting to use the Grease Pencil tool

11. Save the file as `Gidiosaurus_retopology.blend`.

How to do it...

We are now going to start to draw on the character's **head**:

1. Press *Shift + B* and draw a box around the head of the **Gidiosaurus** to zoom to it; then, press the *5* key on the numpad to go into **Ortho** view.

2. Click on the **Draw**, **Line** or **Poly** buttons at the top of the **Grease Pencil** tab in the **Tool Shelf**; alternatively, keep the **D** key pressed (along with left-click) to start to draw the first stroke on the mesh (*Ctrl + D* + left-click and *Ctrl + D* + right-click, respectively for **Line** and **Poly**).

   Because we enabled the **Continuous Drawing** item in the **Tool Shelf**, we can continue to draw without the need to reactivate the drawing mode at each stroke. To quit the sketching session (for example, to change the brush), we can press the *Esc* or the *Enter* keys, so *confirming* the sketching session itself at the same time; otherwise, without the **Continuous Drawing** item enabled, the sketching is confirmed right after each stroke.

3. Start to draw (one half side of the mesh is enough) the strokes; try to make the strokes follow the main, basic, and more remarkable features of the sculpted mesh such as the main **skin folders** going from the **snout** to the **eye sockets** and the bags under the **eyes**, **nostril**, **mouth rim**, and so on.

4. Don't worry too much about the quality or the precision of the strokes; also, don't be afraid to erase (*D* + right-click or the **Erase** button) and/or correct the strokes, if necessary. The **Grease Pencil**, in this case, is just a tool to sketch directly on the mesh the guidelines we will later follow for the re-topology stage:

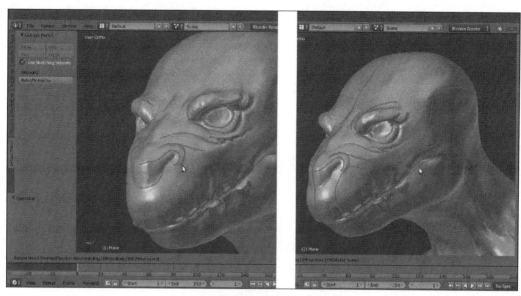

Drawing the head's main features topology

In the case of our **Gidiosaurus**, the topology for a correct deformation is similar to the topology we would use for a human face, but a lot simpler: we just need edge-loops around the **eyes** and in the **eyebrows** area, to give them mobility for expressiveness; a few edge-loops around the **mouth** that, however, in our case, remains quite rigid; and edge-loops following the folders on the top of the **snout**, which can also be important for the *growl* expression.

5. Once the strokes for the main features have been posed, try to join them into a web of edges, as balanced and efficient as possible:

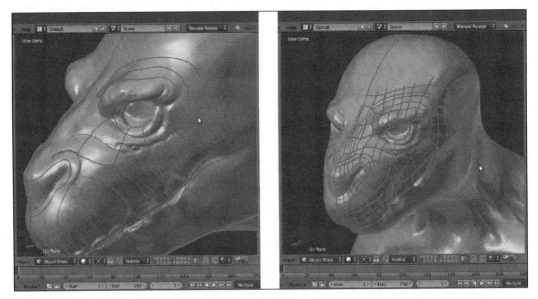

Connecting the strokes

6. At a certain point, when and if the overlapping of the strokes starts to become confusing, you can uncheck the **X Ray** item, which is located to the right side of the **Thickness** slot in the **Grease Pencil** layer subpanel, to disable the visibility of the strokes behind the mesh surface.

7. Forget about the edge-loops of stiff parts such as the cranium; it's enough to plan the position and the flow of the deforming ones. In the screenshot at the bottom right, I have highlighted (in **Gimp**) the main facial edge-loops for the **Gidiosaurus** with different colors:

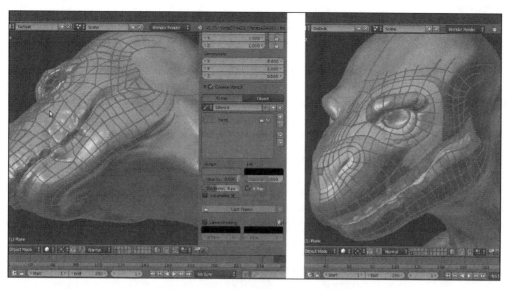

The X Ray button and the highlighted main edge-loops

8. When you think you are done with the **head**, click on the **+** icon button to add a new layer and rename it as **Neck**. Set the values the same you did for the **Head** layer, just change the color of the strokes; I set mine to **RGB 0.106, 0.435, 0.993**, but whatever color you choose, be sure that it stands out in the viewport against the mesh color.

9. In the case of the **neck**, the important thing is to find the correct joining with the **head's** edge-loops under the lower **jaw**, as you can see in the bottom-right screenshot:

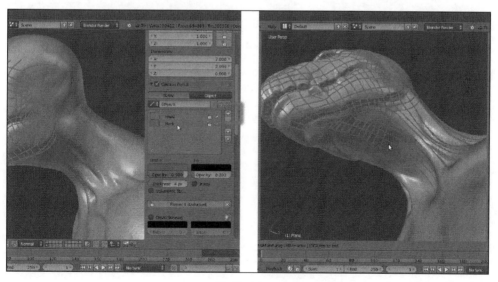

The Neck layer

10. Continue to stroke on the **neck** by drawing parallel horizontal loops along its length and use the vertical strokes to outline the **neck's** muscles (don't look for a **sternocleidomastoid** muscle here; the **Gidiosaurus**, anatomy, although similar in some ways, is not human at all!).

11. Remember that because our character is wearing an **armor**, it is not necessary to re-topologize the whole body, but only the exposed parts; so we can stop the planning just a little beyond the plates outside edges. To verify the correct extension of the strokes, just be sure to have the **X Ray** item enabled in the **Grease Pencil** layers and also the **13th** scene layer enabled to show the **armor**:

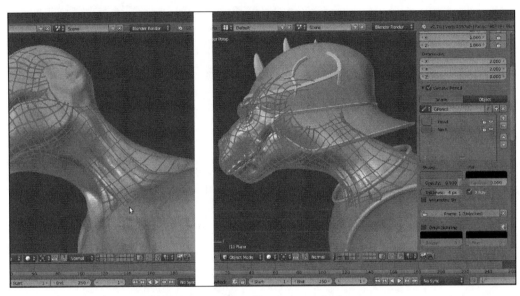

Verifying the extension of the strokes under the armor

12. Click again on the **+** icon button in the **Grease Pencil** subpanel under the **Properties** 3D view sidepanel and rename the new layer as **Arm**. Set the values the same as you did for the **Head** and **Neck** layers, but change the color once more (**R 0.000, G 1.000, B 0.476**); this time, we have to plan the joining of the cylindrical shape of the **arm** with the **shoulder** and the **collar bones** areas:

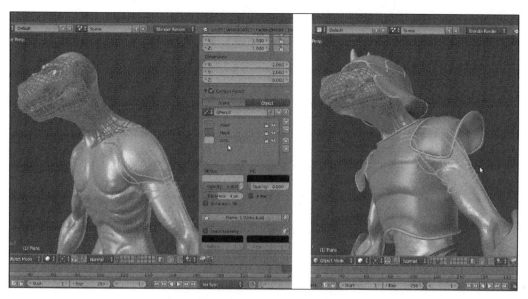

Sketching the guidelines on the arm

13. As before, also in this case, it is not necessary to go beyond the boundaries of the **armor chest** plate, but including also the muscles of the **chest** and **back** in the topology planning can give a more natural result:

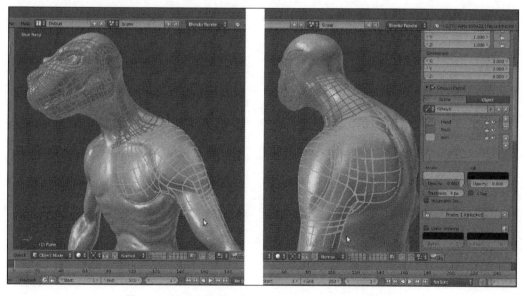

The completed guidelines for the shoulder and the arm joining

14. When you are done, save the file.

At this point, we can stop with the **Grease Pencil** sketching of the topology; the remaining parts of the exposed body are a lot simpler and will be quickly resolved in the successive recipe of this chapter.

There's more...

We can load any already existing **Grease Pencil** layer data blocks even into an empty scene, by clicking on the little arrows on the left-hand side of the **Gpencil** slot (*Freehand annotation sketchbook*) at the top of the **Grease Pencil** subpanel on the **Properties** 3D view sidepanel, and indifferently for **Scene** or **Object**. Actually, the **Grease Pencil** tool can be used as a sketchbook tool, to write quick notes and/or corrections inside the **Node Editor** window or the **UV/Image Editor** window, and even as an animation tool, by drawing inside an empty scene or on the surface of other objects to be used as *templates*.

In the following screenshot, you can see the sketching sessions previously made on the **Gidiosaurus** object's surface, showing *a solo* and keeping the volumes of the character in the 3D space:

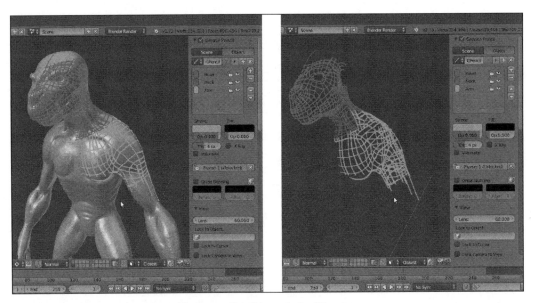

The Grease Pencil layers in the 3D space

See also

► http://www.blender.org/manual/grease_pencil/introduction.html

Using the Snap tool to re-topologize the mesh

In this recipe, we'll use the **Snap** tool to start to re-topologize the sculpted high resolution mesh.

Getting ready

First, let's prepare both, the mesh to be *traced*, which is the high resolution mesh, and the tool itself:

1. Go to the **Outliner** and click on the *Restrict viewport selection* icon, which is the arrow one, to the side of the **Gidiosaurus** item to make it not selectable.

2. Be sure that the **3D Cursor** is at the center of the scene (*Shift + C*) and add a **Plane** primitive.

3. Click on the *Snap during transform* button, the little icon with the magnet, on the 3D view toolbar, or else press *Shift + Tab* to activate the tool.

4. Click on the **Snap Element** button (*Type of element to snap to*) on the close right to select the **Face** item, or else press **Shift + Ctrl + Tab** to make the **Snap Element** pop-up menu appear in order to select the item from:

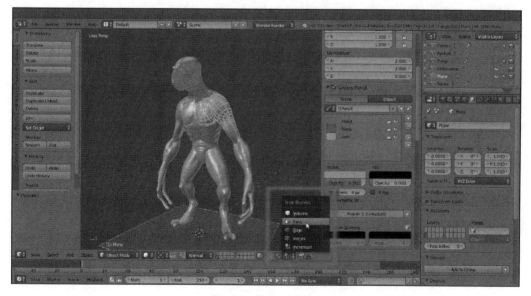

The Snap Element menu

How to do it...

Now, we are going to start the re-topology:

1. With the **Plane** object selected, press *Tab* to go into **Edit Mode**; with all the vertices already selected by default, by pressing *Shift* + right-click, deselect just **one** vertex (anyone of them, it doesn't matter which one).

2. Press *X* to delete the other **three** vertices that are still selected.

3. Select the single remaining vertex and move it onto the **head** of the sculpted mesh, close to the **left eye socket**; as the **Snap** tool is enabled, the vertex stays on the mesh surface.

4. Press the period (.) key on the numpad to zoom the 3D view centered on the selected vertex:

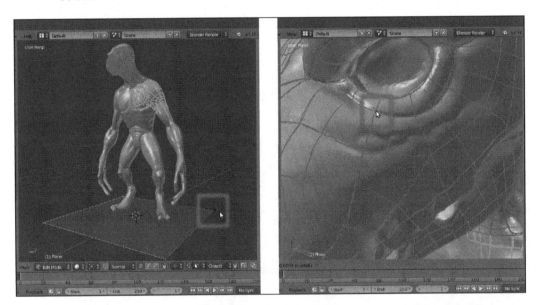

Starting the re-topology process

5. Go to the **Object Data** window and check the **X-Ray** item under the **Display** subpanel in the main **Properties** panel to the right of the screen.

6. Start to extrude the vertex, building an edge-loop around the **eye socket** and following the **Grease Pencil** guideline, both by pressing the *E* key or *Ctrl* + left-click to add vertices; if needed, press *G* to move them at the right location (that is, at the intersections of the guidelines).

7. When you have almost completed the edge-loop around the **eye socket**, select the last and the first vertices and press the *F* key to close it.

8. Select the bottom row of vertices of the edge-loop and extrude them; adjust the position of each vertex on the ground of the strokes guideline:

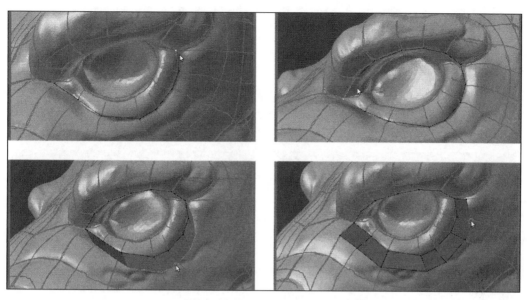

The first re-topology around the eye socket

9. Do the same with the upper row of vertices and then select the free vertices on the right-hand side of the edge-loops and press *Alt + M* to merge them at the center (**At Center**):

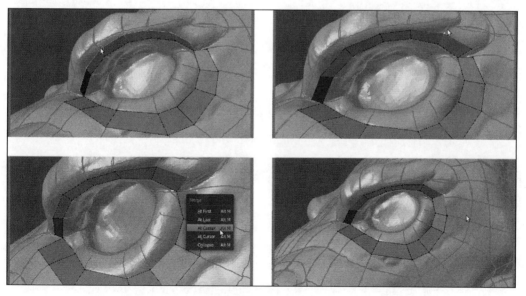

Building the eye edge-loop

10. While still in **Edit Mode**, select all the vertices and press *Ctrl + N* to recalculate the normals.

11. Keep on extruding the edge-loops to build the faces around the **eye socket**. Select the inner edge-loop and extrude it; then, scale it inside and adjust the vertices position as usual.

12. Cut a new edge-loop in the middle of the **eye socket** by pressing *Ctrl + R* and then select each vertex; press *G* and, immediately after, click with the left button of the mouse. This way the newly added vertex stays in place, but is snapped to the underlying surface (sadly, it doesn't work automatically as you cut or add vertices; they must be moved in some way to make the **Snap** tool work).

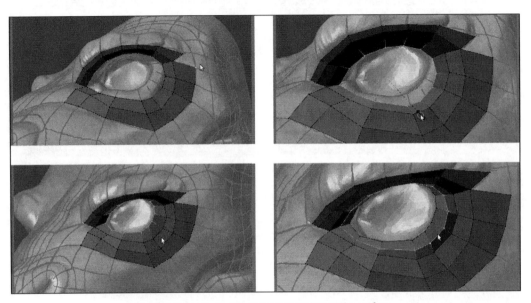

Adding geometry and snapping the vertices to the surface

13. Keep on adding geometry to the mesh, extruding or *Ctrl* + left-clicking, and switch between edges and vertices selection mode to make the workflow faster. Press 5 on the numpad to go into **Ortho** view when necessary. Following the strokes guideline, build faces going towards the median line of the object.

14. As you are arrived to the median line of the object, go to the **Object Modifiers** window under the **Properties** panel and assign a **Mirror** modifier.

15. Click on the *Adjust edit cage to modifier result* icon (the last one in the row to the side of the modifier's name), to activate the modifier during the editing, and check the **Clipping** item.

16. Adjust the vertices you just added to the median line of the mesh to stay on the *y* axis and recalculate the normals.

17. Go to the **Outliner** and rename the **Plane** item as **Gidiosaurus_lowres**.

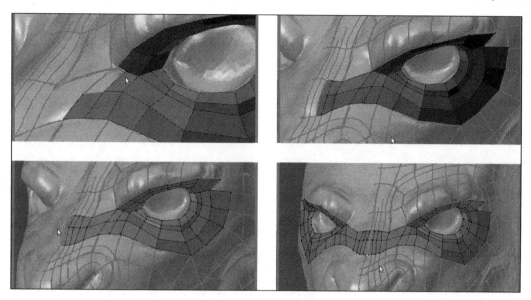

Going towards the median line

18. Build the remainder of the faces the same way, extruding edges or vertices, moving them to react to the **Snap** tool, and adding cuts and edge-loops where needed to keep all quads. **N-gons** faces can be split into quads by dividing an edge to add a vertex in the middle, selecting the new vertex and its opposite one and pressing the *J* key to connect them (see the two screenshots at the bottom row):

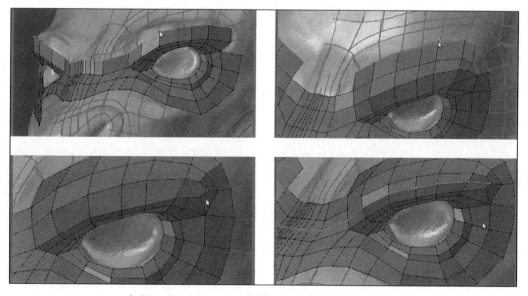

Building the eyebrows and dividing N-gons into two quad faces

19. Assign a **Subdivision Surface** modifier to the low resolution mesh and set **Subdivisions** to **2**. Check the **Optimal Display** item; if you want, click on the *Adjust edit cage to modifier result* icon, which is the last one in the row to the side of the modifier's name. To work with an already smoothed mesh (in the end, the mesh will be subdivided in any case) is a usual workflow; by the way, it depends on your preferences. If you prefer to work without the modifier, occasionally go out of **Edit Mode** to verify how the geometry behaves under the **Subdivision Surface** modifier.

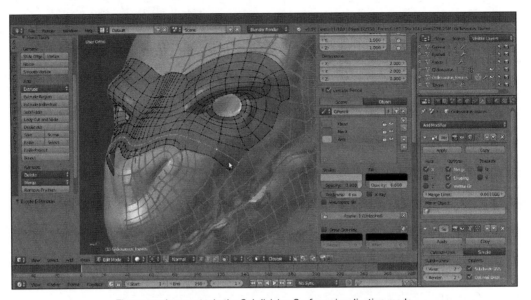

The created geometry in the Subdivision Surface visualization mode

20. Around the eyebrows, it is important to have continuous edge-loops to allow for better mesh deformation; often, it is enough to merge (*Alt + M*) two vertices to obtain the right flow. Note that this creates a pole (check out the screenshot at the top right) that can later be eliminated by a cut and then merges the two tris faces into a quad (*Alt + J*; the two screenshots at the bottom):

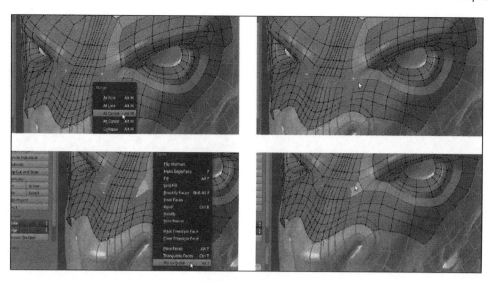

Closing two edge-loops

21. We have almost completed the **Gidiosaurus'** face. Select the vertices of the lower **jaw** and press the *H* key to hide them; select the **upper mouth rim** and extrude it and then adjust the vertices' position.

22. Deselect the vertices, press *Alt + H* to unhide the **mandible**, and press *Shift + H* to hide the unselected vertices (in this case, the **upper face**). Select the **mouth rim** of the **mandible** and extrude and then tweak the position of the vertices.

23. Connect the upper and the lower **jaws** by connecting the last vertices, as shown in the bottom-left of screenshot and then build a face. Tweak the vertices' position:

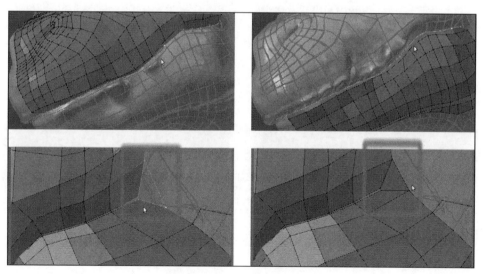

Connecting the jaw to the upper mouth

We can stop using the **Snap** tool at this point and continue with the re-topologizing by using different tools; we'll see this in the upcoming recipes.

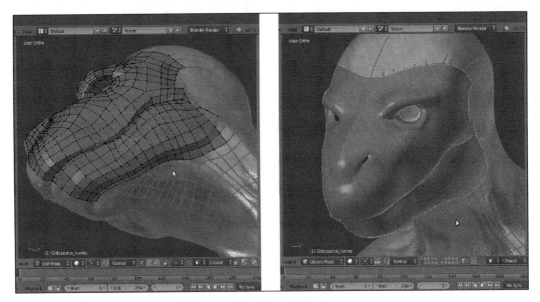

The re-topologized face of the character

How it works...

The main requirement for a re-topology tool is the ability to trace the shape and volume of the high resolution mesh as easily as possible. In this recipe, we used the Blender **Snap** tool that, once set to **Face**, guarantees that every added vertex lies on the faces of any directly underlying object; this way, it is quite simple to concentrate on the flow of the polygons, while their vertices stay anchored to the mesh's surface.

To remark that the strokes are there only as a generic indication, note that in certain areas we are doubling the number of faces sketched with the **Grease Pencil** tool as well as to try to keep the density of the mesh as even as possible.

Using the Shrinkwrap modifier to re-topologize the mesh

Sometimes, the **Snap** tool is not enough or can be quite difficult to use because of a particular shape of the high resolution mesh; in these cases, the **Shrinkwrap** modifier can be very handy.

Getting ready

Basically, the usage of this method is all in the preparation of the modifier:

1. Assign the **Shrinkwrap** modifier to the **Gidiosaurus_lowres** mesh and, in the modifier stack, move it *before* the **Subdivision Surface** modifier.

2. Click on the **Target** field to select the **Gidiosaurus** mesh item and leave the **Mode** option to **Nearest Surface Point** (this seems to be the more efficient mode for this task; by the way, you can experiment with the other two modes that can reveal themselves useful in other situations).

3. Enable the *Display modifier in Edit mode* and *Adjust edit cage to modifier result* buttons (the penultimate one and the last one to the right, with the cube and four selected vertices image and with the upside-down triangle and three vertices image, respectively) and the **Keep Above Surface** item.

4. In **Edit Mode**, if it's necessary to make the low resolution mesh more easily visible against the high resolution one, change the **Offset** value to **0.001**.

5. Having the **X-Ray** item still active, go to the **Shading** subpanel under the **Properties** 3D view sidepanel and check the **Backface Culling** item:

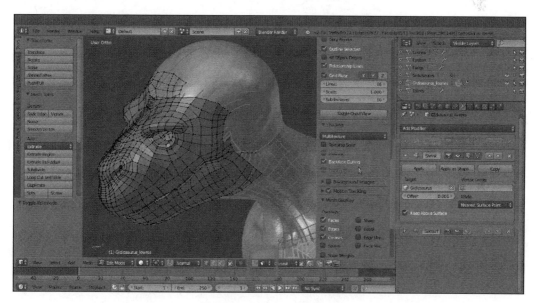

The Shrinkwrap modifier panel

How to do it...

In **Edit Mode**, select, extrude, and move the vertices as required! The **Shrinkwrap** modifier will take care of keeping the vertices adhering to the target mesh surface.

If you are having issues, such as vertices jumping everywhere as you try to move them, try to disable the **Snap** tool. This is not always the case, but sometimes the combination of both the tool and the modifier can give unexpected results; other times, it can be the opposite.

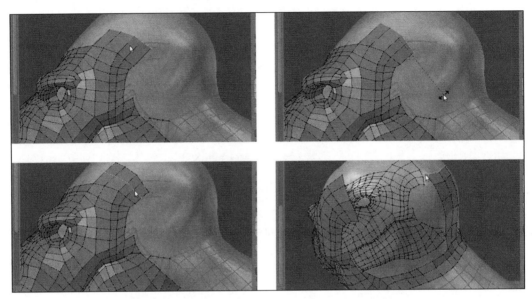

Extruding and cutting an edge-loop under the Shrinkwrap modifier

Remember that if you are using this method to re-topologize, at the end of the process, you *must apply the Shrinkwrap modifier*.

Also, save the file.

Using the LoopTools add-on to re-topologize the mesh

We have already seen the **LoopTools** add-on in *Chapter 3, Polygonal Modeling of the Character's Accessories*. This incredibly useful Python script can even be used for the re-topology!

Getting ready

If the **LoopTools** add-on isn't enabled yet, perform the following steps:

1. Start Blender and call the **Blender User Preferences** panel (*Ctrl + Alt + U*); go to the **Addons** tab.

2. Under the **Categories** item on the left-hand side of the panel, click on **Mesh**.

3. Check the empty little box to the right of the **Mesh: LoopTools** add-on to enable it.

4. Click on the **Save User Settings** button at the bottom-left of the panel to save your preferences and close the panel:

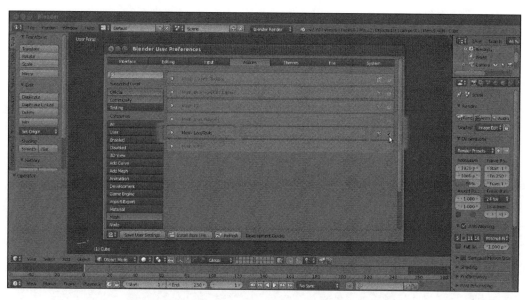

The User Preferences panel and the LoopTools add-on enabled

5. Load the `Gidiosaurus_retopology.blend` file.

6. Click on the *Snap during transform* button on the 3D view toolbar (or else, press *Shift + Tab*) to enable the **Snap** tool again.

How to do it...

In the **LoopTools** add-on, there are at least three tools that can be used for the re-topology: **Gstretch**, **Bridge**, and **Loft** (the last two seem to have almost the same effect so, at least for our present goal, we can consider them to be interchangeable).

Let's first see the **Gstretch** tool:

1. Go to the **Grease Pencil** subpanel under the **Properties** 3D view sidepanel to the right. Be sure that the **Grease Pencil** checkbox is checked and click on the **+** icon button to add a fourth layer after the **Arm** layer (actually, you can also delete the preexisting **GPencil** data block and start with a brand new one, or in any case disable the visibility of the other layers); leave the strokes color as it is by default—that is, pure black.

2. In **Edit Mode**, press *D* and sketch one edge-loop stroke.

3. Select the edges of the low resolution mesh and press *E* to extrude them and then right-click; click on the **Gstretch** button (or press *W* | **Specials** | **LoopTools** | **Gstretch**).

4. In the last operator panel at the bottom of the **Tool Shelf** (or else, press *F6* to make the pop-up window appear at the mouse cursor location), check the **Delete** strokes item.

5. Press *Ctrl + R* to cut the required edge-loops in the new faces:

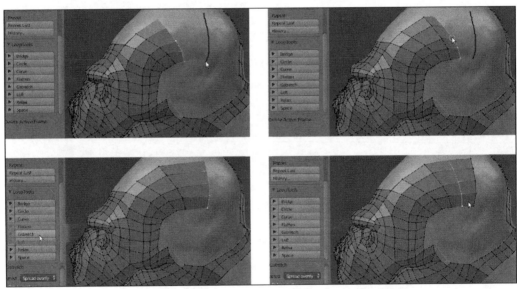

Using the Gstretch tool in conjunction with the Grease Pencil tool

Yes, it's that simple; it's enough to stroke the target position line and the new extruded vertices will be moved to that target position.

Also, now let's see the **Bridge** and the **Loft** tools:

1. Select a group of edges and press *Shift + D* to duplicate them.

2. Move them into a new position and adjust the vertices as required.

3. Select both the new edges as the previous group.

4. Go to the **LoopTools** panel and click on the **Bridge** button (or again, through the *W* key to call the **Specials** menu).

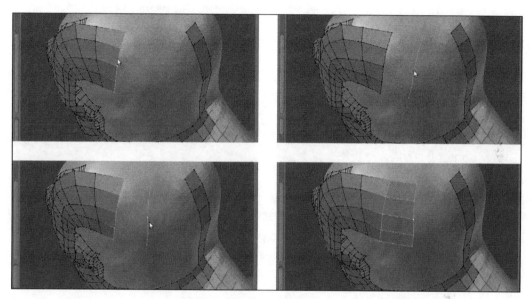

Using the Bridge tool

5. If you need to add cuts, instead of the usual *Ctrl + R* shortcut, go to the last operator panel (*F6*) and change the value of the **Segments** slot to the number required.

It's not mandatory to duplicate new edges, it's enough to select the same number of vertices in the two edge-loops to be connected; here, after the **Bridge** tool operation, we have set the **Segments** value to **3**:

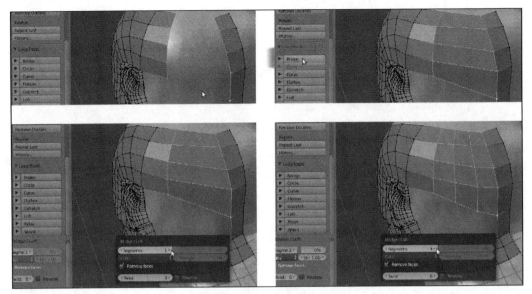

Adding cuts to the bridge operation

You can repeat the operation and the add-on will keep the last values you entered.

Repeat the steps, and this time click on the **Loft** button. The effect is almost the same, but if the new faces come out really messy, just click twice on the **Reverse** checkbox in the last operator panel; this should fix the issue.

You can then use all the other buttons to refine the added geometry; in the following screenshots, I tweaked the new geometry a little bit by selecting the horizontal edges and clicking on the **Space**, **Flatten**, and **Relax** buttons:

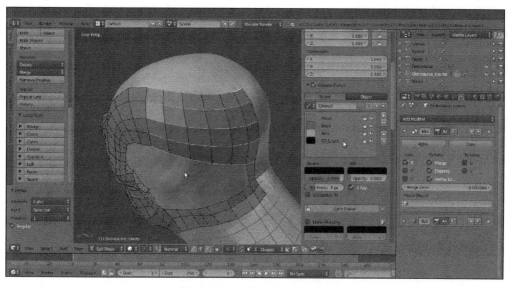

Completing the Gidiosaurus head

Using a mix of all the previous methods, in a short time, we have completed the head and the joining of the neck of our **Gidiosaurus_lowres** mesh; as you can see, particularly in the second screenshot at the bottom, the technique of following the main features and folders of the sculpted surface with the edge-loops can highlight the organic shapes even with a low resolution mesh:

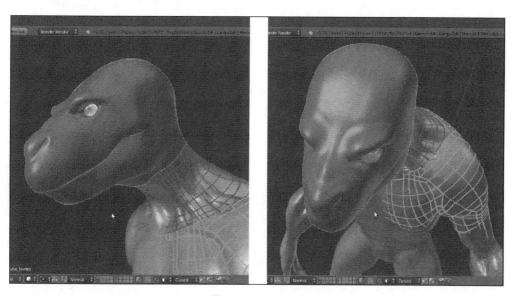

The completed head

Don't forget to save the file and quit Blender.

Concluding the re-topologized mesh

The **Shrinkwrap** modifier method can be the way to quickly finish the rest of the re-topology of the **Gidiosaurus** sculpted mesh, by quickly re-topologizing the simpler cylindrical shapes and then completing the more difficult parts by hand.

Getting ready

If necessary, repeat the steps to set up the **Shrinkwrap** modifier technique:

1. Assign the **Shrinkwrap** modifier to the **Gidiosaurus_lowres** mesh and in the modifier stack, move it *before* the **Subdivision Surface** modifier.

2. Click on the **Target** field to select the **Gidiosaurus** mesh item and leave **Mode** to **Nearest Surface Point**.

3. Enable the *Display modifier in Edit mode* and *Adjust edit cage to modifier result* buttons and the **Keep Above Surface** item.

4. In **Edit Mode**, to make the low resolution mesh more easily visible against the high resolution one, change the **Offset** value to **0.001**.

5. Having the **X-Ray** item still active, go to the **Shading** subpanel under the **Properties** 3D view sidepanel and check the **Backface Culling** item.

6. Then, to conclude the re-topology, we also need to enable the **Copy Attributes Menu** add-on; go to **Blender User Preferences | Addons | 3D View | 3D View: Copy Attributes Menu**.

How to do it...

Let's go on by building the geometry of the **neck**:

1. While still in **Edit Mode**, just select the **head's** last edge loop on the **neck** and extrude it (*E* key) towards the **shoulders**.

2. Press the *Ctrl + R* keys and add at least **7** or **8** widthwise edge-loops:

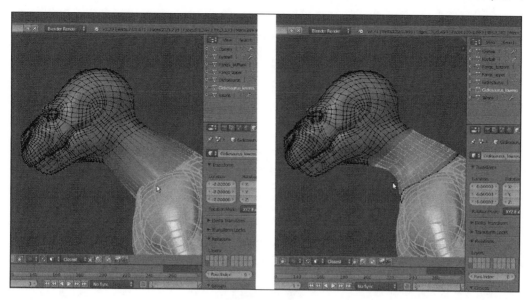

Extruding the neck

3. Also, with the aid of the **Snap** tool, tweak the position of the bottom row of vertices, extrude them to add an edge-loop of faces, and tweak again. Go out of **Edit Mode**.

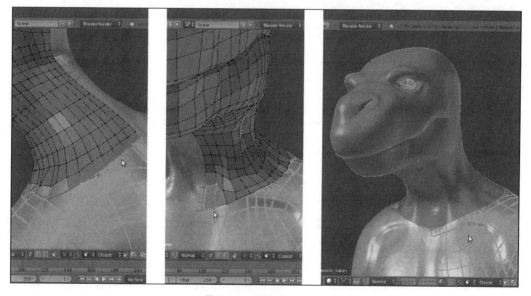

The re-topology of the neck

We can use the same technique as in steps 1, 2, and 3 to quickly re-topologize the left **arm** and **leg** of the character. Instead of extruding the new geometry from the **Gidiosaurus_lowres** mesh, in this case, it's better to add a new simple primitive: a **Circle** or also a **Plane**; whatever the primitive, when you add it, be sure that the **3D Cursor** is at the character's origin pivot point.

As you can see in the following screenshot, at first we just created the geometry only for the *main* cylindrical sections of the **limbs**:

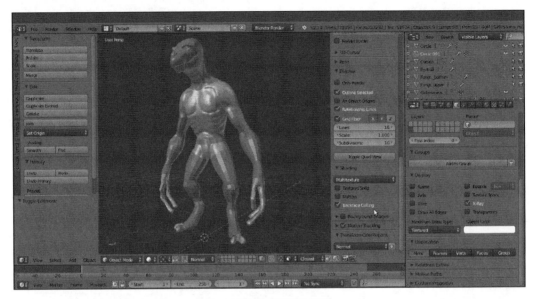

Arms and legs re-topologized

Do the same for the **body**: just a couple of edge-loops placed at the **waist** to extrude the geometry from; remember that the **chest** is covered with the **armor breastplate**, so only the **exposed area** needs to be re-topologized.

One **Mirror** and one **Subdivision Surface** modifier has been assigned to the **three** objects (**head/neck**, **arm**, and **hips/leg**). Also, because of the **Mirror** modifier, the vertices of the half side of the **abdomen's** edge-loops have been deleted.

There's more...

After the main parts have been re-topologized, we can start to tweak the position of the vertices on the **arm** and **leg**, to better fit the flow and shapes of the muscles and tendons in the sculpted mesh.

Thanks to the aid of the **Shrinkwrap** modifier, we can do it quite freely; however, before we start with the tweaking, we require a little bit of preparation for a better visibility of the working objects, to affect and modify the new geometry (visible as a wireframe) and have the underlying sculpted mesh visible at the same time.

To do this, we have two ways:

The first way is as follows:

1. Go to the **Shrinkwrap** modifier panel and set the **Offset** value to **0.002**.

2. Go to the **Object** window and disable the **X-Ray** item; in the **Maximum Draw Type** slot, under the **Display** subpanel, select **Wire**:

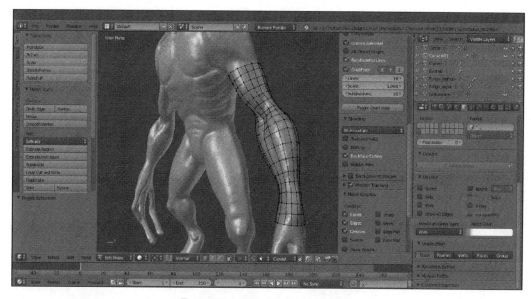

The mesh visualized in wireframe mode

The second way is as follows:

1. Go to the **Shrinkwrap** modifier and set the **Offset** value back to **0.000**.

2. If this is the case, go to the **Object** window and, under the **Display** subpanel, enable the **X-Ray** item. In the **Maximum Draw Type** slot, under the **Display** subpanel, select **Textured**.

3. Go to the **Properties** 3D view sidepanel (press *N* if not already present); if necessary, enter **Edit Mode** and under the **Shading** subpanel, check the **Hidden Wire** item.

4. In both ways (I used the second one), if you want to enable the *Display modifier in Edit mode* and *Adjust edit cage to modifier result* buttons for the **Subdivision Surface** modifier to see its effect in **Edit Mode**, it is better to move the **Shrinkwrap** modifier *after* the **Subdivision Surface** modifier in the stack, to have a better looking result.

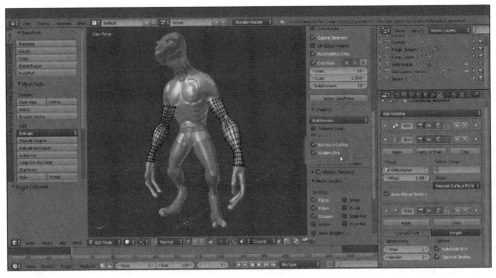

The second wireframe visualization method

We can now start to add the missing parts, by extruding and moving the vertices to better fit the sculpted features and also adding, if necessary, new edge-loops to better define these features:

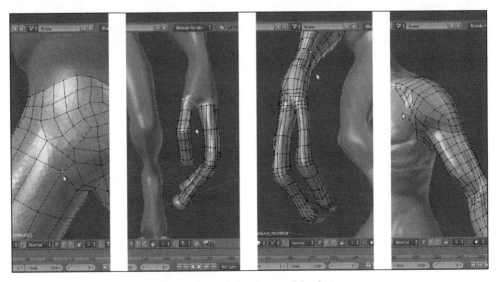

Refining and completing the remaining features

After the **wireframe** setup, it's easy to tweak the low resolution geometry to better fit the character's anatomy:

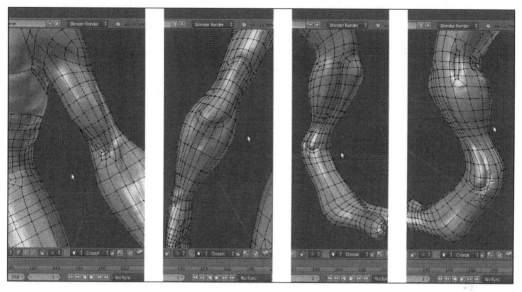

The character's anatomy

The still missing parts are modeled at this stage, such as the inside of the **nostrils** or the **eyelids**, again with the aid of the **Shrinkwrap** modifier; this time, targeted to the **Cornea** object to project the **eyelids** geometry onto it with an **Offset** value of **0.0035**:

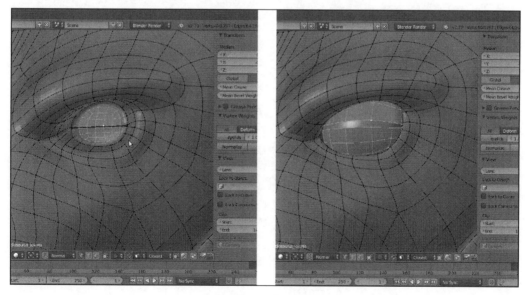

The character's eyelids

Also, we built the **inner mouth** and the **tongue** of our character and refined the **dental alveoli**:

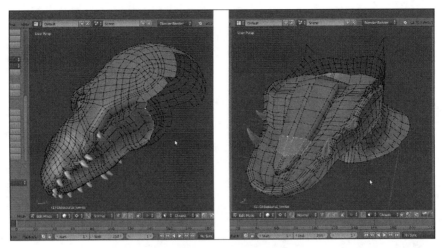

The character's alveoli and tongue

As in every project, we can go on with the refining, adding edge-loops, and so on, and this would seem a never-ending work; instead, at this point, we can consider the **Gidiosaurus** re-topology at the end, so it's time to apply the **Shrinkwrap** modifiers and, if this is the case, select the **Gidiosaurus** body's still separated objects and join them together to have a single mesh.

It's time to do the same with the **armor** that is still waiting on the **13th** scene layer:

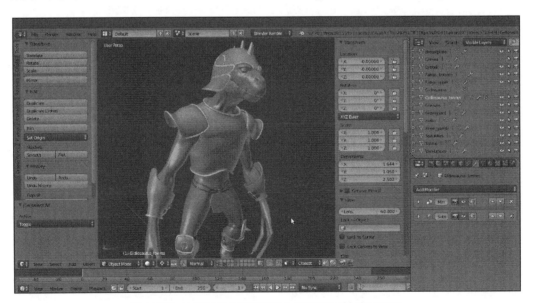

The totally completed re-topologized character with the armor

How it works...

First, we have to quickly build the geometry using the **Shrinkwrap** modifier technique and then set the visibility of this geometry to wireframe (**Wire**), to make the underlying sculpted mesh visible.

The **Shrinkwrap** modifier, in the first case with the **Offset** value set high enough to allow the wireframe visibility over the sculpted surface, ensured that all the moved vertices and the new added geometry are automatically wrapped around the target mesh to preserve the volume.

At the end, we took back the **Offset** value to **0.000** anyway and we applied the **Shrinkwrap** modifier; then, we joined the re-topologized **arm** and **leg** objects together to the **Gidiosaurus_lowres** one.

As you have probably noticed, we haven't applied the **Mirror** modifiers yet. This is because it will still be useful in the next chapter.

5
Unwrapping the Low Resolution Mesh

In this chapter, we will cover the following recipes:

- Preparing the low resolution mesh for unwrapping
- UV unwrapping the mesh
- Editing the UV islands
- Using the Smart UV Project tool
- Modifying the mesh and the UV islands
- Setting up additional UV layers
- Exporting the UV Map layout

Introduction

So, at this point, we have **sculpted** our high resolution character and through the **retopology** process, we have obtained a low resolution *copy*, which is easier to use for rigging, texturing, and animation.

There are several ways to apply textures to a mesh in Blender, as in any other 3D package. In our case, we are going to use **UV Mapping**, which is certainly one of the most commonly used and efficient methods for organic shapes.

Before the unwrapping process, the mesh must be prepared to make the task easier.

Preparing the low resolution mesh for unwrapping

In this recipe, we'll fix the last details such as the position of some of the character's parts (for instance, the **closed mouth**) and in general, anything that is needed to facilitate the unwrapping.

Getting ready

To be more precise, before the unwrapping, we must perform the following tasks in the right order:

1. Join the **teeth** and **talons** to the **body**.
2. Create the vertex group for the **mandible**.
3. Open the **mouth**.
4. Mark the seams to unwrap the **body**.

So, open the `Gidiosaurus_retopology.blend` file and deactivate the layer with the **armor** to hide it; select the **Gidiosaurus** object and save the file as `Gidiosaurus_unwrap.blend`.

How to do it...

The simplest of the *four* tasks just so happens to be the first, joining the **body** with the **teeth** and **talons**.

To join the body parts, follow these steps:

1. Select the **Talons** item in the **Outliner**, and then hold *Shift* and select the **Fangs_bottom**, **Fangs_upper**, and **Gidiosaurus_lowres** items.
2. Press *Ctrl + J* to join them.
3. Right away we will notice that, because the retopologized mesh didn't have any material assigned, the whole object gets the only material available, which is the `Enamel` material we had assigned to the **talons** and **teeth** earlier.
4. To fix this, assign a new material, or you can also assign the already existing `Body` material, to the retopologized mesh before the joining operation.

5. Alternatively, after the joining, click on the **+** icon to the side of the material names, and then select the **New** button in the **Material** window to create a new material. Now, enter **Edit Mode**, put the mouse pointer on the **Gidiosaurus** mesh, and press the *L* key to select all the **connected vertices**. Because the **talons** and **teeth** vertices are joined, *but not connected* to the **face** vertices, they don't get selected; for the same reason, you have to repeat the operation three times to select the **head**, **arm**, **hips,** and **leg** vertices:

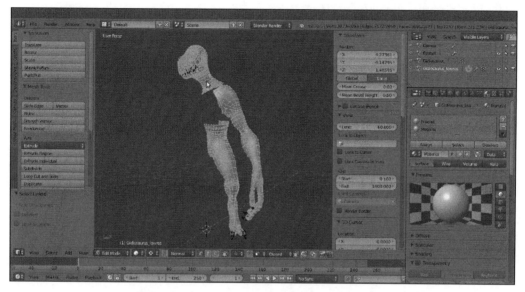

The head, arm and hip/leg vertices selected in Edit Mode

6. Click on the **Assign** button and go out of the **Edit Mode**. Now, edit the name and color of the new material or whatever, or else switch it with the Body one.

   The second task is a bit more complex and is covered in more detail in *Chapter 7, Skinning the Low Resolution Mesh*, which is about the **skinning** process. However, we need to explore this subject a little bit now, as it will help us operate on a small portion of the mesh easily.

   To create a **vertex group** to open the **mouth**, follow these steps:

7. Go to the **Side** view and zoom in on the **head** of the character.

8. Go to the **Object Data** window; under the **Vertex Groups** subpanel, add a new group and rename it mand (short for **mandible**).

9. Press *Ctrl + Tab* to go into **Weight Paint** mode (or left-click on the mode button on the 3D window toolbar to switch from **Edit Mode** to **Weight Paint** mode); press *Z* to go into **Wireframe** viewport shading mode so that you can see the edges of the topology.

10. By using a combination of vertex selection mode, both in **Edit Mode** and by painting with **Weight** and **Strength** as **1.000** in the **Weight Paint** mode, assign vertices to the group of the **mandible** area and the part of the **neck**; obviously, you have to include the vertices of the inner bottom **jaw**, as well as the **tongue** and bottom **teeth**:

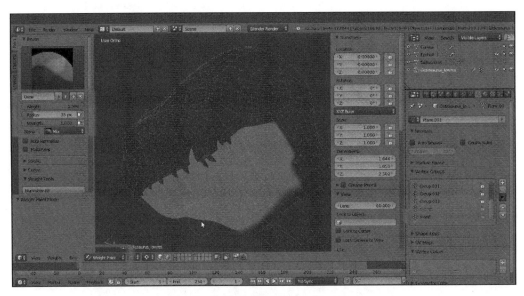

The visualization of the mand vertex group

11. Press *Ctrl + Tab* to exit the **Weight Paint** mode.

    Note that a vertex group can be edited at a later time, so it will be easier to set the exact amount of weight on the vertices by looking at the **Lattice** modifier feedback, which is the next step.

    So, to open the **mouth**, perform the following steps:

12. Add an **Empty** object to the center of the scene (*Shift + A* | **Empty** | **Plain Axes**).

13. Go to the **Side** view (press the *3* key on the numpad). Move the **Empty** to the position where the **mandible** should join the skull (to be precise, I placed it at this location: **X = 0.0000, Y = -0.3206**, and **Z = 2.2644**; go to the **Properties** 3D view sidepanel, and under the **Transform** subpanel, enter the values in the first three slots under the **Location** item).

14. To ensure that the **Empty** cannot be moved anymore, click on the lock icon on the right-hand side of its slot in the **Outliner** and also rename it to `Empty_rot_mand`:

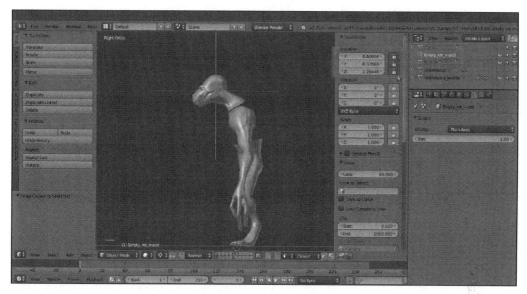

The Empty_rot_mand in place

15. With the **Empty** still selected, press *Shift + S* | **Cursor to Selected**.

16. Add a **Lattice** object to the scene (*Shift + A* | **Lattice**), and in the **Object Data** window, set **Interpolation Type** for **U**, **V**, and **W** to **Linear**; select the **Gidiosaurus** object and go to the **Objects Modifier** window; assign a **Lattice** modifier. Move it before the **Subdivision Surface** modifier.

17. In the **Object** field, select the **Lattice** item; in the **Vertex Group** field, select the **mand** item.

18. In the **Side** view, select the **Lattice** object, go into **Edit Mode**, and select all the vertices and rotate them **35** degrees counterclockwise around the *x* axis:

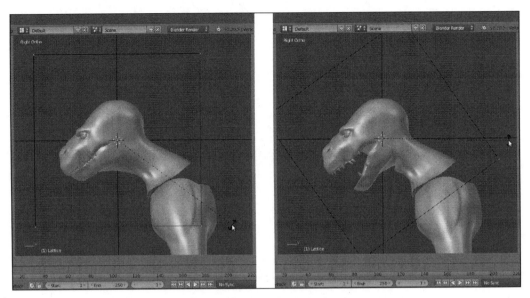

Rotating the Lattice to open the mouth

As you can see, the **Lattice** only affects the vertices inside the **mand** vertex group; however, there is a clear indentation on the throat where the **mand** vertex group ends abruptly, so now we must blur this boundary to keep the smooth curved transition from the bottom **jaw** to the **neck**, and remove the abrupt edge.

19. Go back into the **Weight Paint** mode (*Ctrl + Tab*) and click on the **Brush** icon at the top of the **Tools** tab to switch the **Draw** brush with the **Blur** brush, and then start to blur the boundaries of the **mand** vertex group.

20. Sometimes, blurring the edge weights is not enough, so go back to the **Draw** brush, set the **Strength** to **0.500** (or whatever value you find works best), and paint on the vertices; then refine the transition again with the **Blur** brush:

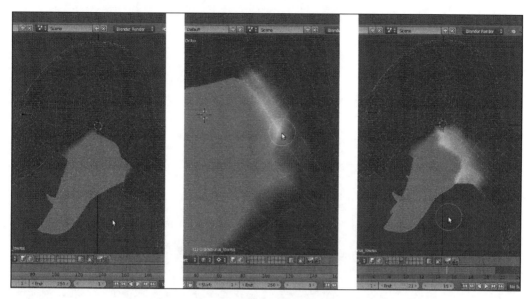

Blurring and painting the weights

21. To make the job easier and faster, you can temporarily disable the **Lattice** modifier, as well as the **Subdivision Surface** modifier.

22. When you are done, go out of the **Weight Paint** mode, apply the **Lattice** modifier, and delete the **Lattice** object.

23. Make sure to keep the **Empty_rot_mand**, which that will turn out to be useful when rigging the character. For now, just hide or move it onto a different layer.

    At this point, we can obviously edit the **throat** area vertices as usual: relaxing and tweaking them and so on. Actually, this is the right moment to tweak all the vertices and any areas that couldn't be done before, such as the inside of the **mouth**, the inner **cheeks**, and so forth, because now we are going to do the last preparation task before the unwrapping.

To mark seams for the unwrapping of the body, we have to perform the following steps. Because our low resolution mesh is actually still only one half side, we don't need to place seams as median cuts, we only need to divide different areas (for example, the **inside of the mouth** from the **outside of the mouth**) and unroll cylindrical parts such as the **arms**, **fingers**, and **teeth**:

24. Go into **Edit Mode** and zoom in to the character's **head**; press *Ctrl + Tab* to call the **Mesh Select Mode** pop-up menu and select the **Edge** item, and then start to select the edge-loop inside the **mouth** (*Alt* + right-click to select an edge-loop); start from the bottom **jaw**, switching direction at the end of the **mouth rim** to go upward, and finish on the inside of the upper **jaw**:

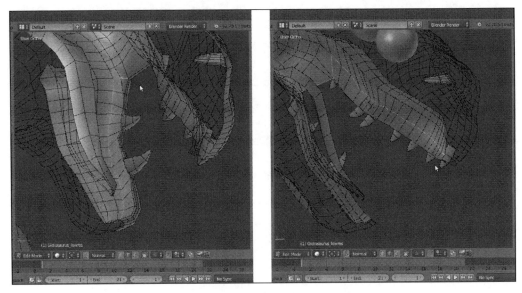

The selected edge-loops inside the mouth

25. Press *Ctrl + E* to open the **Edges** pop-up menu and select the **Mark Seam** item. Alternatively, click on the **Shading / UVs** tab in the **Tool Shelf**, to the left-hand side of the screen, and in the **UVs** subpanel, click on the **Mark Seam** button under the **UV Mapping** item:

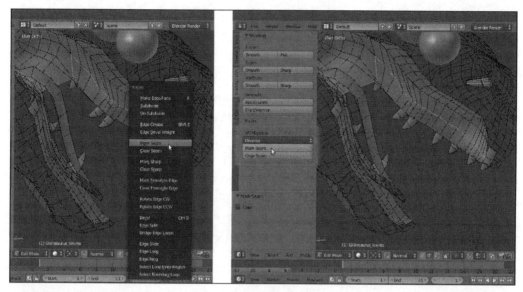

Marking the seams

26. Repeat the procedure for the **arm**; try to place the seams in the less visible areas:

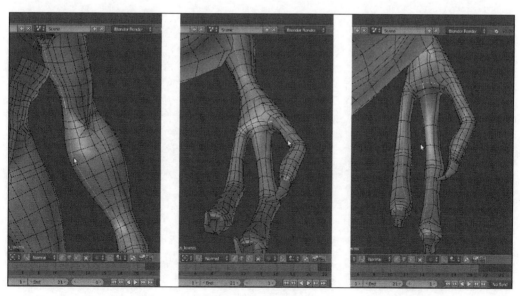

The seams on the arm

27. Do the same for the **pelvis** and **leg**; divide them into two parts with the seams and also try to place the seams inside the natural body folds, if possible:

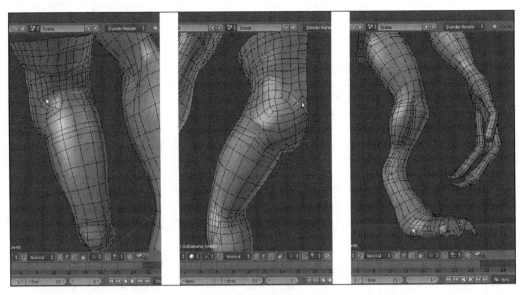

The seams on the pelvis/leg parts

28. It is important to try to place the seams to *divide* parts that would get unwrapped badly if treated as a single object; for example, the inner **nostril** and **tongue** from the **inner mouth**:

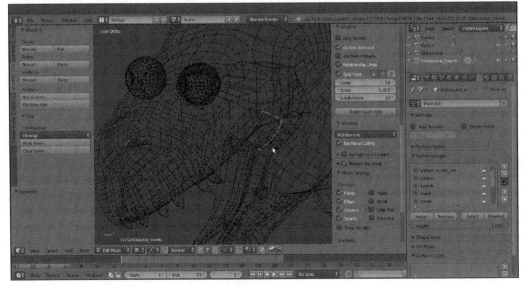

The seams inside the head

29. The final seams to add are for the teeth and talons, which would otherwise get badly unwrapped as squares:

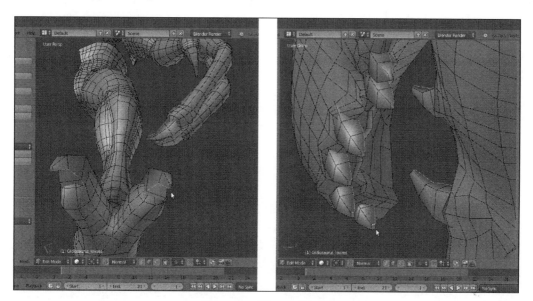

The seams of the small parts

30. Save the file.

UV unwrapping the mesh

At this point, everything is ready for the unwrapping.

Getting ready

Put the mouse pointer on the bottom or on the top horizontal borders of the 3D window. As the mouse pointer changes to a double-arrow icon, right-click and in the **Area Options** pop-up menu select the **Split Area** item; then, left-click to obtain two windows and switch the left one to **UV/Image Editor**.

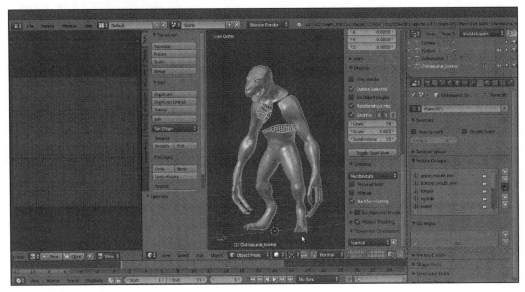

The two windows

How to do it...

To unwrap the mesh in Blender, several options are available; however, the one we are going to use now is the basic unwrap, the result of which we will edit and refine later:

1. Ensure that the **UV/Image Editor** window is not set to **Render Result**, otherwise it won't display the **UV islands**.

2. Select the **Gidiosaurus_lowres** object and enter **Edit Mode**. Select all the vertices (*A* key) and press the *U* key; in the **UV Mapping** pop-up menu, select the first item, **Unwrap**:

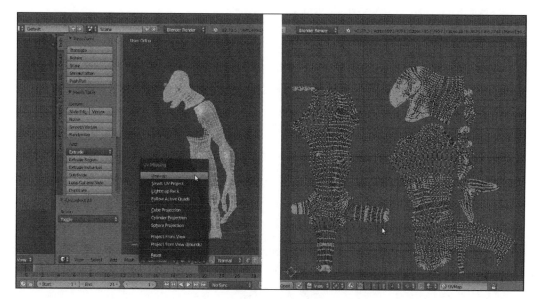

Unwrapping the mesh

After a while, the **UV layer** of the unwrapped mesh appears in the **UV/Image Editor** window; as you can see, several things can be improved. Moreover, we are still using only half of a mesh.

3. Go out of the **Edit Mode** and go to the **Object Modifiers** window; apply the **Mirror** modifier.

4. Go back into **Edit Mode** and press *1* on the numpad to go to the **Front** view; press *Ctrl + R* and place a median seam through the **head** part of the mesh, as well as through the **pelvis** part:

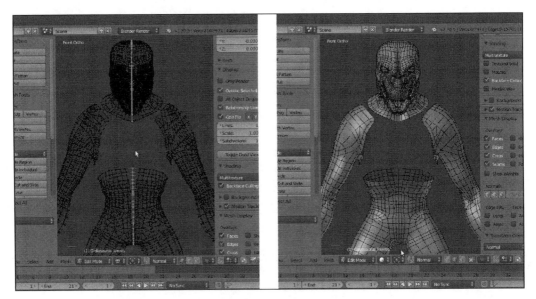

A new loop cut

5. Press *Ctrl + Tab* to switch to vertex selection and press *Z* to go into the **Wireframe** viewport shading mode, and then box-select the vertices on the left-hand side of the mesh (which is the side created by the **Mirror** modifier).

6. Go to the **UV/Image Editor** window; if not already selected, press *A* to select all the **UV islands** of the UV layer, and then press *Ctrl + M | X | Enter* to mirror these selected islands.

7. Press *G* to move them (temporarily) outside the default **U0/V0** tile space, as shown in the following screenshot:

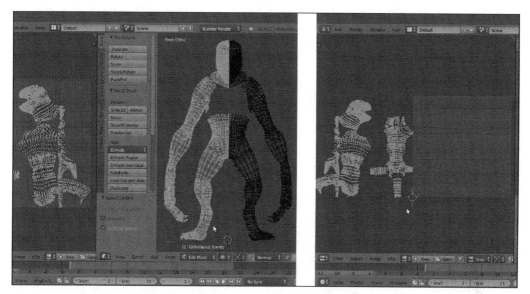

The selected half body vertices and the corresponding UV islands outside the U0/V0 tile space

8. Go to the 3D view and press *A* twice to select all the vertices; go to the **UV/Image Editor** window and press *Ctrl + A* to average the size of all the islands reciprocally.

9. Select all the islands and press *Ctrl + P* to automatically pack all of them inside the UV tile.

10. If you are not satisfied with the result of the **Pack islands** tool, adjust the position (*G* key), rotation (*R* key), and scale (*S* key) of the islands; group together the similar ones (for example, the **teeth**, **talons**, **arms**, and so on), but try to place them to fill the image tile space as much as possible. To select one island, just put the mouse over it and press *L*, and *Shift + L* to multiselect. Use the *X* and *Y* keys to constrain the movements of the islands on the corresponding axis:

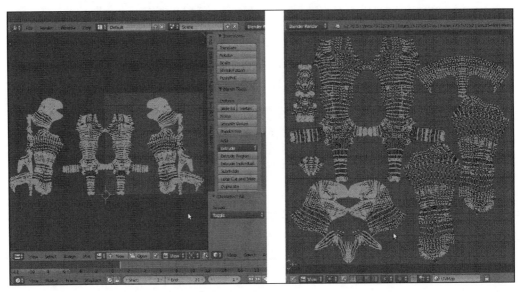

Adjusting the UV islands' position

11. When you are done, ensure that all the vertices of all the islands in the **UV/Image Editor** window are selected, and click on the **New** button on the toolbar of the **UV/ Image Editor** window; in the **New Image** pop-up panel, set **Width** and **Height** to **3072** pixels, and **Generated Type** should be set to **UV Grid**. Then, click on the **OK** button to confirm.

12. Go to the 3D window and press _Z_ to go in the **Solid** viewport shading mode. Then, go to the **Properties** 3D view sidepanel and under the **Shading** subpanel, check the **Textured Solid** item.

13. Go out of the **Edit Mode** and save the file:

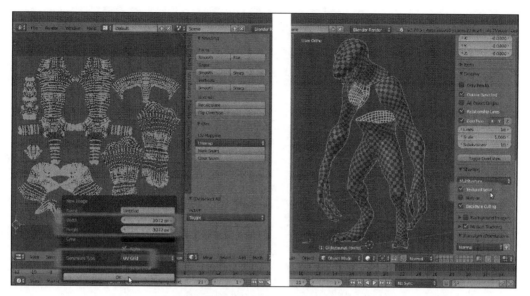

Assigning a grid image to the unwrapped UV islands

This should be enough; even if the halves of the mesh are disconnected, Blender can perfectly solve the mesh painting without visible seams.

However, if we look at the character shown in the **Textured Solid** mode in the 3D view, it's clear that the unwrap of some part of the mesh could be better; for example, you can see a difference in the size of the mapped grid in the **head/neck** area, inside the **mouth**, and on the **arms** and **legs** (look at the arrows in the following images):

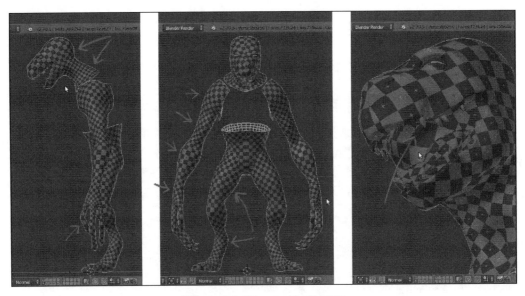

Differences in the mapped grid image

Although this is not a very big issue, the unwrap can be refined further to avoid distortions as much as possible, as well as potential future problems when we'll paint the character textures; we are going to see this in the next recipe.

Editing the UV islands

We are now going to join the two UV islands' halves together, in order to improve the final look of the texturing; we are also going to modify, if possible, a little of the island proportions in order to obtain a more regular flow of the UV vertices, and fix the *distortions* we have seen in the last image of the previous recipe.

We are going to the use the **pin** tool, which is normally used in conjunction with the **Live Unwrap** tool.

Getting ready

First, we'll try to recalculate the unwrap of some of the islands by modifying the seams of the mesh.

Before we start though, let's see if we can improve some of the visibility of the UV islands in the **UV/Image Editor**:

1. Put the mouse cursor in the **UV/Image Editor** window and press the *N* key.

2. In the **Properties** sidepanel that appears by pressing the *N* key on the right-hand side of the window, go to the **Display** subpanel and click on the **Black** or **White** button (depending on your preference) under the **UV** item. Check also the **Smooth** item box.

3. Also, check the **Stretch** item, which even though it was made for a different purpose, can increase the visibility of the islands a lot.

4. Press *N* again to get rid of the **Properties** sidepanel.

All these options enabled should make the islands more easily readable in the **UV/Image Editor** window:

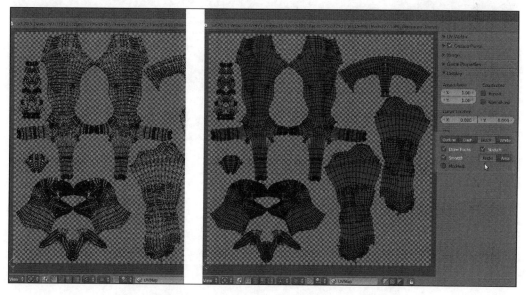

The UV islands made more easily readable by the enabled items

How to do it...

Now we can start with the editing; initially, we are going to freeze the islands that we don't want to modify because their unwrap is either satisfactory, or we will deal with it later. So, perform the following steps:

1. Press *A* to select all the islands, then by putting the mouse pointer on the two **pelvis** island halves and pressing *Shift + L*, multi-deselect them; press the *P* key to **pin** the remaining selected UV islands and then *A* to deselect everything:

 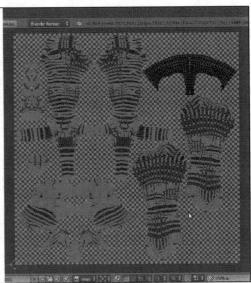

To the right-hand side, the pinned UV islands

2. Zoom in on the islands of the **pelvis**, select both the left and right outer edge-loops, as shown in the following left image, and press *P* to **pin** them.

3. Go to the 3D view and clear only the front part of the median seam on the **pelvis**. To do this, start to clear the seam from the front edges, go down and stop where it crosses the horizontal seam that passes the bottom part of the **groin** and **legs**, and leave the back part of the vertical median seam still marked:

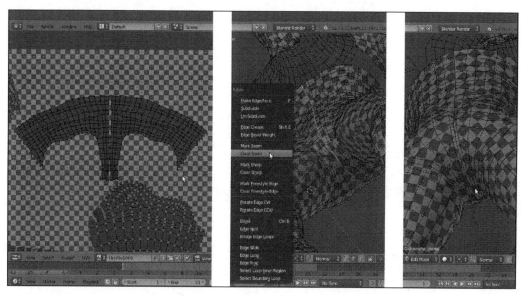

Pinning the extreme vertices in the UV/Image Editor, and editing the seam on the mesh

4. Go into **Face** selection mode and select all the faces of the **pelvis**; put the mouse pointer in the 3D view and press *U* | **Unwrap** (alternatively, go into the **UV/Image Editor** and press *E*):

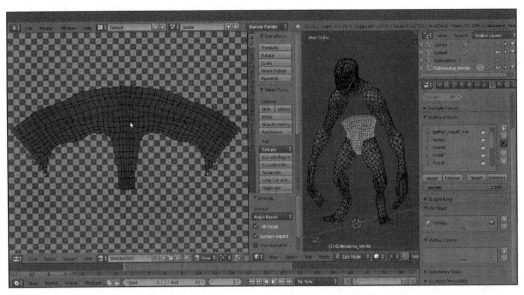

Unwrapping again with the pinning and a different seam

The island will keep the previous position because of the pinned edges, and is now unwrapped as one single piece (with the obvious exception of the seam on the back).

5. We won't modify the **pelvis** island any further, so select all its vertices and press *P* to pin all of them and then deselect them.

6. Press *A* in the 3D view to select all the faces of the mesh and make all the islands visible in the **UV/Image Editor**. Note that they are all pinned at the moment, so just select the vertices you want to **unpin** (*Alt + P*) in the islands of the **tongue** and **inner mouth**. Then, clear the median seam in the corresponding pieces on the mesh, and press *E* again:

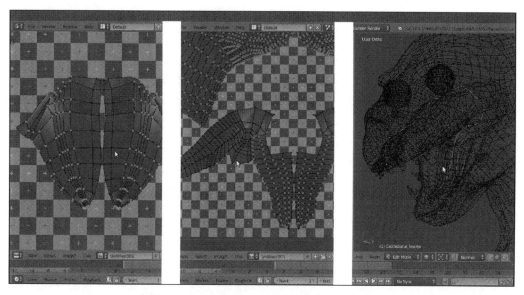

Re-unwrapping the tongue and inner mouth areas

7. Select the UV vertices of the resulting islands and unpin them all; next, pin just one vertex at the top of the islands and one at the bottom, and unwrap again. This will result in a more organically distributed unwrap of the parts:

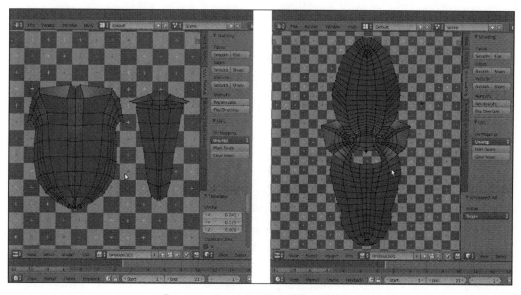

Re-unwrapping again with a different pinning

8. Select all the faces of the mesh, and then all the islands in the **UV/Image Editor** window. Press *Ctrl + A* to average their relative size and adjust their position in the default tile space:

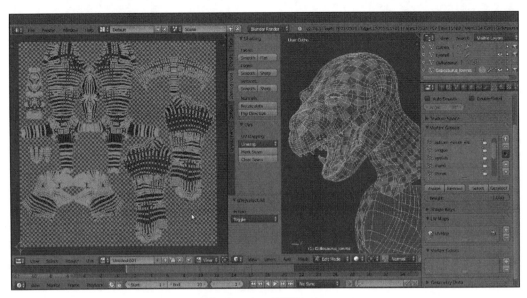

The rearranged UV islands

Now, let's work on the **head** piece that, as in every character, should be the most important and well-finished piece.

At the moment, the **face** is made using two separate islands; although this won't be visible in the final textured rendering of our character, it's always better, if possible, to join them in order to have a single piece, especially in the front mesh faces. Due to the elongated **snout** of the character, if we were to unwrap the **head** as a single piece simply without the median seam, we wouldn't get a nice evenly mapped result, so we must divide the whole **head** into more pieces.

Actually, we can take advantage of the fact that the **Gidiosaurus** is wearing a **helmet** and that most of the **head** will be covered by it; this allows us to easily split the **face** from the rest of the mesh, hiding the seams under the **helmet**.

9. Go into **Edge** selection mode and mark the seams, dividing the **face** from the **cranium** and **neck** as shown in the following screenshots. Select the crossing edge-loops, and then clear the unnecessary parts:

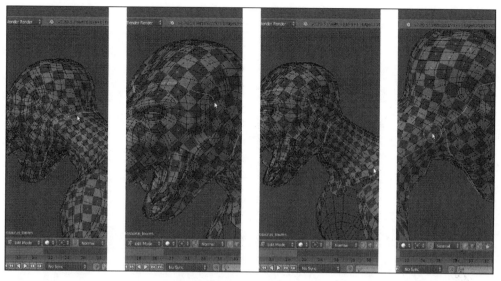

New seams for the character's head part 1

10. Also clear the median seam in the upper **face** part, and under the seam on the bottom **jaw**, leaving it only on the front **mandible** and on the back of the **cranium** and **neck**:

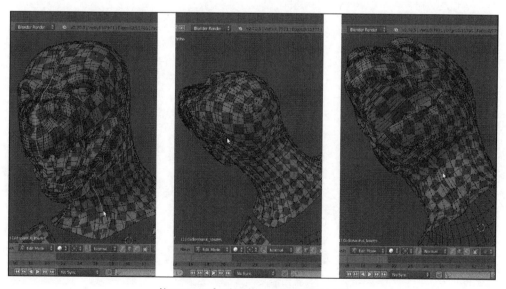

New seams for the character's head part 2

11. Go in the **Face** selection mode and select only the **face** section of the mesh, and then press *E* to unwrap. The new unwrap comes upside down, so select all the UV vertices and rotate the island by **180** degrees:

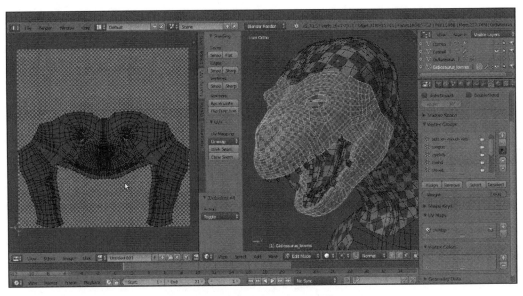

The character's face unwrapped

12. Select the **cranium/neck** section on the mesh and repeat the process:

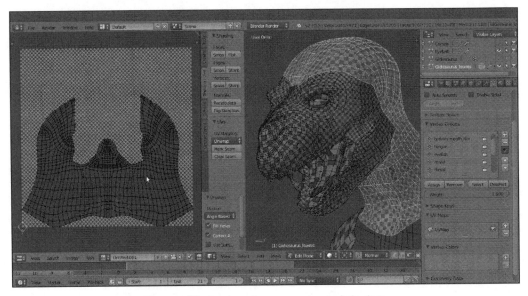

The rest of the head mesh unwrapped as a whole piece

13. Now, select all the faces of the mesh and all the islands in the **UV/Image Editor**, and press *Ctrl + A* to average their reciprocal size.

14. Once again, adjust the position of the islands inside the UV tile (*Ctrl + P* to automatically pack them inside the available space, and then tweak their position, rotation, and scale):

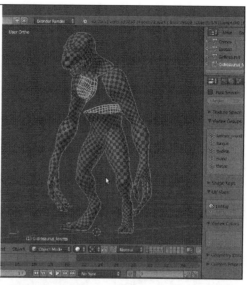

The character's UV islands packed inside the default U0/V0 tile space

How it works...

Starting from the UV unwrap in the previous recipe, we improved some of the islands by joining together the halves representing common mesh parts. When doing this, we tried to retain the already good parts of the unwrap by **pinning** the UV vertices that we didn't want to modify; this way, the new unwrap process was forced to calculate the position of the unpinned vertices using the constraints of the pinned ones (**pelvis**, **tongue**, and **inner mouth**). In other cases, we totally cleared the old seams on the model and marked new ones, in order to have a completely new unwrap of the mesh part (the **head**), we also used the character furniture (such as the **armor**) to hide the seams (which in any case, won't be visible at all).

There's more...

At this point, looking at the **UV/Image Editor** window containing the islands, it's evident that if we want to keep several parts in proportion to each other, some of the islands are a little too small to give a good amount of detail when texturing; for example, the Gidiosaurus's face.

A technique for a good unwrap that is the current standard in the industry is **UDIM UV Mapping**, which means **U-Dimension**; basically, after the usual unwrap, the islands are scaled bigger and placed outside the default **U0/V0** tile space.

Look at the following screenshots, showing the Blender **UV/Image Editor** window:

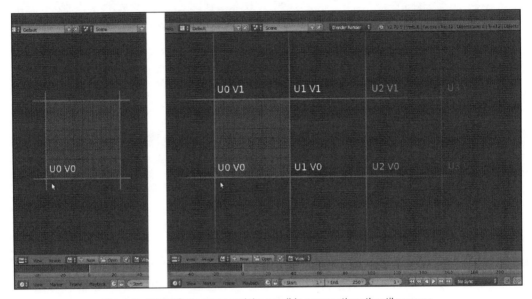

The default U0/V0 tile space and the possible consecutive other tile spaces

On the left-hand side, you can see, highlighted with red lines, the single UV tile that at present is the standard for Blender, which is identified by the **UV** coordinates **0** and **0**: that is, **U** (horizontal) = **0** and **V** (vertical) = **0**.

Although not visible in the **UV/Image Editor** window, all the other possible consecutive tiles can be identified by the corresponding UV coordinates, as shown on the right-hand side of the preceding screenshot (again, highlighted with red lines). So, adjacent to the tile **U0/V0**, we can have the row with the tiles **U1/V0**, **U2/V0**, and so on, but we can also go upwards: **U0/V1**, **U1/V1**, **U2/V1**, and so on.

To help you identify the tiles, Blender will show you the amount of pixels and also the number of tiles you are moving the islands in the toolbar of the **UV/Image Editor** window. In the following screenshot, the **arm** islands have been moved horizontally (on the negative x axis) by **-3072.000** pixels; this is correct because that's exactly the X size of the grid image we loaded in the previous recipes. In fact, in the toolbar of the **UV/Image Editor** window, while moving the islands we can read **D: -3072.000** (pixels) and (inside brackets) **1.0000** (tile) **along X**; effectively, **3072** pixels = **1** tile.

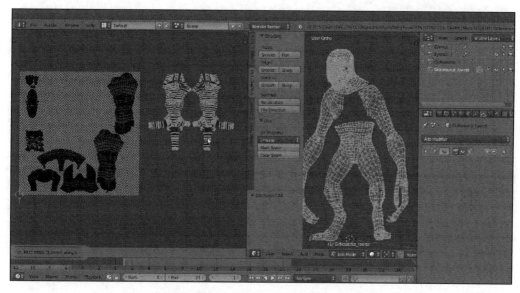

Moving the arm islands to the U1/V0 tile space

When moving UV islands from tile to tile, remember to check that the **Constrain to Image Bounds** item in the **UVs** menu on the toolbar of the **UV/Image Editor** window is disabled; also, enabling the **Normalized** item inside the **Display** subpanel under the N key *Properties* sidepanel of the same editor window will display the UV coordinates from **0.0** to **1.0**, rather than in pixels. More, pressing the *Ctrl* key while moving the islands will constrain the movement to intervals, making it easy to translate them to exactly 1 tile space.

Because at the moment Blender doesn't support the **UDIM UV Mapping** standard, simply moving an island outside the default **U0/V0** tile, for example to **U1/V0**, will *repeat the image you loaded* in the **U0/V0** tile and on the faces associated with the moved islands. To solve this, it's necessary, after moving the islands, to *assign a different material, if necessary with its own different image textures*, to each group of vertices/faces associated with each tile space. So, if you shared your islands over **4** tiles, you need to assign **4** different materials to your object, and each material must load the proper image texture.

The goal of this process is obviously to obtain bigger islands mapped with bigger texture images, by selecting all the islands, scaling them bigger *together* using the largest ones as a guide, and then tweaking their position and distribution.

One last thing: it is also better to unwrap the **corneas** and **eyes** (which are separate objects from the **Gidiosaurus** body mesh) and add their islands to the tiles where you put the **face**, **mouth**, **teeth**, and so on (use the **Draw Other Objects** tool in the **View** menu of the **UV/Image Editor** window to also show the UV islands of the other *nonjoined* unwrapped objects):

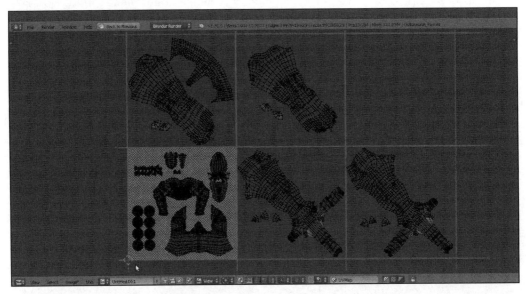

UV islands unwrapped, following the UDIM UV Mapping standard

In our case, we assigned the **Gidiosaurus** body islands to **5** different tiles, **U0/V0**, **U1/V0**, **U2/V0**, **U0/V1**, and **U1/V1**, so we'll have to assign **5** different materials. However, we will cover this in a later recipe.

Note that for exposition purposes only, in the preceding screenshot, you can see the cornea and eye islands together with the **Gidiosaurus** body islands because I temporarily joined the objects; however, it's usually better to maintain the eyes and corneas as separate objects from the main body.

Using the Smart UV Project tool

Now, we are going to use a much easier and faster method to do the unwrapping of the **Armor**: the **Smart UV Project** tool.

Getting ready

The first thing to do is to prepare the **armor** pieces for the unwrap process, so perform the following steps:

1. Starting from the last `Gidiosaurus_unwrap.blend` file you saved, click on the **13th** scene layer to reveal the **armor** and at the same time, hide the **Gidiosaurus_ lowres** object.

2. Go to the **Outliner** and select the first item, the **Breastplate**; then, use *Shift* to multiselect all the other visible objects.

3. Press *Ctrl + J* to join them into a single object, and then in the **Outliner**, rename the result as `Armor`.

4. Go to the **Object Modifiers** window and expand the **Mirror** modifier subpanel; be sure that the **Clipping** item is activated and click on the **Apply** button:

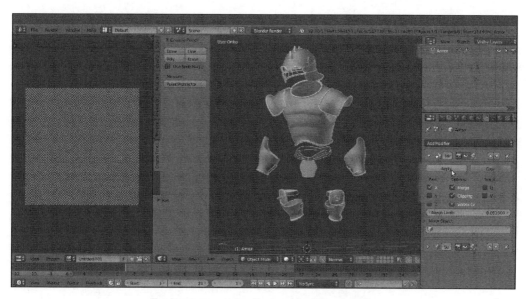

The Armor as a single object and the Mirror modifier

How to do it...

Here is the unwrap process:

1. Press *Tab* to go into **Edit Mode** and press the *A* key to select all the vertices of the **Armor**.

2. With the mouse cursor in the 3D view, press the *U* key, and in the **UV Mapping** pop-up menu that just appeared, select the second item from the top, **Smart UV Project**.

3. A second pop-up appears with some options that you can leave as they are, besides **Angle Limit** (the maximum angle in the mesh used by the tool to separate the islands), which by default is set to **66.00**; raise it to the maximum, which is **89.00**, and then click on the big **OK** button:

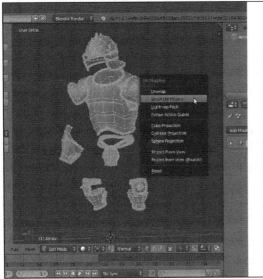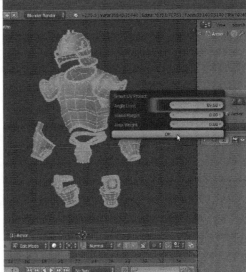

The Smart UV Project tool

The mesh has been divided into several smaller unwrapped parts and is automatically packed inside the **U0/V0** UV tile.

4. Select all the islands in the **UV/Image Editor** window, click on the small double-arrow icon on the toolbar, close to the **New** and **Open** buttons, and select the **Untitled.001** image (the same grid image we used for the **Gidiosaurus** unwrap).

5.   Press *Tab* to go out of **Edit Mode**:

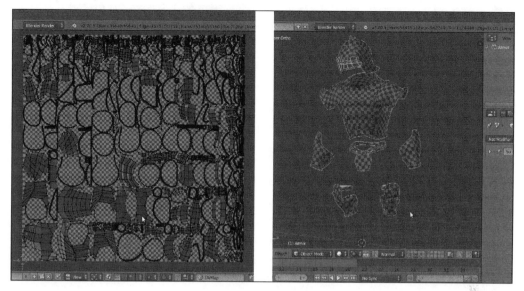

The unwrapped Armor

Considering the amount of tiny islands that the tool created, it's better to separate the big **armor** parts (basically, the **plates**) from the smaller ones (**belts**, **borders**, and so on) and re-unwrap them with the **Smart UV Project** tool, as we did for the **Gidiosaurus** body in the previous recipe; then, place them into two adjacent tiles:

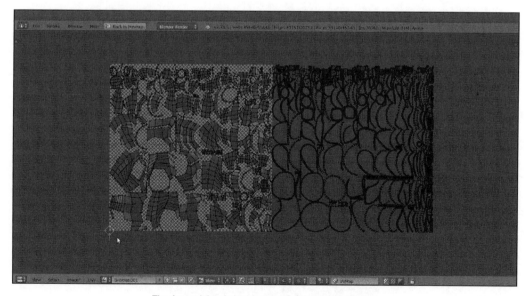

The Armor islands inside the U0/V0 and U1/V0 tiles

Modifying the mesh and the UV islands

At this point, when we look at the **Gidiosaurus** mesh, we realize that some detail in the model is still missing; for example, the **lower teeth**. In fact, we modeled the mouth closed and the **lower teeth**, enclosed in the **upper mouth rim**, weren't visible.

It's now time to add them; in fact, even though we have already done the unwrapping stage, it's still possible to modify the mesh further and also update the UV islands accordingly.

Getting ready

Start from the last `Gidiosaurus_unwrap.blend` file you saved:

1. Press *N* to open the **Properties** 3D view sidepanel, and disable the **Textured Solid** item under the **Shading** subpanel.

2. Click on the **11th** scene layer button to reveal the **Gidiosaurus_lowres** object and select it; go into the **Side** view, zoom in to the **head**, and enter **Edit Mode**. Press the *A* key to select all the vertices of the mesh.

3. Put the mouse pointer inside the **UV/Image Editor**, select all the UV vertices (again the *A* key), and pin them by pressing the *P* key; then deselect everything (the *A* key once more).

How to do it...

We can now start to add new **teeth**:

1. Select the vertices of one **lower tooth** and press *Shift + D* to duplicate it; using the **Transform Orientation** widget set to **Normal**, scale it smaller, rotate and modify it a bit, and then move it in a new position along the **mandible rim**:

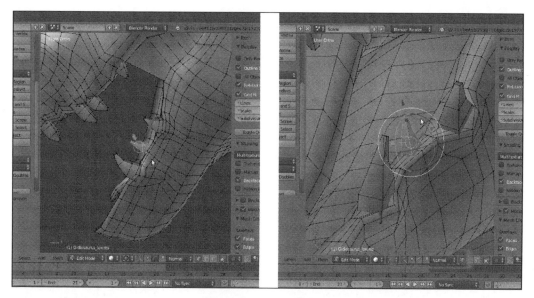

The new added tooth

2. Repeat the process to create the **bottom teeth row** on the left-hand side of the **mandible**:

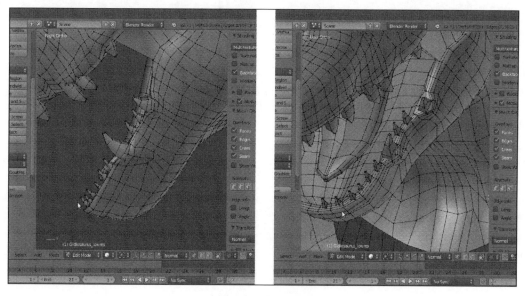

Adding the missing teeth

3. Go out of the **Edit Mode** and put the **3D Cursor** at the pivot point of the mesh (coincidentally, at the center of the scene), and then press the period key (.) to set the **Pivot Point** around the **3D Cursor**.

4. Press *1* on the numpad to go in the **Front** view, enter **Edit Mode** again, and select all the new **teeth**; press *Shift + D* to duplicate them, and then right-click; then, press *Ctrl + M | X | Enter* to mirror them on the x axis to the right-hand side of the **mandible**.

5. Press *Ctrl + N* to recalculate the normals and go out of the **Edit Mode**:

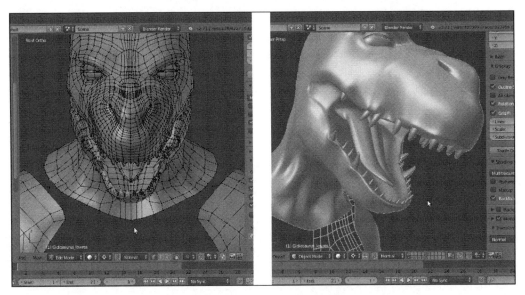

The new teeth mirrored on the x axis

Now, we must adjust the **rim** of the **mandible** where we added the new **teeth**, in order to create the **alveoli**.

6. Go back into the **Edit Mode** and start to add vertical edge-loops on the **lower mouth rim**, in order to create more geometry for the **alveoli**:

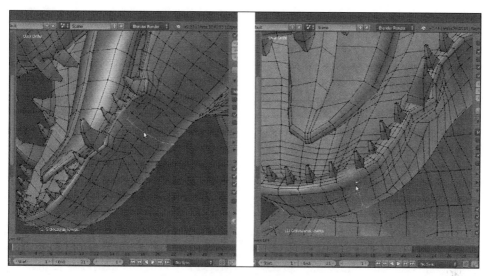

Adding new edge-loops

7. Click on the **Options** tab under the **Tool Shelf** to the left-hand side of the 3D window and enable the **X Mirror** item under the **Mesh Options** subpanel.

8. Tweak the vertices to create the **alveoli** around the **new teeth**; enable the **Subdivision Surface** modifier visibility during **Edit Mode** in order to have better feedback:

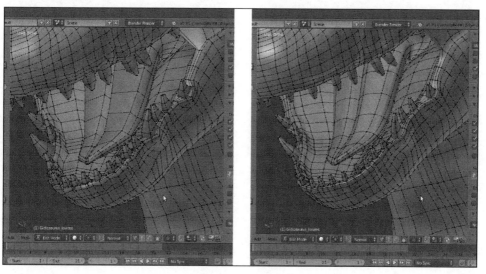

Modeling the alveoli

9. Press *Alt + S* to scale the **teeth** vertices on their normals, in order to thicken them, and add edge-loops where needed to make the transition from the **alveoli** to **inner mouth** as natural as possible.

   When you are done, it's time to update the unwrapped UV layer with the new modifications.

10. In **Edit Mode**, first select the vertices of the **new teeth**. Because we made them by duplicating one of the already unwrapped **fangs**, the **new teeth** will share the same UV island. In the **UV/Image Editor**, press *A* to select all their UV vertices and *Alt + P* to unpin them, and then press *E* for a new unwrap.

11. Scale the new **teeth** islands to **0.200**, and then select the original **teeth** on the mesh; adjust the size and position of the new islands based on the old ones and then pin them.

12. Now, switch to the **Face** selection mode and select the **Gidiosaurus** face; in the **UV/Image Editor** window, unpin all the vertices of its island (*Alt + P*), and then pin only the vertices of certain areas such as the **eyes, nose,** and upper outside edge-loop (*P* key).

With this method, the unwrap of all the new geometry gets recalculated together with the old one. Thanks to the pinned UV vertices, it will keep the previous size and position as much as possible. In the following image, you can see the face island before (left) and after (right):

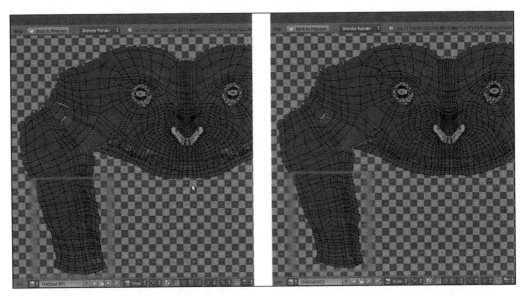

The updated unwrap

Note that you need to recalculate the unwrap for all the islands involved in the mesh's modification, and then save the file.

Setting up additional UV layers

Up until now, we have set just one UV layer whose name is, by default, **UVMap** (go to the **Object Data** window and look under the **UV Maps** subpanel):

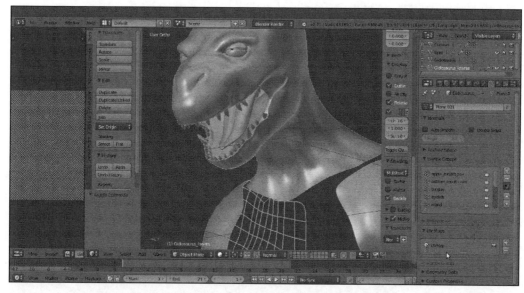

The UV Maps subpanel with the UV Map coordinates layer

Actually, in Blender, it is possible to set more than one UV coordinates layer on the same object in order to mix different UV projections that can eventually also be baked into a single image map.

The names of the UV layers under the **UV Maps** subpanel are important, because they specify which one of the projections a material has to use for the mapping of a texture. By clicking on the **+** icon to the side of the **UV Maps** subpanel, it is possible to add a new UV layer (whose name, in this case, will be **UVMap.001** by default; of course it's possible to change these names by using *Ctrl* + clicking on them and typing the new ones).

Getting ready

We are now going to add a new UV layer to the **Gidiosaurus** object:

1. Ensure that the **Gidiosaurus** object is selected and go to the **Object Data** window under the main **Properties** panel to the right-hand of the screen.

2. Go to the **UV Maps** subpanel and click on the **+** icon to the right-hand side of the names window; a new UV layer is added to the list, right under the first one, and its name is **UVMap.001** (in case you don't see it, it may be because the window is too small; just put the mouse cursor on the **=** sign at the bottom of the window and drag it down to enlarge it):

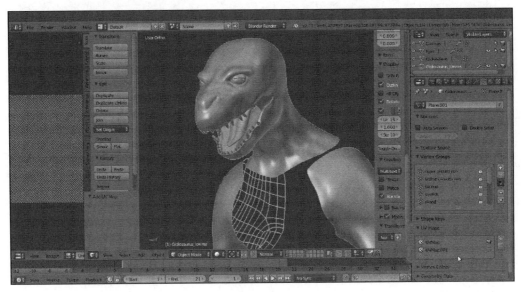

The new UV coordinates layer

3. Use *Ctrl* + left-click on the **UVMap.001** item and rename it as **UVMap_scales**. Then, press *Enter* to confirm.

How to do it...

Now we must set the projection of the UV layer:

1. Go into **Edit Mode**, switch to the **Face** selection mode, put the mouse pointer on the mesh, and press the *L* key to select all the faces of the skin of the **Gidiosaurus** mesh.

2. Go to the **UV/Image Editor** window, select all the visible islands and unpin them (*Alt + P*).

3. Click on the **Image** item on the toolbar and select the **Open Image** item in the pop-up menu (or else, put the mouse cursor in the **UV/Image Editor** window and press *Alt + O*); browse to the `textures` folder and load the `scales_tiles.png` image.

4. With the mouse pointer in 3D view, press *U* and from the **UV Mapping** pop-up menu, select the **Cube Projection** item.

5. In the **UV/Image Editor** window, select all the islands and scale them **5** times bigger (*A | S | 5 | Enter*):

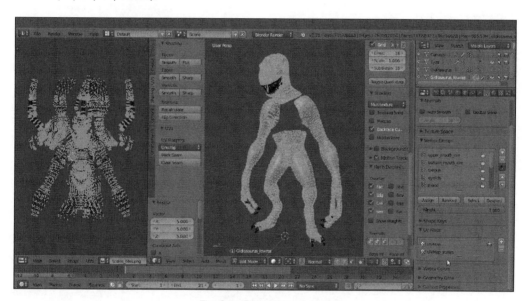

The Cube Projection mapping

6. Go out of the **Edit Mode** and into the **Properties** 3D view sidepanel, enable the **Textured Solid** item under the **Shading** subpanel to see the result of the unwrapping in the 3D viewport:

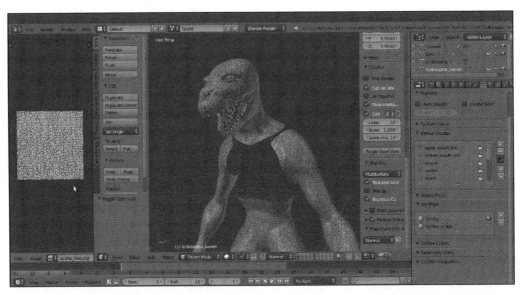

The scales_tiles.png image mapped on the model using the second UV coordinates layer

At this point, as you can see in the **UV Maps** subpanel, the **Gidiosaurus** object has **2** different UV coordinate layers, **UVMap** and **UVMap_scales**. We will use the **UVMap_scales** layer to map the scales image texture on the body and thereby to bake it on the first **UVMap** layer; this will be the one we'll use in the end for the rendering of the model. However, we'll see this in detail in the texturing and baking recipes.

Repeat the process for the **Armor**.

7. Add a new UV layer and rename it **UVMap_rust**; go into **Edit Mode**, select all the vertices and all the islands in the **UV/Image Editor** window, and load the iron_tiles.png image.

8. Switch to the **Face** selection mode, and in the 3D view, press *U* and select **Reset** (the last item) from the pop-up menu. Then press *U* again, and this time select the **Cube Projection** item.

9. Go out of **Edit Mode**.

As you can see, there are a few visible seams. This will be easily fixed during the texturing stage, but for the moment we are done:

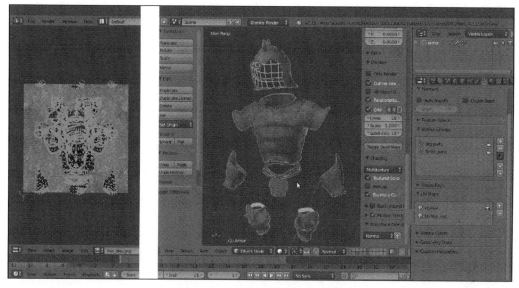

The second UV coordinates layer for the Armor

Exporting the UV Map layout

In this last recipe, we are going to see how to export the UV coordinate layers outside Blender, in order to be used as a guide to paint textures inside any 2D image editing software.

Getting ready

We have seen that the **Gidiosaurus** object and also the **Armor** object have more than one UV coordinate layer, so the first thing to do is to be sure to have set the right layer as the *active* one.

To do this, simply click on the name of the chosen layer inside the **UV Maps** subpanel under the **Object Data** window; if you are in **Edit Mode**, by clicking on the different names, you can also see the different layers switch in real time in the **UV/Image Editor** window.

How to do it...

After you have selected the desired UV layer, do the following:

1. Click on the **UVs** item in the toolbar of the **UV/Image Editor** window, and from the menu, select the **Export UV Layout** item (the top item).

2. You can browse the directory where the `.blend` file is saved, as the directory opens, at the bottom-left side of the screen is the **Export UV Layout** option panel where you can decide on several items: the size and format of the exported image, and the opacity of the islands (by default, for mysterious reasons, it is set to **25 percent** rather than **100 percent**). Moreover, you can decide if you want to export all the islands of the selected object or only the visible ones, and also if you want the modifiers applied to the islands (for example, the **Subdivision Surface** modifier).

3. Browse to the folder where you decided to save the UV layout of your model, or click on the side of the path in the upper line after the slash, and write the name of a new directory. Press *Enter* and click on the pop-up panel with the **OK? Create New Directory** message to confirm (this actually creates a brand new directory).

4. Write the name of the UV layout in the second line and click on the **Export UV Layout** button at the top-right of the screen.

Note that if you want to export all the different tiles placed outside of the default **U0/V0** tile space, as illustrated in the *There's more...* section of the *Editing the UV islands* recipe, at least for the moment, you have to temporarily (using *Ctrl*) move each island at a time to the default **U0/V0** tile space and export it.

6
Rigging the Low Resolution Mesh

In this chapter, we will cover the following recipes:

- Building the character's Armature from scratch
- Perfecting the Armature to also function as a rig for the Armor
- Building the character's Armature through the Human Meta-Rig
- Building the animation controls and the Inverse Kinematic
- Generating the character's Armature by using the Rigify add-on

Introduction

To be able to animate our character, we have to build the rig, which in Blender is commonly referred to as an **Armature**, and this is the *skeleton* that will deform the **Gidiosaurus** low resolution mesh.

The rigging process in Blender can be accomplished basically in two different ways:

- By building the **Armature** by hands from scratch
- By using the provided **Human Meta-Rig** or the **Rigify** add-on

Building the **Armature** manually by hand can be a lot of work, but in my opinion, is the only way to really learn and understand how a rig works; on the other hand, the **Rigify** add-on gives several tools to speed up and automate the rig creation process, and this in many occasions, can be very handy.

Building the character's Armature from scratch

So, the first recipe of this chapter is about the making of the **Armature** by hands for our **Gidiosaurus**.

Getting ready

In this first recipe, we are going to build by hands the **basic rig**, which is the skeleton made only by the **deforming bones**.

However, first, let's prepare a bit the file to be worked:

1. Start Blender and open the `Gidiosaurus_unwrap_final.blend` file.

2. Disable the **Textured Solid** and **Backface Culling** items in the 3D view **Properties** sidepanel, join the 3D window with the **UV/Image Editor** window, and click on the **11th** scene layer to have only the **Gidiosaurus** mesh visible in the viewport.

3. Go to the **Object** window under the **Display** subpanel and enable the **Wire** item. This will be useful in the process in order to have an idea of the mesh topology when in **Object Mode** and **Solid** viewport shading mode. However, for the moment, press the Z key to go in the **Wireframe** viewport shading mode.

4. Press *1* on the numpad to go in the **Front** view, and press *5* on the numpad again to switch to the **Ortho** view.

5. Save the file as `Gidiosaurus_rig_from_scratch_start.blend`.

How to do it...

Let's start:

1. Be sure that the **3D Cursor** is at the origin pivot point of the **Gidiosaurus** mesh. Put the mouse pointer in the 3D view, press *Shift + A*, and in the **Add** pop-up menu, select **Armature | Single Bone**:

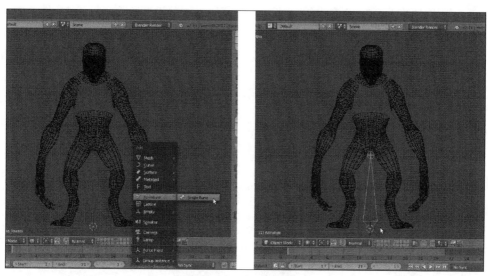

Adding the first Armature's bone

2. Press *Tab* to go into **Edit Mode** and select the whole bone by right-clicking on its **central part**; move the bone upwards to the **Gidiosaurus's** hips area (*G | Z | Enter* or left-click to confirm), and then go in the **Side** view (*3* key on the numpad) and center its position by moving it on the *y* axis:

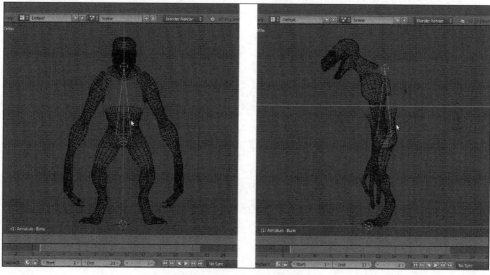

Positioning the bone in Edit Mode

3. Right-click on the **Head** of the bone to select it and by pressing G to move it, scale the bone size to fit the pelvis area:

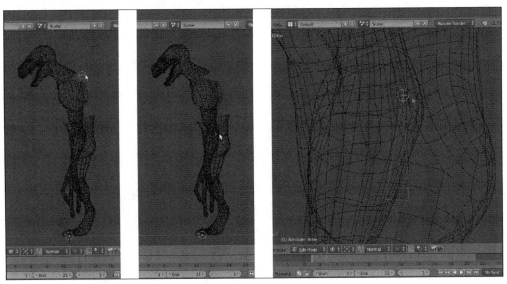

Scaling the bone in Edit Mode

4. Go to the **Item** subpanel under the 3D view **Properties** sidepanel, or in the **Bone** window under the main **Properties** panel to the right-hand side of the screen, and rename **Bone** (default name) as **hips**:

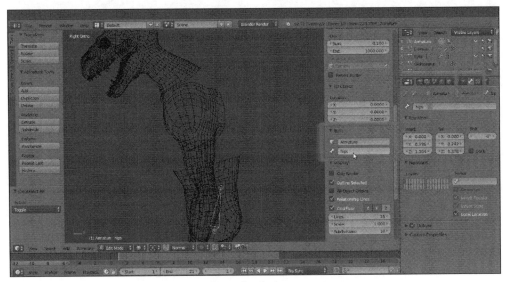

Renaming the bone

5. Press *Z* to go in the **Solid** viewport shading mode, and then go to the **Object Data** window and enable the **X-Ray** item under the **Display** subpanel.

6. With the tip of the bone selected (the **Head**), press the *E* key to extrude it. By this process, and by following the wire topology visible on the mesh as a guide, go upwards to build the **Gidiosaurus spine** (2 bones), **chest** (1 bone), and **neck** (1 bone); as much as possible, try to place the **Heads** (the tips/joints) of the bones aligned with the transversal edge-loops on the mesh's *articulation*:

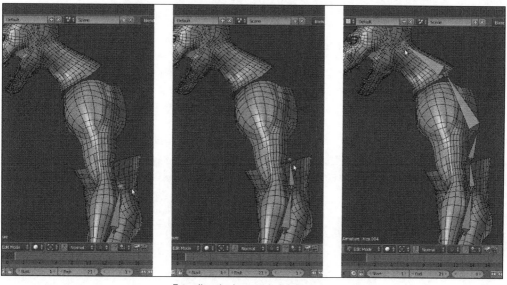

Extruding the bone to build the spine

7. Go again to the **Object Data** window under the **Display** subpanel, and enable the **Names** item (in the following screenshot, all the bones have been selected just to highlight them and their respective names). As you can see in the screenshot, the extruded bones get their names from the previous one, so we have **hips**, then **hips.001**, **hips.002**, and so on:

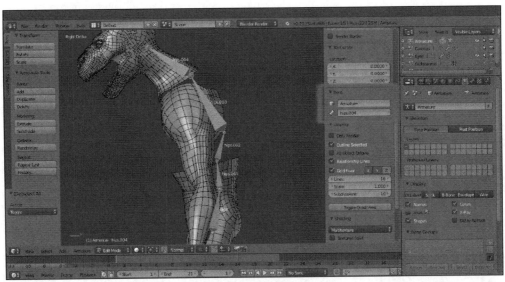

The bones' names

8. Select the **hips.001** bone and rename it **spine.001**; select the **hips.002** bone and rename it **spine.002**.

9. Select the **hips.003** bone and rename it **chest**; select the **hips.004** bone and rename it **neck**.

10. Select the tip of the **neck** bone and extrude it; rename the new bone (**neck.001**) as **head**:

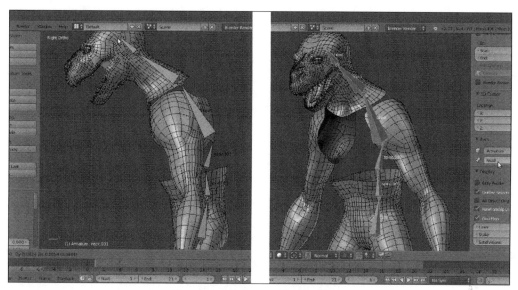

The renamed bones and the head bone

So, now we have built the **spine** - **neck** – **head** part of the **Armature**; actually, one thing is still missing: the bone to animate the **mandible**.

11. Press *Tab* to get out of **Edit Mode**. In the **Side** view, enable the **15th** scene layer on the 3D viewport toolbar, in order to show the **Empty_rot_mand** object; select it and press *Shift + S* to call the **Snap** pop-up menu. Then, select the **Cursor to Selected** item.

12. Reselect the **Armature** and go again into **Edit Mode**. Press *Shift + A* to add a new bone; move its **Head** to resize and fit it inside the **mandible** of the **Gidiosaurus**:

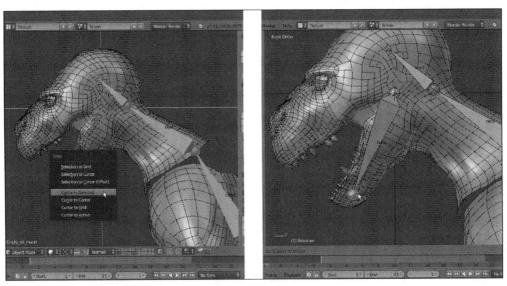

The mandible's bone

13. Rename it **mand** and in the **Bone** window under the main **Properties** panel, in the **Relations** subpanel, click on the **Parent** slot to select the **head** item from the pop-up menu with the bones list. Leave the **Connected** item **unchecked**:

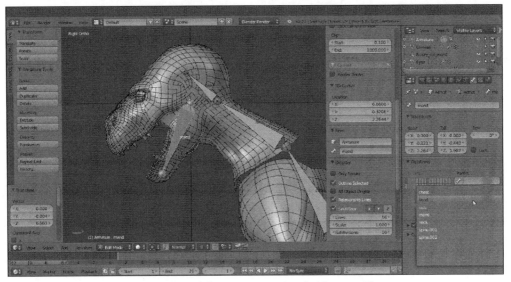

The Parent slot and the pop-up menu to select the parent bone

At this point, we can already see some particular setting to be applied to the bones.

14. Go to the **Object Data** window under the **Properties** panel and in the **Display** subpanel, switch from the default **Octahedral** to the **B-bone** button:

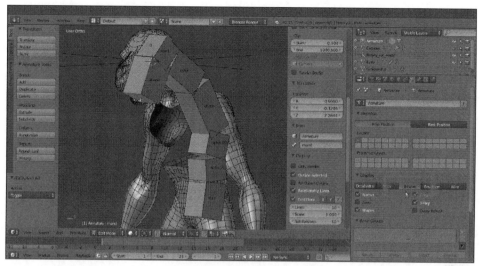

The bones visualized as B-bones

15. Press *A* to select all the bones, and then press *Ctrl + Alt + S* (or go to the **Armature** item in the window toolbar, and then go to **Transform | Scale Bbone**) and scale the **B-bones** to **0.200** (hold the *Ctrl* key to constrain the scaling values; the B-bones scaling works both in **Edit Mode** and **Pose Mode**).

16. Select only the **chest** bone and scale it bigger to **2.500**; select the **head** bone and scale it to **4.000**:

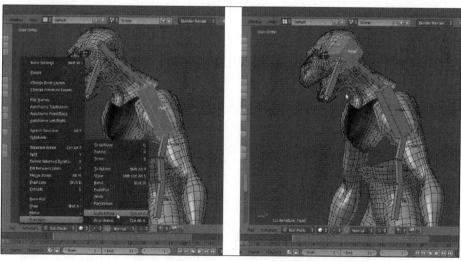

The B-bones scaled for better visualization

17. Go to the **Object** window and under the **Display** subpanel, click on the **Maximum Draw Type** slot (set to **Textured** by default) and switch it to **Wire**.

18. Press *Ctrl + Tab* to switch the **Armature** directly from **Edit Mode** to **Pose Mode**. Right-click on the **chest** bone to select it and go to the **Bone** window under the main **Properties** panel; in the **Deform** subpanel, set **Segments** under the **Curved Bones** item to **3**:

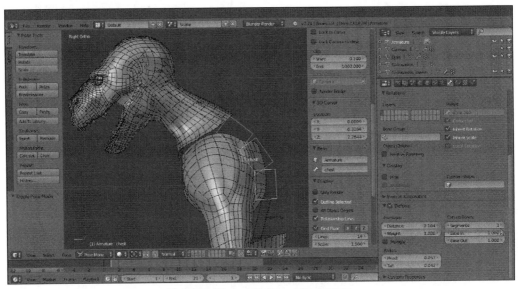

The chest B-bone with 3 curved segments

19. Select the **spine.002** and **spine.001** bones and set **Segments** to **2**. Select the **neck** bone and set **Segments** to **3**.

20. Select the **Gidiosaurus** mesh, go to the **Object** window, and disable the **Wire** item under the **Display** subpanel:

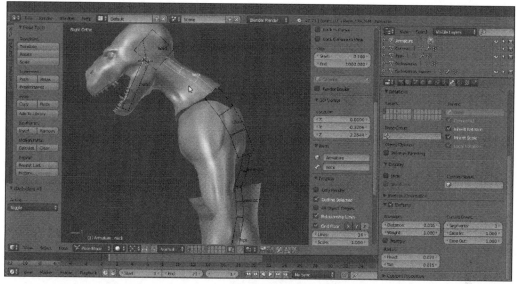

The rig so far

21. Press _Ctrl + Tab_ to go out of the **Pose Mode**, and then _Shift + S_ | **Cursor to Selected** to put the **3D Cursor** at the _rig/mesh/center of the scene_ pivot point.

22. Press _Tab_ to go into **Edit Mode** and press the _1_ key on the numpad to go in the **Front** view; go to the **Object Data** window, under the **Display** subpanel, and switch back from **B-bone** to **Octahedral** (even if the visualization mode is different, the bones set as **B-Splines** still keep their _curved_ properties in **Pose Mode**).

23. Press *Shift + A* to add a new bone at the cursor position. Move and resize it to put it as the **clavicle** bone—almost horizontal and slightly backward oriented, on the left-hand side of the rig. Rename it **shoulder.L** and in the **Parent** slot under the **Relations** subpanel, select the **chest** item:

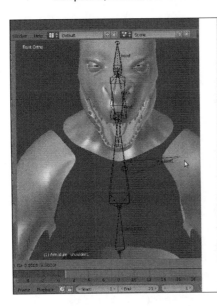
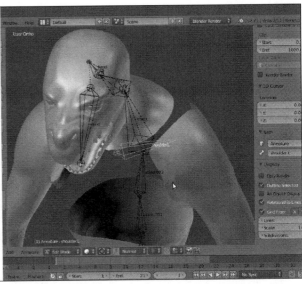

The shoulder.L bone

24. In the **Front** view, select the **Head** of the **shoulder.L** bone and extrude it **3** times to build the bones for **arm**, **forearm**, and **hand**:

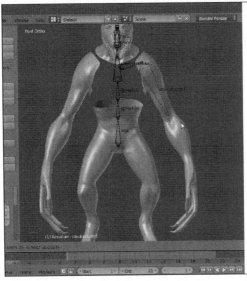
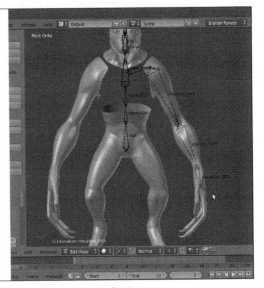

Extruding the shoulder.L bone to obtain the skeleton's bones for the arm

25. Now, exit **Edit Mode** and right-click to select the **Gidiosaurus** mesh; enter **Edit Mode**, select one or more edge-loops at the **elbow** level, and press *Shift + S* | **Cursor to Selected**.

26. Get out of **Edit Mode**, select the **Armature**; go into **Edit Mode**, select the joint between the **arm** and **forearm** bones and press *Shift + S* | **Selection to Cursor**:

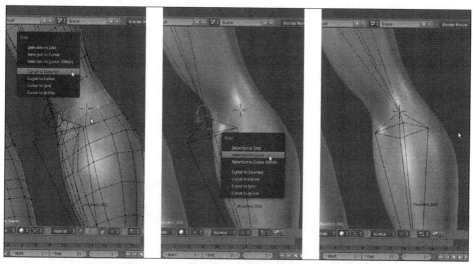

Placing the elbow joint

27. This is the easiest way to correctly align the rig joints with the mesh edge-loops. Do the same for the joint of the **wrist** and the bone of the **hand**; rename the bones as **arm.L**, **forearm.L**, and **hand.L**:

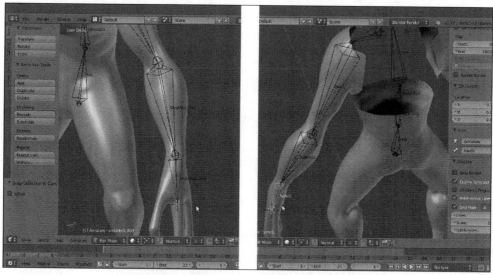

Fixing the position of the wrist joint and hand's bone

28. Select the **hand.L** bone and use *Shift + D* to duplicate it; scale it smaller (*S* | **0.600** | *Enter*), rename it **palm_01.L**, and move it above the joining of the **palm** with the **thumb**. Use *Shift + D* to duplicate it **2** more times and move the new bones above the joining of the other two **fingers**; rename them **palm_02.L** and **palm_03.L**.

29. Use *Shift* to select the three **palm** bones and, as the last one, the **hand.L** bone; press *Ctrl + P* | **Keep Offset** to parent them (**not connected**) to the latter one:

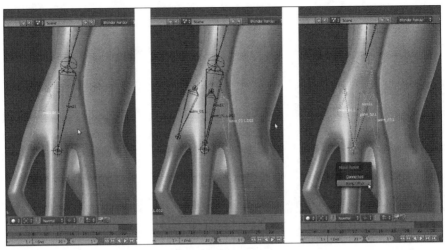

Adding the palm bones

30. Select (individually) the **Heads** of each **palm** bones and extrude the bones for the **fingers**; center their joints with the **3D Cursor/Snap** menu method and rename them properly (**thumb**, **index**, and **middle**):

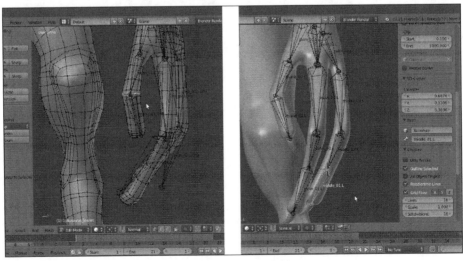

The bones for the fingers

31. Again with the **3D Cursor** at the rig pivot point, add a new bone and shape it to fit inside the left **thigh**, the **Tail** at the top, close to the **hips** bone, and the **Head** at the **knee** location; select it and use *Shift* to select the **hips** bone, and then press *Ctrl + P* | **Keep Offset**. Extrude the bone's **Head** three times to build the **leg – foot** skeleton.

32. Extrude also the bones for the **toes** and repeat the previously described process to center the joints, and then rename all the new bones (**leg, calf, foot, toe inn,** and **ext**):

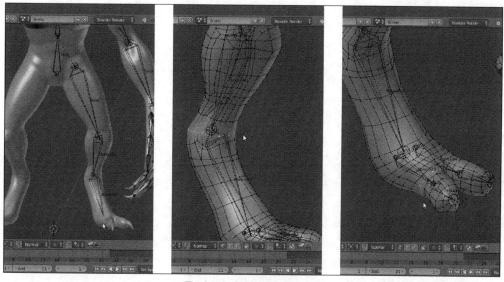

The bones for the leg and toes

In the preceding screenshots, you can see that we have hidden the **talons** vertices in **Edit Mode** (*H* key), in order to have the possibility to easily select the last edge-loops on **fingers** and **toes**.

33. Save the file as `Gidiosaurus_rig_from_scratch_01.blend`.

Building the rig for the secondary parts

Now that we have completed the main body rigging system, it's time to build the rig for **eyes**, **eyelids**, and **tongue**:

1. Get out of **Edit Mode** and select the **Eyes** item in the **Outliner**; press the dot (.) key on the numpad to center the view on the selected object, the *Z* key to go in **Wireframe** viewport shading mode, and *Tab* to go into **Edit Mode**.

2. Press the *A* key to select all the **eye** vertices and then box-deselect (the *B* key and the middle mouse button) the vertices of the **right eye**; use *Shift + S* to call the **Snap** pop-up menu and select the **Cursor to Selected** item to place the **3D Cursor** at the center of the left eye mesh:

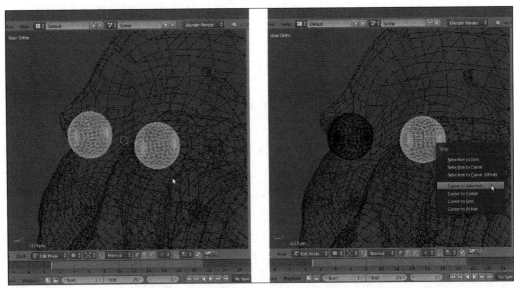

Placing the 3D Cursor at the center of the selected vertices

3. Get out of **Edit Mode**, press the *3* key on the numpad to go in the **Side** view and reselect the **Armature** item in the **Outliner**; press *Tab* to go into **Edit Mode**, and then use *Shift + A* to add a new bone at the cursor position. Press *G* to grab the already selected **Head** of the new bone and move it close to the center of the **eye** to resize it smaller.

4. Get out of **Edit Mode** and select the **Eyes** item; enter **Edit Mode** and deselect all the vertices except for the external last **iris** edge-loop. Then, press *Shift + S* | **Cursor to Selected** and get out of **Edit Mode**.

5. Again, select the **Armature**, go into **Edit Mode**, be sure that the **Head** of the new bone is still selected, and press *Shift + S* | **Selection to Cursor**:

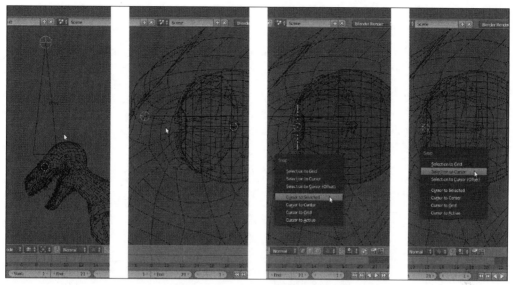

Placing the bone's head at the iris center location

6. Rename the new bone as **eye.L** and in the **Relations** subpanel under the **Bone** window, parent it to the **head** bone (not **Connected**), or use *Shift* to select the **eye.L** and **head** bones and press *Ctrl + P* | **Keep Offset**.

7. Now, select the **Tail** of the **eye.L** bone and press *Shift + S* | **Cursor to Selected** to put the **3D Cursor** on it, and then press the period (.) key to switch the **Pivot Point** around the **3D Cursor**; select the whole **eye.L** bone and use *Shift + D* to duplicate it, and soon after, click with the right mouse button to leave the duplicated bone untouched; rotate it **10** degrees clockwise on the cursor position (*Shift + D* | right-click | *R* | *X* | **10** | *Enter*).

8. Rename the new bone as **eyelid_upper.L**.

9. Reselect the whole **eye.L** bone and repeat the duplication procedure; rotate the new duplicate **10** degrees counterclockwise (*Shift + D* | right-click | *R* | *X* | **-10** | *Enter*).

10. Rename the new bone as **eyelid_bottom.L** (in the following screenshot, all the three new bones—**eyelid_upper.L**, **eye.L**, and **eyelid_bottom.L**—have been selected just to enhance their visibility):

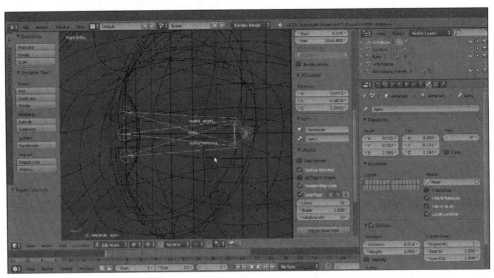

The bones for the eye and eyelids

11. Now, duplicate the **head** bone, resize it smaller, and move it to the joining of the **tongue** with the **inner mouth**; rename it from **head.001** to **tongue.001** and in the **Relations** subpanel, change its parenting from **neck** to **mand**.

12. Select the **Head** of the **tongue.001** bone and press the *E* key to extrude **4** new bones:

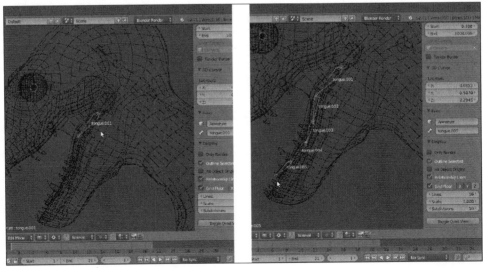

The tongue bones

13. Rename them accordingly, and then use *Shift* to select from the **tongue.001** to **tongue.005** bones and press *Ctrl + R*; move the mouse pointer horizontally to *roll* them on their *y* axis by **180°** (hold *Ctrl* to constrain the rolling to intervals of **5** degrees; alternatively, the roll value can also be set by typing it in the **Roll** button in the **Transform** subpanel under the 3D viewport **Properties** sidepanel).

Completing the rig

At this point, the basic rig building process is almost done, even if it is only for the left-half part of the mesh:

1. Get out of **Edit Mode** and press *Shift + S* | **Cursor to Selected** to place the **3D Cursor** at the median pivot point of the **Armature**.

2. Go back into **Edit Mode**, select only the left-half part bones and *not* the median ones (meaning: leave the **hips, spine, neck, head, mouth**, and **tongue** bones unselected), press *Shift + D* to duplicate them, and then right-click with the mouse button; press *Ctrl + M*, then the *X* key to mirror the duplicated bones on the *x* axis, in order to build the missing right-half part of the rig:

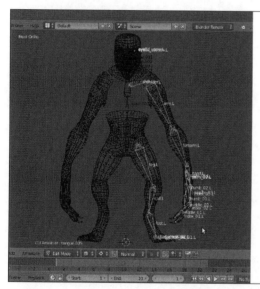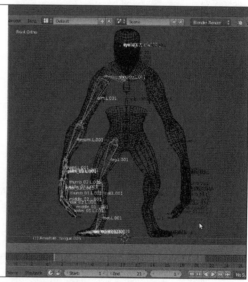

Mirroring the duplicated bones on the x axis

3. With the duplicated bones still selected, go to the **3D window toolbar** and click on the **Armature** item; in the pop-up menu, select the **Flip Names** item to automatically rename them with the correct **.R** suffix:

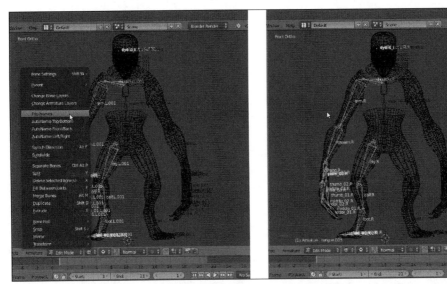

Renaming the suffix of the duplicated bones

As a very last thing for this recipe, we must verify that the alignment of the bones, especially the last duplicated ones, is correct and, just in case, recalculate the roll rotation, that is, the rotation around the y axis of the bone itself.

4. In the **Object Data** window, under the **Display** subpanel, check the **Axes** item to make the bones orientation axes visible (only in **Edit Mode** and **Pose Mode**) in the 3D view.

5. Select all the bones and press *Ctrl + N* to recalculate the rolling of all of them; in the **Recalculate Roll** pop-up menu, there are several different options: because basically the z axis of the bones must match from the left to the right side of the whole rig, with the **Armature** (and the mesh) oriented along the y global axis, as in our **Gidiosaurus** case, the first top item, **Local X Tangent**, can be a good start.

By the way, it is good practice to not trust this automated procedure alone, because sometimes it can give inconsistent results; so, do the following:

6. After the recalculation, check that the axes of each bone are actually correctly orientated in a consistent way; effectively, there are some bones that didn't get consistently oriented, meaning that their x and z local axes are oriented differently from the other bones.

7. In this case, select the incorrectly oriented bone, press *Ctrl + R*, and move the mouse to change the rolling; press the *Ctrl* key to constrain the rolling to intervals of **5** degrees. Alternatively, select the wrong bones, and then use *Shift* to select one bone that is correctly oriented and press *Ctrl + N* | **Active Bone** to copy the rolling from the last selected bone.

By enabling the **X-Axis Mirror** item in the **Armature Options** tab under the **Tool Shelf**, you can recalculate only the bones of one side; the other side bones will follow automatically.

If you want to make sure the bones' orientations are correct and everything is going to work in animation, just go into **Pose Mode** and rotate one bone, for example **leg.L**, and then click on the *Copies the current pose of the selected bones to copy/paste buffer* button (*Ctrl + C*), which is the first left one of the last three buttons to the right-hand side of the viewport toolbar; then, select the symmetrical bone, **leg.R**, and click on the last right button to paste the flipped pose (*Ctrl + Shift + V*); if the **leg.R** bone rotates correctly, then the orientation is OK:

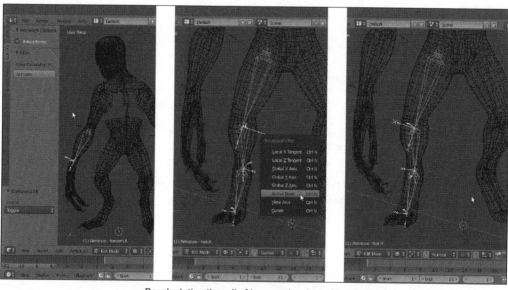

Recalculating the roll of incorrectly oriented bones

8. Now, go to the **Object Data** window under the main **Properties** panel and under **Display**, switch again the bones visualization from **Octahedral** to **B-bone**; select the bones and by pressing *Ctrl + Alt + S*, scale the **B-bones** smaller or bigger, depending on the visual effect you want to obtain:

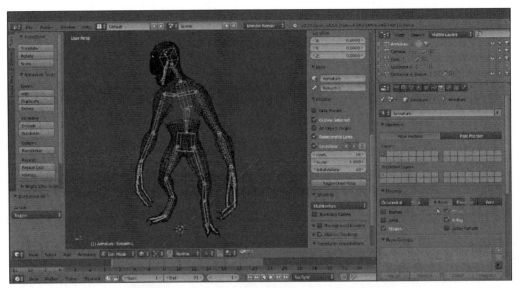

The almost completed Armature in B-bones visualization

9. Press *Ctrl + Tab* to pass directly from **Edit Mode** to **Pose Mode** and select the **forearm.L** bone; in the **Deform** subpanel under the **Properties** panel, set the **Segments** for the **Curved Bones** to **12**, and then set the **Ease In** and **Ease Out** values to **0.000**.

10. Repeat this for the **forearm.R** bone and also for the **calf.L** and **calf.R** bones; repeat also for the **arm.L**, **arm.R**, **leg.L**, and **leg.R** bones.

In the following screenshot, all the eight **B-bones** have been selected to make them more visible. By the way, the highlighted **leg.R** bone is the active one and shows the **Curved Bones** setting in the highlighted **Deform** subpanel to the right-hand side of the screen.

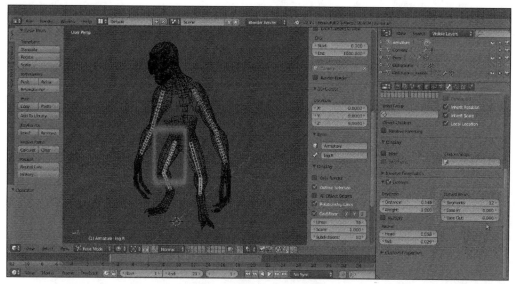

The Segments setting for the leg bone

11. Select the **toe_inn_02.L** bone and in the **Deform** subpanel under the **Properties** panel, set the **Segments** to **6** and leave the **Ease In** and **Ease Out** values to **1.000**.

12. Repeat this for the **toe_ext_02.L** bone; then, do the same also to the **toe_inn_02.R** and **toe_ext_02.R** bones.

13. Select the **toe_inn_01.L** bone and set the **Segments** to **3**; leave the **Ease In** and **Ease Out** values to **1.000**.

14. Repeat for the **toe_ext_01.L** bone; then, do the same also to the **toe_inn_01.R** and **toe_ext_01.R** bones:

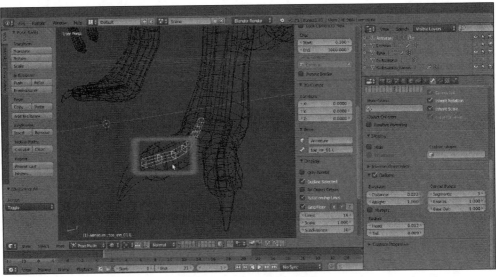

The Segments setting for the toes bones

15. Save the file.

How it works...

Although it's often a really time consuming task, the handmade rigging is quite self-explicative; it is, however, better to explain some of the concepts behind this.

The proper renaming of the bones is important, considering that each deforming bone will affect a vertex group sharing the same name on the mesh; although in some cases, as for the **tongue** bones, the bone naming process can be automated in some way, usually it is better to spend time in giving meaningful names to each bone, in order to avoid mistakes in the following skinning process.

It's also very important to build the hierarchy of the bones so that a bone at a higher level can lead all of the children bones, as it would be in a real skeleton (that is, for example, the **hand** bone leads all the **fingers** bones, the **forearm** bone leads the **hand** bone, and so on).

Parenting a bone and then obtaining the others by extruding and/or duplicating simplifies the work because an extruded bone is automatically parented to the bone it has been extruded from, and a duplicated bone obviously inherits the parenting of the original one; in the case of the **tongue.001** bone, extruding the others has given us a chain with bones automatically parented and named as **tongue.002**, **tongue.003**, **tongue.004**, and **tongue.005**.

B-bones are both a visualization mode for the bones and a way of working; **B-bones**, in fact, can work inside a chain as splines, which means that the bones are curved according to the number of **Segments** and the values of the **Ease In** and **Ease Out** items. For the bones of the **arms** and **legs**, we have set the **Ease In** and **Ease Out** values to **0.000** (default is **1.000**; maximum is **2.000**), in order to have the B-bones rotating only on their **y** axis but remaining straight along their length, and hence, mimic the twisting by not only the rotation (*pronation* and *supination* of the lower arm) of both the *Ulna-Radius* and *Tibia-Fibula* articulation complexes, but also the (limited) rotation of *Femur* and *Humerus*.

In some way, **B-bones** can work as a kind of simulation for a very basic muscle system; in the following screenshot, you can see their effect on the skinned mesh for the **forearm** by rotating the **hand.L** bone on the local *y* axis (to enhance the visibility of the mesh surface's modifications, the *wireframe over solid drawing* item has been enabled in the **Display** subpanel under the **Object** window):

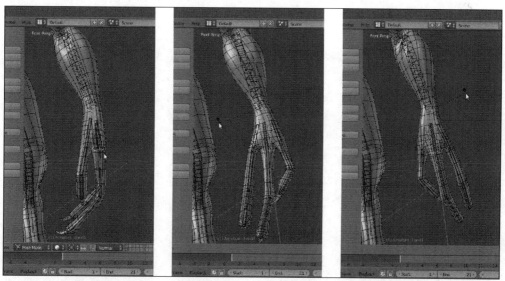

The effect of the rotation of the hand bone on the forearm B-bone and skinned mesh

Here is the effect of the rotation of the **forearm.L** bone on the **Gidiosaurus** high **arm**:

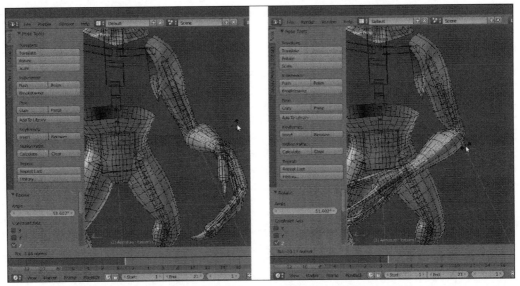

The effect of the rotation of the forearm bone on the upper arm b-bone and skinned mesh

The effect acts on the **shin** as well, by rotating the **foot.L** bone on the global *z* axis:

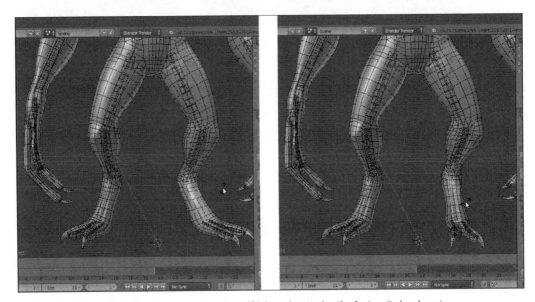

The same effect obtained on the calf b-bone by rotating the foot on its local y axis

Also, the same effect acts on the **thigh** by rotating the **calf.L** bone:

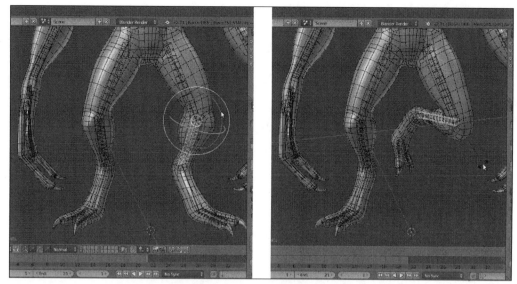

The same effect obtained on the leg b-bone by rotating the calf

Note that the **Gidiosaurus** is a **digitigrade biped humanoid**: the bones that, from our plantigrade point of view, look like the **foot** are actually the **toes**, while the almost vertical structure that we would call an **ankle** is the real **foot** (this is a very common condition among the majority of the terrestrial animals, both still alive and extinct).

Perfecting the Armature to also function as a rig for the Armor

So, in the previous recipe, we have built the body deforming **Armature** for the **Gidiosaurus** character.

However, the **Gidiosaurus** is an (almost) evolved and a civilized creature, and being also a warrior, it wears a metallic **Armor**; this armor will need to be later parented to the rig as well in order to be animated.

Some of the bones that we have already created will be perfect to skin the **Armor** object too, by assigning the right vertex group to the right mesh part (for example, the **head** vertex group for the **Helm** or the **chest** vertex group for the **Breastplate**). However, because the **Armor** is made also by different parts that cannot be simply driven by the already existing bones (for example, the **belts**, **Vambraces**, and especially **Groinguard**), some modification and/or addition to the rig must be done anyway.

Getting ready

Start from the previously saved `Gidiosaurus_rig_from_scratch_01.blend` file:

1. Enable the **13th** scene layer to show the **Armor** object.

2. Select it and go to the **Object Modifiers** window under the main **Properties** panel. Expand the **Subdivision Surface** modifier tab and click on the *Display modifier in viewport* button, the one with the eye icon, to disable it.

3. Go to the **Outliner** and click on the arrow icon to the side of the **Armor** item to make it unselectable.

4. Click on the arrow icon to the side of the **Gidiosaurus_lowres** item to make it unselectable as well.

5. Save the file as `Gidiosaurus_rig_from_scratch_02.blend`.

How to do it...

Let's start by adding bones dedicated to the **Armor**:

1. Go into **Edit Mode** and select the **forearm.L** bone; use *Shift + D* to duplicate it and rename it **vanbrace.L**. Press *M* and in the **Change Bone Layers** pop-up, click on the **2nd** button to move the duplicated bone to that bone layer.

2. Do the same for the **forearm.R** bone (**vanbrace.R**) and for the **calf.L** (**greave.L**) and **calf.R** bones (**greave.R**).

3. Now, go to the **Object Data** window and click on the **2nd** button under the **Layers** item in the **Skeleton** subpanel, in order to show only the four duplicated bones in the 3D viewport; press *Tab* to get out of **Edit Mode**.

4. Select the **vanbrace.L** bone and go to the **Bone** window under the **Deform** subpanel; under the **Curved Bones** item, set back the **Segments** and **Ease In** and **Ease Out** values to default, that is, **1**, **1.000** and **1.000**.

5. Go back into **Edit Mode** and click on the **Connected** item under the **Relations** subpanel.

6. Get out of **Edit Mode** and go to the **Bone Constraints** window under the main **Properties** panel (not to be confused with the **Object Constraints** window); click on the **Add Bone Constraint** button and select a **Copy Rotation** constraint from the pop-up menu (the bone turns light green, in order to show that it has a constraint assigned now).

7. In the **Target** field, select **Armature**; in the **Bone** field, select the **forearm.L** item; in the **Space** fields, select **Pose Space** for both.

Alternatively, for steps 6 and 7, select the **forearm.L** bone and then use *Shift* to select the **vanbrace.L** bone. Hence, press *Shift + Ctrl + C* to call the **Add Constraint (with Targets)** pop-up menu and select the **Copy Rotation** item. This will automatically add the **Copy Rotation** constraint to the **vanbrace.L** bone, with the first select bone (**forearm.L**) as a target; the other setting must be enabled and/or tweaked in the constraint subpanel instead.

8. Click again on the **Add Bone Constraint** button and this time, select an **Inverse Kinematics** constraint (the bone turns yellow, in order to show that an **IK solver** has been assigned). In the **Target** field, select the **Armature** item, in the **Bone** field, select the **hand.L** bone, and set the **Chain Length** to **1**; deselect **Stretch** and select **Rotation**, lowering the weight to the minimum (that is **0.010**):

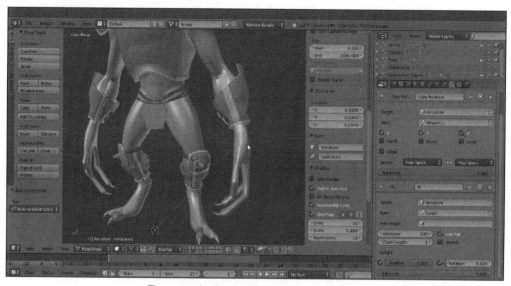

The constraints assigned to the forearm.L b-bone

9. Repeat the steps from 4 to 8 for the other three duplicated bones (obviously, setting the appropriate bones as targets for each pair of constraints; the target bone for the **IK** constraint assigned to the **greave** bones is the respective foot bone).

    The rig can now drive the **vambraces** and **greaves**; let's see the **knee guards** and **Groinguard**.

10. First, switch the **Armature** visualization back to **Octahedral**, then go into **Edit Mode**, select the **hips** bone and use *Shift + D* to duplicate it; in the **Side** view, rotate the duplicate **170** degrees, then move it on the **Groinguard** part of the armor, in order to have the **Head** of the bone placed to the joint of the **plate** with the **ties**; select the **Tail** of the **groinguard** bone and scale it smaller to fit the part.

11. To position the bone more precisely, go to the **Transform** subpanel under the **Properties** 3D view sidepanel and set the following values for the **Head** (of the bone): **X = 0.001, Y = 0.020,** and **Z = 1.147**; for the **Tail** set the following values: **X = 0.001, Y = 0.022,** and **Z = 0.873**.

12. Go to the **Item** subpanel and rename the bone from **hips.001** to **groinguard**:

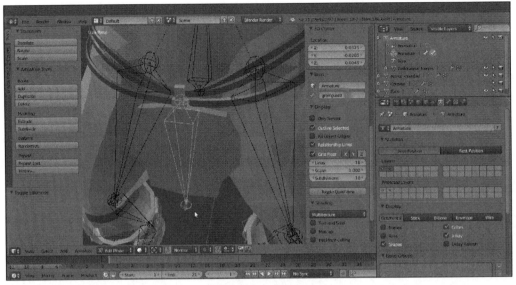

The groinguard bone

13. Go to the **Bone** window in the main **Properties** panel, and under the **Relations** subpanel, click on the **Parent** empty slot to select the **hips** item.

14. Now, select the joint of the **leg.L** bone with the **calf.L** bone and press *Shift + S |* **Cursor to Selected**; press *Shift + A* to add a new bone and rescale it smaller.

15. Select the whole new bone and use *Shift* to select the **calf.L** bone. Then, go in the 3D view toolbar and click on the **Armature** item; go to **Transform | Align Bones** (or else, press the *Ctrl + Alt + A* keys) to align the new bone as the **calf.L** one.

16. Enable the widget (*Ctrl* + spacebar), set the **Transform Orientation** to **Normal**, and the rotation pivot on the **3D Cursor**. Then, rotate the new bone **110** degrees on the normal *x* axis (the red wheel of the widget, or else *R | X | X |* **110** *| Enter*):

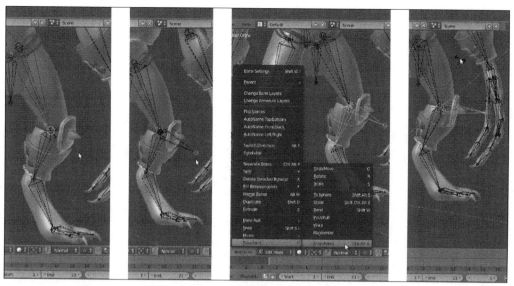

Aligning the new bone

17. Go into **Object Mode** and press *Shift + S* | **Cursor to Selected** to place the **3D Cursor** at the median pivot point of the **Armature**; go back into **Edit Mode**, press *Shift + D* to duplicate the new bone, then *Ctrl + M* | *X* to mirror it on the other side.

18. Rename the new bones as **kneeguard.L** and **kneeguard.R**; enable the axis visibility and recalculate the roll by the *Ctrl + N* | **Active Bone** tool:

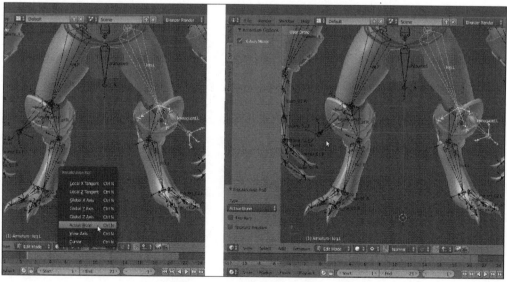

Recalculating the roll angle of the kneeguard bones

19. Parent the **kneeguard.L** bone to the **leg.L** bone and the **kneeguard.R** bone to the **leg.R** one (not connected).

20. Select the **groinguard** bone and use *Shift + D* to duplicate it, and then scale the duplicated bone a little bit bigger and rename it as **groinguard_ctrl**; uncheck the box of the **Deform** subpanel under the **Bone** window:

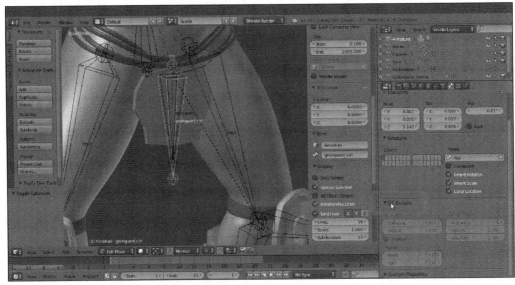

Creating a control bone for the groinguard bone

21. Select the **groinguard** bone, go to the **Relations** subpanel, and click in the **Parent** field to select the **groinguard_ctrl** bone.

22. Get out of **Edit Mode** and in **Pose Mode**, select the **groinguard_ctrl** bone.

23. Go to the **Bone Constraints** window under the main **Properties** panel; click on the **Add Bone Constraint** button and select a **Locked Track** constraint from the pop-up menu.

24. In the **Target** field, select the **Armature** item; in the **Bone** field, select the **kneeguard.L** item. Set the **Head/Tail** value to **0.500**: **To** (*Axis that points to the target object*) = **-X** and **Lock** (*Axis that points upward*) = **Y**. In the **Constraint Name** field, rename it as **Locked Track.L**.

25. Add a new **Locked Track** constraint and repeat everything as in the previous one, except in the **Bone** field, select the **kneeguard.R** item; rename it as **Locked Track.R**.

26. Add a **Damped Track** constraint: **Target = Armature**, **Bone = kneeguard.L**, **Head/Tail = 0.728**, **To = Y**, and **Influence = 0.263**. Rename it as **Damped Track.L**.

27. Add a new **Damped Track** constraint and repeat everything as in the previous one, except again in the **Bone** field, select the **kneeguard.R** item; rename it as **Damped Track.R**.

28. Just to be sure, save the file!

29. Go back into **Edit Mode** and in the **Side** view, select the **chest** bone and use _Shift + D_ to duplicate it. Press _W_ to call the **Specials** pop-up menu and select the **Switch_Direction** item, or else press _Alt + F_ directly:

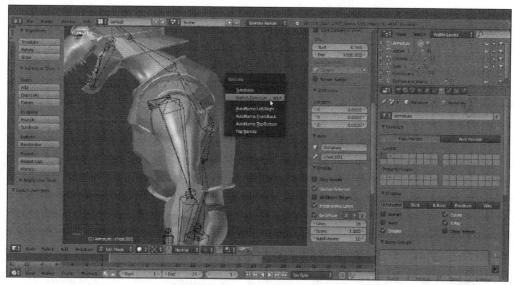

The Specials pop-up menu for the bones

30. Go to the **Bone** window and click on the **Parent** slot under the **Relations** subpanel to select the **chest** item (not connected); then, go to the Deform subpanel and set the **Segments** under **Curved Bones** to **1**. Rename the new bone as **armor_ctrl**.

31. Press *Ctrl + R* to roll the **armor_ctrl** bone, in order to be sure that its local x axis is pointing towards the front of the model; this is important to make the **Transformation** constraints, which we'll add later, work properly:

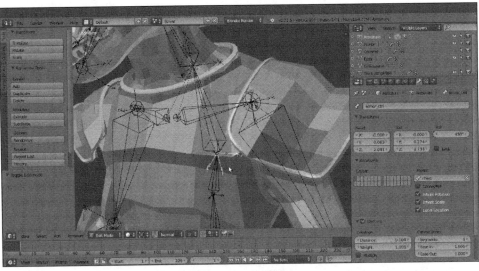

The armor control bone

32. Go in the **Front** view. Note that the **X-Axis Mirror** item in the **Armature Options** panel under the **Tool Shelf** is still enabled; select the **Tail** of the **shoulder.L** bone and extrude a new bone going towards the external edge of the armor **spaulder**. Then, select the extruded bone, press *Alt + P* | **Clear Parent**, and move its **Head** to be positioned above the *joint* of the **spaulder** with the **chest** plate.

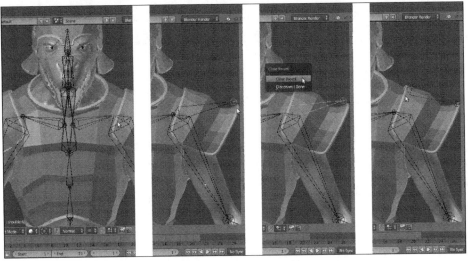

Creating the bone for the spaulder

33. Rename the extruded bone and the corresponding mirrored one as **spaulder.L** and **spaulder.R**; parent them to the **armor_ctrl** bone (enable the **Keep Offset** item).

34. Use *Shift* to select the **spaulder.L** and **arm.L** bones and press *Ctrl + N* | **Active Bone**; do the same with the **spaulder.R** and **arm.R** bones.

35. Now, put the **3D Cursor** at the **spaulder.L** bone's **Head** location, and then set the **Pivot Point** to the **3D Cursor** in the 3D window toolbar. Use *Shift + D* to duplicate the **spaulder.L** bone and rotate the duplicate **70** degrees (in the **Front** view, *R* | **70** | *Enter*).

36. Place the **3D Cursor** at the **shoulder.L** bone's **Tail** location, select the duplicated bone, and press *Shift + S* | **Selected to Cursor**. Rename the duplicated bone and the mirrored one as **rotarmor.L** and **rotarmor.R**. Go to the **Relations** subpanel and set the **rotarmor.L** bone as the child of the **arm.L** bone and the **rotarmor.R** bone as the child of the **arm.R** bone. Disable the **Deform** item for both of them:

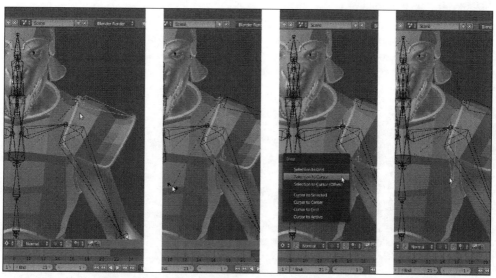

Using the 3D Cursor and the Snap menu to exactly place the bones

37. Go into **Pose Mode**. Select the **spaulder.L** bone and in the **Bone Constraints** window, assign a **Copy Rotation** constraint: **Target = Armature**, **Bone = arm.L**, **Space = Pose Space** to **Pose Space**, and **Influence = 0.200**.

38. Select the **spaulder.R** bone and repeat with the **Bone = arm.R** target.

39. Now, select the **armor_ctrl** bone and assign a **Transformation** constraint. Set **Target = Armature**, **Bone = rotarmor.L**, **Source = Rot**, and **Z Max = 20°**; **Source To Destination Mapping** = switch **X** with **Z**; **Destination = Rot**, **X Max = 4°**, and **Space = Pose Space** to **Pose Space**. Rename the constraint as **Transformation_rot.L** and collapse the panel.

40. Assign a second **Transformation** constraint; set everything as in the previous one, except for the target **Bone = rotarmor.R**, **Source = Rot**, **Z Min = -20°**, and **Destination X Min = -4°**. Rename the constraint as **Transformation_rot.R** and collapse it.

41. Assign a third **Transformation** constraint; set everything as in the first one, except do not switch **X** with **Z**, set **Destination = Loc** and **Z Max = 0.050**. Rename the constraint as **Transformation_move.L** and collapse it.

42. Assign a fourth **Transformation** constraint; set everything as in the second one, except do not switch **X** with **Z**; set **Destination = Loc** and **Z Min = 0.050**. Rename the constraint as **Transformation_move.R** and collapse it.

43. Save the file.

How it works...

We couldn't directly use the **forearm** and **calf** bones to rig the **vanbraces** and **greaves** parts because being subdivided **B-bones**, they would *curve* these **armor** parts along the length as they actually do by deforming organic parts as the **forearms** and **shins**, and this would look awkward, as you can see in the following screenshot:

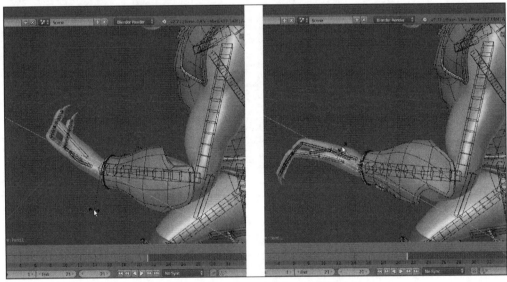

B-bones erroneously deforming stiff objects

Instead, we just duplicated the bones, restored **Segments** and **Ease In** and **Ease Out** to default values, and assigned **2** bone constraints (note that, as already mentioned, the bones have a **Bone Constraints** panel of their own, which is different from the **Object Constraints** one).

The **Copy Rotation** constraint, as the name itself explains, copies the rotation in space of the target **B-bone**; the position inside the chain is granted because the duplicated bones, although not connected, are children of the same bones as the original ones.

The **Inverse Kinematics** constraint—in this case, is used simply to track the **local y** rotation of the **hand** bone in order to rotate correctly on its *y* axis— is necessary because the **Copy Rotation** constraint doesn't seem to read the **local y** rotation of a subdivided **B-bone** (besides the technical details, it makes sense because that's actually not a rotation in space):

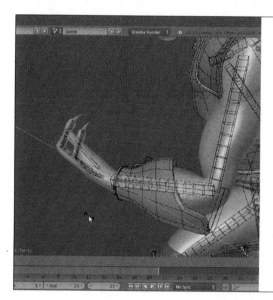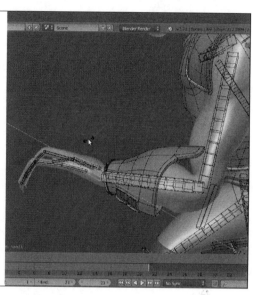

The correct rotation of the stiff armor parts

The constraints assigned to the **groinguard_ctrl** bone are a cheap, but quite an effective, way to fake a rigid body simulation for the **plate** that—in actions, for example, a walk cycle—should interact by colliding with the **Gidiosaurus thighs**. The **Locked Track** constraints, targeted to the **leg** bones, automatically rotate the **plate** according to the **thighs** movements, and the **Dumped Track** constraints, targeted to the **leg** bones as well but with a low influence, add a swinging movement.

The **groinguard** bone, actually the one affecting the **armor plate**, is the child of the **groinguard_ctrl** bone, and so it inherits the constraint's movements but can be used to refine, tweak, or modify the final animation of the plate by hands:

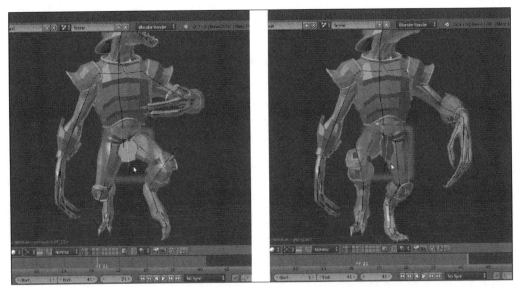

The groinguard bone (and plate) automatically rotating during the walk cycle

The **armor_ctrl** bone is the bone controlling the **armor's Breastplate**; it's the child of the **chest** bone, so it inherits the rotation of the **chest,** but has four **Transformation** constraints.

By using as an input the rotation angle of the **rotarmor.L** and **rotarmor.R** bones (which are children themselves of the **arm.L** and **arm.R** bones), the constraints give to the **Armor chest plate** a slight rotation on the vertical axis and a lateral swinging, driven by the oscillations of the **Gidiosaurus arms**, and simulating of the character's **shoulders** colliding with the **armor plate** during the walk.

Also, the **spaulders** are, in turn, partially rotated by bones with the **Copy Rotation** constraints targeted to the **arms,** but with quite a low influence.

Although better appreciated in motion, the following screenshot will show you the effects as the **arms** rotate backward:

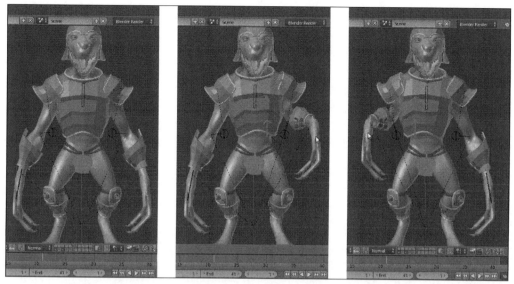

The rotation and swinging of the armor chest plate according to the arms' movements

Building the character's Armature through the Human Meta-Rig

In the previous long and quite complex recipe, we hand-built the deforming elements of an average basic rig for the **Gidiosaurus** character; actually, in Blender, there are other tools to build rigs, particularly meant to facilitate the task, and we'll see them in this recipe and in the following ones.

Now, we are going to take a look at the **Human Meta-Rig** tool.

Getting ready

To be able to use the **Human Meta-Rig** tool, we must first enable the proper add-on:

1. Start Blender and press *Ctrl + Alt + U* to call the **User Preferences** panel. Go to the **Add-ons** tab and under **Categories** on the left-hand side, click on the **Rigging** item. Go to the right-hand side of the panel and check the box to the side of the **Rigging: Rigify** add-on to enable it.

2. Click on the **Save User Settings** button at the bottom-left of the panel and then close it. Because we are starting a rig from scratch again, load the `Gidiosaurus_unwrap_final.blend` file.

3. Disable the **Textured Solid** and **Backface Culling** items in the 3D view **Properties** panel, join the 3D window with the **UV/Image Editor** window, and click on the **11th** scene layer to have only the **Gidiosaurus** mesh visible.

4. Go to the **Object** window and under the **Display** subpanel, enable the **Wire** item; this will be useful in the process to have an idea of the mesh topology when in **Object Mode** and in **Solid** viewport shading mode. However, for the moment, press *Z* to go in the **Wireframe** viewport shading mode.

5. Press *1* on the numpad to go in the **Front** view and *5* on the numpad again to switch to the **Ortho** view.

6. Save the file as `Gidiosaurus_meta_rigging.blend`.

How to do it...

Let's go with the **metarig** itself:

1. Ensure that the **3D Cursor** is at the origin pivot point of the **Gidiosaurus** mesh. Put the mouse cursor in the 3D viewport, press *Shift + A*, and in the pop-up menu, select **Armature | Human (Meta-Rig)**; a biped **Armature**, automatically named **metarig** in the **Outliner**, appears at the **3D Cursor** location:

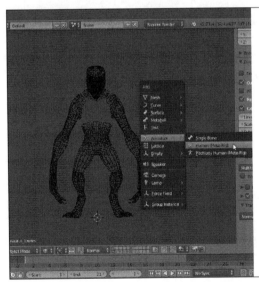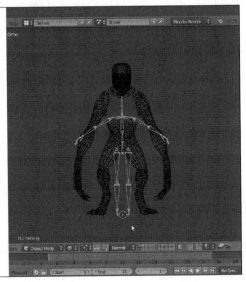

The Human (Meta-Rig) menu and the rig

2. Press the *Tab* key to enter **Edit Mode** and go to the **Options** tab that appeared under the **Tool Shelf** on the left-hand side of the screen; check the box to enable the **X-Axis Mirror** tool under the **Armature Options** item.

3. First, press the period (.) key to set the pivot point around the **3D Cursor** and scale the whole armature bigger while still in **Edit Mode**, and then start to edit locations and proportions of the bones of the **metarig** to fit inside the **Gidiosaurus** shape:

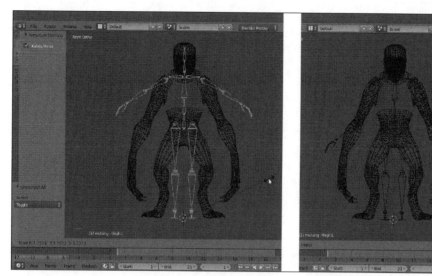

Tweaking the proportions of the bones of the metarig

4. Select the single joints to move them on the right location according to the mesh topology; to do this in a more exact way, just use the snap technique explained in steps 25 and 26 of the *How to do it...* section of the *Building the character's Armature from scratch* recipe. Because of the **X-Axis Mirror** tool we enabled, it's enough to operate only on one side of the **metarig**:

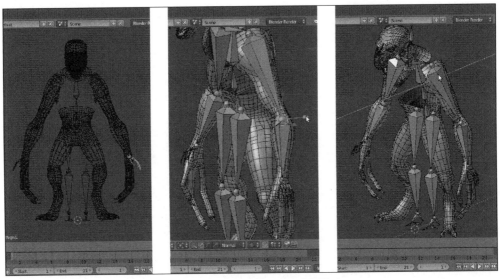

Further tweaking of the bones in Edit Mode

5. Delete the bones that you don't need, for example the extra **fingers** (consider that the **Gidiosaurus** has only three **fingers** in each **hand**), use *Shift + D* to duplicate the bones to be added, for example for the **toes**, and add new bones where missing, for example for the **jaw**, and then parent them. In short, just edit the rig as usual. Again, it should be enough to do all these operations just on one side of the rig:

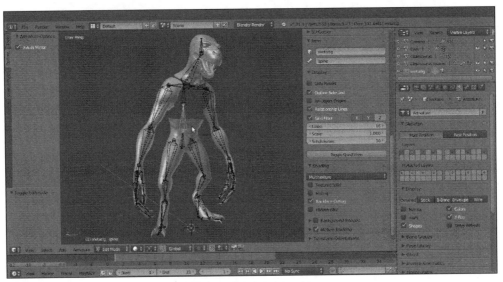

The completed skeleton rig

6. Save the file.

We can also add premade rigging sets, for example a whole new **leg**, **spine**, or **arm**, by going, with the **metarig** still in **Edit Mode**, to the **Rigify Buttons** subpanel under the **Armature** window in the main **Properties** panel. Select the desired item to be added to the rig and click on the **Add sample** button; the new part gets added to the rig's **pivot point** location and must be moved to the right place and tweaked, rotated, and scaled as needed. Also, the new bones must be named with the correct **.R** or **.L** suffix and the top chain bone must be parented to the bottom **metarig** bone; for example, in the case of a **biped.leg** part addition, the **thigh** bone must be parented (*Ctrl + P* | **Keep Offset**) to the **hips** bone:

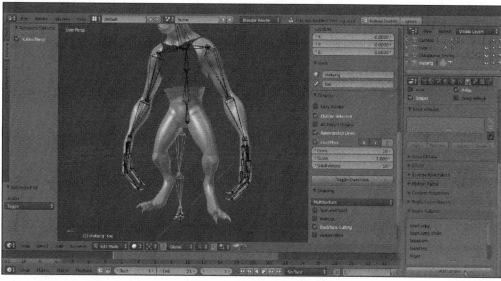

Adding premade rig to the skeleton

How it works...

The **Human metarig** is actually only the first part of a more complex and complete auto-rigging system named **Rigify**, and this we'll see in the next recipe. However, even used by itself, it gives us a readymade humanoid skeleton to be simply tweaked to fit the character's shape: a good shortcut to quickly build the **Armature** rig considering that, at least in its basic form, all the bones are already properly connected and named with the **.L** and **.R** suffices.

Building the animation controls and the Inverse Kinematic

Whether we built the **Gidiosaurus** deforming rig part by hands from scratch or by the **Human Meta-rig**, we must now add the necessary constraints and controls to allow the animators to easily manipulate the character.

 Note that once the mesh is skinned, the rig, as it is at this point, can actually already work by directly selecting the interested bones and rotating them in **Forward Kinematics**; however, to simplify the animator's work (and complicate our life a little bit more), it's good practice to add the **Inverse Kinematic** constraints and the control bones.

Getting ready

Let's start by opening the `Gidiosaurus_rig_from_scratch_02.blend` file; as usual, enter **Edit Mode** to ensure that the **X-Axis Mirror** item in the **Armature Options** subpanel under the **Tool Shelf** is enabled.

How to do it...

We now need to create the control bones; we can do it by extruding from the bones they will drive:

1. Press the *3* key on the numpad to go in the **Side** view and, if not already, select the **Armature**; if necessary, in the **Display** subpanel, change the visualization of the bones from **B-Bone** to **Octahedral**.

2. While still in **Edit Mode**, use *Shift* to select the joints of the **hand** with the **forearm** and the **calf** with the **foot** (it's enough only on one side) and extrude them going backwards (**0.400** along global y axis).

3. Rename the new extruded bones as **ctrl_hand.L**, **ctrl_hand.R**, **ctrl_foot.L**, and **ctrl_foot.R** respectively. Deselect the **Deform** item and unparent them all.

4. Select the **Head** of the **hips** bone and repeat: rename the extruded bone as **MAIN**.

5. Select the **hips** bone and in the **Relations** subpanel, parent it as a child of the **MAIN** bone:

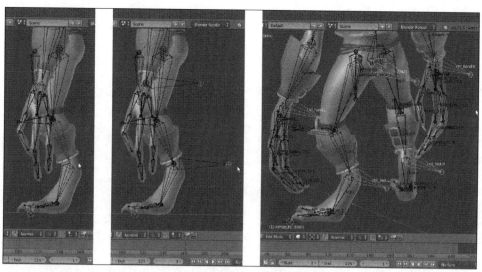

Extruding the control bones part 1

6. Select the **elbow** joint (between the **forearm** and **arm**) and extrude a new bone backwards; rename the extruded bone and the mirrored one as **elbow.L** and **elbow.R**. Disable the **Deform** item and parent them (**Keep Offset**) to the **MAIN** bone. Move them backwards by **0.500** along the global *y* axis.

7. Select the **knee** joint (between the **thigh** and **calf**) and extrude forward; rename the new bones as **knee.L** and **knee.R**. Disable the **Deform** item and parent them (**Keep Offset**) to the **MAIN** bone as well. Move them forward by **-0.500** along the global *y* axis;

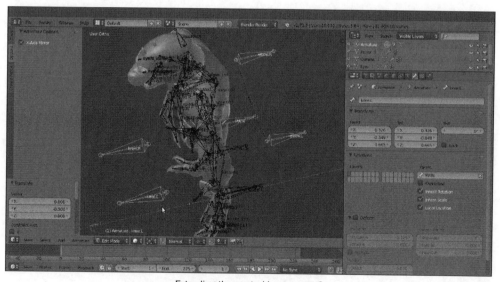

Extruding the control bones part 2

8. Go into **Pose Mode** and select the **forearm.L** bone; go to the **Bone Constraints** window and assign an **Inverse Kinematics** constraint. Set **Target = Armature**, **Bone = ctrl_hand.L**, **Pole Target = Armature**, **Bone = elbow.L**, **Pole Angle = -90°**, and **Chain Length = 2**, and deselect **Stretch**. Repeat the process for the **forearm.R** bone:

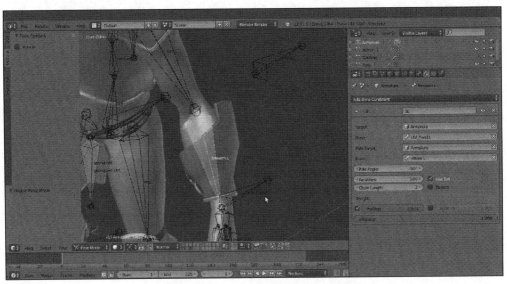

Assigning the IK constraint to the forearm.L bone

9. Do the same for the **calf.L** and **calf.R** bones, using the **ctrl_foot.L** and **ctrl_foot.R** bones as targets and the **knee.L** and **knee.R** bones as poles, but set the **Pole Angle** to **90°** for both.

10. Now, go back into **Edit Mode**, select the **hand** and **foot** bones, and use *Shift + D* to duplicate them. Click on the **Pivot Point** button on the 3D view toolbar, select the **Individual Origins** item, and then scale the duplicated bones smaller to **0.600**:

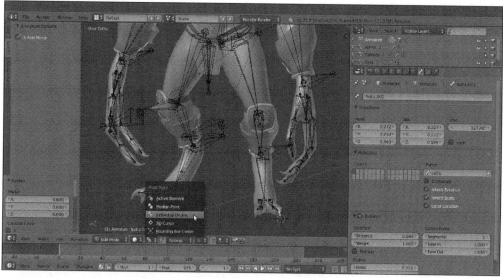

Scaling the bones smaller on their individual origin

11. Deselect the **Deform** item for all of them, and then rename them as: **handrot.L**, **handrot.R**, **footrot.L**, and **footrot.R**.

12. In the **Relations** subpanel (or by the *Ctrl + P* | **Keep Offset** shortcut), parent **handrot.L** to **ctrl_hand.L**, **handrot.R** to **ctrl_hand.R**, **footrot.L** to **ctrl_foot.L**, and **footrot.R** to **ctrl_foot.R**:

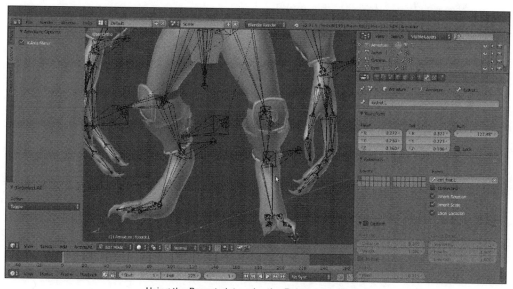

Using the Parent slot under the Relations subpanel

13. Use *Shift* to select the **ctrl_foot.L** bone and the **foot.L** bone and press *Ctrl + Alt + A* to align the first one with the active one; then, select only the **ctrl_foot.L** bone, and by the toolbar widget manipulator set to **Normal** orientation, rotate it **245°** on the x axis:

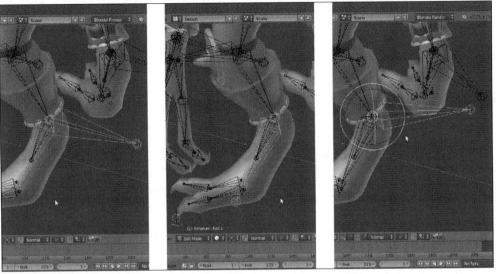

Rotating the bone on the Normal orientation by the widget

14. Go into **Pose Mode** and select the **hand.L** bone; assign a **Copy Rotation** bone constraint with **Target = Armature** and **Bone = handrot.L**, and set **Space = Pose Space** to **Pose Space**.

15. Repeat for the other **hand** bone and **feet**.

16. Select the **Tails** of the **eyelid_upper.L**, **eyelid_bottom.L**, and **eye.L** bones and extrude forward by **0.0600** along the y axis; rename them as **eyelid_ctrl_upper.L**, **eyelid_ctrl_bottom.L**, and **eye_ctrl.L** and the same names with the **.R** suffix for the mirrored ones.

17. Add a new bone in the middle front of the **eyes**, rename it **eyes_ctrl**, and parent it with offset to the **head** bone; then, select the **eye_ctrl.L** and **eye_ctrl.R** bones and parent them with offset to the **eyes_ctrl** bone.

18. Select the **eyelid_upper.L**, **eyelid_upper.R**, **eyelid_bottom.L**, and **eyelid_bottom.R** bones and parent them with offset to the **head** bone:

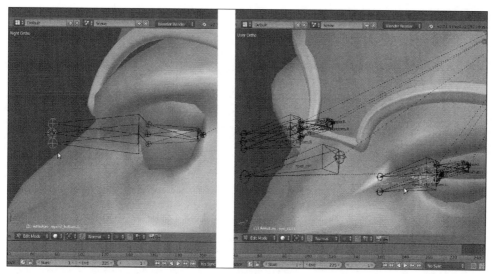

The eyes control rig

19. Select the **Tails** of the **mand** and **tongue.005** bones and extrude; rename the
    extruded bones as **ctrl_mouth** and **ctrl_tongue**. Parent with offset the **ctrl_tongue**
    bone to the **ctrl_mouth** bone and this latter bone to the **head** bone:

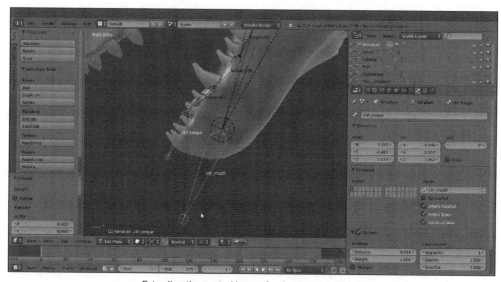

Extruding the control bones for the tongue and jaw

20. Go into **Pose Mode** and assign **Locked Track** constraints to the **eyelid_upper** and **bottom** with target to the respective extruded **ctrl** bones; set **Lock** to **X**:

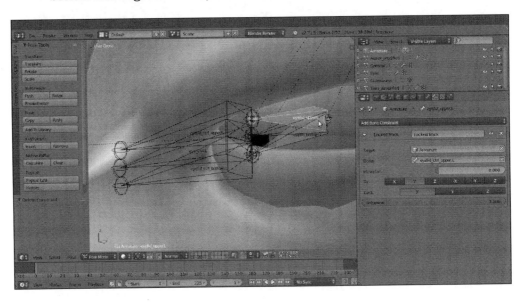

Assigning the Locked Track constraints for the eyelid's controls

21. Assign **Damped Track** constraints to the **eye.L** and **eye.R** bones, again with target to the respective extruded **ctrl** bones:

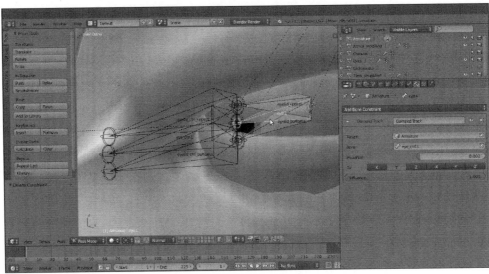

Assigning Damped Track constraints for the eye's controls

22. Assign a **Track To** constraint to the **mand** bone with target to the **ctrl_mouth** bone; check the **Target Z** item box and set **Space = Pose Space** to **Pose Space**:

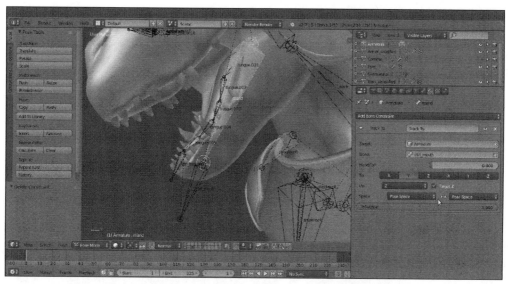

Assigning a Track To constraint to the mand bone

23. Assign an **Inverse Kinematics** constraint to the **tongue.005** bone with target to the **ctrl_tongue** bone; set **Chain Length** to **5**, deselect the **Stretch** item, and then enable also the **Rotation** item;

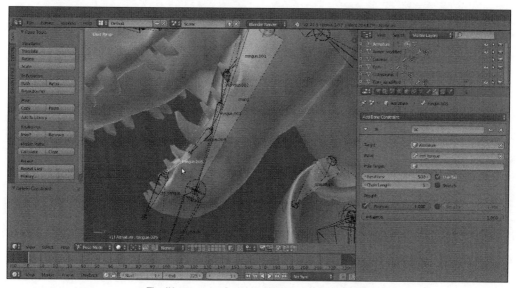

The IK constraint for the bone's chain of the tongue

At this point, the main controls for the **Gidiosaurus** rig are made; still something is missing, for example, the controls to drive **fingers** or/and **toes** bones as a whole, and also a *muscle system* layer of bones with the **Stretch To** constraints that can be added to improve the realism of the model. However, this latter option is quite a complex matter and, for the moment, we will stop here (maybe in another book).

The very last thing to do is to assign **Custom Shapes** (usually, simple meshes located on the last scene layer) to the control and animatable bones widget, and move the rest of the bones to the third **Armature** layer to be out of view.

To see the completed rig with the **Custom Shapes** assigned to the control bones, load the `Gidiosaurus_rig_from_scratch_03.blend` file;

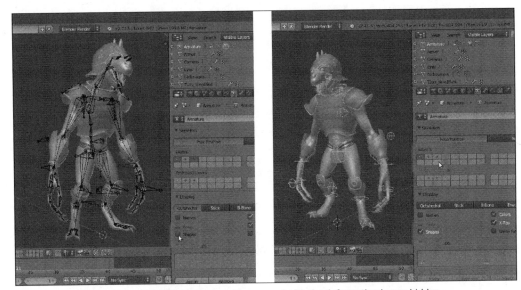

The rig with and without Custom Shapes and with the deformation bones hidden
on the third (disabled) Armature layer

See also

 ▶   `http://www.blender.org/manual/rigging/index.html`

Generating the character's Armature by using the Rigify add-on

We have already seen that the **Human Meta-Rig** armature is part of the **Rigify** add-on. It is a tremendously useful Python script, coded by Nathan Vegdhal, that we enabled two recipes ago, and in this recipe, we are going to use that to build the final rig for the **Gidiosaurus**.

Getting ready

The preparation steps to use the **Rigify** add-on are the same as we did in the *Building the character's Armature through the Human Meta-Rig* recipe: after we have enabled the add-on in the **User Preferences** panel, we load the `Gidiosaurus_unwrap_final.blend` file, add the **Human metarig** to the scene, and then tweak the bone's position, rotation' and size in **Edit Mode** to fit the character's shape and topology.

Also, because the rig generated by the **Rigify** add-on uses some Python script, in the **User Preferences** panel, we must enable the **Auto Run Python Scripts** item (in the **File | User Preference | File** tab, click on the **Auto Run Python Scripts** checkbox).

How to do it...

At this point, in **Object Mode**, we can go to the bottom of the **Armature** window under the main **Properties** panel and click on the **Generate** button in the **Rigify Buttons** subpanel at the bottom of the **Armature** window; the add-on will automatically generate a new **rig** (simply named **rig** in the **Outliner**) using the **metarig** skeleton as an input and adding all the necessary **IK** constraints, the bone's widget controls (generated and located in the last scene layer), and also placing the different bones on different **Armature** layers that are easily accessible through the Python interface created by the script in the 3D window **Properties** sidepanel on the right-hand side (the **Rig Layers** subpanel):

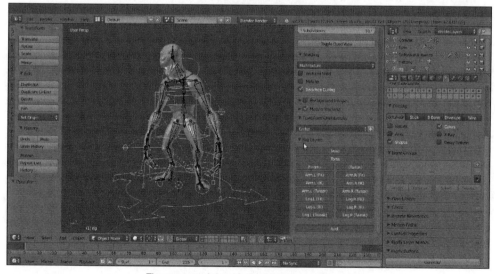

The generated rig with the Rig Layers subpanel

Keep the **metarig** and move it to another layer, just in case we need to do some editing to it in the future; in fact, by testing the generated rig, sometimes you discover that something must be changed to work in a different way. In this case, it is enough to modify the **metarig** and generate the rig again by the add-on that automatically reuses the elements of any already existing rig and the bone's widgets on the last scene layer.

Keep in mind that the generated rig can (and often must) be edited later anyway; after the rig generation, save the file as `Gidiosaurus_rigify_01.blend`.

How it works...

Being conceived to build a rig for a *generic biped humanoid* character, the **Rigify** add-on doesn't generate everything you need automatically: in our case, bones for the **jaw**, **tongue**, **eyes**, and **eyelids** must be added by hands after the rig regeneration and as explained in the *Building the character's Armature from scratch* recipe.

The choice to let face-rig elements, at least initially, out of the **Rigify** add-on has been intentional by Vegdhal, who thinks that a face-rig tool would probably be better as a separate add-on. By the way, in the last Blender releases, it is available, in the **Armature** menu, a **Pitchipoy human rig** option, which is an addition to the **Rigify** script that should help in the face's rig construction (`http://pitchipoy.tv/?p=2026`).

Also, at least for the moment, the **Rigify** add-on doesn't accept custom rig parts, but only the premade parts that we can add to the **metarig** by the **Add Sample** button under the **Rigify Buttons** subpanel in **Edit Mode**; for example, the premade leg rig (**biped.leg**) has only one bone and not two for the toes, as would be necessary for the **Gidiosaurus** character, but in any case, once the final rig is generated by the script, all the necessary additions and modifications can be (quite) easily made by hand.

Obviously, to modify the generated rig, knowing how a rig works in Blender is mandatory: you can rest upon the *Building the character's Armature from scratch*, *Perfecting the Armature to also function as a rig for the Armor*, and *Building the animation controls and the Inverse Kinematic* recipes in this chapter.

In the following screenshot, you can see the **Rigify**-generated rig modified with all the additional bones for the **Armor, eyes, mouth**, and **tongue**, with the necessary added constraints and the **two toed feet** bones; the file is saved as `Gidiosaurs_rigify_02.blend`:

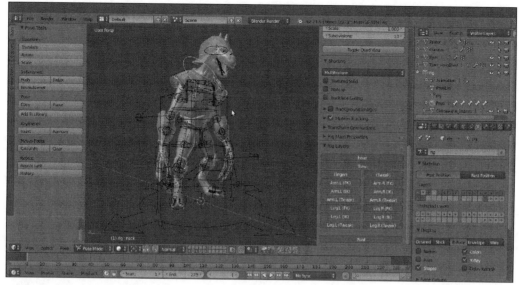

The final total rig

See also

▶   http://blenderartists.org/forum/showthread.php?200371-Rigify-
     Auto-rigging-system-new-and-improved

7

Skinning the Low Resolution Mesh

In this chapter, we will be covering the following recipes:

- ▶ Parenting the Armature and Mesh using the Automatic Weights tool
- ▶ Assigning Weight Groups by hand
- ▶ Editing Weight Groups using the Weight Paint tool
- ▶ Using the Mesh Deform modifier to skin the character
- ▶ Using the Laplacian Deform modifier and Hooks

Introduction

In the previous chapter, we saw the **rigging** stage, that is, how to build the character's rig (which in Blender is called an **Armature**) that will be used to deform the mesh for animations. In this chapter, instead, we are going to see quicker and more effective ways to do the **skinning** that is a necessary step to bind the bones of the **Armature** to the mesh's vertices so that they can be deformed.

To allow an **Armature** to deform a **Mesh**, they must be parented with some kind of relation; in Blender, usually you must select the **Mesh** and then *Shift* select the **Armature** and press *Ctrl + P* to parent them with different options.

This automatically makes the **Mesh** object a child of the **Armature** object and assigns the **Armature** modifier to the **Mesh**. In fact, the parenting would not be strictly necessary; it would be enough to assign an **Armature** modifier to the mesh and manually select the rig as a deforming object, but it's a good habit to use the *Ctrl + P* parenting to have the rig as a parent of the mesh, also in **Object Mode**. This way, whenever you move the **Armature** in **Object Mode**, the mesh will follow it automatically.

For the examples in these recipes, to skin the **Armature** to the **Gidiosaurus** mesh, we are going to use the final version of the rig we have built with our hands: the one saved as `Gidiosaurus_rig_from_scratch_02.blend`.

Anyway, if you want to put this to practice, in this chapter, with a more complex and complete **Rigify** armature (`Gidiosaurus_rigify_02.blend`), the procedure is exactly the same. In this case, even if not strictly necessary, remember that you can enable the **30th Armature layer** (in total there are **32**) to show the deforming bones; instead, disable the visibility of all the other bone layers also by the Python button interface in the **Rig Layers** subpanel under the 3D window **Properties** side panel:

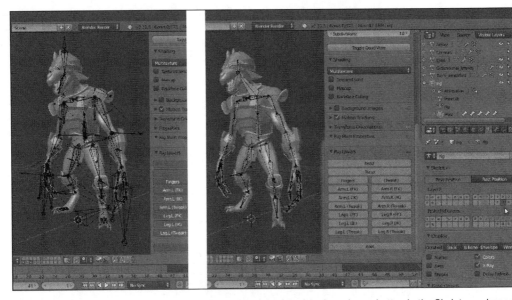

The Rig Layers panel in the N Properties sidepanel and the Armature bone layers button in the Skeleton subpanel under the main Properties panel

Remember to check in your **User Preferences** panel (press *Ctrl* + *Alt* + *U* to call it) if you have, under the **File** tab, the **Auto Run Python Scripts** item enabled; otherwise, the rig based on Python scripts or expressions (like the rigs obtained through the **Rigify** add-on) won't work properly.

In this case, Blender will warn you through an **Auto-run disabled** message visible in the top main header; it's enough to click the **Reload Trusted** button to the right and then confirm by clicking on the **Revert** item in the pop-up menu that appears, to reload the `.blend` file with the scripts enabled and to have everything working as expected:

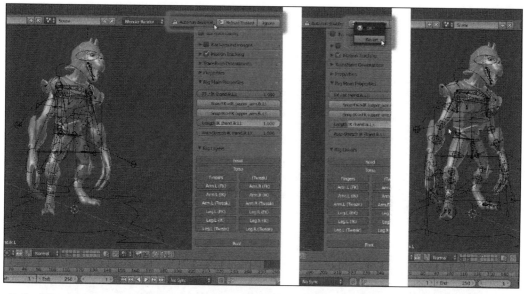

To the left, you can see several bones apparently missing in the rig because it is wrongly oriented, and the "Auto-run disabled" warning in the top main header; to the right, you can see the restored rig

Parenting the Armature and Mesh using the Automatic Weights tool

In this recipe, we are going to see one of the more commonly used parenting options: the handy **Automatic Weights** tool.

Getting ready

Start Blender and open the `Gidiosaurus_rig_from_scratch_02.blend` file.

1. Select the **Armature** item in the **Outliner** and press *Ctrl + Tab* to go out of **Pose Mode** and enter **Object Mode**.

2. Go to the **Armature** window under the **Properties** sidepanel to switch the **Display** mode from **Wire** to **Octahedral** and deselect the **Shapes** item.

3. Enable the third **Armature** layer by clicking on the **3rd** button under the **Skeleton** subpanel.

4. Disable the **13th** scene layer to hide the **Armor**.

5. Go in to **Edit Mode** and *Shift* multi-select the **MAIN** bone, the **pole** bones and the **ctrl** bones; in short, all the bones that don't have to deform anything, but are used to control the rig. Press *Shift + W* and in the **Toggle Bone Options** pop-up panel, select the **Deform** item to disable it for all of them at once:

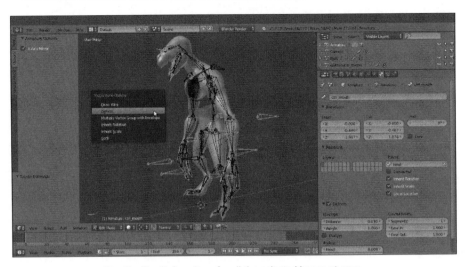

Toggling the Deform item for all the selected bones at once

6. Now, deselect everything and select all the bones that, in the previous chapter, we had added specially to rig the **Armor** object, using the **Armature Layers** buttons: the **armor_ctrl** bone, **groinguard**, **vanbrace.L** and **.R**, **greaves.L** and **.R**, **kneeguard.L** and **.R**, **spaulder.L** and **.R**; again, press *Shift + W* | **Deform** to disable the option.

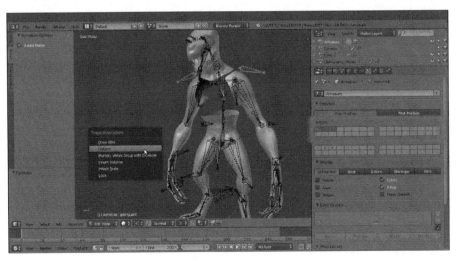

Repeating for the Armor object bones

7. Don't *deselect* the **Armor** bones, simply switch from **Edit Mode** to **Object Mode**.

How to do it...

1. Select the **Gidiosaurus_lowres** object and then *Shift*-select the **Armature**, and press *Ctrl + P*; in the **Set Parent To** pop-up menu; select the **With Automatic Weights** item:

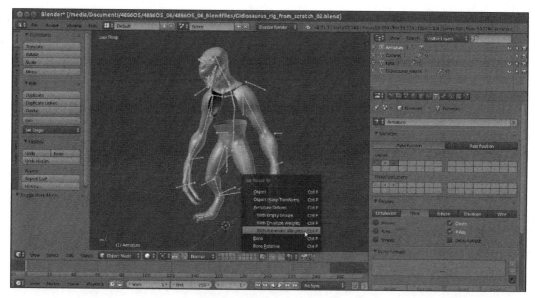

The Set Parent To pop-up menu

2. Reselect the **Armature**, go in to **Edit Mode**, and press *Shift + W* | **Deform** to re-enable the item for the still-selected **Armor** bones; then, go out of **Edit Mode**.

3. Now, reselect the **Gidiosaurus** object; go to the **Object Modifiers** window, move the newly created **Armature** modifier upwards in the stack, and enable the **Preserve Volume** item.

4. Disable the *Display modifier in viewport* button (the one with the eye icon) of the **Subdivision Surface** modifier to speed up the 3D viewport (sadly, Blender still has very bad real-time viewport performances, so even if you have a lot of RAM and a powerful workstation, it's wise to stay as light as you can).

5. Select the **Armature** and under the **Object Data** window, re-enable the **Shapes** item and hide the second and the third **Armature Layer**; press *Ctrl + Tab* to go in **Pose Mode** and try to select some of the control bones to move or rotate them and so control how they are deforming the mesh; temporarily, hide the **Eyes** object in the **Outliner**.

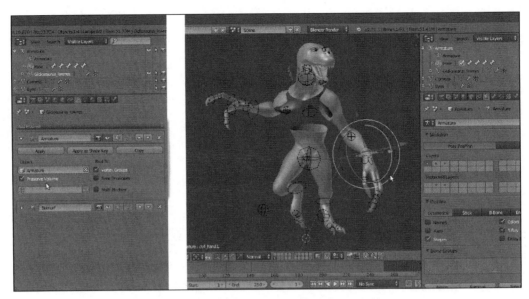

The Armature modifier subpanel and the posed mesh

To rotate the bones on their local axis, enable the **3D manipulator widget** in the 3D view toolbar (*Ctrl + Spacebar*), click on the **Rotate** icon, and set **Transformation Orientation** to **Normal**.

6. Save the file as `Gidiosaurus_autoweights.blend`.

How it works...

The **Automatic Weights** tool creates the necessary **Vertex Groups** based only on the bones that have been set as **Deformers** in the subpanel under the **Bone** window. It then assigns weights inside a range from **0.000** to **1.000** to the vertices contained in these vertex groups, calculating their proximity to the bone with the same name. In short, the **arm.L** bone will deform only the vertices inside the **arm.L** vertex group, and with an intensity based on their weights.

Because we used the **Automatic Weights** tool to skin only the sole **Gidiosaurus** mesh (leaving the skinning of other objects such as the **Eyes** or the **Armor** for the next recipe and method), before the parenting we had to check for any bone erroneously left as a deformer (that is, one of the several control bones in the previous chapter), but, especially we had to temporarily disable the **Deform** item for the **Armor** bones, which otherwise would have also been evaluated by the tool for the **body**.

In most cases, the **Automatic Weights** tool can give quite good results without the need of further tweaking; however in some areas, for example the **head**, where the **head** bone length doesn't fully fit the upper part of the shape of the mesh and where there are also other deforming bones, it can easily fail.

Look at the following screenshot; at first, by rotating the **head** control, the only issue seems to be some of the **teeth** left out from the calculations but then, simply by moving the controls for the **eyes**, **tongue**, and **jaw**, it becomes evident that the tool assigned several vertices to the wrong bones merely based on their proximity to that part of the mesh:

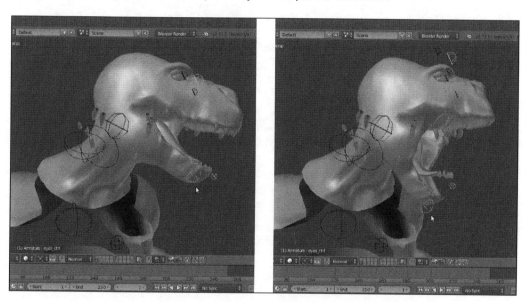

The failure of the Automatic Weights tool parenting

Although at first sight this can appear to be a total mess, it's usually less complex to fix than one might think.

For the moment, by selecting the **Gidiosaurus** mesh and pressing *Ctrl + Tab*, we go in to **Weight Paint** mode, and by right-clicking on a bone (the **Armature** is still in **Pose Mode**), the weights of the corresponding vertex group became visible as colored areas on the mesh; the color **red** corresponds to a weight value of **1.000** and **blue** to a value of **0.000**, with all the intermediate hues corresponding to the intermediate values. For example, **green** = **0.500** and so on.

There's more...

Let's see all this step by step:

1. Select the **Armature** and, while still in **Pose Mode**, enable the visibility of the **third Armature layer** (and therefore of all the deforming bones) and then disable the **Shapes** item again.

2. Select the **Gidiosaurus** mesh and by pressing *Ctrl + Tab*, enter **Weight Paint** mode (or switch to it by the *object interaction mode* button on the toolbar of the 3D view).

3. Click on any one of the deforming bones, for example the **neck** bone, and notice that while the weights appear on the mesh surface, at the same time the corresponding vertex group is highlighted in the **Vertex Groups** subpanel to the right:

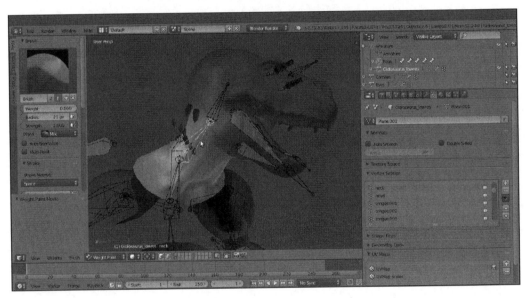

Visualizing the vertex groups on the mesh

By clicking on the **head** bone and/or the **mand** bone, the reasons for the bad deformations are immediately clear: the **Automatic Weights** tool didn't assign the whole upper part of the **head** of the character to the sole **head** vertex group (and therefore to the bone with the same name) with a full value of **1.000**; instead, it assigned part of the **head** mesh to the **eyes** bones, other parts to the **tongue.005** bone, some to the **mand** bone, and so on.

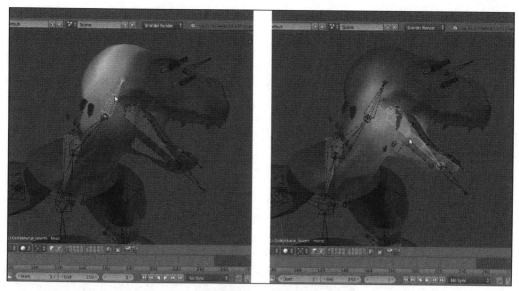

Different weights of the vertex groups associated with different bones

Obviously, this isn't the tool's fault, but it is an *unavoidable issue* due to the particular arrangement of the bones in the **head** area and can be quite easily fixed anyway; we'll see how in the next and the *Editing the Weight Groups by the Weight Paint tool* recipe.

See also

▸ http://www.blender.org/manual/rigging/skinning/obdata.html

Assigning Weight Groups by hand

This technique is the oldest way to assign weights to vertices groups in Blender. Although now there are quicker ways to do the same thing, in some cases it's still one of the best approaches, which can reveal itself to be quite useful mainly because you can precisely select individual or edge-loops of vertices to be weighted inside a group.

Getting ready

Open the Gidiosaurus_autoweights.blend file we saved in the previous recipe.

1. If necessary, press *Ctrl + Tab* to go out of **Weight Paint** mode.
2. Select the **Armature** (which should still be in **Pose Mode**), press the *A* key twice to deselect-select all the bones, and press *Alt + R* and *Alt + G* to clear any rotation or position and restore the default pose.

3. Press the *3* key on the numpad to go in to **Side** view; if necessary, the *5* key on the numpad to go in to **Ortho** view and the *Z* key to go in to **Wireframe** viewport shading mode.

4. Select the **Armature** and disable the **Shapes** item; switch the draw mode of the bones to **Stick** and enable the third **Armature** layer to show the deforming bones.

5. Save the file as `Gidiosaurus_skinning_01.blend`.

How to do it...

First, we are going to use this technique to fix the **head** deformation as follows:

1. Press *Shift + B* to draw a box around the **head** of the **Gidiosaurus** mesh and automatically zoom to it. Select the mesh and enter **Edit Mode**.

2. Press the *C* key, through which the mouse cursor turns into a circle whose diameter can be set by scrolling the mouse wheel.

3. Start to *paint-select* the vertices you want to add to the vertex group; in this case, we must add the whole **upper head** to the **head** vertex group and also include the **upper teeth** that were missing in the group.

4. Be sure that the **head** vertex group is the selected one in the **Vertex Groups** subpanel under the **Object Data** window to the right, and that the **Weight** slider is set to **1.000**; then, click on the **Assign** button.

5. To quickly find a required vertex group, instead of slowly scrolling the list, just click on the grayed out little **+** icon at the bottom of the **Vertex Groups** window (just above the **Assign** button) to expand a blank search field and then write a few letters of the group's name followed by the *Enter* key:

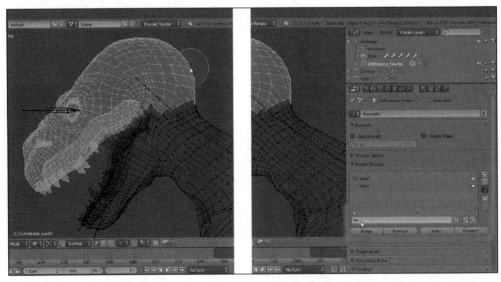

The vertex group names search function

To get the complete list of vertex groups' names back, just erase the letters you wrote in the field and press *Enter*.

6. Now, switch from **Edit Mode** to **Weight Paint** mode again, where the **head** vertex group colors show a lot different than before:

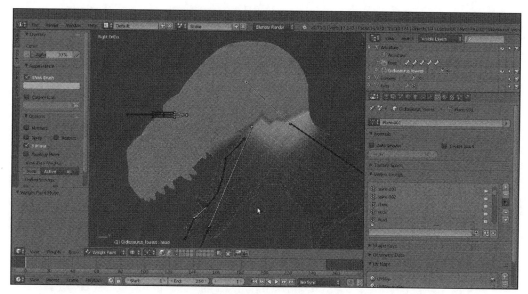

The modified "head" vertex group

7. Now, while still in **Weight Paint** mode, go to the **Tools** tab under the **Tool Shelf** to the left of the screen and, in the **Weight Tools** subpanel, first click on the **Normalize All** button and then on the **Clean** button.

8. Select the **mand** bone, go in to **Edit Mode**, and press *A* to deselect the vertices of the **head** vertex group. Select all the vertices of the **jaw**, including the **bottom teeth**; then go to the **Vertex Groups** subpanel to the right and deselect the **tongue** group by clicking on the, yes, **Deselect** button (we created the **tongue** vertex group chapters ago, during the modeling stage; otherwise, just deselect the tongue's edge-loops manually).

9. Find and select the **mand** group and click on the **Assign** button.

10. Go again in to **Weight Paint** mode and click on the **Normalize All** and **Clean** buttons under the **Weight Tools** subpanel:

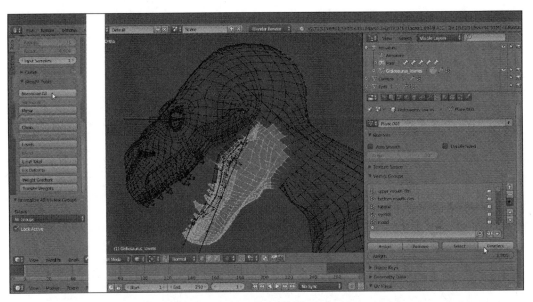

The Weight Tools subpanel and the "mand" vertex group

11. Now, go out of **Weight Paint** mode, select the mesh and, in the **Vertex Groups** subpanel, search for the **eyelid_upper.L** vertex group; enter **Edit Mode** and click on the **Select** button:

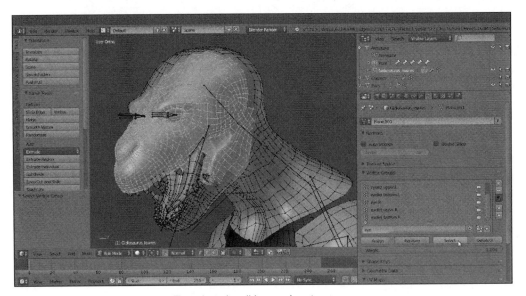

The selected eyelid_upper.L vertex group

We must get rid of all these vertices erroneously assigned to the vertex group by the **Automatic Weights** tool.

12. Click on the **Remove** button and then press the A key to deselect everything.

13. Repeat this for the **eyelid_bottom.L**, **eyelid_upper.R**, **eyelid_bottom.R**, and also for the **eye.L** and **eye.R** vertex groups.

14. Zoom to the **eyes** area. Select an edge-loop (*Alt* + right-click) around the left **eyelids** and then press *Ctrl* and the + key on the numpad to extend the selection; press the *H* key to hide the selected vertices (this is simply to isolate the **eyelids** vertices for easier edge-loops selection):

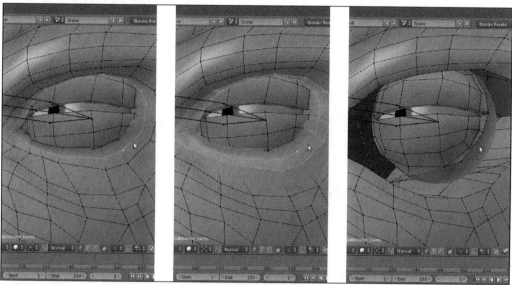

Isolating the eyelids vertices

15. Select the border upper edge-loops and assign them to the **eyelid_upper.L** vertex group with a weight of **1.000**; select the second upper edge-loop and again assign it to the **eyelid_upper.L** vertex group, but with a weight of **0.500** (see the following screenshot).

16. Do the same for **eyelid_bottom.L**:

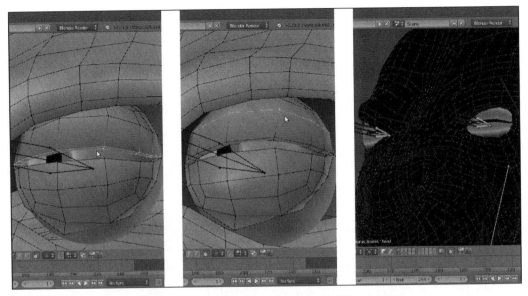

The visualization of the eyelids vertex group with different weights

In the preceding screenshot, to the right, you can see the weights of **eyelid_upper** and **eyelid_bottom** vertex groups on both sides, made visible at the same time by the **Multi-Paint** item enabled in the **Brush** subpanel under the **Tool Shelf**; here it is used only for visualization purposes.

17. Repeat the procedure for the **eyelids** on the right side (**eyelid_upper.R** and **eyelid_bottom.R**).

18. In the **Vertex Groups** subpanel, select the **head** vertex group and then select the border edge-loops of both the **left** and **right eyelids**. Click on the **Remove** button to remove those vertices from the group's evaluation:

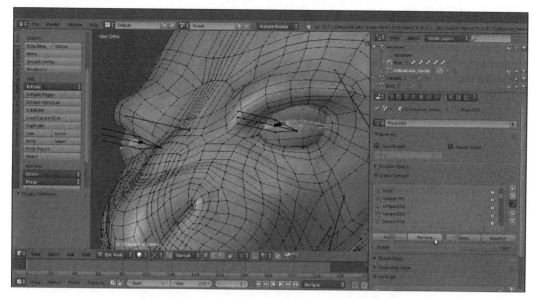

Removing the eyelids vertices from the "head" vertex group

Assigning weights by hand can be a handy method also for other parts, for example, the **eyeballs**, which are separate objects from the **Gidiosaurus** mesh.

19. Go out of **Edit Mode,** and in the **Outliner** select the **Eyes** object; press *Tab* again to go in to **Edit Mode**.

20. Go in to **Front** view and box-select all the vertices of the **left eye**; then, go to the **Vertex Groups** subpanel under the **Object Data** window and click on the **+** icon to the right to create a new group:

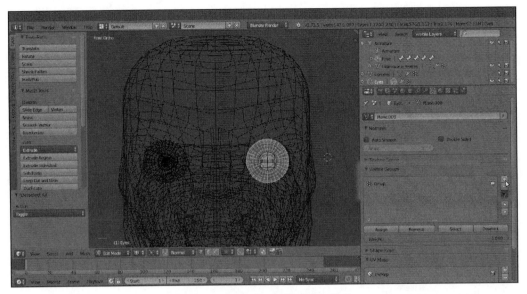

Creating the vertex group for the eyeball

21. *Ctrl* + left-click on the name of the vertex group to rename it as **eye.L** and then click on the **Assign** button to assign all the selected vertices to the group with a value of **1.000**.

22. Deselect everything, select the vertices of the other **eye**, and create a new vertex group; rename it as **eye.R** and assign the vertices.

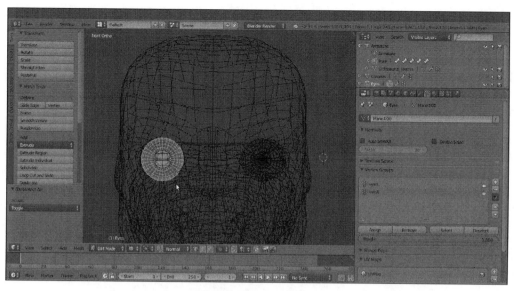

Creating the eye.R vertex group

23. Exit **Edit Mode** (*Tab*) and go to the **Object Modifier** window; assign an **Armature** modifier, move it upwards in the stack, and click on the **Object** field to select the **Armature** item as a deforming object.

24. Temporarily, unhide the **Corneas** object in the **Outliner** and repeat from step 19 to step 23, where we created the **eye.L** and **eye.R** vertex groups and assigned the appropriate mesh vertices and the **Armature** modifier.

    The same process must be applied to the skinning of the **Armor** that, being a single object made of stiff elements, can be easily and ideally divided into different vertex groups; each one is skinned with the full value of **1.000**.

25. Click on the button to activate the **13th** scene layer and show the **Armor**; select it and enter **Edit Mode**.

26. Select all the vertices of the **helm**, including the **decorations**, create the **head** vertex group in the **Armor** mesh (remember that the name must be the one of the deforming bones), and click on the **Assign** button with a weight value of **1.000**:

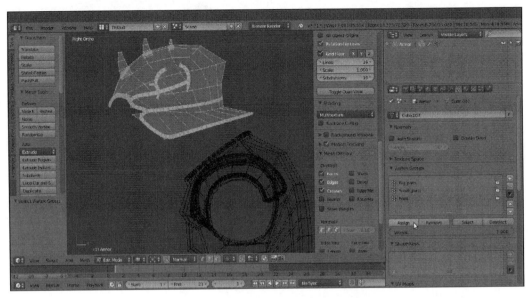

The "head" vertex group for the Armor object

27. Repeat the operation with each part of the **Armor**, so creating, always with a weight of **1.000**, the vertex groups: **vanbrace.L** and **vanbrace.R** (covering the **forearms**), **greave.L** and **.R** (covering the **calves**), **groinguard** (the **front hips**), **kneeguard.L** and **.R**, **spaulder.L** and **.R**, and **armor_ctrl**.

You can use the following screenshot as a guide:

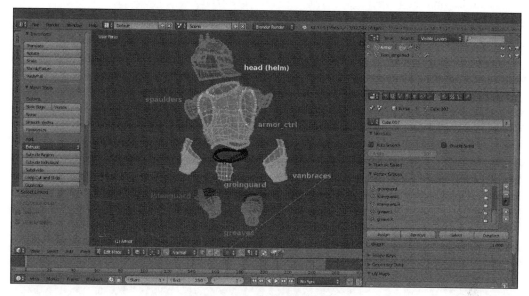

The happy colorful Armor guideline

28. Go out of **Edit Mode**; then, go to the **Object Modifier** window, assign an **Armature** modifier to the **Armor**, move it upwards in the stack, and click on the **Object** field to select the **Armature** item as a deforming object.

29. Disable the *Display modifier in viewport* button (the one with the eye icon) for the **Subdivision Surface** modifier, to speed up the 3D viewport.

For the moment, ignore the **Tiers** (which have been separated by the **Armor** object and simplified by deleting several alternate edge-loops, this we'll skin in the next recipe) and *save the file*.

How it works...

The **Normalize All** button normalizes the weights of all the vertex groups so that their sum is not superior to **1.000**; because we had assigned a weight of **1.000** to the upper head vertices, the vertices in the other groups that were interfering with the **head** deformation have been automatically set to **0.000**.

The **head** group, instead, remained the same because it was locked in the **Options** bottom panel; the **Clean** button, then, took care of removing all the unwanted vertices in the active group, restricting the inclusion of its vertices only to those with a weight greater than **0.000**.

When assigning vertices to a group, the **Weight** slider under the **Vertex Groups** subpanel can obviously be set to any value between **0.000** and **1.000**, so it's also possible to select a single edge-loop or rows of vertices and assign them at different times to the same vertex groups, but with different weight values. For example, a central edge-loop of vertices with the weight of **1.000** can be surrounded by external edge-loops with weight values of **0.750**, **0.500**, **0.250**, and so on. This is what we have done for the **eyelids** after the cleaning of the **eye sockets** area, thanks to the **Select**, **Deselect** and **Remove** buttons. Be aware that the same result can be obtained by painting and/or blurring the weights on the mesh, but we'll see this in the next recipe.

See also

> ► http://www.blender.org/manual/modeling/meshes/vertex_groups/index.html

Editing Weight Groups using the Weight Paint tool

Both the **Automatic Weights** parenting as well as the **Weight Groups** created and assigned by hand must, at a certain point, inevitably be edited for several reasons. As we have already seen, the parenting tool didn't do a perfect job, or maybe the transition between different weights is too sharp and must be blurred to smoothly deform the mesh. In any case, the ideal tool for this editing work is the **Weight Paint** tool.

Getting ready

As usual, let's first prepare the scene to work on:

1. Open the Gidiosaurus_skinning_01.blend file and hide the **13th** scene layer.

2. Enable the 3rd **Armature** layer and then deselect the **Shapes** item.

3. Press the 3 key on the numpad to go in to **Side** view; if necessary, press the 5 key on the numpad to go in to **Ortho** view and the Z key to go in to **Wireframe** viewport shading mode.

4. Save the file as Gidiosaurus_skinning_02.blend.

How to do it...

Also, now let's start with the **Weight Paint** tool itself:

1. Select the **Gidiosaurus** mesh and go in to **Weight Paint** mode; the tabs under the **Tool Shelf** on the left-hand side of the 3D window (press the *T* key in case they are not already present), change to show the **Weight Paint** tools.

2. In the viewport, right-click on the **head** bone to show the **head** vertex group on the mesh's surface.

3. Go to the **Tool Shelf** and click on the **Options** tab to verify that the **X Mirror** item in the **Options** subpanel is activated. Then, go back to the **Tools** tab and click on the big **Brush** window at the top to select a **Blur** brush; set **Weight** to **1.000** and **Strength** to **0.400**.

4. Select the **Auto Normalize** item at the bottom of the **Brush** subpanel.

5. Start to paint on the borderline of the vertex group, blurring the separation between the red and blue colors and trying to obtain, in general, a transition as smooth as possible:

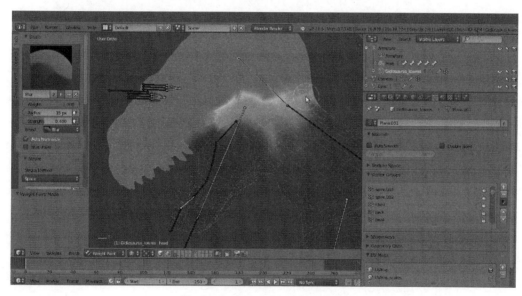

Blurring the edges of the vertex group

6. Switch to the **mand** vertex group by selecting the corresponding bone and smooth the transition again:

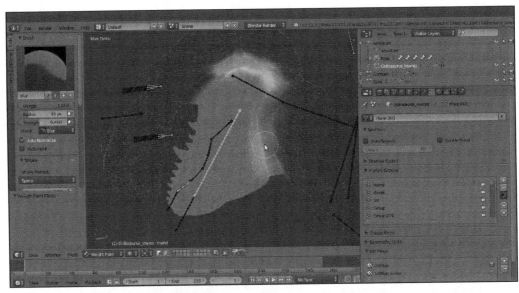

Smoothing the transition of the "mand" vertex group

7. If you need to reduce the weight of a vertex, switch the **Blur** brush with a **Subtract** one, and with a low **Strength** (**0.100** or even less) paint on it. Then, if necessary, blur the area again.

8. Alternatively, instead of using a **Subtract** brush, you can paint on the mesh with a **Mix** brush set with **Strength** = **1.000** and **Weight** = **0.000**.

9. Select the **neck** bone and reduce the weight of the vertices at the **neck** edges to **0.000**.

10. Select the **chest** bone and paint the vertices at the **chest** edges to **1.000**.

11. Repeat the last step also for the **spine.001** and **.002** bones:

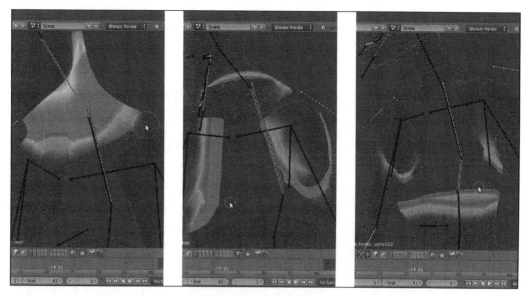

Other vertex groups

To look at exactly how the weights have been edited by the **Weight Paint** tool, open the `Gidiosaurus_skinning_03.blend` file, hide the **Armor**, select the **Gidiosaurus** mesh and press *Ctrl + Tab* to go in to **Weight Paint** mode, and then right-click to select the different bones.

One last thing still remains to be done: we must also skin the **Tiers_simplified** object.

12. Enable the **13th** scene layer to show the **Armor** and the **Tiers**; temporarily hide both the **Armature** and the **Armor** object by clicking on the respective eye icon in the **Outliner**.

13. Select the **Gidiosaurus** mesh, then, *Shift*-select the **Tiers** object and press *Ctrl + Tab* to go in to **Weight Paint** mode.

14. Go to the **Weight Tool** subpanel under the **Tool Shelf** and click on the **Transfer Weight** button, which is the last button at the bottom. After a bit of calculation, the weights of the vertices for the underlying **Gidiosaurus** mesh have been transferred to the corresponding overlaid vertices of the **Tiers** object and the vertex groups as well:

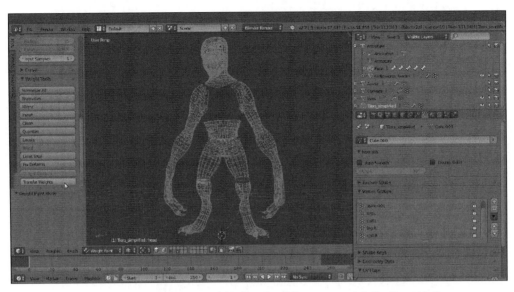

Transferring the vertex group weights from the Gidiosaurus mesh to the tiers object

15. Go out of **Weight Paint** mode and select the sole **Tiers** object. In the **Object Modifiers** window, assign an **Armature** modifier or, if you prefer, just join it to the **Armor** object (**Armor** as an active object and then press *Ctrl + J*). In both cases, just remember to enable the **Preserve Volume** item.

16. Save the file.

See also

▶ http://www.blender.org/manual/modeling/meshes/vertex_groups/weight_paint.html

Using the Mesh Deform modifier to skin the character

The **Mesh Deform** modifier has been introduced in Blender for the production of the short open movie *Big Buck Bunny* and it's a very easy and quick way to skin medium and high resolution characters' meshes. Although the utility of this modifier really shows the skinning of fat, chubby characters, it will be useful to see the way it works even if applied to a quite skinny character such as the **Gidiosaurus**.

Getting ready

First, we must prepare the **deforming cage**, which is a simplified low poly mesh totally enveloping the character's mesh; to do this, in our case, we can start from an already made object:

1. Open the `Gidiosaurus_skinning_03.blend` file.

2. Click on the **File | Append** menu (or press *Shift + F1*), browse to the folder with all the project files, and click on the `Gidiosaurus_base_mesh_02.blend` file. Then, click on the `Object` folder and select the **Gidiosaurus** item.

3. Move the just-appended object to the first scene layer; then, go to the **Outliner** and rename it as **Gidiosaurus_cage**.

4. This is the base mesh we built in the first chapter of this book, so go to the **Object Modifier** window and apply the **Skin** modifier; delete the **Mirror** modifier and disable the **Subdivision Surface** modifier visibility in the viewport by clicking on the eye icon button.

5. Go in to **Edit Mode** and by pressing *Ctrl +R*, cut a median vertical edge-loop at the center of the mesh.

6. Select the vertices of the *missing* half and delete them; then, select the median edge-loop and, with **Pivot Point** set to **3D Cursor** (and the **3D Cursor** located at the center of the scene), scale them to **0.000** along the global *x* axis.

7. Assign a new **Mirror** modifier and enable the **Clipping** item.

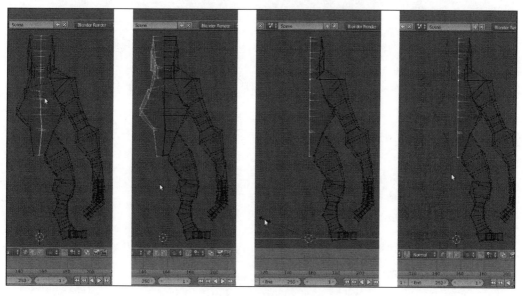

Preparing the deforming cage

8. Now, enable the scene layer with the **Gidiosaurus** mesh, select it, and temporarily disable the **Armature** modifier by clicking on the *Display modifier in viewport* button (the one with the eye icon).

9. In the **Outliner**, click on the eye icon to hide the **Armature**.

10. Reselect **Gidiosaurus_cage**, enter **Edit Mode**, and start to edit. Basically, the cage must be large enough to totally include the character's mesh.

11. Select whole parts such as the **head** or a **hand** and scale the vertices on their normals (*Alt + S*) and move the vertices by hand.

12. Where necessary, add edge-loops (*Ctrl + R*) to refine the cage's shape, but try to keep it as simple and low resolution as possible.

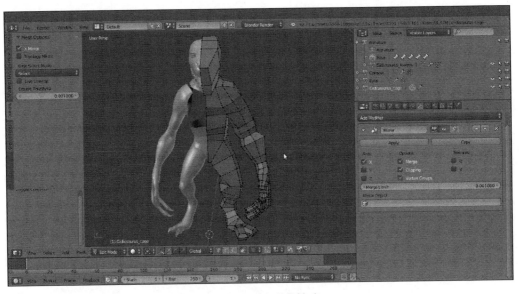

The cage mesh in Edit Mode

13. Once we have confirmed that the **Gidiosaurus** mesh is totally contained in the cage, we can go out of **Edit Mode**.

How to do it...

Now that the **deforming cage** is made, we can go on with the **skinning**:

1. Unhide the **Armature** and select it. Go in to **Edit Mode**, select the bones deforming the **Armor** (see the *Parenting the Armature and Mesh using the Automatic Weights tool* recipe in this chapter for this), and press *Shift + W* | **Deform**. Don't deselect anything because it will be useful later on to have the bones still selected, and go straight back to **Object Mode**.

2. Now, hide the **Gidiosaurus_lowres** object; then, select the **Gidiosaurus_cage** object, *Shift*-select the **Armature**, and press *Ctrl + P* | **With Automatic Weights**.

3. Select the sole **Armature**, go in to **Edit Mode** and press *Shift + W* | **Deform**, and then switch to **Pose Mode**.

4. Reselect the **cage** and go to the **Object Modifiers** window; in the **Armature** modifier, enable the **Preserve Volume** item, but temporarily disable the visibility of the modifier in the viewport (eye icon button):

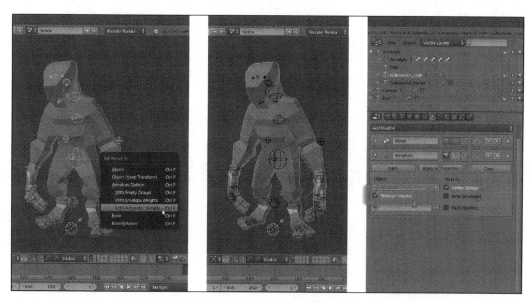

Parenting the deforming cage to the Armature

5. Go to the **Object** window and click on the **Maximum Draw Type** button under the **Display** subpanel to select the **Wire** item. Unhide the **Gidiosaurus_lowres** object.

6. Select the **Gidiosaurus** mesh and go in to **Edit Mode**. In the **Vertex Groups** subpanel under the **Object Data** window, create a new group and rename it as **mdef**; select all the vertices of the **Gidiosaurus** mesh *except feet, fingers, and the head* and assign them to the **mdef** vertex group:

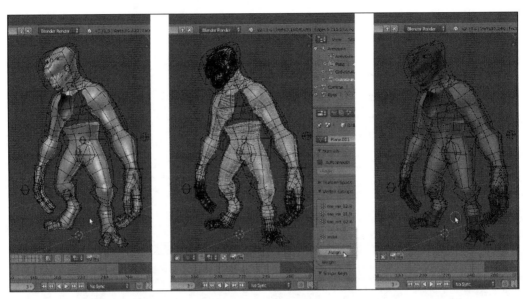

The "mdef" vertex group

7. Go to the **Object Modifiers** window; in the **Armature** modifier panel, click on the vertex group empty field at the bottom (*name of Vertex Group which determines influence of modifier per point*) to select the **mdef** vertex group and then click on the *invert vertex group influence* button to the left (the one with the two arrows pointing in opposite directions). Temporarily, disable the visibility of the modifier in the viewport (eye icon button).

8. Assign a **Mesh Deform** modifier and move it upwards in the stack, before the **Subdivision Surface** modifier but after the **Armature** one.

9. In the **Object** field of the **Mesh Deform** modifier, select the **Gidiosaurus_cage** item; in **Vertex Group** again, select the **mdef** vertex group, check the **Dynamic** item box, and then click on the **Bind** button.

10. Save the file as `Gidiosaurus_mesh_deform.blend`.

How it works...

The **Gidiosaurus_cage** is a very simple mesh. Therefore, it is very easily skinned to the **Armature** (we didn't do it in our case, but obviously, when necessary, the automatic weights assigned by the parenting can be easily edited as in the *Editing the Weight Groups using the Weight Paint tool* recipe) and is therefore deforming, through the binding of the **Mesh Deform** modifier, the more subdivided **Gidiosaurus** mesh.

In fact, if everything went right, now we should have the **Gidiosaurus** body correctly deformed by the **cage** only for the vertices that belong to the **mdef** vertex group, while the **Armature**, which also deforms the **cage**, is still taking care of the vertices outside the group; to check this, just try to pose the rig and alternatively disable, in the **Object Modifiers** window, the viewport visibility of the **Armature** and **Mesh Deform** modifiers for the mesh.

Note that even we didn't apply the **Mirror** modifier to the **cage** object; the **Mesh Deform** modifier works correctly anyway, exactly like the **Armature** one.

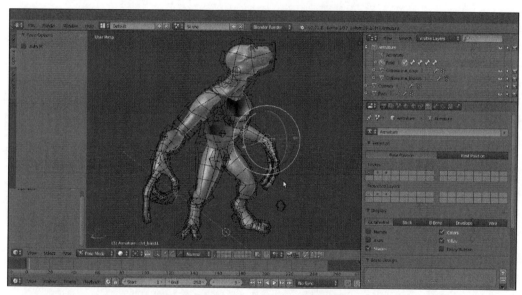

The Gidiosaurus model posed through the Mesh Deform modifier

See also

▸   http://www.blender.org/manual/modifiers/deform/mesh_deform.html

Using the Laplacian Deform modifier and Hooks

One of the last modifiers introduced in Blender, the **Laplacian Deform** modifier shouldn't actually be considered as an effective tool to rig a character, but more as a tool to modify, change, or refine a default pose. Anyway, if set and used smartly it can often give interesting results, so it has been included in this chapter as well.

Getting ready

First, let's prepare the scene:

1. Open the `Gidiosaurus_rig_from_scratch_01.blend` file.

2. Select and then delete the **Armature** in **Object Mode**; then. select the **Gidiosaurus** mesh and delete the **Armature** modifier too in the **Object Modifiers** window.

3. In the **Outliner**, hide the **Eyes** object.

4. Press the Z key to go in the **Wireframe** viewport shading mode.

How to do it...

Now let's go with the **Laplacian** modifier setup:

1. With the **Gidiosaurus** mesh still in **Edit Mode**, select all the vertices of the **hands**, **feet**, **hip**, **head**, plus the **boundary edge-loops** where the mesh is missing (look at the following screenshot).

2. Go to the **Vertex Groups** subpanel and create a new group named as you wish; I named it **lapldef**. Assign the selected vertices with a **Weight** value of **1.000**:

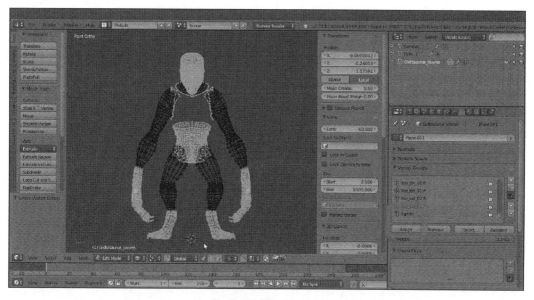

The "lapldef" vertex group

3. Now, box-deselect all the vertices, except the **head** ones; press *Ctrl + H* and in the **Hooks** pop-up menu, select the **Hook to New Object** item:

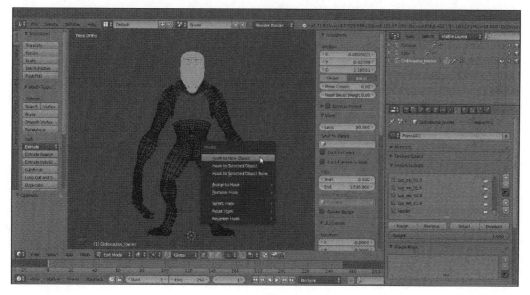

The Hooks menu

4. Click on the **Select** button under the **Vertex Groups** subpanel to the right of the screen and then deselect all the vertices, except the **right hand** ones. Again, press *Ctrl + H* and in the **Hooks** pop-up menu, select the **Hook to New Object** item.

5. Click on the **Select** button again, deselect all the vertices, except the **left hand** ones, and repeat the procedure:

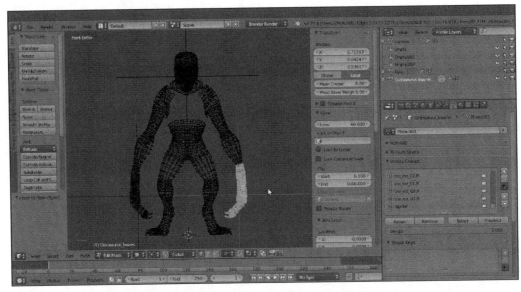

The Hook assigned to the left hand vertices

6. Repeat the procedure separately for the left and the right **feet** and then go out of **Edit Mode**.

7. In the **Outliner**, rename the **Empties** (the **Hooks**) respectively as **Empty_head**, **Empty_hand.L** and **.R**, and **Empty_foot.L** and **.R**.

The Hooks assigned to the mesh's vertices

8. Select the **Gidiosaurus** mesh and go to the **Object Modifiers** window. Collapse all the five **Hook** modifiers for better visibility and assign a **Laplacian Deform** modifier; move it upwards in the stack, just before the **Subdivision Surface** modifier (*but* always after the **Hook** modifiers). Click on the **Anchors Vertex Group** to select the **lapldef** vertex group and then click on the **Bind** button.

9. For better visibility, select each **Hook** and in the **Object Data** window, set the size to **0.40**.

10. Enable the **3D manipulator widget** in the 3D view toolbar (or press *Ctrl* + Spacebar), *Shift*-click on the **Translate** and **Rotate** buttons, and set **Transform Orientation** to **Normal**.

11. Select the **Hooks** and start to move and rotate them using the **3D manipulator widget**, to pose the **Gidiosaurus** mesh:

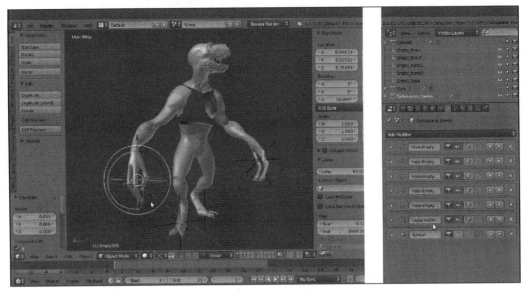

The Gidiosaurus mesh posed through the Hooks and the Laplacian Deform modifier

12. Save the file as `Gidiosaurus_laplacian.blend`.

How it works...

Remember that because they don't work through joints, the **Laplacian Deform** modifier and the **Hooks** don't give a realistic deformation and should be used more to tweak a character pose only inside a limited range. Building a more complex rig, also with **Hooks** at the **elbows** and **knees**, is possible but probably more useful for other types of *unreal* characters' shapes.

It should also be remembered that the **Hooks**, once moved out of their location, can't be simply moved back to their original position by the *Alt + G* shortcut because this command would set them at their original **0, 0, 0** location. Instead, any rotation can be easily removed by the *Alt + R* shortcut.

In any case, the *Ctrl + Z* (**Undo**) shortcut can be used, but first check the number of **Steps** set in the **User Preferences** panel under the **Global Undo** item (there are only **32** by default).

See also

▶ http://www.blender.org/manual/modifiers/deform/hooks.html

▶ http://www.blender.org/manual/modifiers/deform/laplacian_deform.html

8
Finalizing the Model

In this chapter, we will cover the following recipes:

- ▶ Creating shape keys
- ▶ Assigning drivers to the shape keys
- ▶ Setting movement limit constraints
- ▶ Transferring the eyeball rotation to the eyelids
- ▶ Detailing the Armor by using the Curve from Mesh tool

Introduction

In this chapter, we'll see how to create and add **shape keys** (the Blender term for **morphing**) to the model, to create facial expressions for the **Gidiosaurus** and to add shape modifications in a non-destructive way to the model.

Then, we'll see how to set a limit to the **Armature** bones' rotation using constraints and how to slightly transfer a portion of the rotation movement of the **eyeballs** to the covering **eyelids**.

Last, we'll add some detail to the **Armor** by quickly adding **rivets** through a simple and effective technique.

Creating shape keys

In this recipe, we'll set the **shape keys** to create (even if limited) **facial expressions** and to fake the stretching and the contracting effect of the character's **arm muscles**, and we'll add some more shape keys to fix issues in the character's shape.

Getting ready

First, let's prepare a bit the scene and the model:

1. Start Blender and load the `Gidiosaurus_skinning_rigify.blend` file, which is the same as the `Gidiosaurus_skinning_03.blend` file but with the **rig** created by the **Rigify** add-on (and later edited to add the other bones exactly as explained in the last chapter's recipes).

2. In the **Outliner**, click on the respective eye icons to hide the **Armor**, **Eyes**, and **Tiers_simplified** objects and the **Armature**, whose name in this case is **rig**.

3. Select the **Gidiosaurus_lowres** object and press the *1* key on the numpad to go into the **Front** view.

4. Press *Z* to go into the **Wireframe** viewport shading mode and the *5* key on the numpad to switch to the **Ortho** view if it is not already.

5. Enter **Edit Mode** and box-select the **left half** of the mesh vertices (including the **middle vertical edge-loop**) and in the **Vertex Groups** subpanel under the **Object Data** window, create a new vertex group; rename it **left** and assign the selected vertices a weight of **1.000**.

6. Deselect everything and repeat this process for the **right half** of the mesh's vertices to create the **right** vertex group:

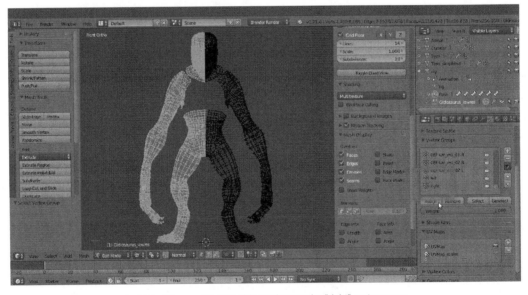

Assigning the mesh's right side vertices to the "right" vertex group

7. Save the file as `Gidiosaurus_shapekeys.blend`.

How to do it...

Let's start now by creating the **facial expressions** shape keys:

1. Exit **Edit Mode** and expand the **Shape Keys** subpanel under the **Object Data** window; click on the **+** icon button to the top left to create the **Basis** shape key (that mustn't be edited), then click once more to create the **Key 1** shape key (that is, instead, the one to be edited):

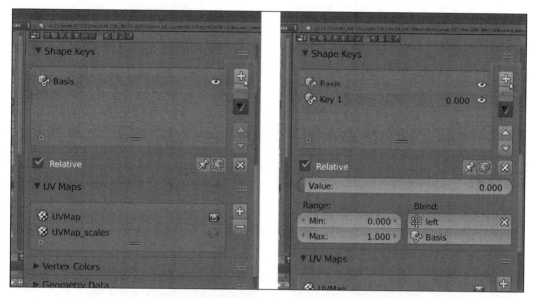

Creating the Basis and the first shape key

2. Be sure that the **X Mirror** item in the **Mesh Options** tab under the **Tool Shelf** is activated and click on the **PET** (**Proportional Editing Tool**) button in the 3D viewport toolbar (or activate it by pressing the O key).

3. Zoom to the **Gidiosaurus** head and again in **Edit Mode**, select some of the vertices at the center of the **snout** area, as indicated in the following screenshot:

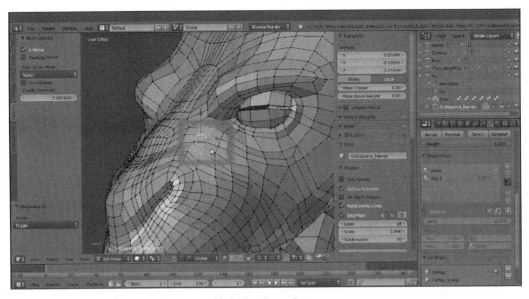

Selecting the vertices

4. Move them upwards and towards the **eye**, set the amount for the **PET** smoothing by scrolling the mouse wheel:

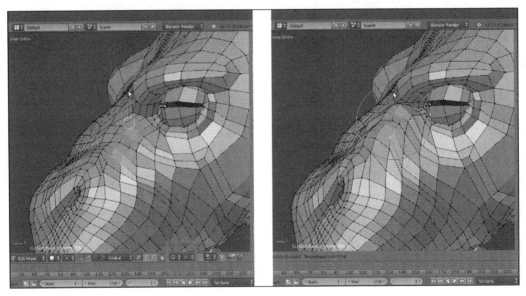

Moving the selected vertices slightly backwards and upwards

Note that we selected two faces instead of the folder edges, because the muscular *scrunching* involves both movement of the skin and a slight folding of the skin as well; the middle edge does not move as much as the selected faces due to **PET** falloff, hence creating a very slight scrunch and a more *naturalistic* skin sliding.

5. If necessary, adjust the position of the single vertices, maybe also disabling the **PET**.

6. Go to the **Shape Keys** subpanel and rename the **Key 1** shape key as **grin**.

7. Click on the *Apply shape key in edit mode* button located right above the **Value** slider to enable it; go into the **Front** view and by moving the **Value** slider from **0.000** to **1.000** and back, check for the correct working of the shape key on both the sides of the character:

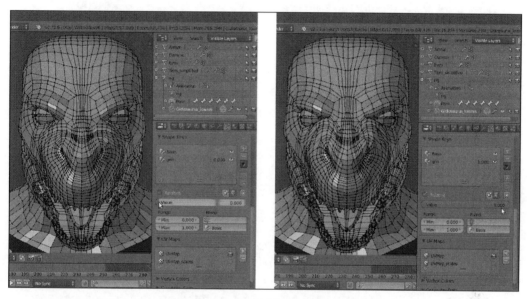

Checking how the "grin" shape key works

8. Go out of **Edit Mode** and just to have better visibility of the shape key modifications, go to the **Object** window to enable the **Wire** item in the **Display** subpanel.

9. Go back to the **Object Data** window and click on the button that has an icon of a downward pointing arrow (*Shape keys specials*); from the pop-up menu select the **New Shape from Mix** item: this adds a new shape key made by the sum of all the active shape keys. In this case, it is just a perfect copy of the sole **grin** shape key (the **Basis** shape key is, well, just the base starting position of the vertices in the mesh). Rename the two shape keys as **grin.L** and **grin.R**.

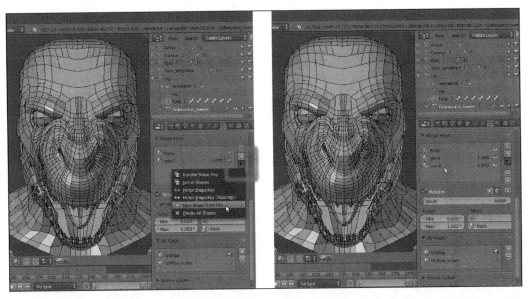

Copying the "grin" shape key to a new one

10. Click on the **grin.L** shape key, set the **Value** slider back to **0.000**, and then click on the *Vertex weight group* slot, the one under the **Blend** item and above the **Basis** one, and select the **left** vertex group.

11. Repeat for the **grin.R** shape key by selecting the **right** vertex group, and then once again set the **Value** slider to **1.000** and ensure it works correctly.

Each shape key now works only on the respective side, according to the selected vertex group:

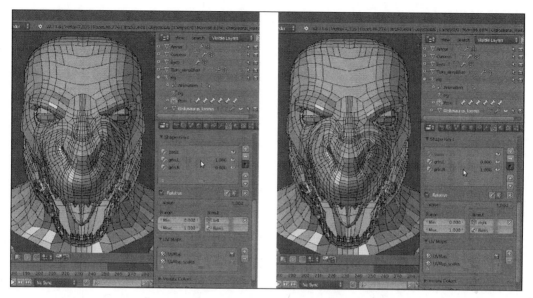

The two "grin" shape keys for the right and the left sides

This was for the **grin** expression; now we need to add at least two or three more kinds of shape keys, namely: two for the **eyebrows** (up and down) and one for the **nostrils**, multiplied for each side.

This means **six** more shape keys in total, but as you have seen, the procedure is quite quick and simple.

12. Set the **Value** slider for the **grin.L** and **grin.R** shape keys back to **0.000** and click on the **+** icon button to add a new shape key.

13. Rename it **eyebrow_up.L** and enter **Edit Mode**; grab some vertices on the left eyebrow and, still with the **PET** activated, move them upward; you can use the mouse wheel to set the influence of the **PET**:

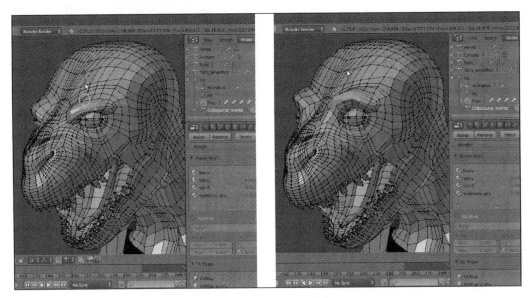

Moving the eyebrow upward

14. Repeat the steps from 9 to 11 to create the **eyebrow_up.R** shape key.

15. Repeat the steps from 3 to 11 to create the **eyebrow_down.L** and **eyebrow_down.R** shape keys:

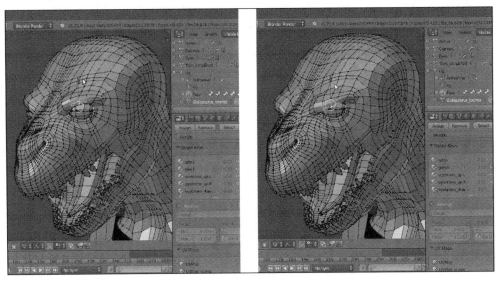

Moving the eyebrow downward

16. Finally repeat step 3 to step 11, this time selecting the vertices around the **nostrils** and scaling them to be bigger, creating the **snare.L** and **snare.R** shape keys:

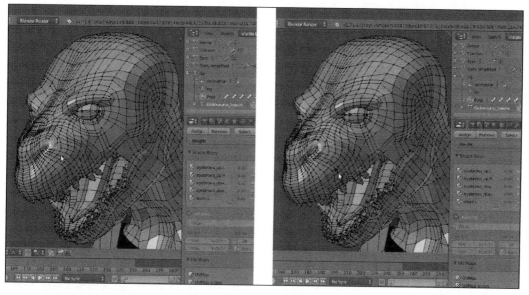

The nostril flaring

Note that, when naming the shape key for the enlargement of the nostrils, I erroneously wrote **snare**; it should have been something like *snarl* or *flaring*, but in the end it's just a naming convention and therefore, this little mistake doesn't pose a real problem.

We are done with the facial expressions; now let's add one more shape key to enhance some of the body features of the **Gidiosaurus** a bit; these are not meant to be animated during the animation, but are simply a way to apply non-destructive modifications to the model.

17. Add a new shape key and rename it **prop** (for *proportions*).

18. In **Edit Mode**, select the vertices of the **left foot**, excluding the **feet talons**, and press *Alt + S* to scale them *on their normals*; if you are using the **PET**, just be sure to be in the **Connected** mode (so that the **PET** has influence only on the vertices connected to the selected ones, otherwise the unselected **feet talon** vertices will also be modified):

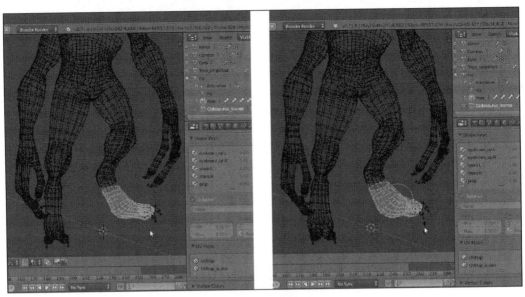

Modifying the feet proportions

19. Disable the **PET** and adjust the transition between the scaled vertices and the surrounding ones, the area between the two **toes**, and so on.

20. If you wish, you may also make additional modifications; in my case, besides the bigger **feet**, I simply enhanced the **knuckles** on the **hands** and at the **fingers'** joints. Also, I tweaked the rim shape of the upper and bottom borders of the **mandibles** a bit:

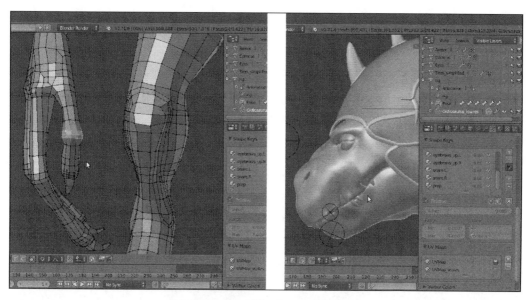

Enhancing some of the character's features

21. When you are done, set the **Value** slider of the **prop** shape key to **1.000**.

Now, let's add a couple of shape keys to mimic the movement of the main muscles of the arms, specifically of the **biceps** and of the **triceps** muscles:

22. Add a new shape key, then go to the **Gidiosaurus** mesh; select some of the vertices in the middle area of the **bicep** muscle and after enabling the **PET** again, move them forward and also scale them to be bigger, to make the muscle *grow*:

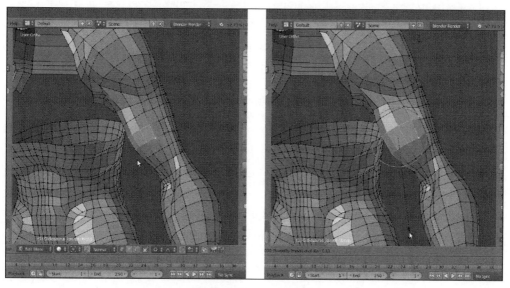

Making the bicep muscle grow

23. Rename the shape key **bicep.L**, and then repeat the steps from 9 to 11 to create the **bicep.R** shape key.

24. Add a new shape key and repeat everything by selecting vertices on the back of the arm, in the **triceps** area, to create the **triceps.L** and the **triceps.R** shape keys.

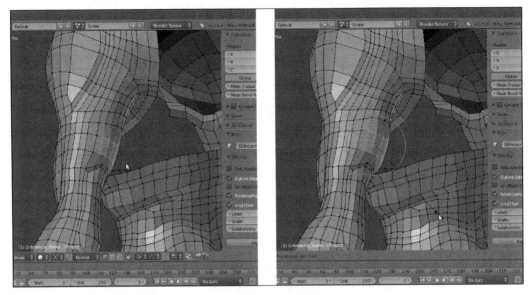

Making the triceps muscle grow

25. Leave the values of these last four shape keys as **0.000** and exit **Edit Mode**.

    More shape keys could be added to simulate a complete muscle system, but in our case we stop here with the **Gidiosaurus** mesh; now let's concentrate on the **Armor**.

26. Go to the **Outliner** and unhide both **Armor** and **rig**.

27. Select the **rig** and then press *N* to call the **Properties** 3D view sidepanel; scroll to the bottom and first go to the **Rig Main Properties** subpanel to set both the slider for **FK/IK (hand.ik.L)** and **(hand.ik.R)** to **1.000**, then go down to the **Rig Layers** subpanel and deselect everything except for the **Arm.L (IK)** and **Arm.R (IK)** buttons.

 Note that if the **FK/IK sliders** don't appear, it's because you have to select one of the hand (**ik** or **fk**) bones in the viewport first.

28. Go to the 3D viewport and select the **hand.ik.L** and **hand.ik.R** handle bones, go into the **Side** view and move them towards the upper back.

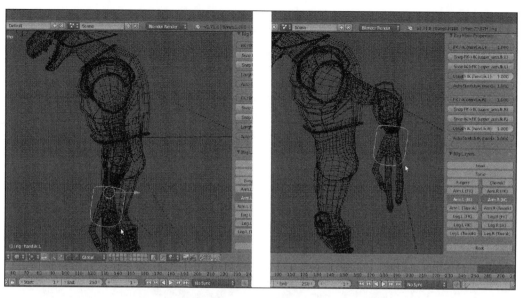

Moving the arm control bones backward using the Inverse Kinematics

29. Now press *Ctrl* + numpad *1* to go in **Back** view and move the **hand.ik.L** bone to **0.200** along the global *x* axis; select the **hand.ik.R** bone and move it to **-0.200**:

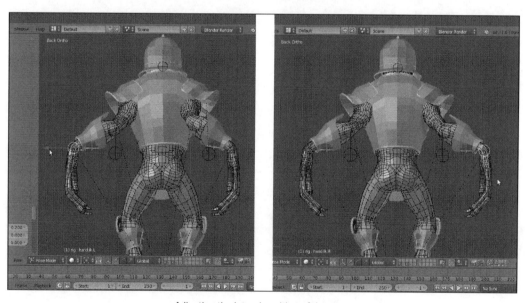

Adjusting the lateral position of the arms

30. Now select the **Armor** object and add the **Basis** shape key in the **Shape Keys** subpanel under the **Object Data** window, and then add **Key 1**.

31. Enter **Edit Mode** and press the slash key (/) on the numpad to go in **Local** view; this way only the selected objects are visible in the viewport, in our case only the **Armor**. Using the **Proportional Editing** mode, start to enlarge the back section of the opening for the **arms**, adjust the position of the surrounding vertices as required, and also raise the back vertices of the **spaulders** a bit, to avoid interpenetration with the borders of the **chest plate** and the **shoulder** as well.

32. Press the numpad slash (/) key again to go out of the **Local** view and check for the correction with the **Gidiosaurus** mesh:

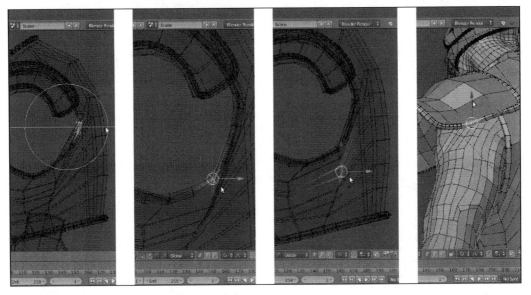

Editing the position of the Armor vertices for a new shape key

33. When you are done, just exit **Edit Mode** and set the **Value** slider of the **Key 1** shape key for the **Armor** to **1.000**:

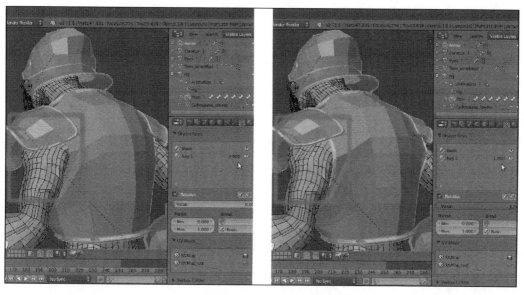

The shape key working as a fix for the Armor

34. Rename the **Key 1** shape key as **Armor_fix** and save the file.

How it works...

Although technically there are no differences, we could say that we created three different types of **shape key**:

- One type to fix shape errors or make improvements in the mesh, for example, with the **prop** and the **Armor_fix** shape keys
- The second type to modify the mesh only at certain established moments during the animation process, in our case just to animate facial expressions
- The third type to simulate muscle movements in the character

Shape keys work in **linear space**; that means that it's not possible to make vertices rotate around a pivot through a shape key, but only to move them *from point A to point B*. That's why we didn't use shape keys for stuff like the **eyelid** movements, for example, or the opening/closing of the **jaw**, but only for actions including muscles sliding above the bones such as the **eyebrows**, the **grin**, and the **nostrils**, as well as the **bicep/triceps** movements.

Thanks to shape keys, we also made *last minute* modifications and improvements to the **Gidiosaurus** mesh and to the **Armor**; being included inside a shape key, all these modifications are *non-destructive* and can be turned on or off at will, or their influence can be set at an intermediate strength value.

When modifying a mesh using a shape key, be careful not to change too much of the mutual proportions of articulated parts of a *to-be-deformed* mesh; for example, it's usually problematic to scale a whole part such as the **hands** or the **head** of a character, both smaller or bigger, unless you also scale the corresponding bones of the rig and the joints' position accordingly as well.

Beyond a certain threshold, the bones of the **fingers**, or of the **eyes** and **jaw**, start to be *out of register* compared to the respective mesh's edge-loops and you'll have to fix this by re-positioning the joints of the **Armature's** bones (just in case, remember: always do this in **Edit Mode**).

In our example, with the **prop** shape key, we just restricted ourselves to enhance the hands' **knuckles** and to make stronger **feet** by simply making the vertices' positions grow in the direction of their normals.

Assigning drivers to the shape keys

In the previous recipe, we created three different types of **shape keys**. Besides the *fixing* shape keys, that have a fixed value (no pun intended), we now need a way to set the amount of influence of the other two types of shape keys, facial expressions, and the muscle movements during the animation. This is accomplished by setting **drivers**, though with different kinds of controls.

Getting ready

Start from the previously saved `Gidiosaurus_shapekeys.blend` file:

1. Go to the **Outliner** and hide the **Armor** object.

2. Select the **Armature** rig, switch to the **Octahedral** bones draw mode, and press *Tab* to enter **Edit Mode**; zoom to the character **head** and add **six** bones located as follows: **two** bones close to both the right and the left **eyebrows**, **two** bones close to both the sides of the **grin snout** area, and **two** bones close to the **nostrils**. Enable the **Names** item in the **Skeleton** subpanel under the **Object Data** window and rename the bones accordingly and with the correct **.L** or **.R** suffix, then be sure to have them located on the first bone layer by pressing the *M* key to call the **Change Bone Layers** pop-up.

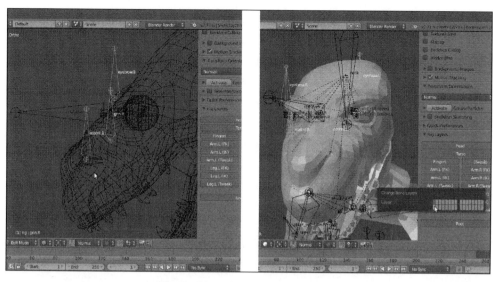

The new bones for the shape key drivers

3. Exit **Edit Mode** and select the **Gidiosaurus** mesh.

4. Go to the **Shape Keys** subpanel under the **Object Data** window and expand the list window by left-clicking on the = icon at the bottom and dragging it downward.

5. Now right-click on the value (**0.000**) at the right side of the name of the first shape key (**grin.L**) and from the pop-up panel, select the **Add Driver** item; the value is enhanced, in violet, to show that now it has a **driver** associated.

6. Repeat the same for all the shape keys in the list except for the **prop** one, which has a fixed value of **1.000**:

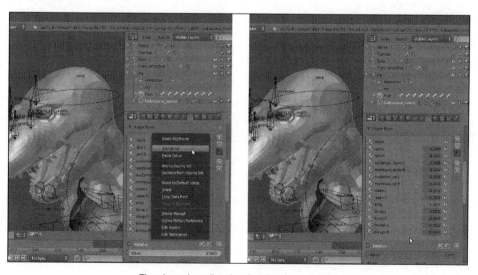

The shape keys list showing they have drivers

7. Split the 3D viewport horizontally into two parts, change the upper part into a **Graph Editor** window, or simply switch the screen to the **Animation** layer (in the **two** files provided with the cookbook, there are actually two prepared animation screens, **Animation1** and **Animation2**). Click on the *Editing context being displayed* button in the toolbar of the **Graph Editor** window and change it from **F-Curves** to **Drivers**.

How to do it...

Let's start with the **expressions shape keys**:

1. If not already present, press the *N* key to open the **Properties** sidepanel of the **Graph Editor** window, then click on the **Value (grin.L)** top item in the drivers list at the top-left of the screen:

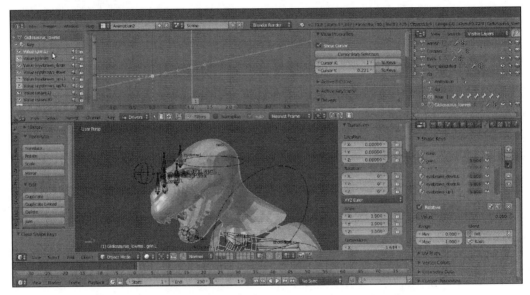

The Graph Editor window, at the top of the screen, with the driver f-curve

2. Go to the **Properties** panel of the **Graph Editor** and, by scrolling down, find the **Drivers** subpanel. In the *Driver* **Type** slot, switch from the **Scripted Expression** item to the **Averaged Value** one.

3. In the **Ob/Bone** slot, select **rig** and in the under slot (*Name of PoseBone to use as target*), select the **grin.L** bone.

4. Going downward, in the *Variable* **Type** slot, select the **Y Location** item and in **Space**, select **Local Space**.

5. Click on the **Update Dependencies** button at the top of the **Drivers** subpanel (the **Update Dependencies** function works particularly for **Scripted Expression**; it is quite important to use it to refresh the new setups each time).

6. Go even further down and click on the **Add Modifier** button in the **Modifier** subpanel; from the **Add F-Curve Modifier** pop-up menu, select the **Generator** item.

7. In the *Coefficient for polynomial* – **x** slot, change the value **1.000** to the value **20.000** (this is to re-map the declivity of the **f-curve** and therefore the speed of the corresponding shape key):

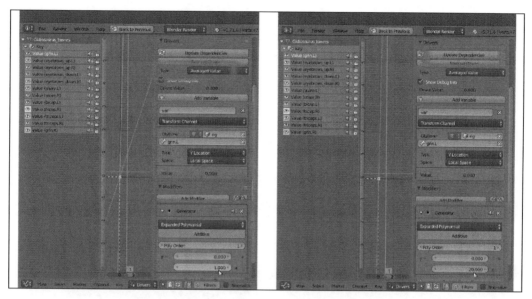

The N Properties Graph Editor sidepanel for the selected driver

8. Now select the **grin.L** bone and in **Pose Mode**, move it upward to see the **grin.L** shape keys being animated on the character's **snout**.

9. Go to the **Shape Keys** subpanel and right-click on the value to the right side of the **grin.L** shape; from the pop-up menu, select the **Copy Driver** item.

10. Select the **grin.R** shape key and right-click on the value to the right; from the pop-up menu, select the **Paste Driver** item.

11. Go to the **Animation** screen and switch the **grin.L** to the **grin.R** bone in the **Ob/Bone** field under the **Drivers** subpanel.

12. Copy and paste the drivers for the **eyebrows_up.L** and **eyebrows_up.R** shape keys, then replace the driver bones names in the **Ob/Bone** field under the **Drivers** subpanel.

13. Go to the **Shape Keys** subpanel under the **Object Data** window and set the **Max** value under the **Range** item to **0.600** for both the **eyebrows_up.L** and **eyebrows_up.R** shape keys; this is to limit the movement of the shape keys to avoid any intersection with the character's **helm**.

14. Copy and paste the drivers for the **eyebrows_down.L** and **eyebrows_down.R** shape keys. This time, leave the same driver bone names and instead change the value of the *Coefficient for polynomial* – **x** to negative and **-20.000** to *invert* the direction of the **f-curve**.

15. Repeat the procedure for the **snare.L** and **snare.R** shape keys, this time switching the *Variable* **Type** from **Y Location** to **X Location** and assigning a negative **-20.000** value to the **snare.L** driver and a positive **20.000** value to the **snare.R** one.

    At this point, all that is left is to assign automatic drivers for the *shape keys to stretch and grow muscles* we created for the character's **arms**.

16. Click on the **Value (bicep.L)** item in the drivers window at the left top of the **Graph Editor** and then go to the **Properties** panel on the right and then to the **Drivers** subpanel. In the *Driver* **Type** slot, select the **Averaged Value** item again; in the *Variable* **Type** slot, switch to **Rotational Difference**.

17. In the **Bone1** slot, select **rig** and in the slot below (*Name of PoseBone to use as target*), select the **DEF-forearm.01.L** bone; in the **Bone2** slot, select **rig** again, and then **DEF-upperarm.02.L**.

18. In the **Graph Editor**, click on a point of the **f-curve** to select it and then press the *L* key to select all the points of the **f-curve**; move them downward, on the *y* axis, by **-1.400** (*G* | *Y* | **-1.4** | *Enter*).

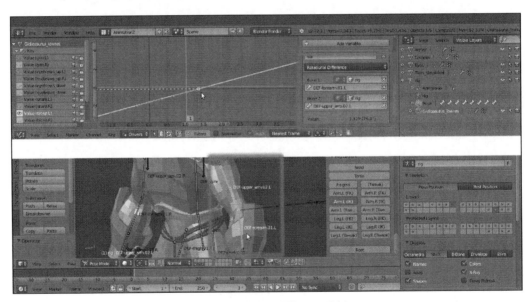

The triceps Rotational Difference driver

19. Copy and paste the driver to the **bicep.R** shape key, then change the **.L** suffixes of the bones to the **.R** ones.

20. Copy the **bicep.L** driver and paste it to the **triceps.L** shape key; click on the **Add Modifier** button under the **Modifier** subpanel; and from the **Add F-Curve Modifier** pop-up menu, select the **Generator** item.

21. In the *Coefficient for polynomial – y* slot, write the value **2.300** and in the **x** slot, write the value **-1.000** (remember that all these values in the recipe are not universal and are valid just for this **Gidiosaurus** model in this particular setup; the drivers values could change from character to character, so always test them on your model).

22. Copy and paste to the **triceps.R** shape key, and change the suffixes of the bones.

23. Click on the **Update Dependencies** button at the top of the **Drivers** subpanel and save the file.

How it works...

Drivers assigned to bones as controllers for the shape keys are not only an effective way to create a device for animation but also a mandatory technique in the Blender pipeline workflow, where a character is usually linked into the scene from a different file and the rig gets **proxified** (we'll see how to do this in the next chapter). The only possible way to have access to the shape keys in a linked character is through the **drivers** and the **rig**.

As you probably already know, shape keys are often used not only for **facial expressions** but also to mimic the stretching and the growing of the body's **muscles** according to the movement of a character's **limbs**. In this case, their influence is automatically driven by the rotation of the respective bones through the **Rotational Difference** drivers that, as the name itself says, base their influence on the difference of rotation between two bones; more precisely, on the **angle** between them.

The **Generator** modifier we added is a multiplier we used to *virtually* modify the slope inclination of the **f-curves** of the drivers. The default inclination of the **f-curve** wasn't enough to fully map the curve itself to a driver bone movement of (almost) just one or two Blender Units (it was too slow, resulting in a required driver movement of several units to have an appreciable effect), so we increased the declivity by a factor of **20.000** to have a faster correspondence.

However, the same modifier was also used to reverse the direction of the **f-curve**, by using a negative value of **-20.000**, for example to drive the downward movement of the **eyebrows**, or to change the location of the curve along the *y* axis so as to tweak the timing of the driver influence, like in the **triceps** shape keys.

Therefore, by copying and pasting a driver and giving an opposite declivity at the slope of the copied one, it is possible to drive two opposite shape keys through the same bone, as for the **eyebrows** shape keys:

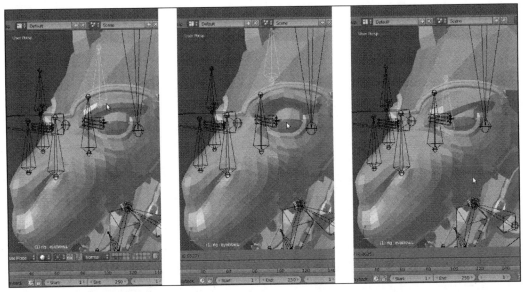

The same bone moving in two opposite directions to drive two opposite shape keys

There's more...

To add shape keys and the respective drivers to the **Gidiosaurus** model, we used the `Gidiosaurus_skinning_rigify.blend` file, with the **rig** created by the **Rigify** addon. The control bones of a **Rigify** rig have pre-made **Custom Shapes** to make their identification and selection easier and are usually located in the last scene layer.

So, for the last step, I just modeled a new simple custom shape, a small **Circle** mesh with **16** vertices. I named it **Widget_generic4** and I assigned it to all the *driver* bones:

The driver bones with the new Custom Shape

See also

▶ http://www.blender.org/manual/animation/basics/drivers.html

Setting movement limit constraints

Often, it is very useful to put movement limitations on the bones of a rig, for several reasons—usually, to make them easier to work with, but also to establish a maximum range for the rotation of the **limbs** or other parts like in the **mandible** or the **eyelids**.

Two types of limits for the bones are: by the **Transform** locks, and by **bone constraints**.

Getting ready

Load the Gidiosaurus_shapekeys.blend file, select the **Armature**, and go in **Pose Mode**.

Finalizing the Model

How to do it...

Let's start with the **Transform** locks:

1. Select the **eyebrow.L** bone and if not already present, press the *N* key to call the 3D viewport **Properties** sidepanel. Go to the **Transform** subpanel, which is the first entry at the top, or also to the **Transform Locks** subpanel under the **Bone** window in the main **Properties** panel to the right of the screen:

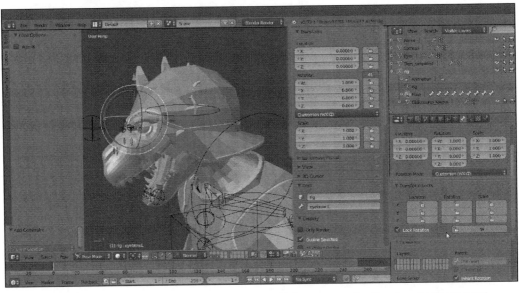

The Transform subpanel in the N Properties sidepanel and the corresponding Transform Locks subpanel under the main Properties panel

2. Click on the lock icon to the right side of the properties; for this bone (which, if you recall, is the driver control object for the left up and down **eyebrow** shape keys), we want to lock all the possible transformations *except* for the movement on its *y* axis, so the **Location Y** lock button is the only one that should remain untouched:

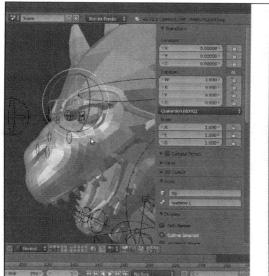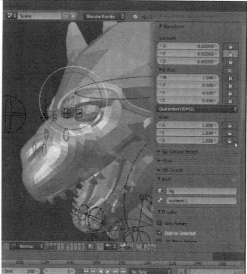

Setting the axis Transform locks for the Location, Rotation, and Scale

If you now try to move the **eyebrow.L** bone, you will notice its movement is constrained only to its local *y* axis; the movement is directed by the **Roll** orientation of the bone in **Edit Mode** (and not by the **Normal** item enabled in the **Transform Orientation** button on the viewport toolbar); enable the **Axes** item in the **Display** subpanel under the **Object Data** window to see this.

Having locked the other two axes, it's no longer necessary to use the widget arrow to move the bone on its local *y* axis but it's enough to simply press the G key and then move the mouse instead.

And now, let's see limits by **constraints**.

3. Go to the **Bone Constraints** window and assign a **Limit Location** constraint to the **eyebrow.L** bone.

4. Check the **Minimum X** and **Maximum X**, **Minimum Y**, and **Maximum Y**, and **Minimum Z** and **Maximum Z** items. Leave the values for the *x* and *z* axes as they are, change **Minimum Y** to negative **-0.050**, and change **Maximum Y** to positive **0.050** (again, remember that these values are valid just for this file).

5. In the **Convert** slot, change the **Owner Space** item to **Local Space**:

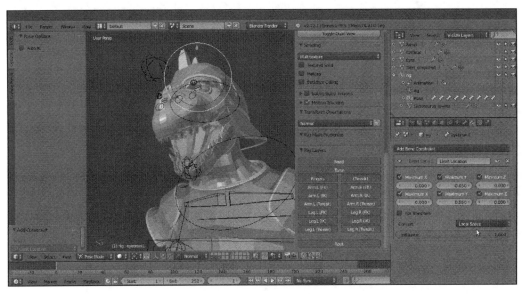

The assigned Limit Location constraint subpanel under the main Properties panel

In *Chapter 1, Modeling the Character's Base Mesh*, we enabled the **Copy Attributes Menu** add-on in **User Preferences** and then we saved the **User Settings**, so I'm taking for granted that you have the script still enabled.

Therefore, we do the following:

6. Select the **eyebrow.R** bone and then *Shift*-select the **eyebrow.L** bone. Press *Ctrl + C* and from the **Copy Attributes** pop-up menu, select the **Copy Bone Constraints** item.

7. Select the **grin.L** and **grin.R** bones and then *Shift*-select the **eyebrow.L** bone. Once again, press *Ctrl + C* | **Copy Bone Constraints**, and in the two copied constraints, set the **Minimum Y** value to **0.000**.

8. Select the **nostril.L** and **.R** bones and *Shift*-select the **grin.L** bone, then press *Ctrl + C* | **Copy Bone Constraints**. This time, set both the **Y** values to **0.000** and **Minimum X** for the **nostril.L** bone to negative **-0.050** and the **Maximum X** for the **nostril.R** bone to positive **0.050**.

9. Save the file.

Several other movement constraints have been added to different bones in the rig, for example the **jaw** bone, or the **eyelid** controllers, but especially to the **eye** bones, to limit the range of possible rotations. To have a look at the various settings, just open the Gidiosaurus_limits.blend file.

▶ http://www.blender.org/manual/animation/techs/object/
constraint.html

Transferring the eyeball rotation to the eyelids

This is a really simple trick that can add a lot of life to the facial expressions of an animated model, making the **eyelids** follow some of the movement of the **eyeballs**.

Getting ready

Following on from the previous recipes, open the Gidiosaurus_limits.blend file:

1. If not already selected, select the **Armature** and enter **Pose Mode**.

2. In the **Object Data** window, go to the **Skeleton** subpanel and enable the **30th** bone layer, to show the deforming bones.

3. In the **Display** subpanel, switch the bones' drawing mode from **Wire** to **Octahedral**:

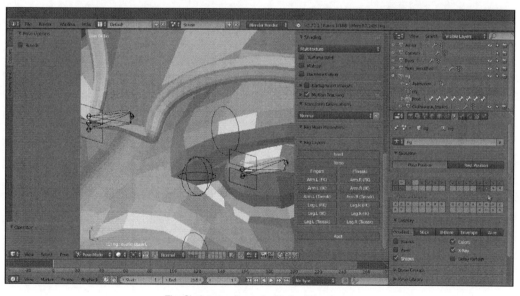

The Skeleton subpanel with the bone layers

How to do it...

Now zoom to the character's **head** and continue with the following steps:

1. Select the **eyelid_upper.L** bone and go to the **Bone Constraints** window; assign a **Copy Rotation** constraint.

2. In the **Target** field, select the **rig** item, and in the **Bone** field, select the **eye.L** bone item. Set **Space = Pose Space** to **Pose Space**.

3. Set the **Influence** slider value to **0.300**.

4. Select the **eyelid_bottom.L** bone and *Shift*-select the **eyelid_upper.L** bone, then press *Ctrl + C* | **Copy Bone Constraint**.

5. Select the **eyelid_upper.R** bone and repeat the procedure but with **eye.R** as the target bone; copy the constraint to the **eyelid_bottom.R** bone:

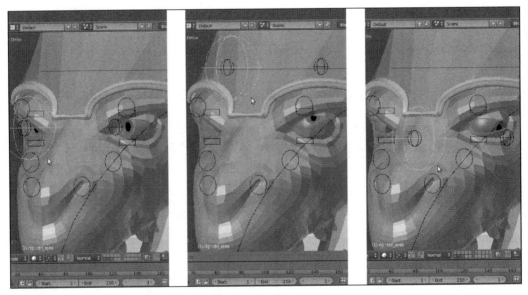

The eyelids slightly following the eye movements

6. Save the file.

Detailing the Armor by using the Curve from Mesh tool

In *Chapter 3, Polygonal Modeling of the Character's Accessories*, in the *Using the Mesh to Curve technique to add details* recipe, you already saw how to use this technique as a modeling tool. In this recipe, we'll use the same technique but in the opposite direction—to add **rivets** around the perimeter of the borders of the different **Armor** parts.

Getting ready

Re-open the `Gidiosaurus_limits.blend` file; the first thing to do is to model a very lowpoly **rivet** object to be duplicated on the **Armor** surface:

1. Switch to an empty scene layer, press *Shift + C* to place the **3D Cursor** at the center of the grid, and add a **Cube** primitive mesh. Enter **Edit Mode** and delete the bottom face, then scale the remaining faces by a value of **0.100** twice, then one last time by **0.500**. Move the top face downward to flatten the overall shape a bit and scale the same face by **0.700**.

2. Press *A* to select all the vertices and *W* to choose the **Subdivide Smooth** item from the **Specials** pop-up menu, then delete the middle horizontal edgeloop.

3. Put the pivot on the **3D Cursor** and while still in **Edit Mode**, rotate all the vertices by **90°** on the x axis.

4. Select the bottom edgeloop and press *Shift + S* | **Cursor to Selected**. Exit **Edit Mode** and click on the **Set Origin** button under the **Tool** tab to select the **Origin to 3D Cursor** item.

5. Click on the **Smooth** button under the **Shading** item and in the **Outliner**, rename the **rivet** object. Once again, place the **3D Cursor** at the center of the grid and the **rivet** at the **Cursor** location; press *Ctrl + A* to apply the **Rotation & Scale** option.

6. Enable the scene layer with the **Armor** on it, and in the **Outliner**, hide the **rig**.

How to do it...

Now, let's create the *guides* to duplicate the rivets on:

1. Select the **Armor** object and press *Shift + D* to duplicate it, then place the duplicate **Armor.001** object on the scene layer of the **rivet**. Go to the **Shape Keys** sidepanel under the **Object Data** window and delete the **Armor_fix** first and then the **Basis** shape keys.

2. Go to the **Object Modifiers** window, remove the **Armature** modifier, and apply the **Subdivision Surface** modifier with a **Subdivision** level of **2**.

3. Enter **Edit Mode** and start to select the edgeloops on the different **Armor** parts in areas where you want to add the **rivet** rows (*Alt* + right-click for the first one, then *Alt* + *Shift* + right-click). As usual, it's enough to work only on one half of the mesh:

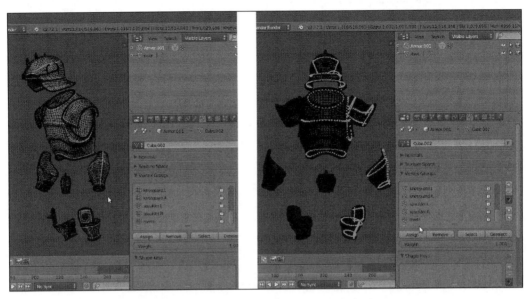

The Armor mesh in Edit Mode with the selected edge-loops

4. Press *Shift* + *D* and soon after, click the right mouse button to duplicate the selected edgeloops without moving them, then press the *P* key to separate them from the **Armor.001** object (in the **Separate** pop-up menu, choose the **Selection** item).

5. Exit **Edit Mode** and delete the **Armor.001** object, or if you don't have problems with big file sizes, move it to a different scene layer to keep it for future refinements. In this case, you can save the edge-loops selection as a vertex group named **rivets**.

6. Select the **Armor.002** object (the duplicated and separated edgeloops) and enter **Edit Mode**; make the necessary adjustments to the edgeloops by deleting the unnecessary vertices, for example the backsides of the plates, and disconnect the welded edgeloops by deleting the common vertices or connecting them where required edges are missing:

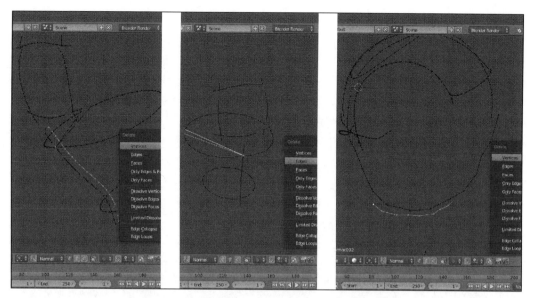

Cleaning the edge-loops of the duplicated Armor.002 mesh

7. Press _A_ to select all the vertices and then go to the **Tools** tab under the **Tool Shelf**. Go to the **LoopTools** subpanel and press the **Space** button to evenly space the vertices along the edgeloops.

8. Exit **Edit Mode** and press _Alt + C_; in the **Convert to** pop-up menu, select the first item, **Curve from Mesh/Text**. The mesh edgeloops actually get converted into a **Curve** object, as you can see in the **Object Data** window under the main **Properties** panel to the right of the UI. Click on the **Fill** slot to select the **Full** item.

9. Now the tedious part (but not difficult, just a little tedious); in **Edit Mode** again, put the mouse on one of the points and by pressing the _L_ key, select each separate part of the **Curve**, then press _P_ to separate the whole selected part. This way, you are going to obtain **16** separated **Curve** objects.

10. Select the **rivet** object and go to the **Object Modifiers** window; assign an **Array** modifier with **Fit Type** = **Fit Length**, **Length** = **0.50**, and **Relative Offset X** = **3.000**. Collapse the panel.

11. Assign a **Curve** modifier, then in the **Object** field select the **Armor.002** curve. Leave the panel expanded.

12. Assign a **Mirror** modifier and collapse the panel:

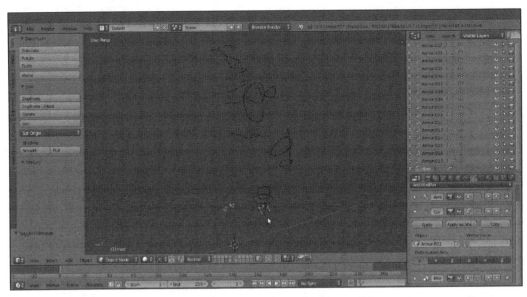

The rivet object instanced on the mirrored curve object

13. In the viewport area, zoom to each curve to check for the correct tilting of the points; if necessary, select the curve, enter **Edit Mode**, select all the points, press *Ctrl + T*, and move the mouse to rotate the tilting of the curve's points until the instanced **rivets** are correctly rotated/aligned with the surface of the main **Armor** mesh:

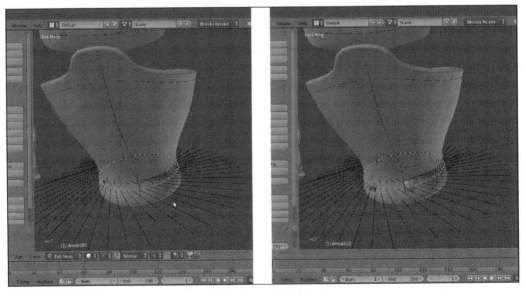

Tilting the curve's points

If necessary, you can also select individual points of the curve to tweak the orientation of only a part of the instanced rivets, even of single rivets at once; this has been done for part of the **helm** and for the **spaulders**, especially.

14. In the **Outliner**, re-select the **rivet** and press *Shift + D* to duplicate it, then in the **Object Modifiers** window, under the **Curve** modifier panel, select the **Armor.003** item in the **Object** field.

15. Once again, zoom to the curve and if necessary, fix the curve tilting and also adjust the **Length** value of the **Array** modifier (for the **Armor.003** curve it has been raised to **0.59**) and the **Relative Offset** value. By selecting all the points and pressing *W*, you can also select the **Switch Direction** item in the **Specials** menu.

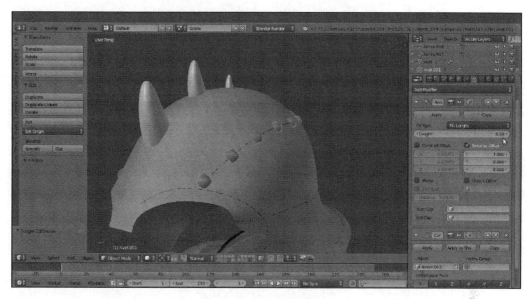

The rivets on the helm object

16. Duplicate the rivet and repeat the procedure changing the curve name in the modifier for each curve object and so on. At the end, you should have **16** copies of the rivet as well.

   At this point, if required, we can still make some modification to the rivet mesh; in my case, I just subdivided it a bit more, then deleted some useless edgeloop, made it rounder, and extruded the open side a bit more.

   Now that the rivet is ready, select all the rivet copies (so that the *modified one* is the active object, that is *the last selected*) and press *Ctrl + L* | **Object Data** to share the modifications between them.

   Leaving everything selected, press *U* | **Object & Data** to make them single users again (this is necessary for the next step with the modifiers).

17. When you are done, select all the rivets *one at a time* in the **Outliner** and apply all the **Array** and the **Curve** modifiers.

18. Join all the rivets into a single object (select all and press *Ctrl + J*) and in **Edit Mode**, delete the unnecessary or overlapping ones, keeping only the rivets that really add to the **Armor** look. Then, apply all the **Mirror** modifiers:

The completed rivets

19. Select the **Armor** object and then *Shift*-select the rivets object, press *Ctrl + Tab* to go in **Weight Paint** mode and click on the **Transfer Weights** button under the **Tools** tab.

20. Exit **Weight Paint** mode and assign an **Armature** modifier to the **rivets** object, select **rig** in the **Object** field.

21. Save the file as Gidiosaurus_final_detailing.blend.

There's more...

At this point, the **Gidiosaurus** model is ready to be animated, but some minor adjustments are still missing and can be added.

I won't go into the details about these additions, they are all processes you have already seen in the previous chapters and recipes, so this is simply a showcase:

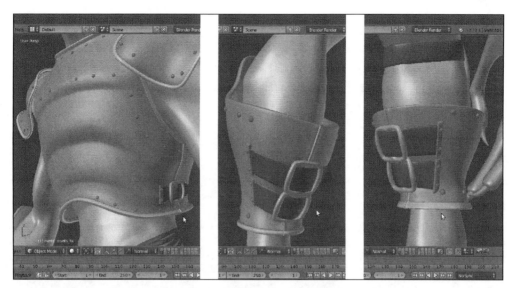

The modeled tiers and the rivets

1. The tier attachments on the **Armor's vambraces** and on the **greaves** have been refined by adding smaller **rivets**, and new tiers have been added to the sides of the **Armor chest plate**. Also, the opening seams in the **Armor** parts have been modeled under each tier location.

2. The **Armor** decorations have been separated as a new object (the **Armor_ decorations** item in the **Outliner**) and simplified by deleting as many edgeloops as possible without altering their basic shape:

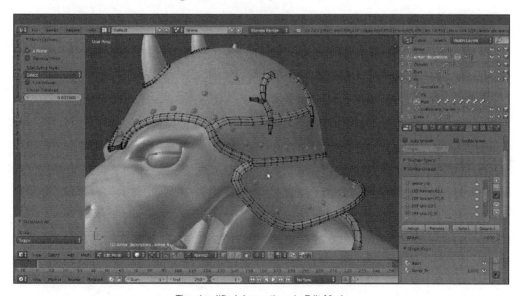

The simplified decorations in Edit Mode

3. The **Armor's** shape also has been tweaked even further through the **Armor_fix** shape key to adjust some overlaps that were occurring during the movements of the **spaulders** and in the **stomach** area too. The same shape key has been repeated also on the **decorations** and on the **rivets** objects for the areas of interest.

4. A bit of asymmetry has been introduced in the **Gidiosaurus** mesh by assigning a **Lattice** modifier to the character, and slightly modifying the shape on the left side, then applying the modifier as a shape key (the **Apply as Shape Key** button):

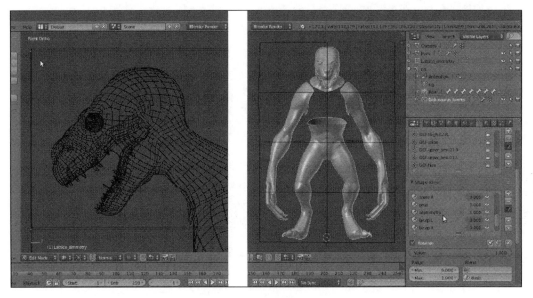

The asymmetry lattice

5. Finally, after some test renders, I realized that the **teeth** and the inside of the **mouth** of the **Gidiosaurus** still needed refinements, so I made some more adjustments to the **prop** shape key by making the **teeth** bigger and bolder, and the **inner mouth** more organic-looking and smooth:

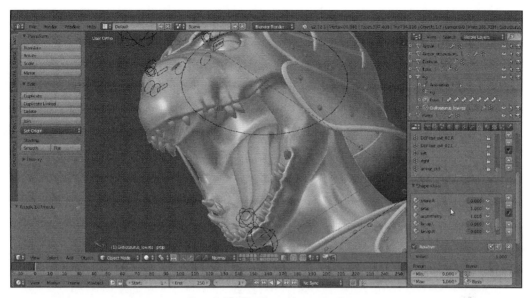

The modified teeth and inner mouth

Be aware that almost in every modeled object there is still room for improvement, and that's okay, it's not a sign of a bad job! This sort of improvement is done all the time and is simply part of the working experience.

See also

▶   http://www.blender.org/manual/modeling/curves/index.html

9

Animating the Character

In this chapter, we will cover the following recipes:

- ▸ Linking the character and making a proxy
- ▸ Creating a simple walk cycle for the character by assigning keys to the bones
- ▸ Tweaking the actions in Graph Editor
- ▸ Using the Non Linear Action Editor to mix different actions

Introduction

There are literally a *plethora* of tutorials and manuals about animation principles in general, and in Blender in particular, on the Web and in bookstores, so this one is going to be just a very *easy* chapter, mainly about the **technical aspects** of creating a simple animation with the rigged **Gidiosaurus** character, following the most usual pipeline commonly used in Blender (at least for the **open movies**).

Linking the character and making a proxy

The habit of linking assets from library files is the most useful and used, I would say, not only in a Blender based workflow, but also in the *industry*. A linked asset, in our case a creature character, can be placed and animated even if not already completed in all its parts, thus it allows a team to work almost *at the same time* on the different aspects. In our case, the **Gidiosaurus** is still missing **texturing** and **shaders**, but can already be placed *on stage* and animated anyway.

To link an asset in Blender and keep the possibility of animating it through a rig, we must make a proxy of the **rig** itself. A **proxy object** overrides the animation controls of a linked object in a non-destructive way, so that an animator can animate it locally to the .blend file the rigged character has been linked to. This way, the linked character object retains all its original information and is *only locally* altered by the proxy object scene.

Getting ready

As the first thing, we must prepare the **library**, so open the Gidiosaurus_final_ detailing.blend file:

1. Go to the **Outliner** and select the **Gidiosaurus_lowres** mesh, then also *Shift*-select the **Armor**, the **Armor_decorations**, the **rivets**, the **Eyes**, and the **Corneas** objects.

2. Press *Ctrl + G*, and all the selected objects are outlined in green to show that now they belong to a **group**, in this case, to the same group we created just now.

3. Go to the **Object** window and in the **Groups** subpanel, change the generic default **Group** name to **Gidiosaurus**.

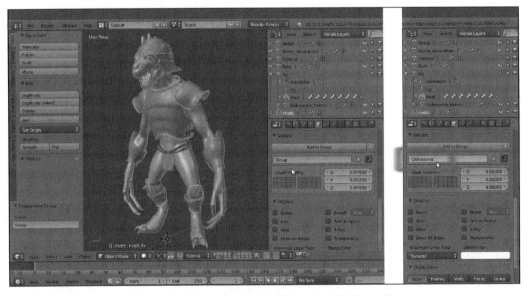

Creating a Group and assigning all the selected objects to it

4. Go to the **Outliner** and click on the eye icon to the side of the **rig** item to make it visible again, and then click on the **rig** item itself to select it.

5. Press *Ctrl + Tab* to go out of **Pose Mode** and go to the **Groups** subpanel under the **Object** window again. Click on the **Add to Group** button and in the pop-up menu, select the **Gidiosaurus** item (in this case, the only group already created). The **rig** is outlined in green as well:

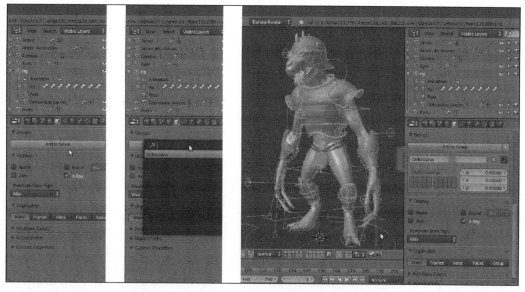

The rig assigned to the group as well

6. Click again on the *Restrict view-port visibility* button (the one with the eye icon) to the side of the **rig** item to hide it and save the file as Gidiosaurus_library.blend.

How to do it...

1. Click on the **File** item in the main menu bar, select the **New** item, and confirm by clicking on the **Reload Start-Up File** pop-up (or just press *Ctrl + N*).

2. Select the default **Cube** and delete it, then go to **File | Link** (or press *Ctrl + Alt + O*). Browse and click on the Gidiosaurus_library.blend file, then click on the **Group** folder item, and finally click on the **Gidiosaurus** item. Click on the **Link from Library** button to the top right of the screen.

A new object has appeared at the **3D Cursor** location (that should be placed at the center of the scene), and what we have got at this point is the **linked Gidiosaurus group**; this means that the character and any other object inside the **Gidiosaurus** group in the library file are now linked and *instanced* on an **Empty** that is named **Gidiosaurus** as well:

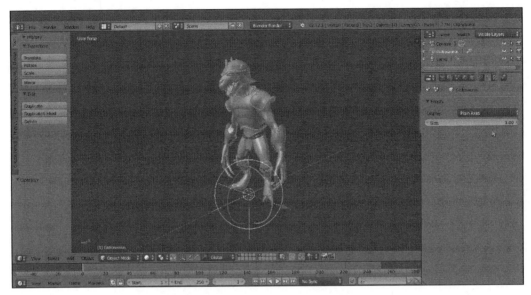

The Gidiosaurus group linked and instanced on the Empty

Remember that in the library file, inside the **Gidiosaurus** group we put also the **rig**, which for the moment is not visible in the linked group because it is *hidden in the library file*.

3. Press *Ctrl + Alt + P*, and a new pop-up appears where we can select the item we want to *proxify* (although all the objects inside the group appear in the list, at the moment only an **Armature** can be proxied). Click on the **rig** item:

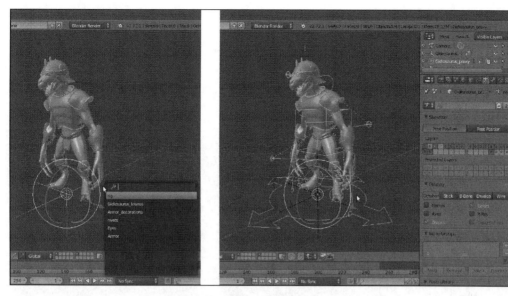

The proxified rig

The **rig** appears as a separate object in the **Outliner**, identified by the name **Gidiosaurus_proxy**; at this point, it is possible to only select the **rig** (which is still in **Object Mode**) and move it to a different layer.

4. Select the **Gidiosaurus_proxy** object and move it to the **11th** scene layer (use the _M_ key). _Shift_-click to enable the layer and then go to the **Display** subpanel, under the **Object Data** window, to enable the **X-Ray** item.

5. Press _Ctrl + Tab_ to go into **Pose Mode** and the _N_ key to call the viewport **Properties** sidepanel.

6. Save the file as `Gidiosaurus_proxy.blend`.

    At this point, looking at the viewport **Properties** sidepanel, we will see the **Rig Layers** interface usually created by the **Rigify** addon, _but_ if we save the file and reopen it, the interface is gone.

    This is because, at least for the moment, the Python script that draws the rig interface doesn't get automatically linked with the rig, so it's something we must do by hand. This is not a big issue, and by the way, the procedure is incredibly simple:

7. Click again on **File | Link** in the main header menu (or press *Ctrl + Alt + O*).

8. Browse to the `Gidiosaurus_library.blend` file, click on it, and then click on the **Text** item. Click on the **rig_ui.py** item (the Python script for the interface) and then on the **Link from Library** button.

9. Save the file and reopen it; the rig interface is visible again on the viewport **Properties** sidebar:

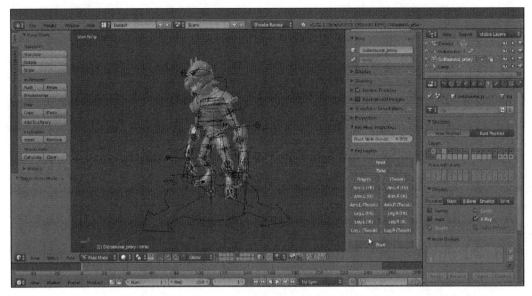

The rig interface at the bottom of the Properties sidepanel

See also

▸ http://wiki.blender.org/index.php/Template:Release_Notes/2.43/ Animation/Proxy_Objects

▸ http://www.blender.org/manual/data_system/linked_libraries. html?highlight=proxy#proxy-objects

Creating a simple walk cycle for the character by assigning keys to the bones

We are now going to create a simple **walk cycle** for the **Gidiosaurus** character by assigning **position** and **rotation** (and in some cases, also **scaling**) keys to the **control bones** of the **rig**.

Getting ready

In Blender, there is already a **preset screen** layout named **Animation** that you can switch to and start animating. By the way, I usually prefer to set up my screen layout for the required task, and animating is no exception, so let's first prepare the scene and the screen for the job:

1. Open the `Gidiosaurus_proxy.blend` file.

2. If necessary, enable the **3D manipulator widget** in the toolbar of the 3D view (press *Ctrl* + Spacebar), click on the **Translate** icon button, and set **Transform Orientation** to (just for the moment) **Global**.

3. Split the 3D view horizontally into two windows and change the bottom one into a **Dope Sheet** window. Click on the *Editing context being displayed* button on its toolbar to switch from **Dope Sheet** to the **Action Editor** context **Mode**.

4. Go to the **Properties** sidepanel of the 3D viewport (use the *N* key to make it appear if necessary) and under the **Rig Layers** subpanel, disable the **Arm.L (FK)**, **Arm.R (FK)**, **Leg.L (FK)**, and **Leg.R (FK)** buttons.

5. Select the **Gidiosaurus_proxy** rig, making sure you're in **Pose Mode**, and select the **hand.ik.L** control bone. Go to the **Rig Main Properties** subpanel under the **Properties** panel and set the **FK / IK (hand.ik.L)** slider to **1.000**:

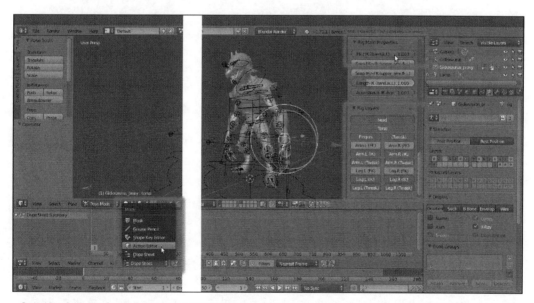

Switching from the Graph Editor to the Action Editor and setting the Inverse Kinematics in the Rig Layers subpanel

6. Repeat for the **hand.ik.R** bone and for the **foot.ik.L** and **foot.ik.R** control bones as well.

7. Go to the **Scene** window, enable the **Simplify** subpanel, and set the **Subdivision** level to **0** (or, if you have a more powerful machine than my laptop, also to **1**).

8. Go into the **Side** view and press the 5 key on the numpad to go into the **Ortho** view.

9. Click on the **red button icon** (*Automatic keyframe insertion for Objects and Bones*) in the **Timeline** toolbar.

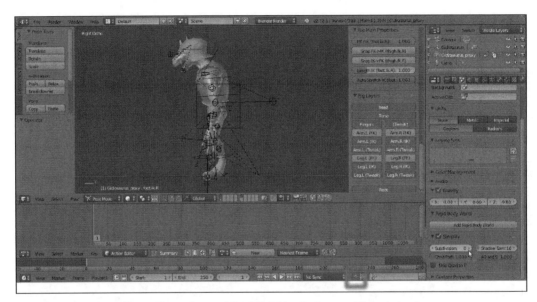

The red button icon and the Subdivision Surface modifier subpanel

10. Save the file as `Gidiosaurus_walkcycle.blend`.

How to do it...

To create a walk cycle, it's important to first establish the start and the end poses of the walk, so let's pose our character for his first step:

1. Be sure to be in the first frame (which in Blender is frame **1** and not **0**), both by clicking on the *Jump to first/last frame in frame range* left button on the **Timeline** toolbar or by pressing the *Shift + Left Arrow* keys.

2. Select the **foot_ik.R** control bone and, by using the widget, move it backward on the global *y* axis to around **0.350**.

   As you release the mouse button, an **Action** datablock, automatically named **Gidiosaurus_proxyAction**, is created and a keyframe for the **foot_ik.R** bone is automatically added in the first frame in the **Action Editor** window. We can also see the value for the movement on the *y* axis in the **Transform** subpanel.

Note that all the transformation value slots turned yellow; this is to show that at the current frame, an animation keyframe exists for all those values:

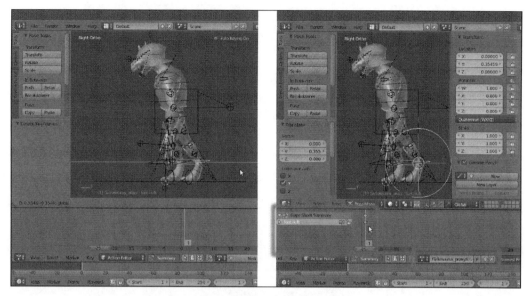

Setting the first key at frame 1

3. Temporarily, switch **3D View** to the **Graph Editor** window:

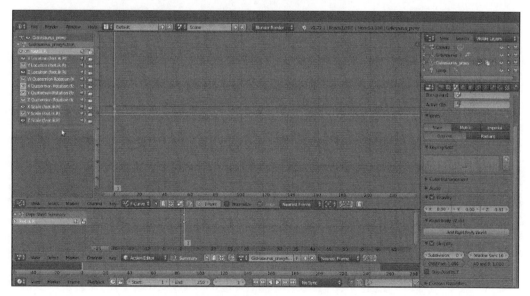

The Graph Editor window

As you can see, because we enabled the **red button icon** (*Automatic keyframe insertion for Objects and Bones*) in the **Timeline** toolbar, every time we move, rotate, or scale a bone, a keyframe for **Location**, **Rotation**, and **Scaling** is automatically added to the **Action**. This can be handy, but also results in a lot of useless keyframes, for example, for most of the rig bones, we need to set keys for the **Location** and/or the **Rotation**, but very rarely for the **Scaling**.

4. Put the mouse cursor inside the **Curve Editor** area of the **Graph Editor** and press the *A* key to deselect everything.

5. *Shift* + left-click on the **Scale** and **Quaternion Rotation** items in the **Gidiosaurus_ proxy** Channel Region to select them, then press *X* to delete them:

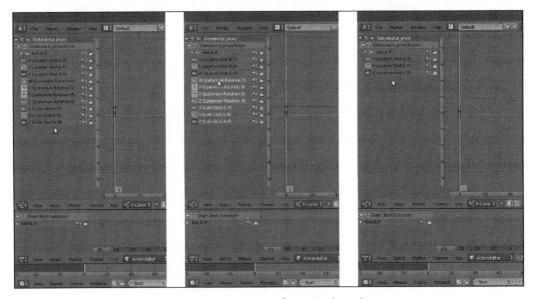

Deleting the useless transformation channels

6. Switch back to the **3D View**, and in the **Transform** subpanel in the **Properties** sidebar (and in the **Transform** subpanel under the **Bone** window in the main **Properties** panel), now only the **Location** slots are highlighted in yellow.

7. Disable the **red button icon** (*Automatic keyframe insertion for Objects and Bones*) in the **Timeline** toolbar.

8. Go to frame **21** by grabbing and moving the **Time Cursor** inside the **Timeline** window or the **Action Editor** window, or by typing the frame number inside the *Current Frame* button on the **Timeline** toolbar.

9. Select the **foot_ik.R** control bone and by using the widget, move it forward on the global *y* axis for around **-0.440**.

10. Press *I* and in the **Insert Keyframe Menu**, select the **Location** item; this adds a second key to the **foot_ik.R** bone at frame **21**, but this time only for **Location**:

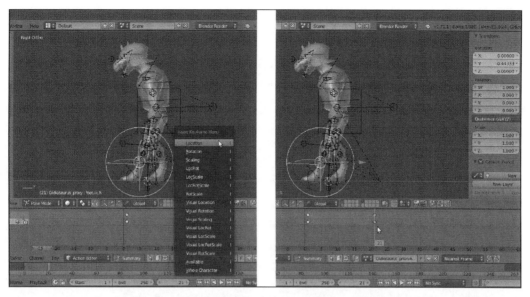

Setting a Location only key through the Insert Keyframe Menu pop-up

11. Go to frame **41**, right-click to select the key at frame **1** in the **Action Editor** window, and press *Shift* + D to duplicate it, then move the duplicated key to frame **41**.

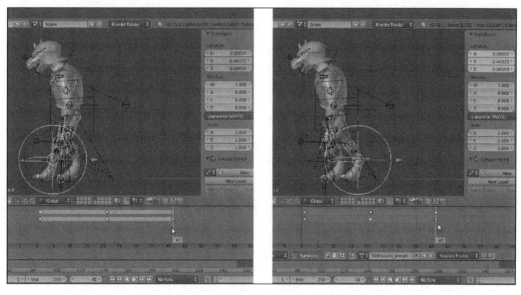

Creating poses at different frames by duplicating keys

12. Put the mouse cursor in the **Timeline** and press the *E* key to set the total length of the animation to the current frame position:

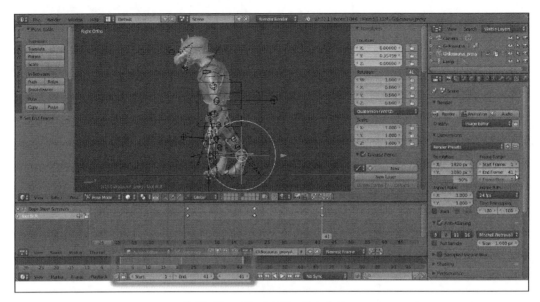

Setting the action total length in frames

13. Still at frame **41** (but this being a cycle, frame **1** could also be fine) and with the **foot_ik.R** bone selected, click on the *Copy the current pose of the selected bone to copy/paste buffer* button on the 3D viewport toolbar.

14. Go to frame **21** and select the **foot_ik.L** bone, then click on the *Paste the stored pose on to the current pose* button at the extreme right side of the 3D viewport toolbar to paste a **mirrored pose**.

15. Press the *I* key and in the pop-up menu, click on the **Location** item to add a new key:

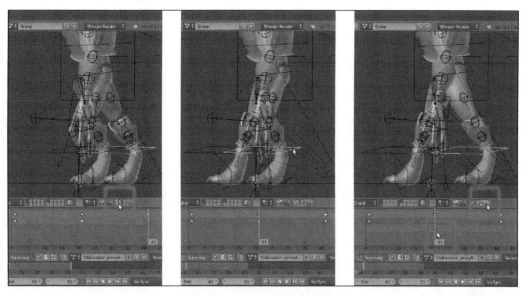

Copying a pose and pasting it reversed

16. Now, still at frame **21**, select the **foot_ik.R** bone and click on the *Copy the current pose of the selected bone to copy/paste buffer* button on the 3D viewport toolbar.

17. Go to frame **1**, select the **foot_ik.L** bone, and again click on the *Paste the stored pose on to the current pose* button to paste the reversed pose, then press *I* and insert a **Location** key.

18. Select and duplicate the new key at frame **1** for the **foot_ik.L** bone and move the duplicated one to frame **41**:

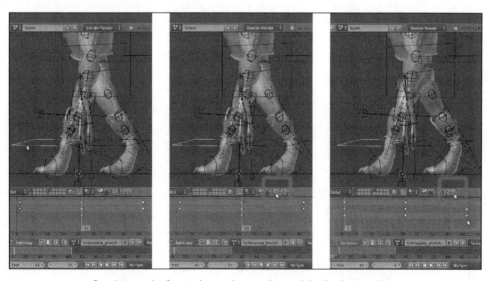

Creating new keyframes by copying, pasting, and duplicating pose keys

At this point, by scrolling the **Time Cursor** in the **Timeline**, in the **Action Editor** window, or by clicking on the *Play Animation* button in the **Player Control** on the **Timeline** toolbar, we can already see a complete *shuffling* cycle of the movement of the feet of the **Gidiosaurus**:

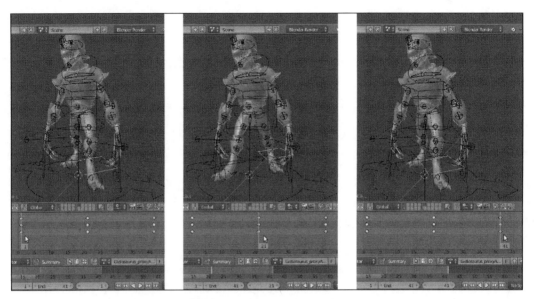

The Gidiosaurus' walk cycle with sliding feet

19. Now go to frame **1**, select the **torso** bone, and lower it on the *z* axis for almost **-0.200**, then assign a position key.

20. Select the just added **torso** bone key in the **Action Editor** window, press *Shift + D* to duplicate it, and move the duplicate to frame **21**, then repeat for frame **41**:

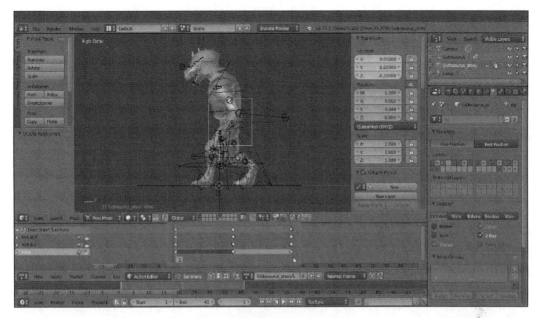

Animating the torso

21. Go to frame **11**, select the **foot_ik.R** bone, and move it on the z axis for **0.200**, then assign a position key.

22. As we already did at steps 16 and 17, copy the bone pose, go to frame **31**, and paste it reversed, then assign a position key to the **foot_ik.L** bone.

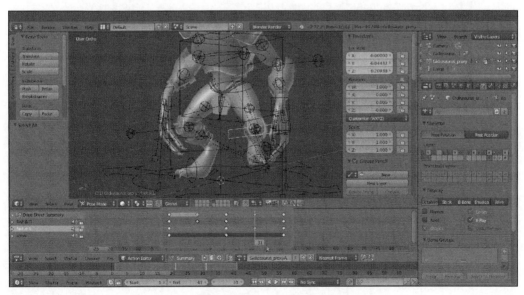

Assigning more translation keys

23. Working in the same manner, select the **hand_ik.R** and **.L** bones and animate them according to the **Gidiosaurus'** walk (note: as for any average walk cycle, in the opposite position with respect to the feet):

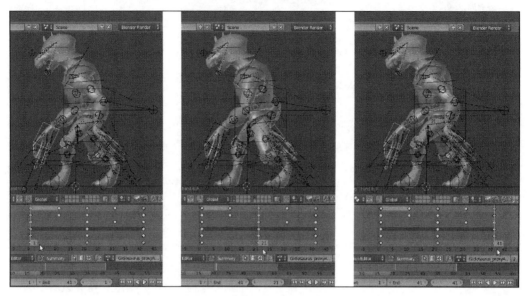

Animating the arms to complete the walk cycle

24. Reselect the **torso** bone, go to frame **1**, and move it forward for **0.240** on the y axis. Assign a new position key (to overwrite the old one), then delete the keys at frames **21** and **41** and substitute them with duplicates of the new frame **1** key.

25. Go to frame **11** and move the **torso** bone for almost **0.200** upward on the z axis. Duplicate the key for frame **31**.

26. Go to frame **1** and select the **toe.R** bone, then assign a rotation key. Go to frame **11** and rotate the bone on the normal x axis (the red circle in the widget tool with **Transform Orientation** set to **Normal**) for **75°**. Go to frame **21** and press *Alt + R* to clear the rotation pose and assign a rotation key. Use *Shift + D* to duplicate the last added key and move the duplicated one to frame **41**.

27. Select the **toe.L** bone and assign a rotation key at frame **1**, then go to frame **21** and repeat. Copy the **toe.R** pose at frame **11** and paste it reversed for the **toe.L** bone at frame **31**, then assign a cleared rotation pose key at frame **41**:

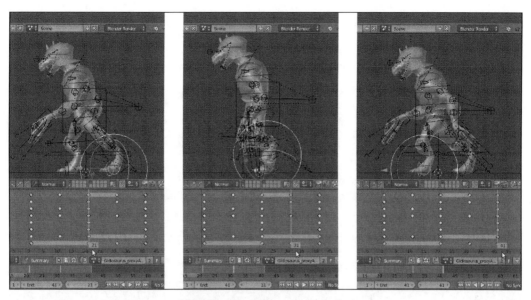

Adding the in-between poses for the feet

28. Following the previous procedures, set keys for the position and/or the rotation of all the affected bones, also adding movements such as the rotation of the **torso** and of the **hips**, the position of the **pole target** for **legs** and **arms**, the swinging of the **head** to compensate for the body's lateral movements, the closed **mouth** and the open **eyelids**, and so on:

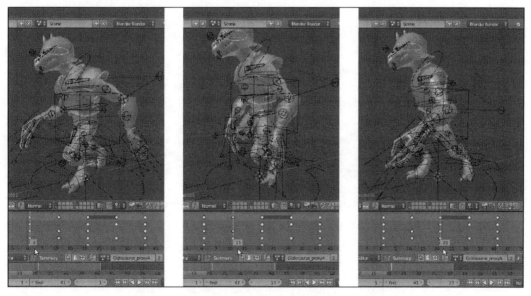

The first phase of the walk cycle animation is almost done

The animation cycle, at this point, looks really stiff and *robotic*. This is simply because everything *happens at the same time*, that is, in the same frame, as you can easily see in the **Action Editor** window (to enlarge a window, put the mouse cursor inside it and press *Ctrl* + Up Arrow; to go back, press *Ctrl* + Down Arrow):

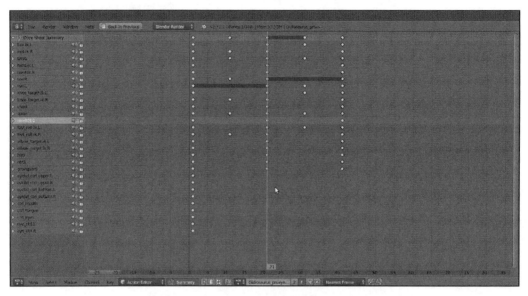

The maximized Action Editor window with the walk cycle action

To make the animation look more realistic and natural, we must offset some of the keys to make the different actions *happen at different times;* for example, the **torso** bone goes down a few frames later than the **foot** touching the ground, and goes up a few frames later as well, the same for the **head** swinging, and so on.

29. To offset the affected keys, simply select and/or *Shift*-select and move them for the required frames, forward or backward in the **Action Editor** window. Here, a bit of testing is needed to reach the right number of frames (usually in the range of **3-5** frames, by the way).

30. Where a *hole* happens at frame **1** in the action channel for a bone because of the dislocation of the keys, simply duplicate the last right side key of that bone and move it to the appropriate **negative frame** position. That is, to the left side of frame **0**, and be sure that the relative item, **Allow Negative Frames**, is enabled in the **Editing** tab of the **User Preferences** panel, as you can see in the following screenshot for the **torso** and for the **elbow_target_ik** bones:

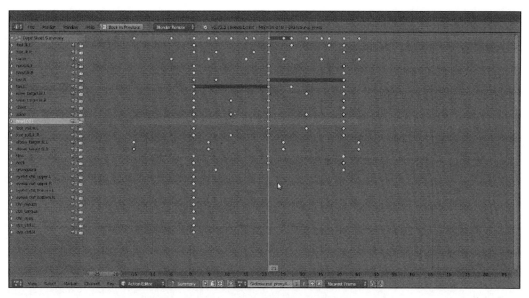

Duplicated keys moved to the Negative Frames space

31. Rename the action `Gidiosaurus_Walkcycle`. To better check the playing animation, go to the **Timeline** toolbar to set the end frame for the total length of the animation to **40** frames, because frame **1** and frame **41** are the same poses.

32. Save the file.

    At this point, we have made our first action with the **Gidiosaurus** character, and it's a **41** frame-long walk cycle meant to be repeated in loops for longer animations.

    Because in the next recipe we are going to use the **Non Linear Action Editor** (**NLA Editor**) to re-use the **action datablocks** to build the final animation, we need now to create some more actions to be mixed with the walk cycle one.

33. Activate the **Fake User** for the **Gidiosaurus_Walkcycle** action by clicking on the **F** icon button to the side of the action datablock on the **Action Editor** toolbar, then click on the **X** icon button to unlink the action datablock.

34. Put the mouse cursor in the 3D viewport and press the **A** key to select all the control bones, then press *Alt + G*, *Alt + R*, and *Alt + S* to clear any position, rotation, or scale and restore the rig default pose (actually, the only control bones using the **scale** operator for the animation are the **fingers**, which we haven't animated so far).

35. Be sure to be at frame **1** and zoom to the character's **head**, select the **head.001** and **neck** bones, and assign a rotation key, then select the **ctrl_mouth** bone and assign a position key.

36. Rename the action `Gidiosaurus_Roar`, then enable the **Fake User**; use *Shift + D* to duplicate the keys and move the duplicated ones to frame **21**.

37. Go to frame **15** and rotate the **head.001** and **neck** bones clockwise to raise the **head**, then open the **mouth** wide by moving the **ctrl_mouth** bone down.

38. Go to frame **7** and rotate the **head.001** and **neck** bones counterclockwise a bit to lower the **head**:

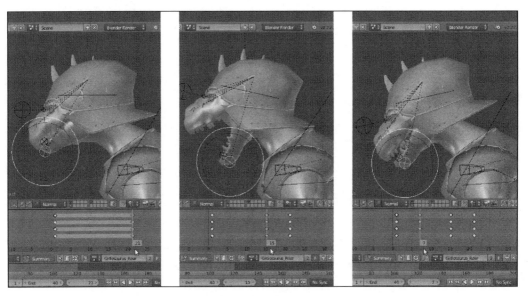

The Gidiosaurus_Roar action

We have now built a roar action for the **Gidiosaurus**, but it happens in only **21** frames, so it's really too fast. Although it is possible to scale any action strip in the **NLA Editor** window, in this case it's better to do it directly in the basic action itself.

39. In the **Action Editor** window, put the **Time Cursor** to frame **1**, then press the A key to select all the keys of the action. Press S | X | **2** | *Enter* to scale the action of the double to frame **41**:

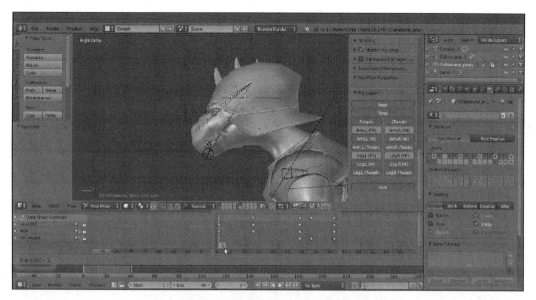

Scaling the action on the position of the Time Cursor

40. Now that the action length has been doubled, we can move some keys of a few frames and also animate the movement of the character's **tongue** a bit during the *roar*:

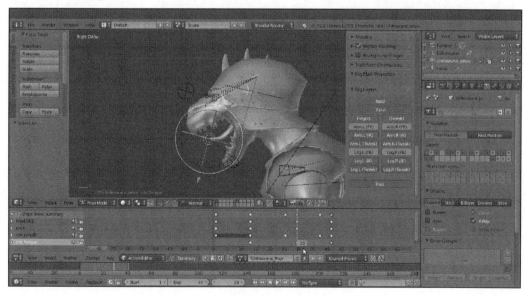

Animating the tongue

41. Again, click on the **X** icon button to unlink the action datablock, select all the bones, then press *Alt + G* and *Alt + R* to clear the poses.

42. *Shift*-select the **thumb.R** and **.L**, **f_index.L** and **.R**, and **f_middle.L**, and **.R** control bones and add a **Scaling** key. Rename the newly created action `Gidiosaurus_ Fingers` and enable the **Fake User**:

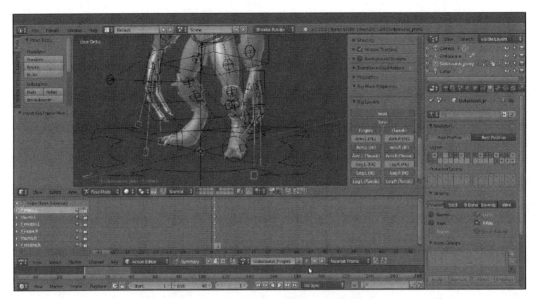

Renaming the fingers action and enabling the Fake User

43. Now *Shift*-select for both the **.L** and **.R** bones, **thumb.01**, **thumb.02**, and **thumb.03**, **f_index.01** and **f_index.02**, **f_middle.01** and **f_middle.02**, and the **palm** control bones, then add a **Rotation** key:

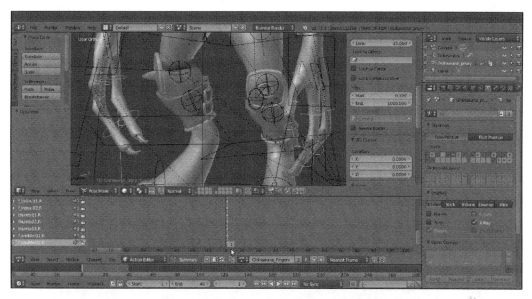

Adding a first rotation key for all the fingers at the same time

44. Now that we have all the finger bones' names in the **Action Editor** list-tree to the left (the **Channel Region**), start to click on the bone names to highlight them, for example, click on the **thumb.L** item, then press *Shift + PageUp* keys to move it to the top of the list.

45. Then highlight the **thumb.01.L** bone and by pressing the *PageUp* arrow, move it right after the **thumb.L** bone (press *Shift + PageUp* to eventually go directly to the top). Repeat with the **thumb.02.L** and the **thumb.03.L** bones, then go to the **thumb.R** bone, and so on. To move an item downward in the list-tree, simply press the *PageDown* key instead (or *Shift + PageDown* to go directly to the bottom).

46. Repeat the ordering until you have *grouped* the bones' names *by finger* in the list-tree, to make it easier to individuate them in the **Action Editor** window, then use *Shift + D* to duplicate all the keys and move the duplicated ones to frame **41**.

47. Go to frame **21**, select **thumb.L, .R, f_index.L, .R, f_middle.L**, and **.R** bones and press S to scale them to **0.900**. Assign a **Scaling** key, then select and rotate the other control bones, and assign **Rotation** keys (be aware that the previous scaling bones can also be rotated). Also, by using the *Copy/Paste* technique already shown, build a kind of *creepy hands* animation:

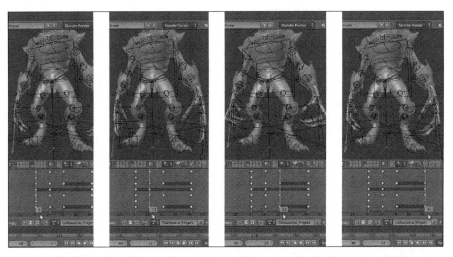

The "creepy hands" animation made by rotating and scaling the bones controls

48. When you are done, thanks to the re-ordering we made in the **Channel Region**, go to the **Action Editor** window and move groups of keys based on their finger group; in short, to avoid the *everything-at-the-same-time* issue, dislocate the timing of one finger with respect to the others:

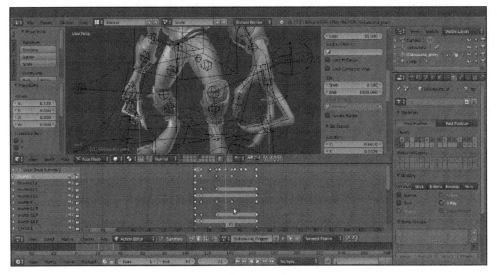

Offsetting the finger' keys

49. After this, click on the *Display number of users of this data* button to create a new copy of the action and change the name to **Gidiosaurus_Fingers.L**. In the **Channel Region**, *Shift*-select all the **.R** bones items and delete them (*X* key), then enable the **Fake User**.

50. Click on the double arrows icon to the left side of the datablock name (*Browse Action to be linked*) and reselect the **Gidiosaurus_Fingers** action.

51. Again, click on the *Display number of users of this data* button to create a new copy of the action and change the name to **Gidiosaurus_Fingers.R**. *Shift*-select all the **.L** bones items and delete them. Enable the **Fake User** and click on the **X** icon button to unlink the action datablock.

52. Save the file.

To have a look at the completed walk cycle of the **Gidiosaurus** and the other actions, open the `Gidiosaurus_walkcycle_final.blend` file provided with this cookbook.

How it works...

An **Action** is a bones **F-Curves** datablock created at the same moment any animation key is added through the **Insert Keyframe Menu** (*I* key) or the **red button icon** (*Automatic keyframe insertion for Objects and Bones*) in the **Timeline** toolbar. The newly created **Action** automatically takes the name from the object itself (**Gidiosaurus_proxy** in this case) plus the **Action** suffix.

The **Actions** are stored inside the `.blend` file, but thanks to the **Fake User** they don't necessarily need to be linked to the rig to be preserved after saving and closing the file.

Note that the scaling operation for the selected keys of an **Action** in the **Action Editor** window (and the same for the **Graph Editor** and the **NLA Editor**) use the **Time Cursor** position as the pivot point. Also note that even though we did it in our recipe, it wasn't mandatory in this case to declare the *x* (horizontal) axis for the scaling.

There's more...

Organizing the bones' names in the list inside an action in the **Action Editor** window is a good way to quickly find the required item, but it can be improved even further by **Bone Groups**:

1. Open the `Gidiosaurus_library.blend` file and go to the **Outliner**; click on the eye icon to the side of the **rig** item to unhide it.

2. Select the **rig** and go to the **Object Data** window, then in the **Bone Groups** subpanel, click on the **+** icon to add a **bone group**.

3. Double click on it to rename it **thumbs**, then go into the 3D viewport and *Shift*-select all the **thumbs'** bones.

4. Click on the **Assign** button, then click on the **Color** slot to choose a **Theme Color Set** from the pop-up menu:

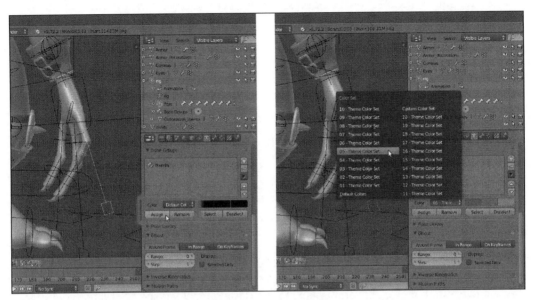

Choosing a Theme Color Set for the Bone Group

5. Repeat the steps from 2 to 4 for the other two fingers, thus creating the **indexes** and **middles** bone groups and selecting a different **Theme Color Set** option for each group:

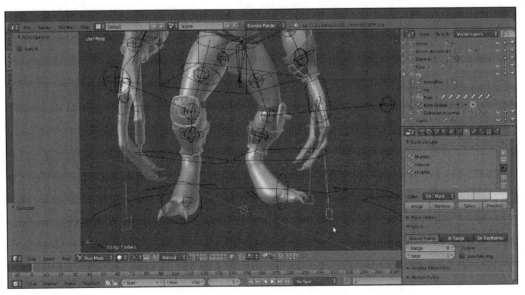

Three different Bone Groups

6. In the **Outliner**, hide the **rig** item again and save the file.

7. Re-open the `Gidiosaurus_walkcycle.blend` file; the colored bones don't show in the **proxified rig**, and this is because we had already proxified it and only later assigned the **bone groups** to the library file.

8. The solution to fix this is simply to select the affected bones one at a time and by going to the **Relations** subpanel under the **Bone** window, click on the **Bone Group** empty field to select the name of the appropriate group:

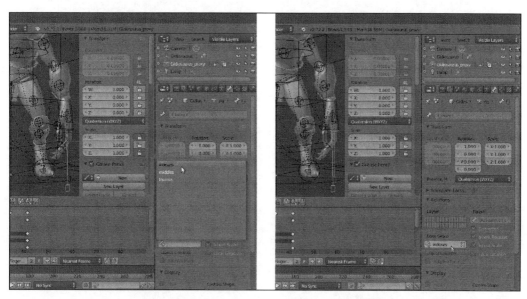

Reassigning the Theme Color Set to the proxified bones

By the way, it is always better to do the **Bone Groups** before the **proxy**, if possible.

The colors of the **Bone Groups** also show as *background color* for the bone channels inside the **Action Editor** window, making it a lot easier to select all the bones of a group; just be sure to have the **Show Group Colors** item enabled in the **View** menu on the **Action Editor** toolbar:

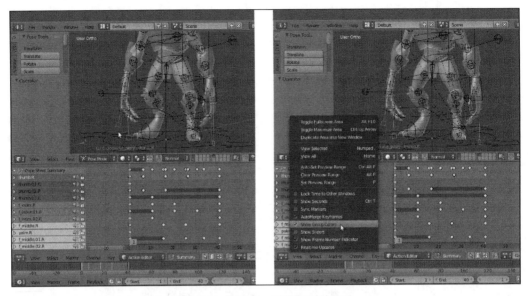

The Group Colors enabled for the bones

You can find the library with the colored fingers' control bones under the alternative file named `Gidiosaurus_library_colors.blend`.

See also

The walk cycle and the other actions we built in this recipe are, from an *animation point of view*, very simple and basic, not meant to teach you *how to animate* but only to show enough of Blender's tools for you to easily start animating a rigged character.

If you want to go deeper into the animation process, in Blender or not, here are some links to visit:

- `http://www.fjasmin.net/walk_cycle_tutorial/index.html`
- `http://cgcookie.com/blender/2010/01/24/learning-basic-animation-and-a-walk-cycle/`
- `http://wiki.blender.org/index.php/Doc:2.6/Manual/Animation`
- `http://wiki.blender.org/index.php/Doc:2.6/Manual/Animation/Techs`

Tweaking the actions in Graph Editor

In the previous recipe, we built **Actions** by setting position, rotation, and/or scaling keys, which Blender **interpolates through F-Curves** to create the character's animation. In this recipe, we are going to see the **Graph Editor** window, a tool to modify these **F-Curves** to fix errors or fine-tune the movements of the animated character.

Getting ready

Open the `Gidiosaurus_walkcycle.blend` file.

1. If it's not already loaded, in the **Action Editor** window, load the **Gidiosaurus_ walkcycle** action.

2. Go to the top main window header and click on the two little arrows to the left side of the button labeled as **Default**. In the pop-up menu, select the **Animation** item to change the screen layout:

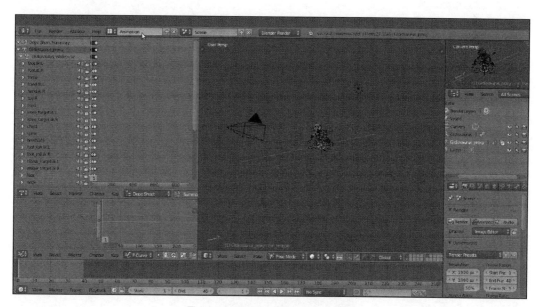

The premade Animation screen layout

3. Press the *Ctrl* key and left-click on the **top right corner** of the **Dope Sheet** window, then drag the mouse towards the **Graph Editor** window below to switch the two windows.

4. Go to the 3D viewport and zoom to the character to select the **foot_ik.L** bone; the **F-Curves** for the selected bone appear in the **Graph Editor** window:

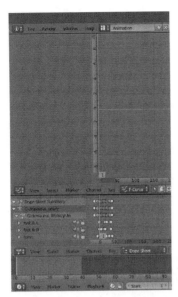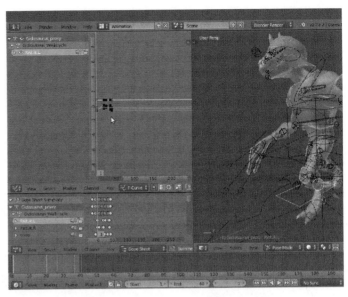

The F-Curve of the animation keys of the selected bone in the Graph Editor window

5. Expand the **foot_ik.L** item in the **Graph Editor** list-tree by clicking on the little arrow to the side of the item itself, then click on the **View** item in the toolbar and select the **View All** item to better visualize the curves inside the **Curve Editor** area:

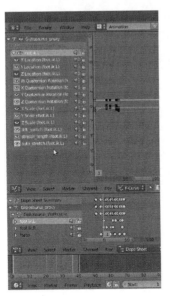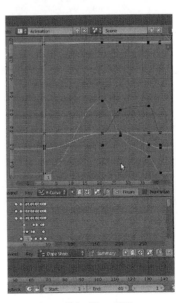

The list of the available F-Curves for the selected bone and the automatic zoom through the View All item

6. Hide (by clicking on the eye icon) and/or delete (select using left-click and the _X_ key) the unnecessary curve items such as (at least in this case) **X Scale**, **Y Scale**, **Z Scale** or **ikfk_switch (foot_ik.L)**, and so on. Join the unnecessary windows together and adjust the size of the **Edit Area** (the part with the keyframes) in the **Dope Sheet** to make them more easily readable. Optionally, enable the **Normalize** item in the **Graph Editor** toolbar to show all the **F-Curves** in a normalized **-1** to **1** range.

7. Save the file as `Gidiosaurus_F-Curves.blend`:

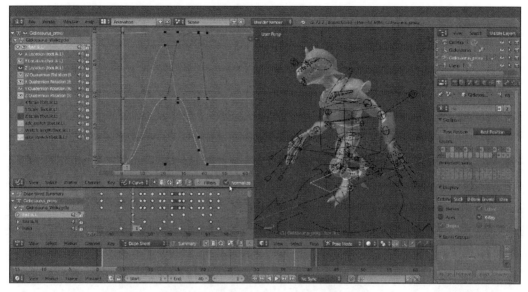

The Animation screen with a bit of customization

How to do it...

By selecting a curve name item and/or hiding the others in the **Graph Editor** list-tree, we can concentrate on one curve at a time. For example, what if we want to change the position of the **right foot** at frame **27** on the global x axis, when it's high off the ground?

1. Just left-click on the **X Location (foot_ik.L)** item in the list to highlight it and/or simply hide the others. Right-click on the curve keyframe/control point at frame **27** to reveal the **handles**, then press G | Y to move the keyframe handles on the vertical axis and see the foot move accordingly in the viewport on the global x axis:

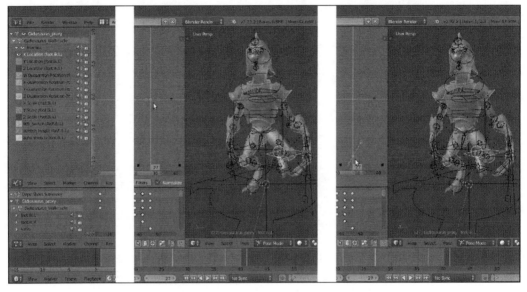

Editing the points of the F-Curve to tweak the bone's position

2. Or else, right-click only on one of the handles of the keyframe to move it and change the curve's envelope:

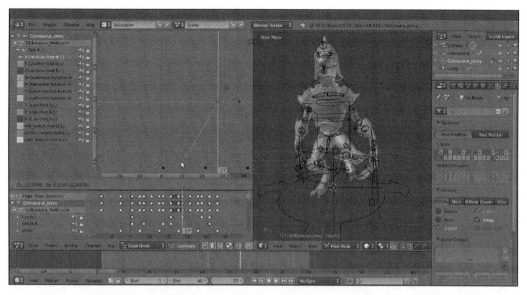

Changing the envelope of the F-Curve by modifying one of the point's handles

3. By *Shift*-selecting two or more keyframes of an **F-Curve** and pressing the *T* key, it is possible to set the **interpolation** type through the **Set Keyframe Interpolation** pop-up menu; by default the **F-Curves** are **Bezier**, but they can be switched to **Linear** or **Constant**. There are also **Easing** and pre-made **Dynamic** effects:

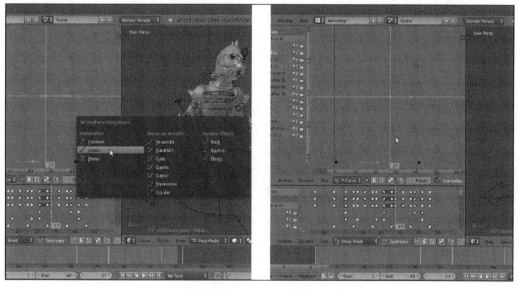

Changing the F-Curve Interpolation mode

4. Finally, the handles' type can also be set through the **Set Keyframe Handle Type** menu by pressing the *V* key; by default the handles are **Aligned**, but they can be set as **Free**, **Vector**, **Automatic**, and **Auto Clamped** too:

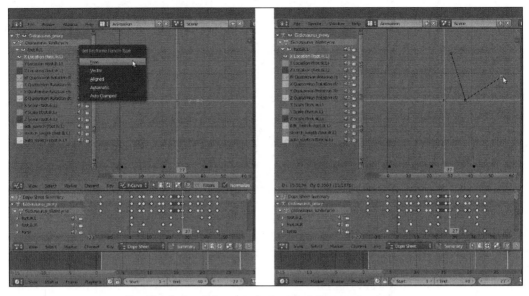

Changing the handle's type to further tweak the curve's envelope

See also

▶ http://wiki.blender.org/index.php/Doc:2.6/Manual/Animation/
   Editors/Graph

Using the Non Linear Action Editor to mix different actions

It's finally time to use the **NLA Editor** to compose a longer animation using the actions we built in the previous recipes.

Getting ready

As usual, first let's prepare the screen:

1. Start Blender and press *Ctrl + Alt + U* to call the **User Preferences** panel; in the **Editing** tab, enable the **Allow Negative Frames** item.

2. Click on the **Save User Settings** button and close the panel.

3. Load the Gidiosaurus_F-Curves.blend file and switch the **Graph Editor** to the **NLA Editor** window, and the **Dope Sheet** below it with the **Action Editor** window.

4. If necessary, click on the **X** icon button in the **Action Editor** window toolbar to unlink any action from the rig and clear the pose:

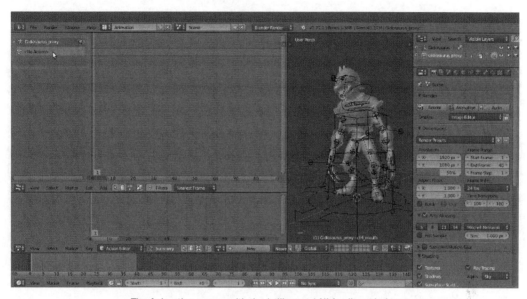

The Animation screen with the (still empty) NLA editor window

How to do it...

We are going to add **Action strips** to the **Gidiosaurus_proxy** rig, so it's mandatory to have at least one bone selected (any one, but in this case, it's the **ctrl_mouth** bone):

1. Put the mouse cursor in the **Track Region (NLA-stack)** of the **NLA Editor** window, right under where it shows **Gidiosaurus_proxy | <No Action>** items, and press *Shift + A* to add **a NlaTrack** channel:

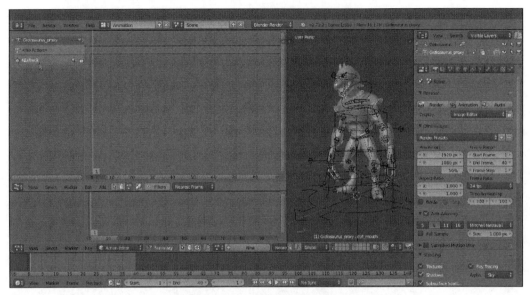

Adding a first track to the NLA Editor window

Now, take a moment and load the **Gidiosaurus_walkcycle** action in the bottom **Action Editor** window to see the action extension; it starts at frame **-15** and ends at frame **45**.

2. Unlink the action in the **Action Editor** and move the **Time Cursor** to negative frame **-15**; put the mouse cursor in the **Strip Edit** area to the right side of the **NlaTrack** item and again press *Shift + A*. From the pop-up menu, select the **Gidiosaurus_Walkcycle** item:

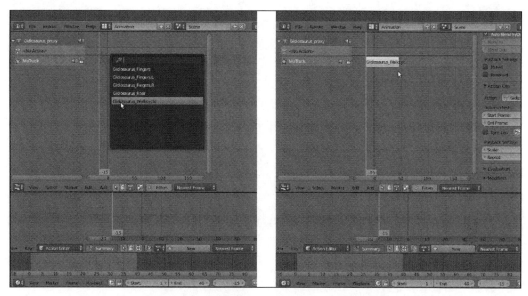

Loading the Gidiosaurus_walkcycle action into the track

A yellow action strip, with the **Gidiosaurus_Walkcycle** name superimposed, is added to the track at the **Time Cursor** location (the vertical green bar showing the frame number. If you now press the **Play** button in the **Player Control** on the **Timeline** toolbar, the animation starts at frame **1** and because the animation is only **40** frames long, it loops correctly, exactly as if the action was loaded in the **Action Editor** window.

3. If not already present, press the *N* key to call the **Properties** sidepanel of the **NLA Editor** window, right-click on the action strip to select it, and then go to the **Action Clip** subpanel. Under **Playback Settings**, set the **Repeat** value to **3.000**.

4. Click on the **End** button in the **Timeline** toolbar and change the frame value from **40** to **120** (**40** frames x **3**):

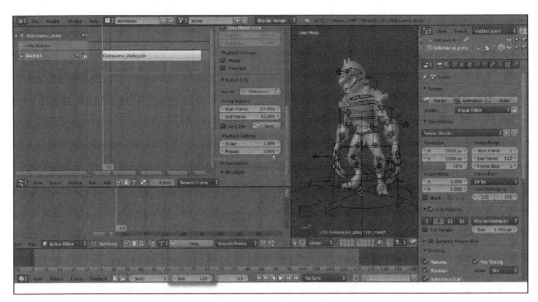

The Gidiosaurus_walkcycle action set to be repeated three times

If you press the **Play** button now, the animation is repeated **3** times *but* it doesn't loop correctly anymore because the **negative frames** keys are also included, in both the second and third repetitions. This is because we loaded the action at frame **-15**, so this is the **Start Frame** value for **Action Extents** (**Start Frame** = **-15**, **End Frame** = **45**).

Hence, some adjustment must be done to the action strip:

5. First, move the **Time Cursor** to frame **1**; with the strip selected, press the *Tab* key to go into **Edit Mode** and make the inner keys of the strip visible, both above the strip in the **NLA Editor** window, and as an **Action** in the **Action Editor** window. This way it's simpler to understand what keys are at what frame, and so on.

6. Second, go to the **Active Strip** subpanel and under the **Strip Extents** item, set the **Start Frame** value to **1.000**.

7. Go to the **Action Clip** subpanel and under the **Action Extents** item, set **Start Frame** to **1.000** as well and the **End Frame** value to **41.000**:

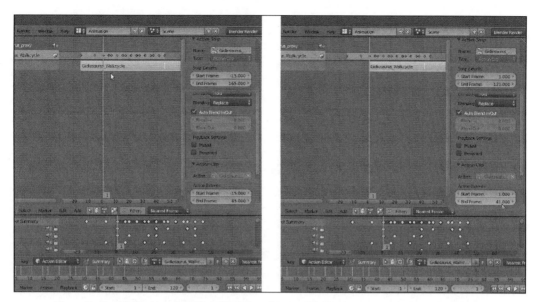

The action in Edit Mode and the Strip Extents and Action Extents values in the Properties subpanel of the NLA window

8. Press *Tab* to go out of **Edit Mode**.

Now, the walk cycle animation loops correctly for all the **120** frames, and obviously it is also possible to loop it even more by raising the **Repeat** value.

So, the correct and fastest procedure would have been, from the start:

1. At frame **1**, load the action strip in the **NLA Editor** window.

2. In the **Properties** sidepanel, under the **Action Extents** item in the **Action Clip** subpanel, set the **Start Frame** value to **1.000** and the **End Frame** value to **41.000**.

3. Under **Playback Settings**, set the **Repeat** value to **3.000** and the total length of the animation to **120** frames in the **End** button of the **Timeline** toolbar:

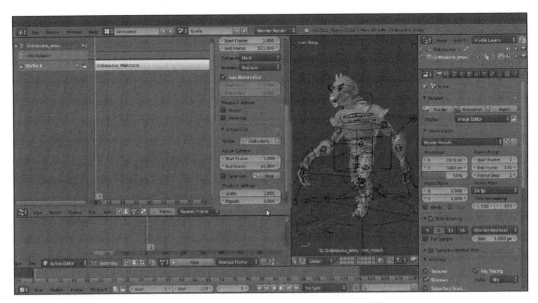

Recapitulating the action extents values to be set

Now, let's see how to add the other actions:

1. Put the mouse cursor under the **NlaTrack** item and press *Shift + A* to add a new track (**NlaTrack.001**); load the **Gidiosaurus_Roar** action strip and move it (*G* key) to start at frame **10**.

2. Select the **Gidiosaurus_Walkcycle** strip and in the **Active Strip** subpanel, disable the **Auto Blend In/Out** item but leave the values as **0.000**. Select the **Gidiosaurus_Roar** strip and disable the **Auto Blend In/Out** item as well, then set the **Blend In** value to **10.000** and the **Blend Out** value to **5.000**.

3. Add **two** more tracks, select the **NlaTrack.002** track and load the action strip **Gidiosaurus_fingers.L**, then select the **NlaTrack.003** track and load the action strip **Gidiosaurus_fingers.R**.

4. Select the **Gidiosaurus_fingers.L** strip and in the **Active Strip** subpanel, disable the **Auto Blend In/Out** item, and leave the values as **0.000**; repeat for the **Gidiosaurus_fingers.R** strip.

5. Move the two strips separately in different positions inside the **120** frames animation range.

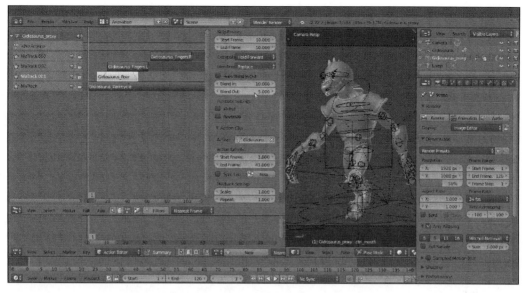

Setting the Blend In and Blend Out values to mix the other actions

6. Press the **Play** button in the **Player Control** on the **Timeline** toolbar to watch the composited animation and save the file as Gidiosaurus_NLA.blend.

At this point it could be possible to start to render at least some **OpenGL** preview to see the result, but there are still several steps missing in our workflow before we reach the final goal, from the **texturing** to the **shaders**, **lighting**, and finally **beauty-rendering** and **compositing**; all stuff that we'll see in the next few chapters.

See also

▶   http://wiki.blender.org/index.php/Doc:2.6/Manual/Animation/
    Editors/NLA_Editor

10

Creating the Textures

In this chapter, we will cover the following recipes:

- ▸ Making a tileable scales image in Blender Internal
- ▸ Preparing the model to use the UDIM UV tiles
- ▸ Baking the tileable scales texture into the UV tiles
- ▸ Painting to fix the seams and to modify the baked scales image maps
- ▸ Painting the color maps in Blender Internal
- ▸ Painting the color maps in Cycles

Introduction

In this chapter, we are finally going to create the textures for the **Gidiosaurus** character, meaning all the image textures that we'll need later, to build the **shaders** for the body and for the **armor**. Basically, the essential images we need are:

- ▸ A grayscale reptilian scales image to be used as a bump map and to color the skin
- ▸ Painted image textures for the skin diffuse coloration
- ▸ A tileable image for the worn armor metallic surface
- ▸ A bump image for the armor decoration patterns

In this chapter, we'll focus on the skin of the **Gidiosaurus**, and the last two textures for the **armor** will be treated in the next chapter.

The most difficult and tedious part is, no doubt, rendering the **scales** on the **Gidiosaurus** skin; I mean, if we had to paint the scales one by one. Instead, we'll try to obtain the complex scales pattern with the minimum effort possible, using a couple of techniques to speed up the work.

Trying to keep things clear, from now on we'll use *two different texture folders*: the usual `textures` one and a `textures_making` folder, where the latter is used to contain the images we need during the process to produce the final image textures.

Making a tileable scales image in Blender Internal

So, the first thing to do is to obtain a **tileable** grayscale **reptilian scales** image; we'll start from an already existing image obtained from an old and larger texture I had painted in **Gimp** for a dinosaur model some years ago... but that's a different story.

In any case, if you prefer, you can paint a new reptilian scales image from scratch by using painting software such as **Gimp** or **Photoshop** or open source applications such as **MyPaint** (`http://mypaint.intilinux.com/`) or **Krita** (`https://krita.org/`).

Getting ready

We are taking for granted that in your **Blender User Preferences** window, you still have the **Import Images as Planes** addon enabled; if not, start Blender and just enable it as already explained in *Chapter 1, Modeling the Character's Base Mesh*. Then, follow these steps:

1. Select and delete the default **Cube** primitive in the scene. Select the **Camera** and the **Lamp** and move them to the **6th** scene layer.

2. Click on the main **File** menu and then on the **Import** item; select the **Images as Plane** item.

3. Browse to the `textures_making` folder and select the provided `scales.png` image texture, which is a gray painted scales image:

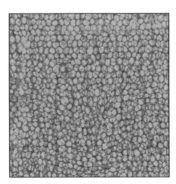

The "scales.png" image provided with this cookbook

4. Press the period (.) key on the numpad to center the view on the selected **Plane** and then the *7* key on the numpad to switch to the **Top Ortho** view.

5. Go to the **Object Modifiers** window and assign an **Array** modifier to the **Plane**; check the **Merge** item and leave all the other settings as they are.

6. Click on the **Copy** button to assign a new identical **Array** modifier, and in the new **Array** modifier, under the **Relative Offset** item, change **X** to **0.000** and **Y** to **1.000**.

7. Save the file as 48860S_10_scales_tiles_01.blend.

8. Press the period (.) key again on the numpad to center the view on the *enlarged* **Plane**, then switch the **Viewport Shading** mode to **Texture** (*Alt + Z*):

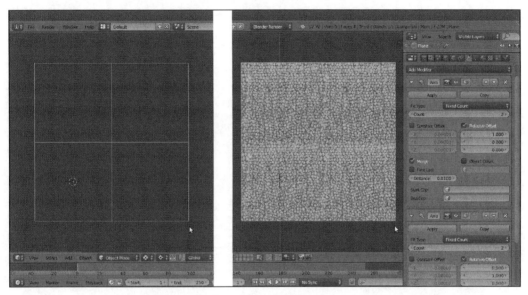

The UV mapped Plane with the Array modifiers assigned

As you can see in the preceding screenshot, the mapped **Plane** is now repeated **4** times.

By zooming towards the middle seams, it's clear that the mapped scales image is not tileable yet:

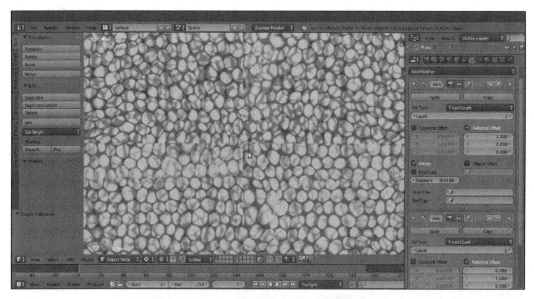

The visible seams at the borders of the Plane instances

Just in case the previous screenshot is not readable enough, open the provided 4886OS_10_scales_tiles_01.blend file to have a better look.

How to do it...

At this point, the file is ready and we can start to paint on the image to make it tileable:

1. Click on the mode button (*Sets the object interaction mode*) on the viewport toolbar to select the **Texture Paint** mode item.

2. Put the **mouse cursor** on a bright value in the scales image and press the S key to sample it, then go near the color selector in the **Brush** subpanel under the **Tool Shelf** to the left and click on the *Toggle foreground and background brush colors* button (the one with the two opposing arrows) to switch the active color. Otherwise, simply press the X key, put the mouse cursor on a dark area, and press S again to sample it as the opposite color.

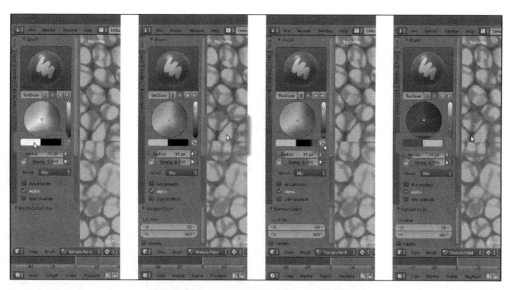

Sampling the light and dark colors of the image

3. Set the brush's **Radius** and **Strength** values, and if you are using a **graphic tablet**, be sure to have the **two** *tablet pressure sensitivity* buttons at the sides of the previous items enabled.

4. Start to paint by fixing the scales on the image at the seams areas. Because we can also paint on the **Planes** duplicated by the **Array** modifier, and because we are always painting on the same instanced image, it's quite simple to visually join the scales at the four sides, actually making the image tileable:

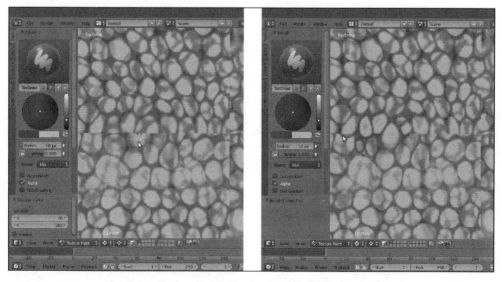

Painting on the image at the borders to make the scales seamless

It's enough to fix the areas along the middle horizontal and vertical axes of the **Planes** to cover all the four edges (in fact, fixing **two** edges is automatically fixing **four**).

5. When you are done, go back into **Object Mode** and open a new window with **UV/ Image Editor**; press *Tab* to go into **Edit Mode**, make the revised image appear, and save it (by clicking on **Image | Save as Image** in the toolbar or simply press the *F3* key) in the textures_making folder as scales_tiles.png:

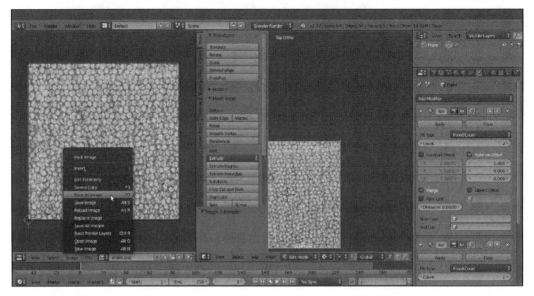

Saving the tileable scales image with a different name

6. Save the file as 4886OS_10_scales_tiles_02.blend.

<h2>How it works...</h2>

You might wonder why we didn't use the **Make Seamless** filter of **Gimp** (**Filters | Map | Make Seamless**) to obtain a tileable image in one click; well, the answer is simple: the **Make Seamless** plugin actually offsets and blends together whole areas of the image, and this can work in several cases, but not for a complex pattern made by scales, where a simple fading is not good enough. In this case, I prefer to paint the joining line between them by hand.

Preparing the model to use the UDIM UV tiles

In the previous recipe, we made the scales image texture seamless, ready to be seamlessly mapped on our model. If you go back to *Chapter 5, Unwrapping the Low Resolution Mesh*, you'll remember that we assigned **two** different sets of **UV coordinate** layers to it: the **UVMap** layer, divided into **5 different tiles** (this is called **UDIM UV Mapping**; it's a popular standard in the industry and means **U-Dimension**), and the **UVMap_scales** layer, set up to repeat the `scales_tiles.png` image pattern at the right size on the model:

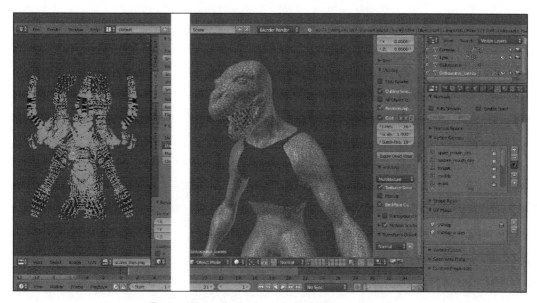

The two UV coordinates layers in the UV Maps subpanel

By zooming in and looking carefully at the result of the tiling (in **Textured Solid** mode, which is enabled under the **Shading** subpanel of the *N* viewport sidepanel), you can see that although we used a tileable scales image, we still have seams in some areas. This is obviously due to the fact that the **UVMap_scales** layer (as you can see in **UV/Image Editor** in the **Edit Mode** after selecting all the mesh's vertices) is made up of separated and overlapping islands to obtain a randomly distributed mapping of the scales on the **Gidiosaurus** skin:

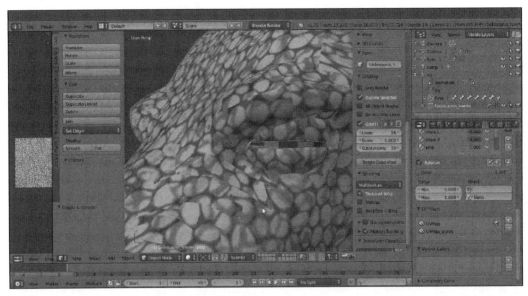

The seams on the Gidiosaurus scales skin

A simple solution to fix these seams is to bake the random scales pattern on the **5** tiles of the **UVMap** layer and then use the **Paint Tool** to adjust the gaps. This a step that we have to do in any case to allow further texture modifications such as the painting of befitting facial scales around the **eyebrows**, the **eyes**, the **nostrils**, and so on, but let's go in order.

To be able to bake and then paint on the different tiles in real time through the 3D viewport, we must prepare the file a bit.

Getting ready

Start Blender and open the `Gidiosaurus_library.blend` file; save it as `Gidiosaurus_baking_scales_01.blend`:

1. *Shift*-click on the **13th** scene layer to disable it and hide the **Armor** object, then enable the **6th** scene layer to show **Camera** and **Lamp**. Split the 3D view into two windows and change the left one into a **UV/Image Editor** window (if it shows the **Render Result** image datablock, just click on the **X** icon button to unlink it).

2. Put the mouse in the 3D viewport and press the *T* key to hide the **Tool Shelf** panel, and then maximize the **UV/Image Editor** window as much as possible. Go to the **Outliner** and click on the eye icon to the side of the **Camera** item to disable its visibility in the viewport.

3. Go to the **UV Maps** subpanel under the **Object Data** window and be sure to have the **UVMap** layer selected (the one with the **5** different space tiles); if necessary, click on the camera icon to the right to enable it as the active UV coordinates layer.

How to do it...

Now, let's prepare the materials; remember that, at the moment, we are under the **Blender Render** engine and not under **Cycles**:

1. Go to the **Material** window and out of **Edit Mode**, click on the – icon button to the right of the materials datablock window (*Remove the selected material slot*) to unlink both the Enamel and the Body material datablocks.

2. Now click on the **+** icon button to add **5** material slots, and then add **5** materials by selecting each slot and clicking on the **New** button.

3. Starting from the top one, rename the **5** materials as Material_U0V0, Material_U1V0, Material_U2V0, Material_U0V1, and Material_U1V1.

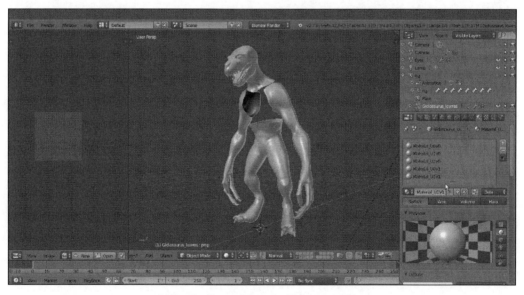

Adding the 5 materials to the Gidiosaurus object

4. Select the `Material U0V0` slot and go to the **Textures** window to click on the **New** button and add a texture.

5. Scroll down the vertical panel by rotating the middle mouse wheel and click on the **New** button under the **Image** subpanel; in the **New Image** pop-up panel, click on the **Color** slot to set the **Alpha (A)** value to **0.000**, then *Ctrl* + click on the **Width** slot and right after the default value of **1024**, type `*3`, then press *Enter* (in Blender, you can do a math calculation for any parameter like this anywhere). Copy and paste (*Ctrl + C* and *Ctrl + V*) the result of the multiplication, **3072**, into the **Height** slot; click on the **Name** slot to write the texture name as `blank_U0V0`, then press the **OK** button at the bottom of the panel:

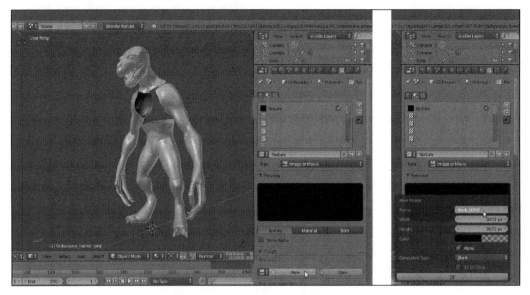

Adding a blank image texture to the first material

This adds a blank (*alpha background*) **3072** x **3072** pixels image as a texture on the material.

6. *Ctrl* + left-click on the *Unique datablock ID name* slot right above the **Type (Image or Movie)** slot, and rename the default **Texture** name as `U0V0`. Go down to the **Mapping** subpanel and click on the **Map** slot to select the **UVMap** item:

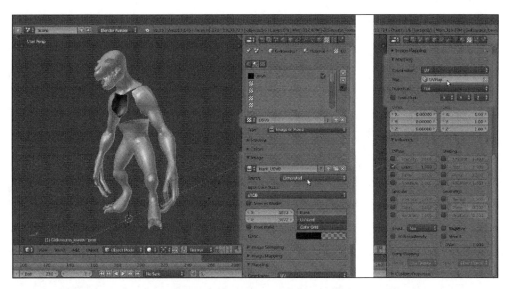

The "Unique datablock ID name" slot, the Image subpanel, and the Mapping subpanel

7. Go to the **UV/Image Editor** to the left side of the screen and click on the double arrows to the side of the **New** button in the toolbar; from the pop-up menu select the **blank_U0V0** item. Slide the toolbar to the right and click on the **Image** item. In the pop-up menu, select the **Save as Image** item (or press the *F3* key) and save the image in the `texture_making` folder as `blank_U0V0.png`, then click on the pin icon button to the right to activate it (*Display current image regardless of object selection*):

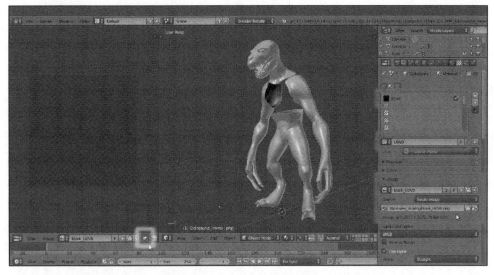

The assigned blank image loaded in the UV/Image Editor window and pinned to be displayed regardless of the object selection

As the image is saved under the **Image** subpanel, the **Source** slot caption changes from **Generated** to **Single Image**.

8. Repeat the procedure for all the remaining four materials, assigning and saving a blank image texture for each material. So inside the `texture_making` folder, you have saved the images: `blank_U0V0`, `blank_U1V0`, `blank_U2V0`, `blank_U0V1`, and `blank_U1V1`.

9. Start to split the **UV/Image Editor** window until you have **5 UV/Image Editor** windows. Press the *Tab* key to go into **Edit Mode** with the mesh; put the mouse in the 3D viewport and press the *A* key to select all the mesh's vertices and therefore show the UV islands in all the **UV/Image Editor** windows.

10. Enlarge one **UV/Image Editor** window as much as possible and enable the *Keep UV and edit mode mesh selection in sync* button on the toolbar.

11. If it's the case, deselect everything, then box-select the islands (*B* key then left-click and drag the mouse) in the **U1V0** tile space. In the **Material** window, select the `Material_U1V0` slot and click on the **Assign** button. Go to the top right **UV/Image Editor** window and click on the **X** icon button on the toolbar to unlink the current image datablock (which is still **blank_U0V0**). Then click on the **Image** item on the toolbar and from the drop-down list, select the `blank_U1V0` image.

12. Press the *A* key to deselect everything and box-select the islands in the **U2V0** tile; select the `Material_U2V0` slot and again click on the **Assign** button. Go to the following image editor and unlink the current image datablock to load the `blank_U2V0` image.

13. Repeat for the other two missing tiles and material slots (note that this is not necessary for the **U0V0** ones, which are, by default, first assigned to the whole mesh and the first created material and so still remain associated to `Material_U0V0`). Then go out of **Edit Mode**.

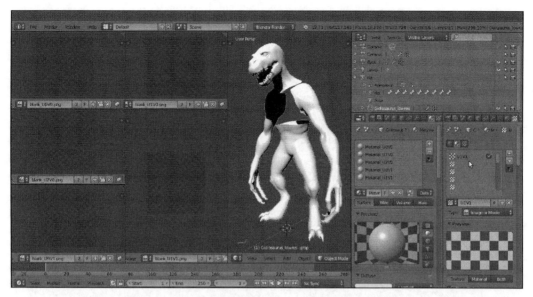

The work-space prepared with the 5 UV/Image Editor windows with their respective blank images

As you can see, by selecting the vertices of the UV islands in **UV/Image Editor**, the corresponding vertices on the mesh are also selected. Moreover, this makes all the UV islands visible in the image editor, even though, we haven't selected a single vertex on the mesh yet (normally, you see only the islands of the selected vertices in the image editor). This way, it's simple to associate a certain UV island with a certain material and a certain group of vertices on the mesh.

14. Go to the **Material** window and select the `Material_U0V0` slot. Go to the **Texture** window and click on the second texture slot right under the **U0V0** one. Click on the **New** button, scroll down to the **Image** subpanel, and click on the **Open** button to browse to the `texture_making` folder and load the `scales_tiles.png` image.

15. Go to the **Mapping** subpanel and in the **Map** slot, select the **UVMap_scales** UV coordinates layer. Rename the `Unique datablock ID name` slot as `scales_tiles`. Click on the checkbox to the side of the **U0V0** texture slot to disable it (this is just temporary but mandatory for the baking, otherwise it would create a dependency loop, that is, the *Circular reference in texture stack* message in the top main header and in the **Terminal** panel as well):

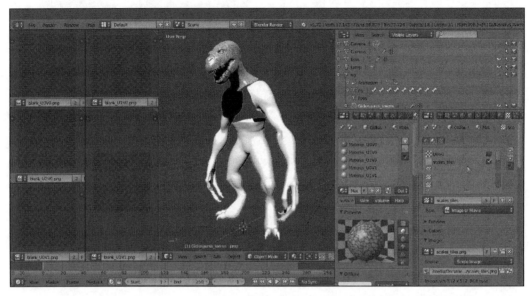

Disabling the blank texture image and loading the "scales_tiles.png" image in the first material

16. Click on the button with a black arrow pointing downward, right after the **+** and **−**icon buttons, and from the pop-up menu, select the **Copy Texture Slot Setting** item. Select the `Material_U1V0` slot and then click on the second texture slot right under the **U1V0** one and click on the **New** button. Click again on the black arrow button and this time, select **Paste Texture Slot Setting**:

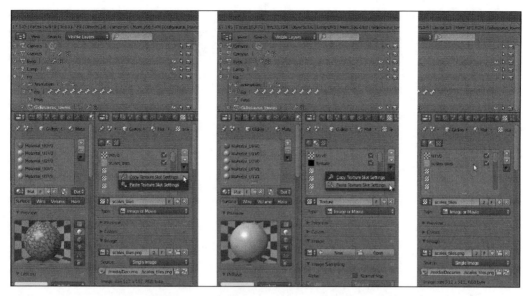

Copying and pasting the "scales_tiles" texture slot to the other materials

17. Repeat this copy and paste for the other three materials, and also remember to disable the first texture slot for all the materials.

18. Press *Tab* to go out of the **Edit Mode** and save the file.

How it works...

Thanks to the pin icon button that is enabled for each loaded image, it's possible to keep the different images visible at the same time. At this moment, the **5** different PNG images are blank, so this isn't particularly evident; it will be a lot more clear when we start to actually paint on the model through the 3D viewport.

Baking the tileable scales texture into the UV tiles

What we have to do now is to bake the `scales_tiles.png` image map (used in all the materials and mapped on the **UVMap_scales** coordinates layer) on the **5** tiles of the **UVMap** coordinates layer.

Getting ready

At this moment, Blender is not able to bake automatically outside of the default **UOVO** tile space yet, so a bit of additional work is needed; nothing particularly difficult by the way. The steps are as follows:

1. Press *Tab* to go into **Edit Mode** again and then put the mouse in the **blank_UOVO UV/Image Editor** window; press the *N* key to call the **Properties** sidepanel and under the **Display** subpanel, check the **Normalized** item:

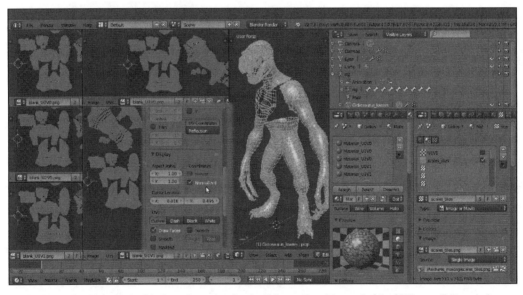

The Normalized item in the Display subpanel under the N Properties sidepanel of the UV/Image Editor window

2. Press *N* again to hide the **Properties** sidepanel. Go to the **UV Maps** subpanel under the **Object Data** window and click on the **+** icon button to the right to add a new UV coordinates layer (**UVMap.001**), then rename it **UVMap_temp** (or whatever you prefer).

How to do it...

We are now going to create a new UV coordinates layer for the baking by moving all the islands in the outside tiles to the space of the default one; but before we go on, we must be sure about two things:

▸   In the toolbar of the **blank_U0V0** image editor window, the _Keep UV and edit mode mesh selection in sync_ button must now be disabled

▸   In the pop-up menu, accessible by clicking on the **UVs** item in the image editor toolbar, the **Constrain to Image Bounds** item must be deselected:

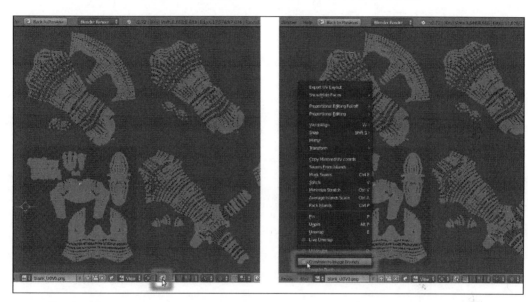

The "Keep UV and edit mode mesh selection in sync" button and the Constrain to Image Bounds item

Go to the **blank_U0V0** image editor window; if you prefer, maximize it (mouse cursor into the window and press *Ctrl* + Up Arrow). If necessary, press *A* to deselect all the islands.

1. Now, box-select the islands on the **U1V0** tile, and move them to the default **U0V0** tile space (*G* | *X* | **-1** | *Enter*):

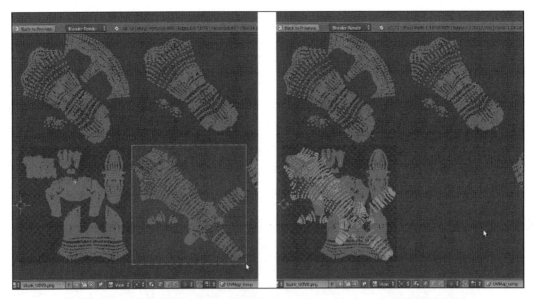

The UV islands of the U1V0 tile space, box-selected and moved to the default U0V0 tile space

2. Deselect everything and box-select the islands at **U2V0**, then move them to the default space, which is the same as the previous one (*G* | *X* | **-2** | *Enter*).

3. Repeat for the last **2** islands tiles (*G* | *Y* | **-1** | *Enter*) and (*G* | *X* | **-1** | *Enter* and then *G* | *Y* | **-1** | *Enter*), then rearrange the image editor windows.

4. Go to the **Object Data** window and in the **UV Maps** subpanel, be sure to have the **UVMap_temp** layer, the **last one**, enabled as the active one, that is, the **camera icon** to the right side of the **UVMap_temp** item must be the one enabled and visible (*Set the map active for rendering*):

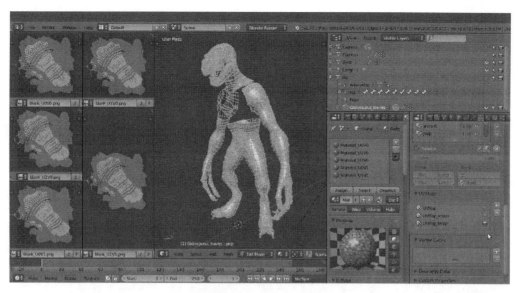

The new UVMap_temp coordinates layer

5. Out of **Edit Mode**, go to the **Render** window and then go to the **Bake** subpanel (usually at the bottom of the panel). If necessary, click on the **Bake Mode** slot to select **Textures**, then set the **Margin** value to **8** or higher; and check the **Clear** item flag. Be sure to have the **Gidiosaurus** object still selected and press the **Bake** button.

After a while, the baked scales textures appear on the **5** PNG images, baked according to the **UV** islands of the **5** tiles of the **UVMap** layer:

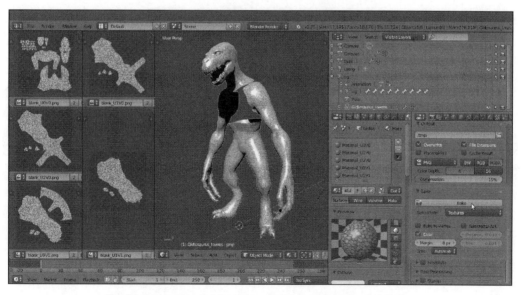

The 5 baked images and the Bake subpanel under the Render window

6. Click on the **Image** item on the **UV/Image Editor** toolbar and from the pop-up menu, select the **Save All Images** item or if you want to preserve your blank images (we are going to use them again later), just save each image at a time (**Save As Image** item or *F3* key) with the names `baked_U0V0.png`, `baked_U1V0.png`, and so on:

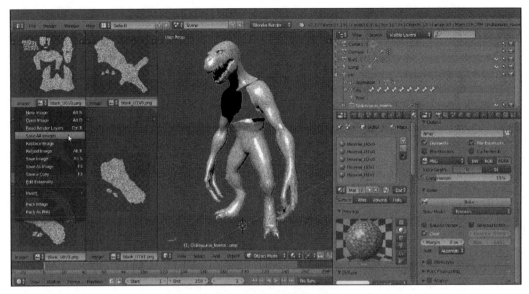

Saving the baked image maps

Opening the `texture_making` folder on your desktop, you will now find the baked textures:

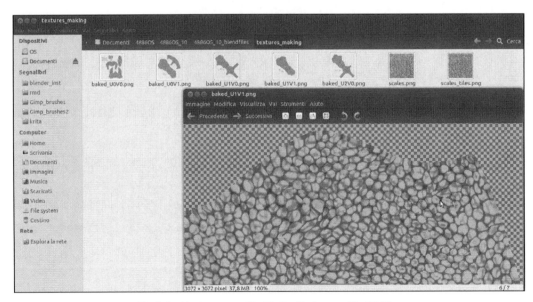

The baked textures saved inside the "texture_making" folder

As you can see in the information bar at the bottom of the **GNOME** image viewer (I'm working in **Linux Ubuntu**), each image saved from Blender is **37.8** megabytes.

The large size of the images can of course be reduced (a lot) by opening them in **Gimp** (or any other 2D application) and re-saving.

How it works...

All the UV islands have been moved to the default **U0V0** tile space, which is the only one where the baking happens, but because each image is associated with a different part of the mesh, each image is correctly baked with the right islands and textures.

In fact, inside Blender, and in our case, the location of each tile in the UV space doesn't actually matter; we made a new UV coordinates layer and kept the old one just in case the model should be exported to a different 3D application.

To move the islands exactly by the correct number of pixels, we enabled the **Normalized** item in the **Display** subpanel of the image editor *N* sidepanel to display the UV coordinates from **0.0** to **1.0**, rather than in pixels. Anyway, without the **Normalized** item enabled, it would have been enough to move the islands by **3072** pixels, that is, the width (or/and height) in pixels of the assigned blank image.

There's more...

As with any other software, Blender is not free from bugs; particularly, the baking section seems to have an annoying bug, which is very difficult to fix because it happens very rarely and randomly, so that it cannot easily be reproduced and consequently submitted to the Blender bug tracker (`https://developer.blender.org/maniphest/project/2/type/Bug/`).

It's difficult to understand the reason for this, but sometimes the software refuses to do the baking, claiming that *No objects or images (are) found to bake to* (the message appears on the top right main header and in the **Terminal** panel as well); in our case, this seems to happen when you switch the *active for rendering* UV coordinates layers.

If this happens, one thing you can do is check that all the images assigned in the **UV/Image Editor** windows to the different materials under one UV layer, also appear correctly assigned under the other UV layer (it shouldn't make a difference, but who knows), eventually re-assigning them one at a time.

If the baking still fails, there is a simple workaround; switch to the **UVMap** coordinates layer instead, rather than the **UVMap_temp** one, and just move the islands to the default **U0V0** space and bake them *one at a time*. To do this, first bake the islands of the **U0V0** tile space and save the image, then move the islands of the **U1V0** tile space to the **U0V0** tile space, bake and save as a different image, and so on with the islands of all the tiles.

Painting to fix the seams and to modify the baked scales image maps

In the previous recipe, we baked the *randomly* tiled scales image map on the **5** tiles of the **UVMap** coordinates layer. This was necessary for the next step to be able to fix seams and modify certain areas of the baked scales images through the **Paint Tool**.

In order to paint in real time on both the model and on all the images assigned to the **5** different UV tiles, and at the same time, once again we need to first prepare the file. To be more precise, we must assign **5** different materials to the mesh, one for each tile and each one with the appropriate image texture.

Getting ready

Start Blender and re-open the `Gidiosaurus_baking_scales_01.blend` file; save the file as `Gidiosaurus_baking_scales_02.blend`.

1. Minimize the image editor windows on the left as much as possible, then also minimize the **Outliner**, the **Material**, and the **Texture** windows on the right to make room for the 3D viewport.

2. Click on the **Viewport** Shading button in the 3D viewport toolbar and switch the shading mode from **Material** to **Solid**, then press the *T* key to call the **Tool Shelf**. Then switch from **Object Mode** to **Texture Paint** mode by clicking on the mode button in the toolbar:

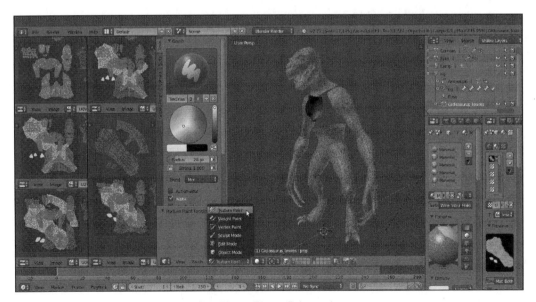

Switching to Texture Paint mode

3. Click on the **Options** tab inside the **Tool Shelf** and under the **Project Paint** subpanel, enable the **Occlude**, **Null**, and **Normal** items:

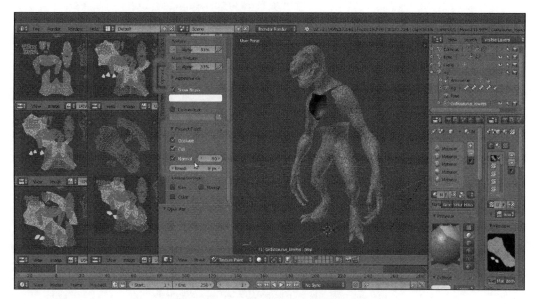

Items to be enabled under the Options tab

4. Click on the **Tools** tab inside the **Tool Shelf** to go back to the **Brush** subpanel options.

How to do it...

At this point, we are ready to start to paint both directly on the model in the 3D viewport or also in the **UV/Image Editor** windows (just for all eventualities, I suggest you make a copy of the baked scales images before starting to paint):

1. Zoom in on a part of the **Gidiosaurus** object in the 3D viewport, for example, the **head**.

2. Put the **mouse cursor** on a bright value of the scales image on the model and press the S key to sample it, then go near the color selector in the **Brush** subpanel under the **Tool Shelf** to the left and click on the *Toggle foreground and background brush colors* button (the one with the two opposing arrows) to switch the active color. Otherwise, simply press the X key, put the mouse cursor on a dark area, and press S again to sample it as the opposite color.

3. Scroll down and click on the **New** button (*Add new palette*) at the bottom of the **Brush** subpanel; **+** and **−** icon buttons will have appeared above the color switcher. Click on the **+** icon button to add the active color to the palette, then switch the colors and click on the **+** button again to add a new color to the palette.

4. Set the brush's **Radius** value to **6** and **Strength** value to **1.000**, and if you are using a **graphic tablet**, be sure to have the **2** *tablet pressure sensitivity* buttons at the sides of the previous items enabled. Change the default **Palette** name in **Scales**.

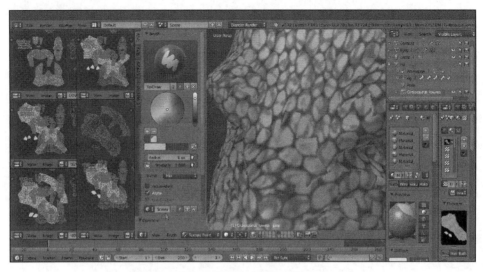

Setting a palette and the brush strength and radius

5. Simply start to paint on the model, re-drawing the scales where there are seams by flipping the color as you need to, by pressing the *X* key and painting the dark folds and the light scales. The two colors we sampled, used with the pressure sensitivity enabled, should be enough, but feel free to sample new ones and add it to the palette as you go on:

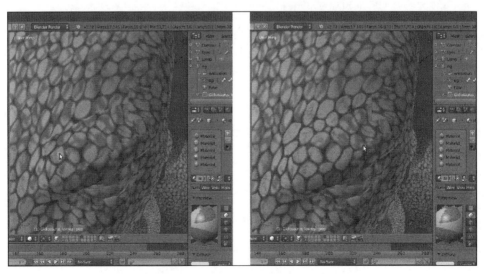

Painting on the model to fix the image texture seams

6. From time to time, click on the **Slots** tab in the **Tool Shelf** and click on the **Save All Images** button.

7. Do most of the fixing you can, across the entire **Gidiosaurus** body, keeping in mind that it's quite useless to spend time fixing seams in areas that will later be covered by the **Armor** (for example, the top of the head).

8. When you are done, *be sure to have saved all the edited images* as explained in step 6 (but you can also do it one image at a time through the **Image | Save Image** item in each editor window toolbar or by pressing the *Alt + S* shortcut).

9. Now, be sure to have the Material_U0V0 slot selected as active in the **Material** window and go to the **Texture** window; left-click on the empty slot right under the **U0V0** one and then click on the **New** button to add a new image texture.

10. Scroll down to the **Image** subpanel and click on the **New** button. In the **New Image** pop-up panel, write added_scales_U0V0 in the **Name** slot, then set the **Width** and **Height** values to **3072** and the **Alpha** (**A**) value to **0.000** (basically add a new blank and background transparent image as shown in step 5 of the *How to do it...* section of the *Preparing the model to use the UDIM UV tiles* recipe):

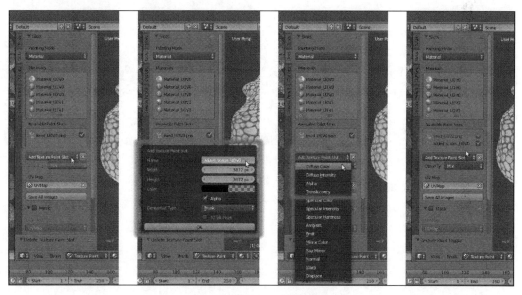

Adding a new texture paint slot layer

11. Go to the **Shading** subpanel of the **Material** window and enable the **Shadeless** item for the Material_U0V0 slot. Then go to the 3D viewport toolbar and change **Viewport Shading** from **Solid** to **Material**.

12. If not selected already, click on the **Slots** tab in the **Tool Shelf** panel and select the `added_scales_U0V0` item that appears under the `U0V0.png` once inside the **Available Paint Slots** window.

13. Directly in the 3D view, start to paint new scales on the **eyebrows** to replace the randomly distributed ones; use the light color of the palette to conceal the old scales on the first layer, and the dark color to draw the new ones. Try to build a consistent pattern, also using photos of real reptiles as references. When you are done, save the image in the `texture_making` folder:

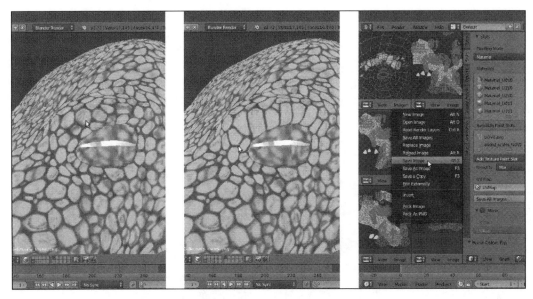

Painting new scales on the eyebrow

14. Draw new scales around the **nostrils** and the **rim** of the **mouth**:

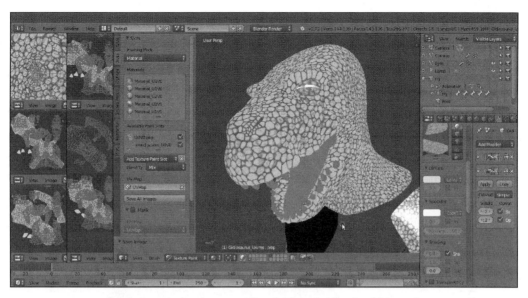

Painting new scales also around the nostrils and at the rim of the mouth

The Blender **Paint Tool** also has other handy brushes; a particularly useful one is the **Smear** brush, which smudges the borders or any blotch in the scales.

To access the brushes, just click on the big window in the **Brush** subpanel under the **Tool Shelf** and click on the chosen one to select it:

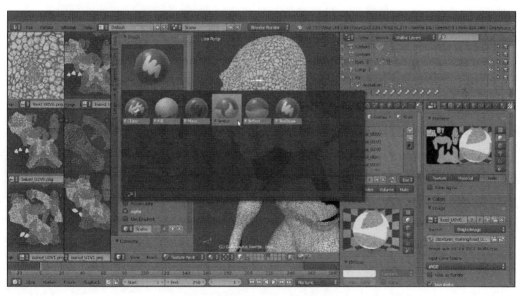

The brushes selection pop-up menu

Remember to always save the painted images before closing Blender, otherwise you'll lose them.

Also remember that if you have more than one texture layer to save, it's necessary to load each one of them into an **UV/Image Editor** window. This is actually very quick and easy, just select each layer in the **Available Paint Slots** window (in the **Slots** subpanel under the **Slots** tab) to make it appear in the image editor window and save it through the **Image | Save As Image** menu in the editor toolbar.

Once saved the first time, it's possible to re-save all of them in one single click, through the **Save All Images** items, both in the tab, as well as in the toolbar menu.

15. Save the file as `Gidiosaurus_painting_scales_fix.blend`.

 In the textures and blend files provided with this cookbook, you'll find textures fixed only in the **head** area; I leave the task of finishing the fixing and drawing of new scales on the rest of the body (for example, bigger scales can be added to the upper side of the hand **fingers**, **feet**, **shoulders**, and so on) to you.

How it works...

The new Blender **2.73** texture paint layering feature works simply by adding a new texture slot to the material, and automatically setting it as required, by the type of texture you selected in the **Add Texture Paint Slot**; in fact, by going to the **Texture** window, it is possible to see the added new texture slot and also, if necessary, to change the settings:

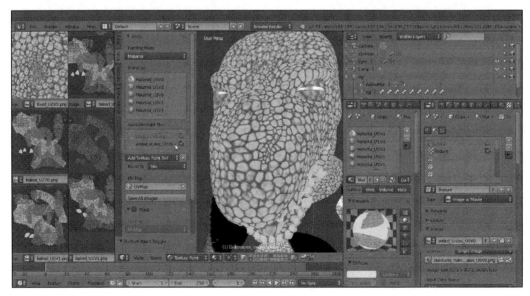

The added texture paint slot also appearing as a texture slot in the Texture window

Nonetheless, it is a great addition to Blender that can simplify the texture painting workflow a lot.

There's more...

To bake the added scales as a single image with the background scales images, perform the following steps:

1. Enter **Edit Mode** and click on the **Select** button for `Material_U0V0` to select the vertices assigned to that tile.

2. Go to the top left **UV/Image Editor** window and press *Alt + N* to call the **New Image** pop-up menu; add a new blank image of **3072** x **3072** pixels named `baked_scales_U0V0`, and save it inside the `textures_making` folder.

3. Go out of **Edit Mode** and if it's the case, click on the double arrows icon to the left side of the image name datablock to re-assign the just-created `Untitled` image.

4. Repeat for the other four materials, naming the new images according to the tile and saving them inside the `texture_making` folder as well.

5. Go to the **UV Maps** subpanel under the **Object Data** window to make the **UVMap_temp** coordinates layer active.

6. Go to the **Render** window, and be sure that the **Bake Mode** under the **Bake** subpanel is set to **Textures**, then click on the **Bake** button.

7. After the baking is done, click on the **Image** item in the toolbar of one of the image editors and select the **Save All Images** item.

Not necessarily everything has to be fixed by painting in Blender; for example, it would be enough to fix the scales on only the half of the **head**, export the painted image texture, and open it in **Gimp** (or any other 2D image editing software):

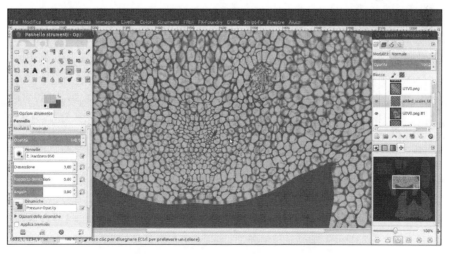

The scales "U0V0.png" image map and the "added_scales_U0V0.png" layer in Gimp

Then, by duplicating the layer and mirroring it, plus a little bit of painting to adjust the seams, it's really simple to obtain the missing half of the new scales texture:

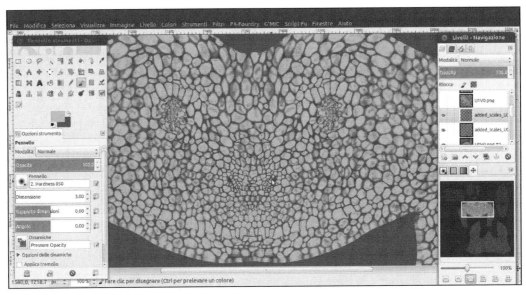

The duplicated and mirrored "added_scales_UOVO.png" layer in Gimp

Of course, if you want to fix every side and part by hand-painting on the model in Blender to obtain a more natural looking result, no one is going to stop you!

See also

▶ http://wiki.blender.org/index.php/Doc:2.6/Manual/Textures/ Painting

▶ http://wiki.blender.org/index.php/Dev:Ref/Release_Notes/2.72/ Painting

▶ http://docs.gimp.org/en/gimp-tutorial-quickie-flip.html

Painting the color maps in Blender Internal

After having obtained the scales textures, we must now paint the diffuse color of the **Gidiosaurus** character.

Getting ready

Start Blender and open the `Gidiosaurus_baking_scales.blend` file:

1. Go to the main **Properties** panel and be sure to have the **UVMap** coordinates layer selected and active, in the **UV Maps** subpanel under the **Object Data** window.

2. Go to the **Material** window and select the `Material_U0V0` slot, then go to the **Texture** window and be sure to have the **scales_tiles** texture slot selected; left-click on the **X** icon button to the right side of the name datablock to unlink it (*Shift* + left-click to remove it from the file):

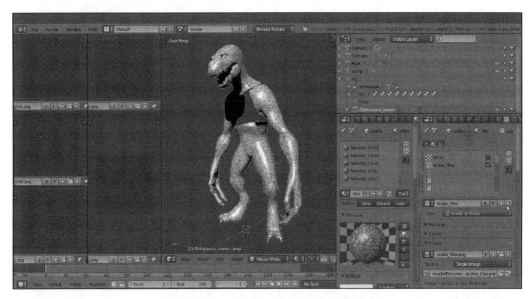

Unlinking the scales_tiles texture slot datablock

3. Select and enable (by clicking on the checkbox to the right) the **U0V0** texture slot. Repeat the procedure at steps 2 and 3 for all **5** materials.

   I'll take for granted that you have preserved your blank images and that they are the ones loaded into the current file; otherwise, substitute them with new blank images (you have to do this both in the **Texture** window as well as in the **UV/Image Editor** windows) by following steps 5 and 7 of the *Preparing the model to use the UDIM UV tiles* recipe in this chapter.

4. Minimize the image editor windows to the left and the **Material** and **Texture** panels to the right as much as possible, then click on the mode button (*Sets the object interaction mode*) on the toolbar to go into **Texture Paint** mode. Press *T* with the mouse pointer over the 3D view to call the **Tool Shelf** and click on the **Viewport Shading** button on the toolbar to switch to **Solid** mode:

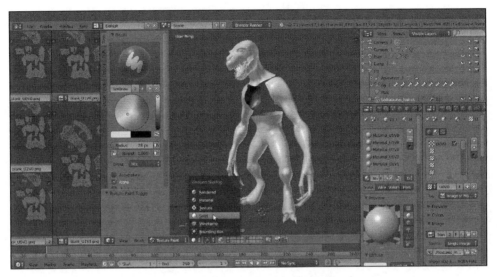

Switching to Solid viewport shading mode

5. Just to verify that everything works correctly, select a black color (or any other one) in the color wheel under the **Brush** subpanel and trace a continuous stroke in the 3D viewport that envelopes all the **Gidiosaurus** body parts:

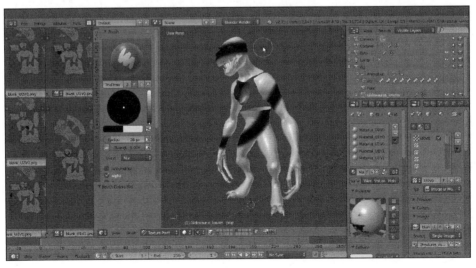

Testing that everything works correctly with a single stroke on the mesh

By enlarging the **UV/Image Editor** windows, you will see that after the stroke, each image has been updated with the corresponding painting (pay no attention to the over-imposed and *repeated for each window* UV islands):

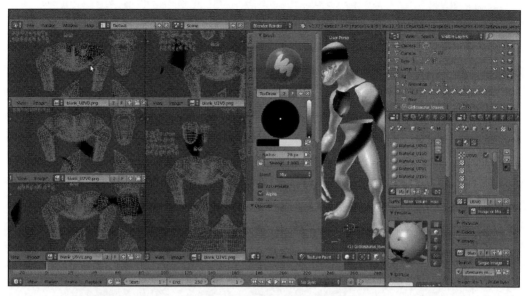

The test stroke correctly visible inside each one of the UV/Image Editor windows

6. Rearrange the image editor windows, then press *Ctrl + Z* to undo the stroke and save the file as `Gidiosaurus_painting_BI.blend`.

How to do it...

We are now ready to paint the basic color for the **Gidiosaurus** character. But first, one more little thing:

1. Select the **Gidiosaurus** object and enter **Edit Mode**; select the vertices of all the **teeth** and all the **talons**, then assign a new vertex group renamed **enamel**; press *Ctrl + I* to invert the selection and go out of **Edit Mode**.

2. Now, start by selecting a medium dark greenish color (**R 0.349, G 0.510, B 0.435**) in the color wheel under the **Brush** subpanel. Scroll down and go to the bottom of the subpanel and click on the **New** button to create a new palette, then click on the **+** icon button (**Add Swatch**) above the **Foreground Color** slot (the left one) to add the color to the palette. Rename the default **Palette** name as `Gidiosaurus_colors`.

3. In the 3D viewport toolbar, click on the *Face selection masking for painting* button to enable the masking tool; now it's possible to paint only on the part of the mesh that has selected vertices in **Edit Mode**, so in this case we want to paint only on the skin, leaving the teeth and the talons blank.

4. Click on the **Brush** window and select the **Fill** brush; if necessary, click on the greenish color box added to the palette (called **Swatch**) to load it as the **foreground color** (note that with the **Fill** brush, the background color swatch disappears and the foreground color swatch becomes the only one available). Set the **Strength** value to **1.000** and click on the **Gidiosaurus** object in the 3D viewport.

   After a while, all the *paintable* parts of the mesh are filled with the active color (and therefore also the textures in the **UV/Image Editor** windows; there are weird straight lines, probably a bug, but not a problem in this case because they don't show on the mesh and we can fill in the texture's backgrounds later anyway). If any tiny part is left out, just click on one of the parts again to fill it:

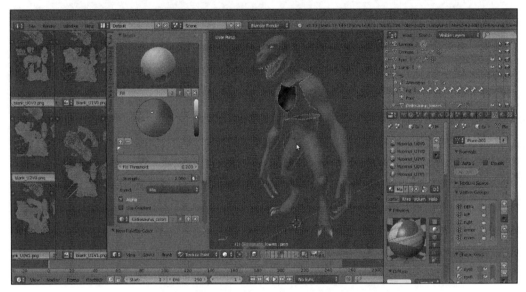

The Fill brush and the Mask button in the 3D view toolbar

5. Now select the **TexDraw** brush and a darker and more saturated green color (**R 0.129, G 0.275, B 0.125**) as the foreground color, and add it to the palette.

6. Under the **Tool Shelf**, go to the **Options** tab and be sure to have the **Occlude, Cull** and **Normal** items disabled still; then go into the **Ortho Side** view.

7. Now it's time to use a tablet, if you have one; enable both the tablet pressure sensitivity buttons to the side of the **Radius** and **Strength** items and start to shade the **Gidiosaurus** body on the **head, shoulders, arms**, and **legs**:

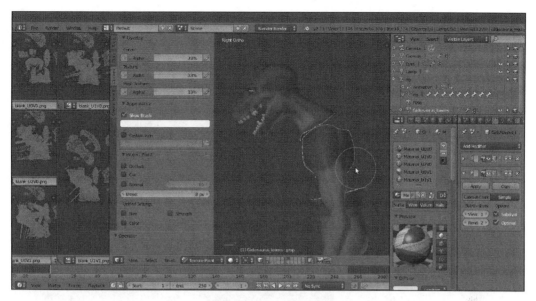

Painting colors on the model

8. Select a brownish color (**R 0.204**, **G 0.188**, **B 0.133**) and add it to the palette; disable the tablet pressure sensitivity for **Radius** and lower the **Strength** to **0.500**. Go into the **Front** view, maximize the 3D viewport (mouse pointer in the window and press _Ctrl_ + Up Arrow), and keep on adding shades to the **hands**, **feet**, and **legs**:

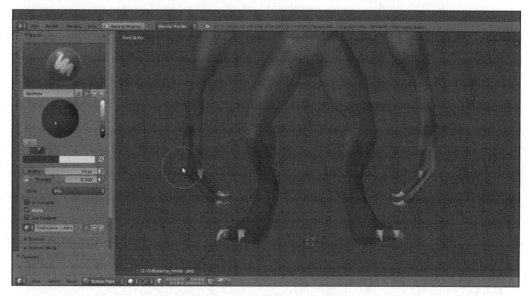

Shading the character's limbs with darker hues

9. Increase the **Radius** value to **100** (using the slider or by pressing the *F* key and moving the mouse pointer in the 3D view) and painting on the **head** and the **shoulders**:

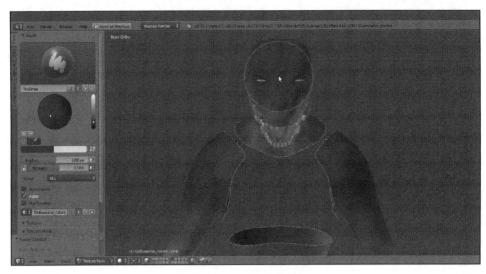

Shading the head and shoulders

10. If, for any reason, it becomes difficult to paint directly on the model through the 3D viewport, you can maximize the involved **UV/Image Editor** window (mouse pointer in the window and press *Ctrl* + Up Arrow), click on the **Mode** button (*Editing context being displayed*) in the toolbar (which by default shows **View**), and switch it to **Paint**. Press *T* to call the **Tool Shelf** and go on with the painting, smudging, or whatever, directly on the texture image:

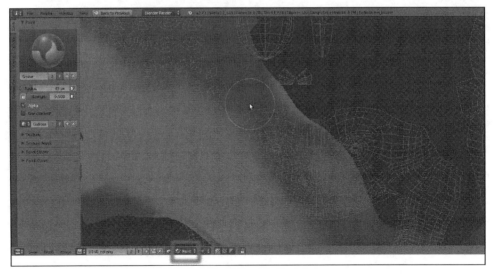

Painting directly on the image map in the UV/Image Editor window

For example, this is the way I painted the inside of the **mouth** and the **tongue**, then went back to the 3D viewport to smudge and soften the joining line of the pink tissue with the green skin at the borders:

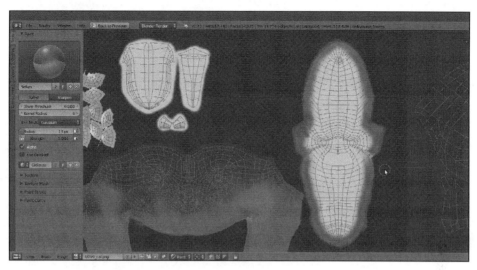

Working on the inside of the mouth in the UV/Image Editor window

I'm not going to show you every step in this process, but basically this is the procedure I used to paint the diffuse coloration for the character. I also added lighter and warmer colors for the face's areas close to the **mouth** and more bluish and colder hues to de-saturate the brownish **hands** and **feet**, and then inverting the **enamel** vertex group to paint in **Edit Mode**, through the use of the **Mask** tool, the **teeth** and **talons** as well:

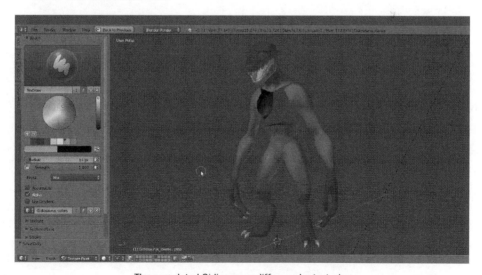

The completed Gidiosaurus diffuse color texturing

To have a look at the final **Gidiosaurus_colors** palette, open the `Gidiosaurus_painting_BI_02.blend` file provided.

11. When you are done, go to the top left **UV/Image Editor** window, **blank_UOVO**, and click on the **Image** item in the toolbar. Save the image texture in the `textures_making` folder as `UOVO_col.png`, and do the same with the other **4** image textures.

12. To keep the palette, save the file.

How it works...

There is not that much to explain about this recipe, except I just want to highlight the fact that we disabled the **Occlude**, **Cull**, and **Normal** items in the **Options** tab under the **Tool Shelf**. This is so we were able to paint (from the **Side** view) on both sides of the model at the same time; in fact, with these settings disabled, the mesh is *not occluding itself*. It seems that all three items must be disabled for this to work.

Instead, to smear and/or soften the texture on some parts, for example, the inside of the **mouth**, we had to re-enable them, in order to prevent our mouth-painting from accidentally overwriting our skin-painting.

Remember, the **Occlude**, **Cull**, and **Normal** items should always be enabled if you want to paint only on the model's surface right under your brush. You can disable them to paint on the front/outer and the back/inside of the mesh at the same time.

See also

▶ http://www.cgmasters.net/free-tutorials/layered-painting-in-blender-2-72/

▶ http://blender.stackexchange.com/tags/texture-painting

Painting the color maps in Cycles

There are no differences in painting in **Blender Internal** or in **Cycles**, because the **Paint Tool** is exactly the same; the only difference is in the preparation of the materials.

In this recipe, we are not going to repeat the procedure already explained in the previous one; we'll just set up the file for the painting and test whether it's possible to paint in real time on all **5** image textures at the same time, as it is in **Blender Internal** (*spoiler:* it is).

Let's start with the `Gidiosaurus_painting_BI.blend` file; in that file, we already have the **UV/Image Editor** windows set and the **5** materials assigned to the **5** different **UDIM** tiles and parts of the mesh.

In case you want to start with a brand new file, here you need to repeat the steps of the *Preparing the model to use the UDIM UV tiles* recipe in this chapter. Then, continue with the following:

1. Be sure you're in **Object Mode**.

2. Go to the main top header and click on the *Engine to use for rendering* button; switch from **Blender Render** to **Cycles Render**.

3. Split the 3D view into two horizontal rows and change the top one into a **Node Editor** window; press the *N* key to get rid of the **Properties** sidepanel.

4. In the **Material** window, select the **Material_UOVO** slot; click on the **Use Nodes** button or select the **Use Nodes** checkbox in the **Node Editor** toolbar:

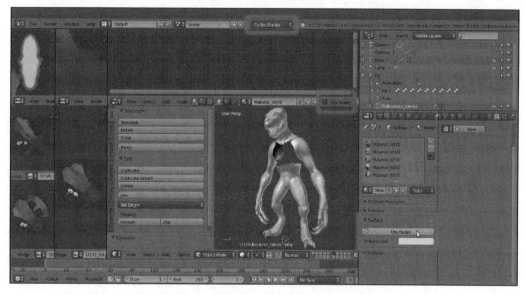

Enabling the nodes for the materials under Cycles

5. Put the mouse pointer inside the **Node Editor** window and add an **Image Texture** node (press the *Shift + A* keys and in the pop-up menu, go to the **Texture** item to select **Image Texture**). Connect its **Color** output to the **Color** input socket of the **Diffuse BSDF** node.

   At this point, if we haven't already painted the color textures in **Blender Internal**, we should load the `blank_U0V0.png` image in the **Image Texture** node and then do the same for the other **4** materials.

   Instead, because we already have the color textures, let's load them in the **Cycles** materials. To see whether everything works as it should, we'll paint on them through the 3D viewport.

6. Click on the double arrows to the side of the **Open** button in the **Image Texture** node and select the **U0V0_col.png** item from the pop-up menu (remember that the **5** color textures are already loaded inside the blend file):

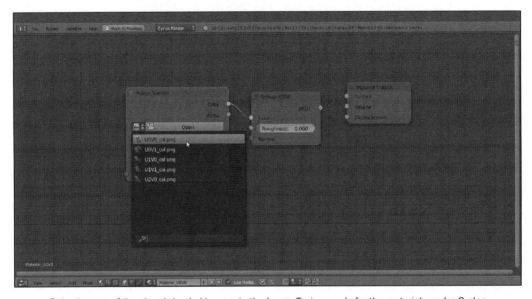

Selecting one of the already loaded images in the Image Texture node for the materials under Cycles

7. Repeat step 4 to step 6 for the other **4** materials.

How to do it...

Now, the steps are really simple:

1. Go to the **Brush** subpanel and switch the foreground color with the background black color.

2. Trace in the 3D viewport, a continuous stroke enveloping all the **Gidiosaurus** body parts:

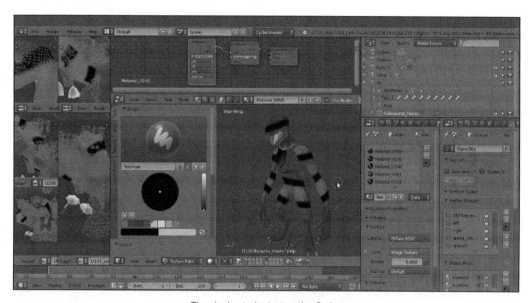

The single stroke test under Cycles

This is the proof that it works exactly as in **Blender Internal**.

3. Press _Ctrl + Z_ to undo the stroke and save the file as `Gidiosaurus_painting_ Cycles.blend`.

11
Refining the Textures

In this chapter, we will cover the following recipes:

- ▸ Sculpting more details on the high resolution mesh
- ▸ Baking the normals of the sculpted mesh on the low resolution one
- ▸ The Armor textures
- ▸ Adding a dirty Vertex Colors layer and baking it to an image texture
- ▸ The Quick Edit tool

Introduction

In *Chapter 10, Creating the Textures*, we have prepared the **color** and **bump** texture images for the **Gidiosaurus** skin. In this chapter, we'll see the process for creating some additional (but equally important, nonetheless) textures, both for the character and the iron **Armor**.

Sculpting more details on the high resolution mesh

In *Chapter 2, Sculpting the Character's Base Mesh*, we sculpted the **Gidiosaurus** character's features, obtaining a high resolution mesh that we re-topologized in the following *Chapter 4, Re-topology of the High Resolution Sculpted Character's Mesh*, to have a low resolution mesh for easy rigging and texturing.

Because in the following recipe (*Baking the normals of the sculpted mesh on the low resolution one*) we are going to bake the normals of the sculpted mesh on the low resolution one, we should now add as much detailing and finishing to the sculpted model.

I'm not going to explain every step in detail, here, because the procedure is the same as already seen in the *Chapter 2, Sculpting the Character's Base Mesh*, so just a quick tour to show what I've done should be fine.

Getting ready

Let's start by preparing the file:

1. Start Blender and load the `Gidiosaurus_painting_BI.blend` file; if necessary, go out of **Texture Paint** mode back to **Object Mode** and save the file as `Gidiosaurus_details_sculpt.blend`.

2. Collapse all the **UV/Image Editor** windows on the left of the screen and then join them with the 3D viewport (put the mouse pointer on the edge of one of the two windows; as it changes into a two opposite arrows pointer, right-click and in the **Area Options** pop-up menu, left-select the **Join Areas** item; then, move the mouse pointer towards the window to be eliminated and left-click to join them).

3. Join the **Material** and **Texture** windows in the main **Properties** panel, switch to the **Object Data** window, and enlarge the 3D viewport as much as possible.

4. Click on the **File** item in the main top header and then select the **Append** item (or else, directly press the *Shift + F1* keys); navigate to the `Gidiosaurus_retopology_02.blend` file, click on it, and then click on the **Object** item (folder) to select the **Gidiosaurus** item.

5. Click on the **Append from Library** button on the top-right of the screen and then go to the **Outliner** window to click on the **eye** and the **arrow** icon buttons (*Restrict view-port visibility* and *Restrict view-port selection*) and enable both the object visibility and selection in the 3D viewport.

6. Move the appended high resolution **Gidiosaurus** mesh to the **14th** scene layer (*M* key):

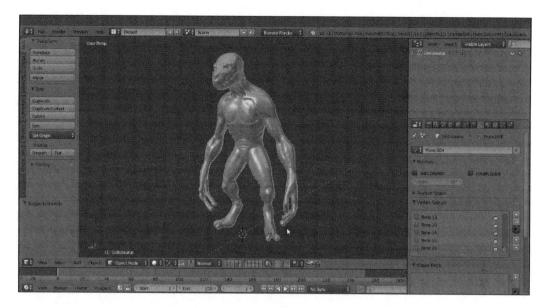

The appended, sculpted Gidiosaurus mesh

7. Press *N* to call the **Properties** sidepanel and in the **Display** subpanel, enable the **Only Render** item; go down to the **Shading** subpanel, enable the **Matcap** item, and then select your favorite matcap type (mine is always the brick red colored **Zbrush**-like).

8. Enable the **12th** scene layer to show the **Eyes**; however, in the **Outliner**, just to be sure, disable the selection arrow icon button.

9. Press *N* again to hide the **Properties** sidepanel and then switch to **Sculpt Mode** and save the file.

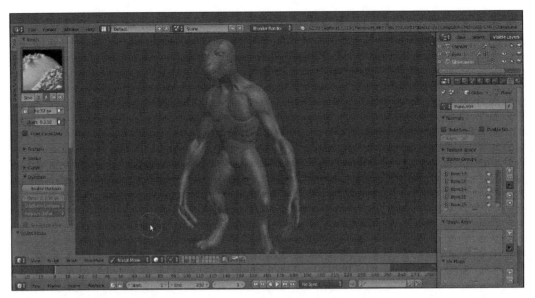

The Gidiosaurus object ready for the new sculpting session

How to do it...

We are now ready to sculpt again on the **Gidiosaurus** mesh; first, let's do some more settings pertinent to the sculpt tools:

1. Go to the **Dyntopo** subpanel under the **Tool Shelf** and click on the **Enable Dyntopo** button; set **Detail Size** to **1.60** px and check the **Smooth Shading** box.

2. Go down to the **Symmetry / Lock** subpanel to be sure that **Mirror** is enabled for the x axis.

3. Click on the **Options** tab and go to the **Options** subpanel to enable the **Fast Navigate** item (the **Threaded Sculpt** item should be already enabled by default).

4. Go back to the **Tools** tab and click on the **Brush** windows; select the **Crease** brush (press the *Shift + C* or *5* keys), zoom to the **Gidiosaurus's head**, and start to add **expression folds**:

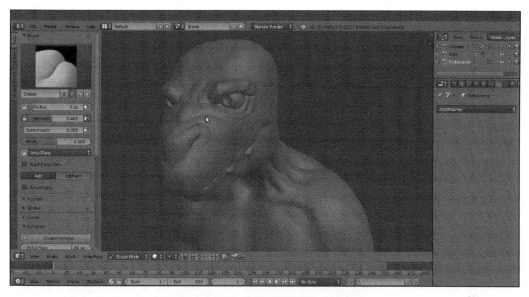

Adding expression folds with the Crease brush

5. Move to the **throat**, in the **Tool Shelf** panel, switch the effect of the brush from **Subtract** to **Add** through the buttons at the bottom of the **Brush** subpanel (or simply by pressing the *Ctrl* key while sculpting), and add veins to the area:

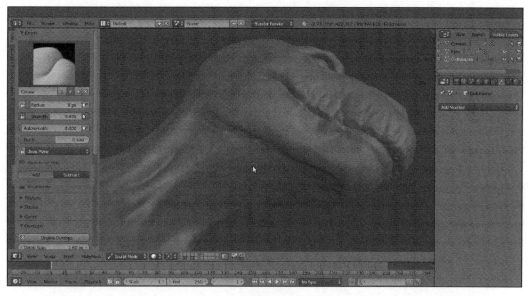

Adding veins under the jaw and on the neck by using the Crease brush again, but with inverted effect

6. By using the same technique, add **veins** also on the **shoulders** and the **biceps**; then, select the **Polish** brush (*Shift + 4*) and refine the **elbow** a bit:

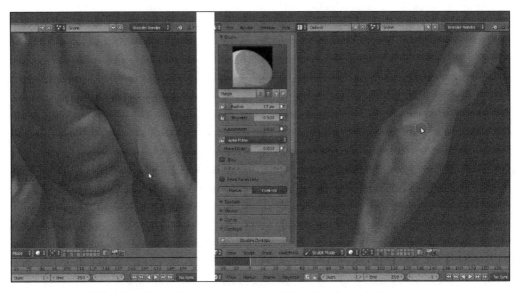

Adding the veins on the arm muscles and polishing the elbow's bulging muscle

7. By using the **Clay** brush (*C* or *3* keys) and also the **Crease** (*Shift + C* or *5* keys) and **Pinch** (*P* or *Shift + 3*) brushes, refine the shape and the folds of the **palm** and add details to the back of the **fingers**. The **Clay** brush can be used in **Subtract** mode too, to carve shapes:

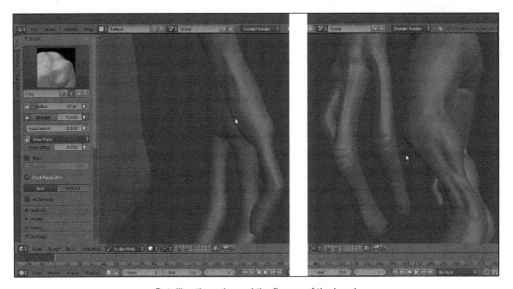

Detailing the palm and the fingers of the hand

8. Similarly, add details and refine the back of the **foot** and the **sole**:

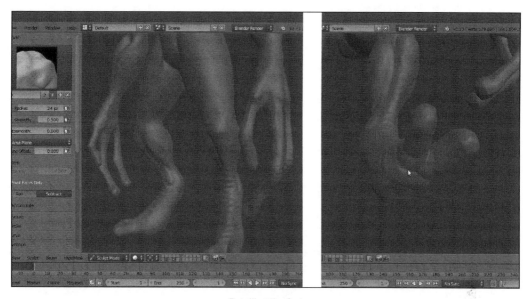

Detailing the feet

9. Use the **Smooth** brush (*S* or *Shift* + *7* keys) to gently soften the character's features; when you are done, save the file.

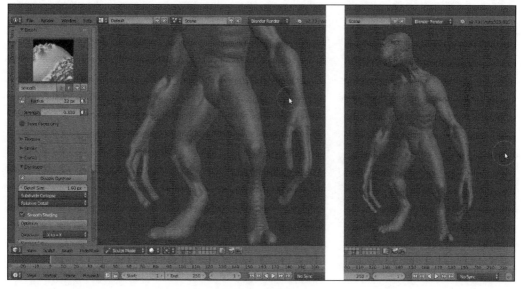

Smoothing the added features

Now, as we have detailed the body of the **Gidiosaurus**, it would be a good idea to refine the **Armor** also.

10. Switch to the **13th** scene layer; select the **Armor** object and go to the **Shape Keys** subpanel under the **Object Data** window.

11. Select the **Basis** shape key and then click on the – icon button to delete it (this leaves the only remaining shape key, **Armor_fix**, as the base one, so permanently applying the morph to the mesh); then, also select the **Armor_fix** shape key and delete it.

12. Repeat the previous steps for the **rivets** and the **Armor_decorations** objects as well.

13. Through the **Outliner** window, *Shift*-select the **rivets, Armor_decorations**, and **Armor** objects; then, press *Ctrl + J* to join them as a single object.

14. Go to the **Vertex Groups** subpanel and add a new vertex group; rename it as **shrinkwrap**.

15. Enter **Edit Mode** and select the vertices on the outside of the **armor body plates**, leaving the **inside faces** of the **plates**, the **bottom** of the **spaulders**, the **decorations**, the **rivets**, and the **tiers**, unselected; if necessary, use the **seams** to help you to divide the outer from the inner parts of the mesh. Click on the **Assign** button at the bottom of the **Vertex Groups** subpanel:

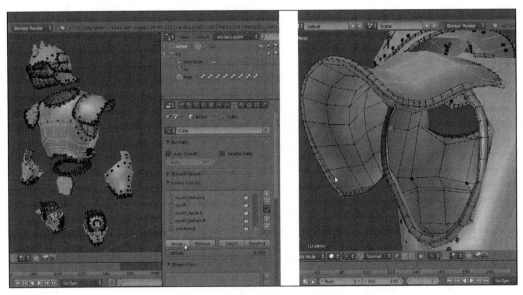

Selecting the outer parts of the Armor

16. Split the 3D view into two windows and change the left one into a **UV/Image Editor** window.

17. Go to the **UV Maps** subpanel under the **Object Data** window, click on the **+** icon button to add a new UV coordinates layer, and rename it as **UVMap_norm**. Then, click on the camera icon on the right-hand side of the name to make it the active UV layer.

18. Put the mouse pointer in the 3D viewport and press *U*; in the **UV Mapping** pop-up menu, select the **Smart UV Project** item; in the pop-up panel, click on the **Island Margin** value (default = **0.00**) and set it to **0.001**. Leave the other values as they are and click on the big **OK** button at the bottom of the panel.

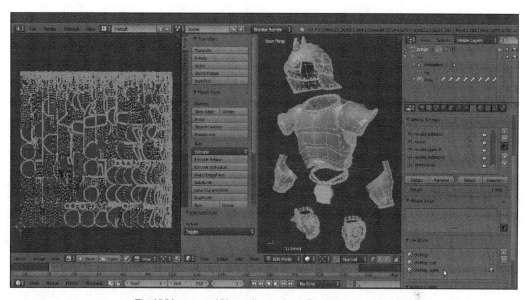

The UVMap_norm UV coordinates layer for the Armor object

19. Go out of **Edit Mode** and minimize the **UV/Image Editor** window as much as possible; press *Shift + D* to duplicate the **Armor** object and move the duplicated one to the **3rd** scene layer.

20. Enable the **3rd** scene layer; go to the **Object Modifiers** window and delete the **Armature** and the **Subdivision Surface** modifiers; in the **Outliner**, rename the new object (now **Armor.001**) as **Armor_detailing**.

21. Assign a **Multiresolution** modifier. Click on the **Subdivide** button until it reaches level **3**; then, check the **Optimal Display** item and go in **Sculpt Mode**. Using the same procedure as before, add scrapes, bumps, deformations, and so on, to the **armor** surface; add some kind of engraving also, for example, on the **groinguard**.

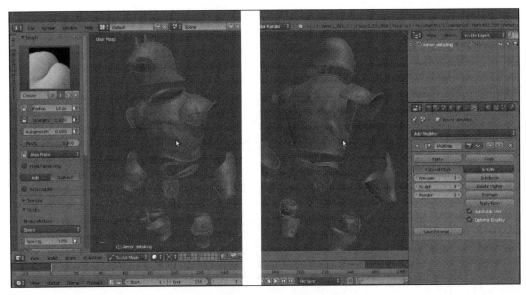

Sculpting the Armor_detailing object

22. Save the file.

Baking the normals of the sculpted mesh on the low resolution one

At this point, we can transfer all the details sculpted on our high resolution meshes (the **Gidiosaurus** and the **Armor** objects) to the low resolution assets; to do this, we have to **bake** these details as **normal maps**.

Getting ready

Continue from the previous `Gidiosaurus_details_sculpt.blend` file:

1. Split the 3D viewport into **two** windows and change the left one into a **UV/Image Editor** window.

2. Go to the **11th** scene layer and select the **Gidiosaurus_lowres** object; press the *Tab* key to enter **Edit Mode** and, if necessary, press *A* to select all the vertices.

3. Go to the **UV Maps** subpanel under the **Object Data** window, click on the **+** icon button to add a new UV coordinates layer, rename it as **UVMap_norm**, and click on the camera icon to make it the active UV layer.

4. Put the mouse pointer in the 3D viewport and press *U*. In the **UV Mapping** pop-up menu, select the **Smart UV Project** item; in the pop-up panel, click on the **Island Margin** value (default = **0.00**) and set it to **0.001**. Leave the other values as they are and click the big **OK** button at the bottom of the panel.

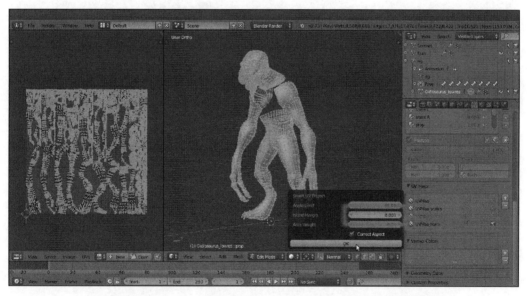

The UVMap_norm UV coordinates layer for the low resolution Gidiosaurus mesh

5. Deselect all the vertices (the *A* key again) and zoom to the **head**; *Shift*-select the vertices of all the parts that don't actually exist in the high resolution sculpted model such as the inside of the **mouth**, the **mouth inner rims**, the **tongue**, the **eyelids**, the inside of the **nostrils**, the **teeth**, and the **talons**:

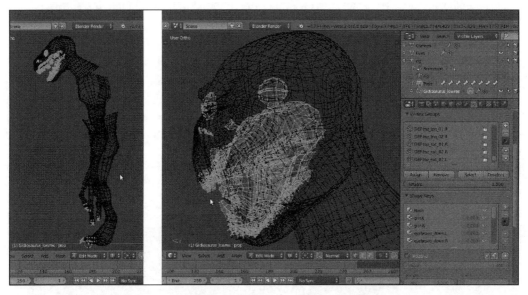

Selecting the low resolution mesh parts that don't have a counterpart in the high resolution sculpted mesh

6. Go to the **Vertex Groups** subpanel under the **Object Data** window and click on the **+** icon button to add a new vertex group; rename it as **shrinkwrap**.

7. Press *Ctrl + I* to invert the selection and then click on the **Assign** button below the vertex group list window in the **Vertex Groups** subpanel:

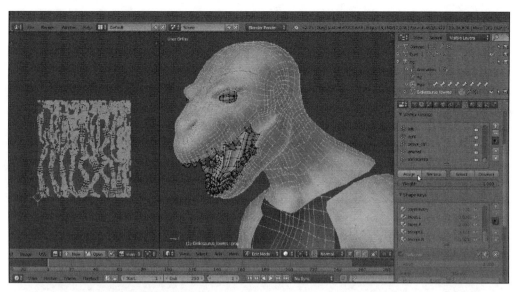

Assigning the inverted selection to the "shrinkwrap" vertex group

8. Go out of **Edit Mode** and press *Shift + D* to duplicate the **Gidiosaurus_lowres** object; move the duplicate to the **4th** scene layer and in the **Outliner** window, rename it as **Gidiosaurus_for_baking**.

9. In the **Outliner**, enable the 3D viewport visibility of the **rig**; select and move the **ctrl_mouth** bone upward to close the **Gidiosaurus's** mouth and then hide the **11th** scene layer.

10. Reselect the **Gidiosaurus_for_baking** object and go to the **Object Modifiers** window; click on the **Apply as Shape Key** button of the **Armature** modifier.

11. Go to the **Shape Keys** subpanel under the **Object Data** window to find a new shape key at the bottom of the list: **Armature**, with the value of **0.000**.

12. Rename the new shape key as **closed_mouth** and set the value to **1.000**:

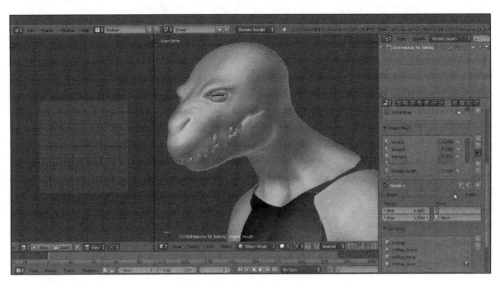

The closed_mouth shape key

13. Go to the **Object Modifiers** window and assign a **Shrinkwrap** modifier to the **Gidiosaurus_for_baking** object; as **Target**, select the **Gidiosaurs_detailing** object and then click on the **Vertex Group** slot to select the **shrinkwrap** vertex group.

In the following screenshot, you can see the effect of the **Shrinkwrap** modifier on the low resolution mesh with the **Subdivision Surface** modifier enabled also for the 3D viewport:

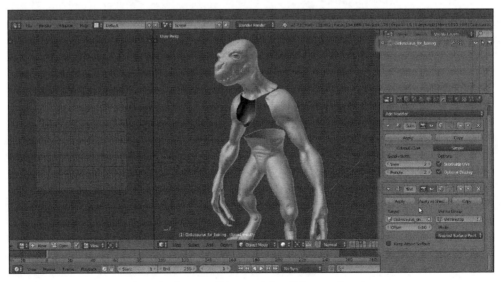

The "shrinkwrapped" low resolution Gidiosaurus mesh

After this quite *intensive* file preparation, let's go with the baking itself:

1. Enter **Edit Mode** and select all the mesh vertices; in the **UV/Image Editor** window, add a new **3072** x **3072** blank image and rename it as `norm`.

2. Go out of **Edit Mode**, enable the **14th** scene layer, select the **Gidiosaurus_detailing** object, and then *Shift*-select the **Gidiosaurus_for_baking** object.

3. Go to the **Render** window, scroll the panel down and, in the **Bake** subpanel, check the **Selected to Active** item. Set **Margin** to **8** pixels, the **Bake Mode** to **Normals**, and the **Normal Space** to **Tangent**; click on the **Bake** button to start the baking:

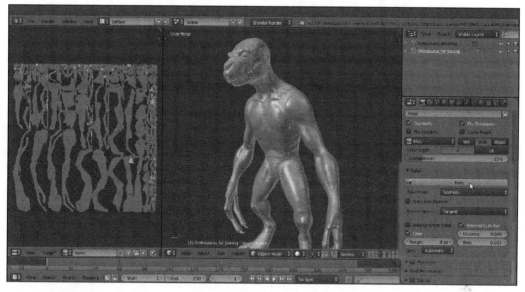

The baked normals' image map, the two overlapping and selected objects, and the Bake subpanel

4. Click on the **Image** item in the **UV/Image Editor** window toolbar to save the baked image as `norm.png` inside the `texture_making` folder.

How it works...

To close the **mouth** (to conform it to the sculpted mesh), we moved the control bone in the rig and then applied the **Armature** modifier as a **shape key**; be aware that a modifier cannot be applied to a mesh with shape keys (you get a warning message), so we had to use the **Apply as Shape Key** option or delete all the shape keys with drivers and redo them later. In this case, however, it wouldn't have been necessary to duplicate the **Gidiosaurus** low resolution mesh, but we did it anyway to keep things simpler and cleaner.

Right before the baking, a **Shrinkwrap** modifier has been assigned to the lowres **Gidiosaurus_for_baking** object, to conform its surface to the high resolution sculpted **Gidiosaurus_detailing** object and avoid any possible intersection between the two meshes (that would give ugly artifacts in the baked image); we used the **shrinkwrap** vertex group to keep the vertices that don't have a counterpart on the high resolution mesh (**teeth, eyelids, inner mouth,** and so on) out of the modifier influence.

As you can see in the following OpenGL screenshot, comparing the sculpted and the low res **Gidiosaurus** meshes, the result of the baked normals on the low resolution object is pretty good and effective:

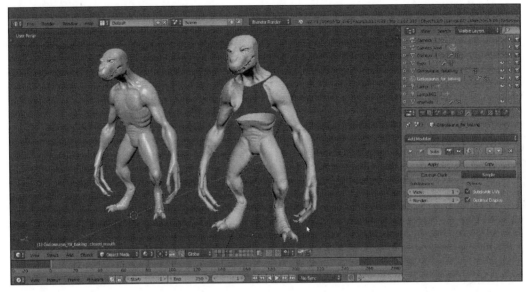

Comparison between the high resolution sculpted mesh and the low resolution object with the baked normal map

There's more...

As we reopen the **mouth** by lowering the **close_mouth** shape key value to **0.000** or also by simply assigning the baked normal map to the **Gidiosaurus_lowres** object, we see that something is wrong inside the **mouth** (and, actually, also on the **teeth** and **talons**): the normals have been calculated for those parts too, but they show wrong and weird artifacts because there were no counterparts to take the normals from in the sculpted high resolution mesh.

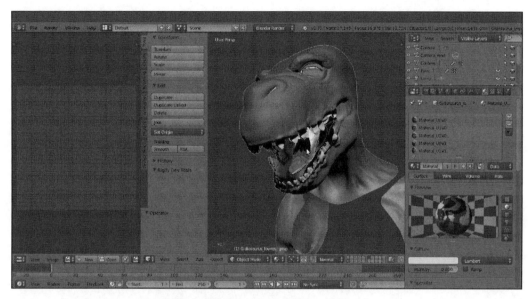

Artifacts of the normal map in some mesh parts

The solution in this case is very simple: we must paint the areas on the baked normal map corresponding to the afflicted parts, such as the **teeth**, the **tongue**, and so on, with a *flat normal* color (**R 0.498**, **G 0.498**, **B 1.000**) to *flatten* and therefore erase the unwanted details.

We can do this directly in Blender, by selecting the vertices of the areas to be painted on and enabling the **mask tool** in the 3D viewport toolbar:

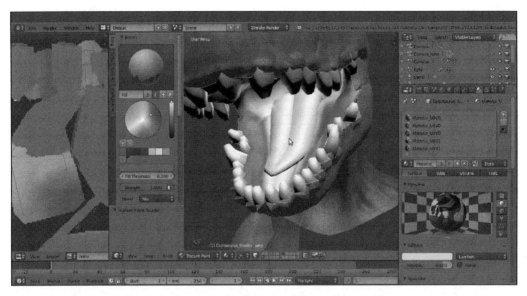

Flattening the unwanted artifacts by painting on the normal map

Alternatively, we can do it in an external painting software program such as Gimp; in this case, just delete the vertices of the parts that you don't want to change in the mesh and export the UV layer of all the remaining parts to be used as a guide to paint.

The Armor textures

The same procedure used in the previous recipe must be used for the **Armor** object, to bake the normals of the sculpted high resolution version on the low poly one.

Getting ready

So, in short, we will do the following:

1. Enable the **13th** scene layer; select the **Armor** object and go to the **Object Modifiers** window.

2. Temporarily, disable the **Armature** modifier both for rendering, and the viewport, and be sure that the **Subdivision Surface** modifier levels are both set to **2**.

3. Assign a **Shrinkwrap** modifier with a target to the **Armor_detailing** object; in the **Vertex Group** slot, select the **shrinkwrap** vertex group and, just to be sure, also check the **Keep Above Surface** item.

Also, in this case, thanks to the **shrinkwrap** vertex group, only the outside of the **armor** mesh is conformed to the sculpted mesh; the insides are not important and can even be deleted (only for the baking and, of course, on a duplicated **armor** object, as we did with the **Gidiosaurus_for_baking** object). In any case, they will be barely visible.

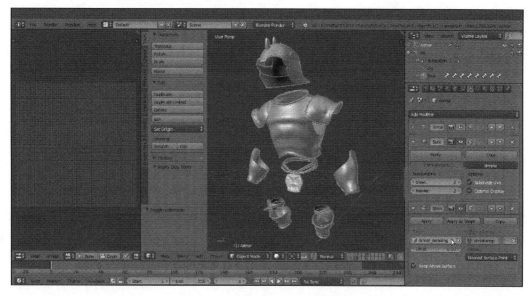

The Armor object prepared for the baking

How to do it...

Let's now bake the sculpted geometry in a few steps:

1. Enter **Edit Mode** and select all the mesh vertices; in the **UV/Image Editor** window, add a new **3072** x **3072** blank image and rename it as `norm2`.

2. Go out of **Edit Mode**, enable the **3rd** scene layer and select the **Armor_detailing** object, and then *Shift*-select the **Armor** object.

3. Go to the **Render** window, scroll the panel down; in the **Bake** subpanel, check the **Selected to Active** item, and set the **Margin** to **8** pixels, the **Bake Mode** to **Normals**, and the **Normal Space** to **Tangent**. Then, click on the **Bake** button.

4. Click on the **Image** item on the **UV/Image Editor** window toolbar to save the baked image as `norm2.png`, inside the `texture_making` folder.

5. Save the file as `Gidiosaurus_baking_normals.blend`.

In the following OpenGL screenshot, you can see the comparison between the sculpted and the low resolution **Armor** objects with the assigned normal map:

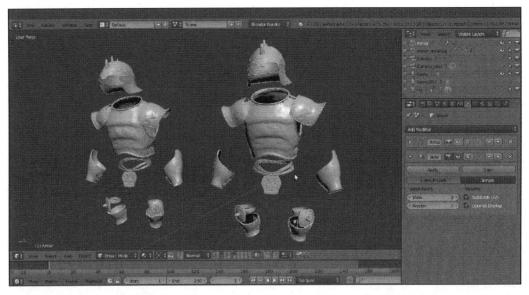

A comparison between the sculpted and the normal map versions of the Armor

There's more...

Inside the `texture_making` folder provided with this cookbook, there is also an already seamless `iron_tiles.png` image to be used for the **Armor**; it has been made seamless in **Gimp**, but after the mapping on the model, we'll need to fix some visible seams again by using the **Clone** brush of the Blender **Paint Tool**.

I won't go through all the required steps here, because this would be a repetition of recipes already explained in *Chapter 10, Creating the Textures*.

Just remember that all we have to do is to bake the seamless `iron_tiles.png` image, which is mapped on the **UVMap_rust** coordinates layer, on the **UDIM UVMap** coordinates layer; in this case, shared into **two** tiles spaces and then fix the visible seams on the baked images.

So, we have to add two materials to the **Armor** object; each one with its own image texture and assigned to the vertices corresponding to each tile, and then also add the `iron_tiles.png` image to each affected material.

In short, we have to replicate the steps of the *Preparing the model to use the UDIM UV tiles*, *Baking the tileable scales texture into the UV tiles*, and *Painting to fix the seams and to modify the baked scales image maps* recipes from *Chapter 10, Creating the Textures*.

To use the **Clone** brush (press the *1* key to call it after entering **Texture Paint** mode), press *Ctrl* + left-click on the area of the mesh you want to clone from; this will place the **3D Cursor** in that location. Then, left-click on the seams to clone the texture from the area under the **3D Cursor**:

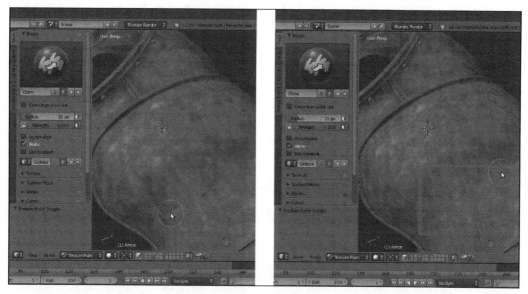

The Clone brush is cloning the texture area at the 3D Cursor location

Besides the **Clone** brush, in this case, it is also possible to fix the seams with the **Smear** brush (*4* key).

When you are done, save the two iron images as `iron_U0V0.png` and `iron_U1V0.png` inside the `texture` folder.

See also

Be aware that the first following link is for Blender version **2.6** (seems there is very little official documentation for version **2.7** at the moment), and a few things in the **Paint Tool** have changed; in any case, I think it can still be an interesting reading:

- `http://wiki.blender.org/index.php/Doc:2.6/Manual/Textures/Painting`

- `http://www.blender.org/manual/render/blender_render/textures/painting.html`

Adding a dirty Vertex Colors layer and baking it to an image texture

Let's see now how to add a *dirty* map through the **Vertex Colors** tool and how to bake it to an image texture; such a texture map can be useful for the creation of the shaders (which we'll see in the next chapter).

Getting ready

To do this, we are going to use an already set `.blend` file:

1. Start Blender and open the `Gidiosaurus_baking_normals.blend` file; save it as `Gidiosaurus_baking_dirty.blend`.

2. Put the mouse pointer in the 3D view and press the *Z* key twice to switch into **Solid** viewport shading mode; click on the **14th** scene layer to enable the visibility of the **Gidiosaurus_detailing** object.

How to do it...

Let's first go with the creation of the **Vertex Colors** layer:

1. In the **Outliner**, select the **Gidiosaurus_detailing** object and then click on the mode button in the 3D viewport toolbar to select the **Vertex Paint** mode:

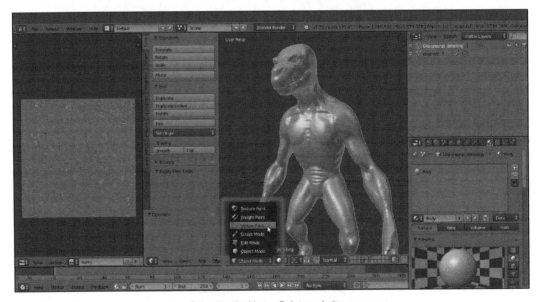

Selecting the Vertex Paint mode item

2. Now, click on the **Paint** item in the 3D viewport toolbar and from the menu, select the **Dirty Vertex Colors** item; the **Gidiosaurus** mesh, first filled with a plain white color, gets shaded in grayscale tones:

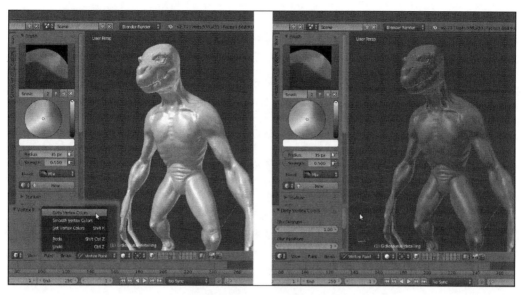

Using the Dirty Vertex Colors tool

3. Expand the last operation panel at the bottom of the **Tool Shelf** and press *Ctrl*+click on the **Dirt Angle** slot to enter the value **90°**; the grayscale shading on the mesh gets a lot more darker and contrasted:

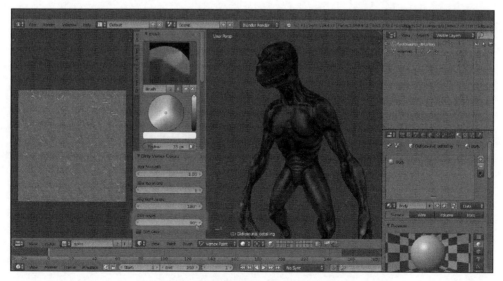

Tweaking the settings for the Dirty Vertex Colors tool

4. Go back in **Object Mode** and then move to the **Material** window, where the **Body** material is already assigned to the high resolution mesh. Scroll down the panel to reach the **Shading** subpanel and enable the **Shadeless** item; then, reach down the **Options** subpanel and enable the **Vertex Color Paint** item:

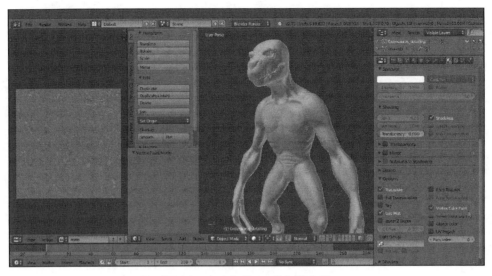

The Shadeless and the Vertex Color Paint items

To understand the effect of the items we enabled in the **Material** window, just switch to the **Rendered** viewport shading mode; the mesh surface is self-illuminating and showing the dirty **Vertex Colors** layer:

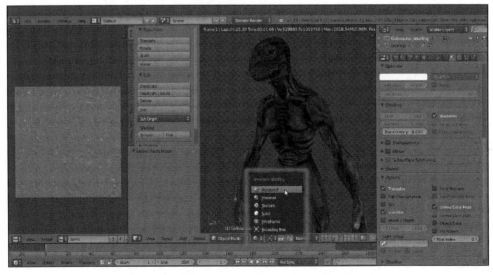

The Dirty Vertex Colors layer visualized in the Rendered preview

Note that the **Shadeless** item is not actually mandatory for the baking, but is only required to see the object in the **Rendered** viewport shading mode as in the previous screenshot.

5. Also, enable the **4th** scene layer (*Shift*+left-click) and in the **Outliner** window, select the **Gidiosaurus_for_baking** object. Go to the **Object Data** window to be sure that the **UVMap_norm** layer is the active one and then go to the **Render** window and scroll down to the bottom, to the **Bake** subpanel; click on the **Bake Mode** slot to select the **Textures** item from the pop-up menu:

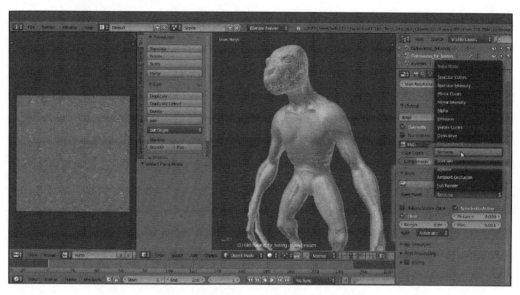

Baking the Dirty Vertex Colors layer to Textures

6. With the **Gidiosaurus_for_baking** object still selected, enter **Edit Mode** and select all the vertices; in the **UV/Image Editor** window, add a new **3072 x 3072** blank image renamed as `vcol`.

7. Go out of **Edit Mode** and in the **Outliner**, select the **Gidiosaurus_detailing** object; then, *Shift*-select the **Gidiosaurus_for_baking** object and go to the **Bake** subpanel under the **Render** window to click on the **Bake** button:

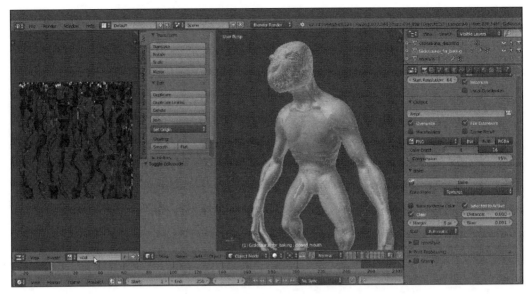

The final baked "vcol.png" image map

8. Save the baked image as vcol.png into the texture_making folder.

9. Enable the **3rd** scene layer, select the **Armor_detailing** object, and repeat the procedure; save the baked image as vcol2.png in the texture_making folder and also save the file:

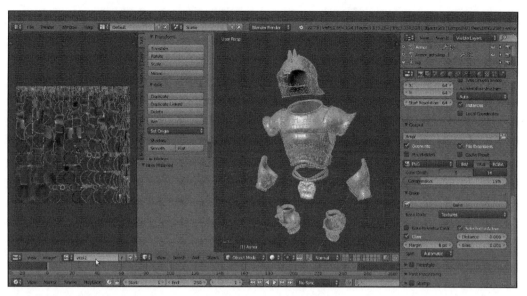

The baked vertex color layer for the Armor

How it works...

The **Vertex Colors** tool can add a color to each vertex of the mesh, so it's actually possible to paint an object without the need for an image texture; the denser the mesh, the better this works.

The **Dirty Vertex Colors** tool uses the proximity and the depth of folds and creases on the mesh surface to calculate grayscale values to be assigned to the vertices; thanks to the **Vertex Color Paint** item, enabled in the **Material** window, this grayscale shows up in the rendering and so it's also possible to bake it into an image.

See also

- ▶ http://wiki.blender.org/index.php/Doc:2.6/Manual/Materials/ Special_Effects/Vertex_Paint

- ▶ http://www.blender.org/manual/render/blender_render/materials/ special_effects/vertex_paint.html

The Quick Edit tool

It's time to talk a bit about a very useful Blender tool: the **Quick Edit** tool.

Through this tool, it's possible to export a screenshot of the model in our favorite 2D painting software (**Gimp** or **Photoshop**, or whatever), paint on it using a new alpha background layer, and reassign the painted layer to the model in Blender, which is UV-mapped on the selected UV coordinates layer. All this, in just a few clicks.

Getting ready

In our case, we don't actually need to use this tool to refine the textures for the **Gidiosaurus**, so this recipe is going to be just an example. By the way, to fully understand how to use the tool, I suggest you to follow all the steps; just don't save the file at the end (or save it with a different name in a different directory if you want to keep it). So, carry on with the following:

1. Start Blender and call the **User Preferences** panel (*Ctrl + Alt + U*); go to the **File** tab and, in the **Image Editor** slot (*Path to an image editor*), write the path to your 2D image painting software installation (this is also done by clicking on the open/browse button at the right end of the slot). The path, of course, changes based on your OS; in my case, in **Linux Ubuntu**, it's enough to write `gimp`:

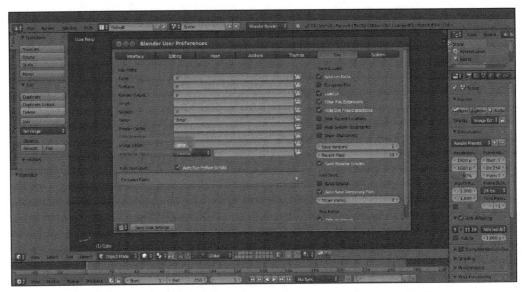

The Image Editor path in the File tab of the User Preferences panel under Linux Ubuntu

2. Click on the **Save User Settings** button at the bottom-left of the panel and close it.

How to do it...

Once you've set the path to the image editor, let's load our **Gidiosaurus** file:

1. Load the `Gidiosaurus_painting_BI.blend` file and maximize it as much as possible in the 3D viewport.

   You can use both the **User** or the **Camera** view; it doesn't make any difference for the tool to work. By the way, it would be a good idea to use the **Camera** view so as to have a fixed point of view for any other case.

2. If necessary, press the *T* key to call the **Tool Shelf** panel; select the **Gidiosaurus** object and then go in **Texture Paint** mode.

3. Go to the **External** subpanel under the **Tools** tab; set a size for the screenshot to be exported (by default, it's **512** x **512** pixels; I set it to **3072** x **3072** pixels) and then click on the **Quick Edit** button:

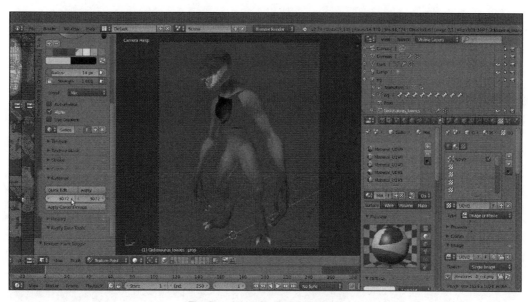

The External Image Editor subpanel

After a while, the image editor automatically starts (in my case, it's **Gimp 2.8**) and opens the screenshot of the model:

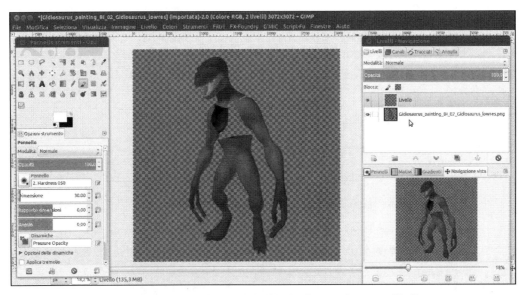

The screenshot previously visible in the Blender Camera view opened in Gimp

4. Add a new transparent layer and start to paint on it, adding some kind of tribal make-up decoration to the **Gidiosaurus**:

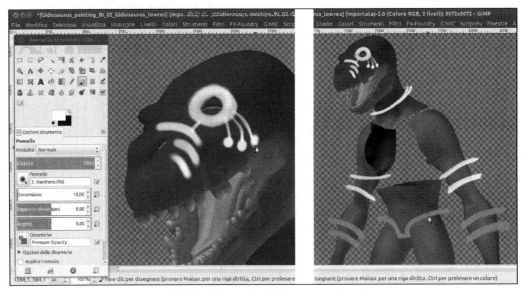

Tribal painting on the Gidiosaurus warrior

5. When you are done, deselect the visibility for the export layer and export the transparent painted one *by saving it with the same name as the exported one*. That is, the **Quick Edit** tool exported the screenshot by saving a `.png` image inside the blend file directory with the name `Gidiosaurus_painting_BI_02_Gidiosaurus_lowres.png`; export the painted layer by saving it as `Gidiosaurus_painting_BI_02_Gidiosaurus_lowres.png` as well:

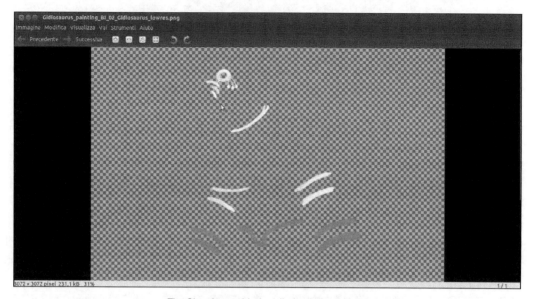

The Gimp layer with the tribal painting "a solo"

This is necessary for Blender to find it in the next step.

6. Back in Blender, click on the **Apply** button under the **External** subpanel and watch the new layer added to the model in the 3D viewport:

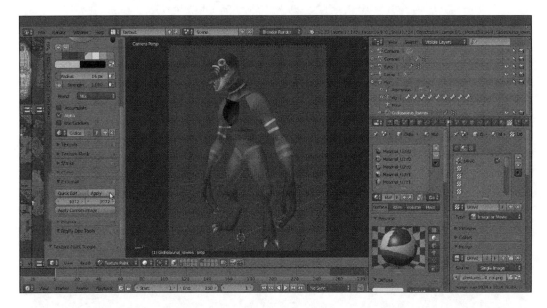

7. To make the textures editing permanent, click on the **Save All Images** button, both under the **Slots** tab and the **Image** item on the **UV/Image Editor** window toolbar:

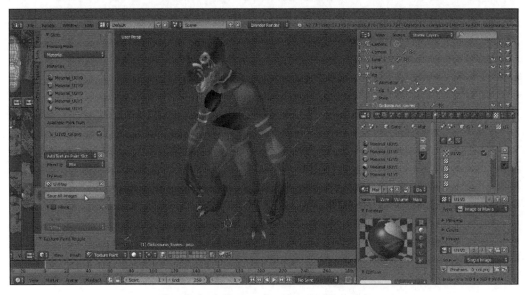

The tribal painting transferred on the 3D model

The editing we did in **Gimp** is now correctly transferred on the image textures:

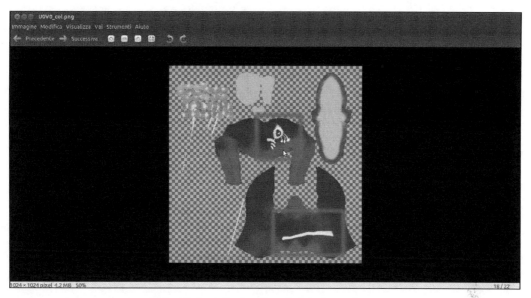

The tribal painting transferred on the image map

How it works...

As you have seen, the **Quick Edit** tool worked like a charm on all the **5** different materials assigned to the **Gidiosaurus** model for the painting. Be careful that, at least at the moment, this doesn't seem to work with **nodes materials** (which we'll see in the next chapter).

12
Creating the Materials in Cycles

In this chapter, we will cover the following recipes:

- ▶ Building the reptile skin shaders in Cycles
- ▶ Making a node group of the skin shader to reuse it
- ▶ Building the eyes' shaders in Cycles
- ▶ Building the armor shaders in Cycles

Introduction

In *Chapter 10*, *Creating the Textures*, and in *Chapter 11*, *Refining the Textures*, we have prepared all the necessary texture images for the **Gidiosaurus** skin and for the iron **Armor** (the creation process for some textures, specifically the two textures for the character's **eyes**, hasn't been described, but basically it's a process similar to what we have already seen).

In this chapter, we'll see how to use these textures and how to set up the materials for the **Gidiosaurus** and the **Armor** in the **Cycles Render** engine.

A rendered example of the Cycles' shader final result

Building the reptile skin shaders in Cycles

So, let's start with the **Gidiosaurus** skin.

Getting ready

But first, as usual, we must prepare the file:

1. As the very first step, go to the `texture_making` folder and move the textures `vcol.png`, `vcol2.png`, `norm.png`, and `norm2.png` to the `textures` folder.

2. Then start Blender and open the `Gidiosaurus_baking_normals.blend` file we saved in *Chapter 11, Refining the Textures*.

3. Switch the left **UV/Image Editor** window with a **Node Editor** window and press the *N* key to get rid of the **Properties** sidebar. Put the mouse pointer in the 3D viewport to the right and press the *T* key to get rid of the **Tool Shelf** panel, then press the *Z* key twice to go in **Solid** viewport shading mode.

4. Enable the **3rd** scene layer, select and delete the **Armor_detailing** object (press the *X* key, then left-click to confirm).

5. Enable the **4th** scene layer and select and delete the **Gidiosaurus_for_baking** object as well. Enable the **14th** scene layer, and also select and delete the **Gidiosaurus_detailing** and the **enamels** objects.

6. Enable the **11th** scene layer and right-click on the **Gidiosaurus_lowres** object to select it.

7. It's not mandatory but, in case it is not already disabled, it is best to go to the **Object Modifiers** window and disable the **Armature** modifier visibility in the viewport by clicking on the eye icon button.

8. Go to the **UV Maps** subpanel under the **Object Data** window and select the **UVMap** coordinates layer (the first one); press *Tab* to enter **Edit Mode**, then click on the **+** icon button to the right side of the **UV Maps** subpanel to add a new coordinates layer; rename it **UVMap2**.

9. Go to the left window and change it into a **UV/Image Editor**; one by one, select the UV islands of the **talons** (at the moment these are placed inside the other **UDIM** tile spaces), and move them to the default **U0V0** tile, to overlap the location of the **teeth** islands. The reason for this will be clear later, when we will reuse the same color map both for the teeth and for all the talons.

10. If necessary, remember to disable the *Keep UV and edit mode mesh selection in sync* button on the **UV/Image Editor** toolbar:

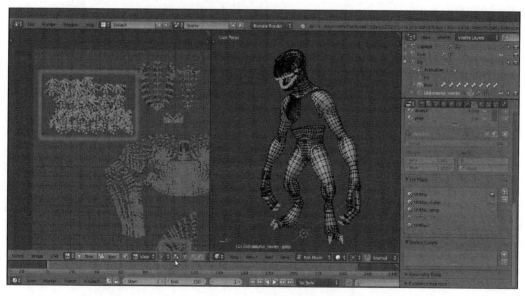

Moving the talon islands to overlap the teeth islands inside the default U0V0 tile space

11. Go out of **Edit Mode** and switch the **UV/Image Editor** window back to a **Node Editor** window.

12. Click on the *Engine to use for rendering* slot on the main top header to switch to the **Cycles Render** engine.

13. Also, enable the **6th** scene layer to show the **Lamps**. Go to the **Outliner**, unhide and delete the **Lamp.001** object and select the **Lamp** object; in the **Object Data** window, change the type to **Spot** and then click on the **Use Nodes** button. Set the **Strength** to **10.000** and the **Color** to **R 1.000, G 1.000, B 0.650**, then set the **Size** to **0.500** and enable the **Multiple Importance** item (the **Multiple Importance Sampling** helps in reducing noise for big lamps and sharp glossy reflections, at the cost of the samples rendering a bit slower).

14. Put the mouse pointer in the 3D viewport and press *N* to call the **Properties** sidepanel; in the top **Transform** subpanel, type: **Location X = 6.059204, Y = -9.912249** and **Z = 7.546275**, and **Rotation X = 55.788944°, Y = 0°** and **Z = 30.561825°**.

15. Go to the **Render** window and, under the **Sampling** subpanel, set the **Samples** to **400** for **Render** and **300** for **Preview**.

16. Go down to the **Light Paths** subpanel and disable the **Reflective Caustics** item, then set **Filter Glossy** to **1.000**.

17. Re-select the **Gidiosaurus_lowres** object and go to the **Material** window:

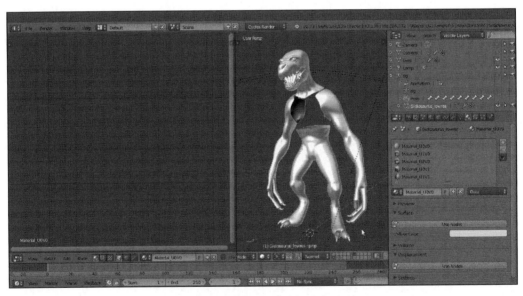

The 5 materials under the Cycles render engine

As you can see in the previous screenshot, the **Gidiosaurus_lowres** object has already assigned the **5** materials corresponding to the **5 UDIM** tile spaces (see *Chapter 5, Unwrapping the Low Resolution Mesh*, and *Chapter 10, Creating the Textures*).

The materials have been created under **Blender Internal** so, switching to **Cycles**, they show but aren't *initialized* as **node materials** yet; besides this, just before starting the creation of the first Cycles material, we must add **two** more materials.

18. Click the **+** icon button **twice** (*Add a new material slot*) to the right side of the **Material** window to add **two** new material slots.

19. Select the penultimate slot and click on the **New** button; rename the new material as Material_enamels. Select the last slot, click on the **New** button and rename it as Material_wet_UOVO.

20. Press *Tab* to enter **Edit Mode** and select all the vertices of the **teeth** and the **talons**; assign them to the Material_enamels slot.

21. Zoom on the **Gidiosaurus** head; select the vertices of the inner **nostrils**, of the inner edges of the **eyelids** and of the **tongue**, as shown in the following screenshot, and assign them to the Material_wet_UOVO slot:

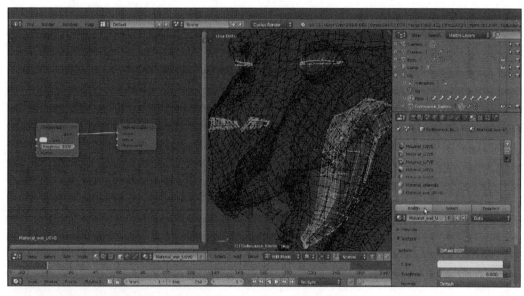

Selecting the vertices of the "wet" areas of the character's head to assign them to the "Material_wet_UOVO" slot

22. Save the file as Gidiosaurus_shaders_start.blend file.

How to do it...

We know that the skin of our character is shared in **5** different materials; we are going to focus on the **head** (Material_UOVO), as the more representative one.

Once we are happy with the result, we will also copy (with all the due differences) the material to the other **body** parts.

Therefore, the steps are as follows:

1. In the materials list inside the **Material** window, select the `Material_U0V0` (the first top one) and press *Ctrl* + left-click on it to rename it as `Material_skin_U0V0`; then, move down and click on the **Use Nodes** button inside the **Surface** subpanel.

   Immediately, a **Diffuse BSDF** shader node (already connected to a **Material Output** node) appears inside the **Node Editor** window to the left of the screen and listed in the **Surface** slot inside the **Surface** subpanel to the right:

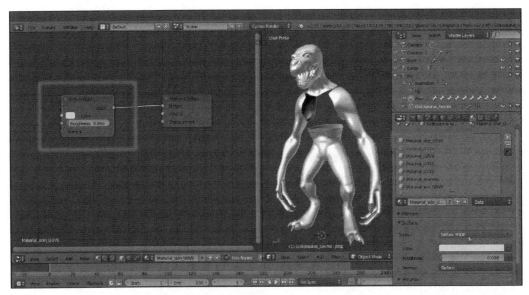

The Diffuse BSDF shader node connected to the Material Output node

2. In the **Surface** subpanel, under the **Material** window, click on the **Surface** slot that now shows the **Diffuse BSDF** shader: in the pop-up menu that appears, select a **Mix Shader** node:

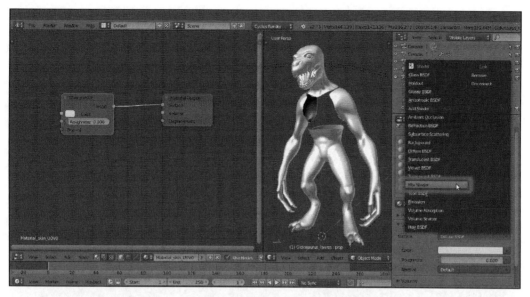

Switching the Diffuse BSDF shader node with a Mix Shader node through the Material window drop-down list

The **Surface** slot now shows the **Mix Shader** node item, and right below there are two new **Shader** slots that at the moment show the **None** item; in fact, looking at the nodes inside the **Node Editor** window, we see that the **Diffuse BSDF** shader node has been replaced by a **Mix Shader** node, and that the two (green) **Shader** input sockets are still empty:

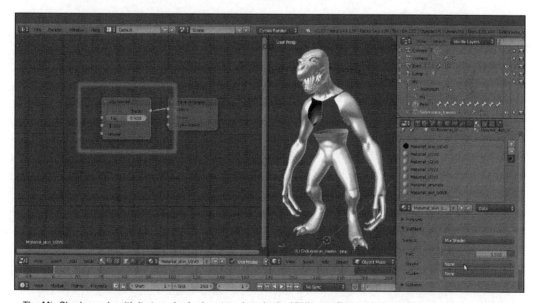

The Mix Shader node with its two shader input sockets in the UV/Image Editor window and in the Material window

3. Click on the first **Shader** slot under the **Surface** subpanel to select, again from the pop-up menu, a **Diffuse BSDF** shader node; click on the second **Shader** slot and select a **Mix Shader** node; both the two new nodes are added and connected to the proper input socket, as we can see in the **Node Editor** window:

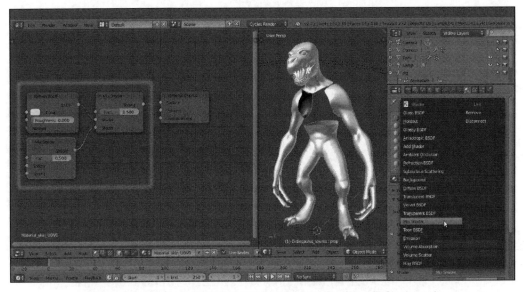

Two new nodes connected to the two shader input sockets of the Mix Shader node

At this point, to avoid confusion, it's already better to start to label the various nodes with meaningful names.

4. Put the mouse pointer inside the **Node Editor** window and press the *N* key to call the **Properties** sidepanel.

5. Select the last **Mix Shader** node we added to the material and then go to click on the **Label** slot inside the top **Name** subpanel of the side **Properties** panel: type **Mix Shader1**:

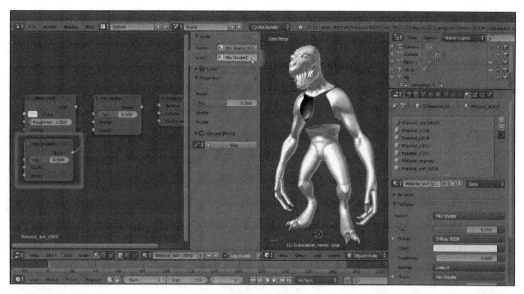

Labeling the nodes

6. Select the other **Mix Shader** node (the *old* one) and repeat the procedure by labeling it as **Mix Shader2**:

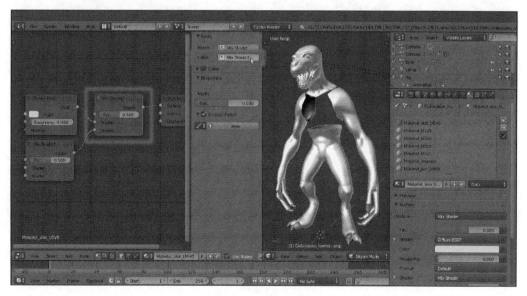

Labeling the nodes again

7. Put the mouse pointer on the 3D viewport and press the 0 key on the numpad to enter the **Camera** view.

8. Press *Shift + B* and by left-clicking draw a box around the **head** of the **Gidiosaurus** character to crop the area that can be rendered.

9. Zoom to the red square by scrolling the mouse wheel and then press *Shift + Z* to switch the **Viewport Shading** mode to **Rendered**:

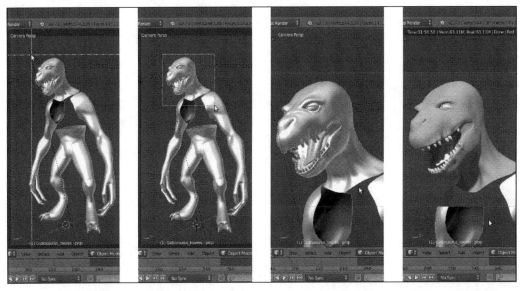

Cropping the renderable area and zooming to it

10. Put the mouse pointer inside the **Node Editor** window and press *Shift + A*. In the pop-up panel that appears, navigate to **Shader** and then click on the **Glossy BSDF** item to add the node; as it appears, move the mouse to place it to the left side of the **Mix Shader1** node.

11. Label it as **Glossy BSDF1**, connect its output to the first top **Shader** input socket of the **Mix Shader1** node, and set **Distribution** to **Beckmann**:

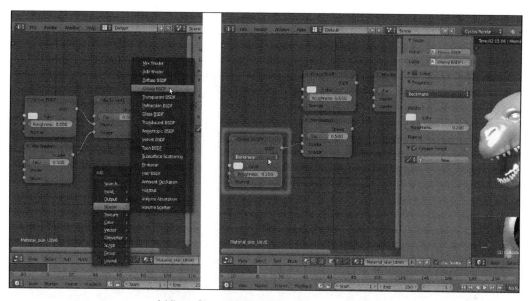

Adding a Glossy BSDF shader node and labeling it

12. Add a second **Glossy BSDF** shader node (*Shift + A* | **Shader** | **Glossy BSDF**) and place it right under the previous one; label it as **Glossy BSDF2**, connect its output to the second **Shader** input socket of the **Mix Shader1** node, and set **Distribution** to **Beckmann** as well and the **Roughness** to **0.400**.

13. Set the factor value (**Fac**) of the **Mix Shader1** node to **0.350**:

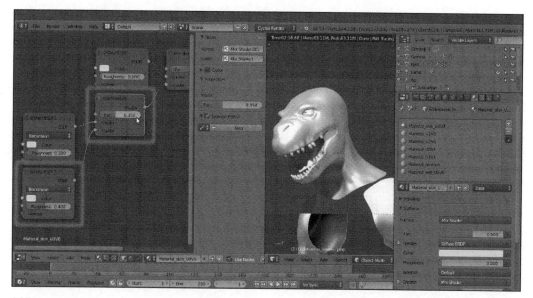

Adding a second Glossy shader node and blending it with the first one through the Fac value of the Mix Shader1 node

14. Add a **Fresnel** node (*Shift + A | Input | Fresnel*) and connect its **Fac** output to the **Fac** input socket of the **Mix Shader2** node; set the **IOR** value to **3.840**. Set the **Roughness** value of the **Diffuse BSDF** shader node to **0.500**:

Adding a Fresnel node to set the Index of Refraction value to blend the diffuse with the glossy components

15. Add a **Subsurface Scattering** node (*Shift + A | Shader | Subsurface Scattering*) and an **Add Shader** node (*Shift + A | Shader | Add Shader*). Move this last one to the link that connects the **Mix Shader2** node to the **Material Output** node in order to paste it automatically between the two nodes (automatically when the connection line becomes highlighted):

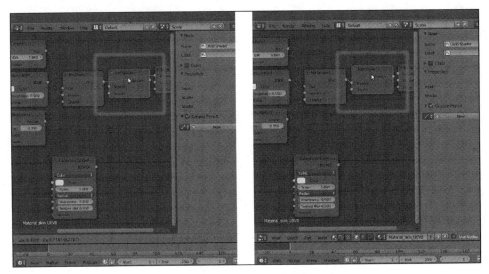

Automatically joining the Add Shader node

16. Connect the output of the **Subsurface Scattering** node to the second **Shader** input socket of the **Add Shader** node. In the **SSS** node, change **Fallof** from **Cubic** to **Gaussian**, set the **Scale** to **0.001** and click on the **Radius** button to set the **RGB** to **9.436**, **3.348** and **1.790**:

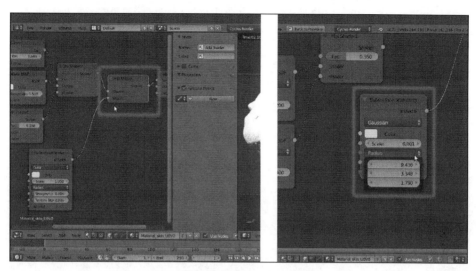

Connecting and setting the SSS node

17. Add a new **Mix Shader** node (*Shift + A* | **Shader** | **Mix Shader**) and label it as **Mix Shader3**. Connect the output of the **Mix Shader2** node to the first **Shader** input socket of the **Mix Shader3** node, and the output of the **Add Shader** node to its second **Shader** input socket. Set the **Fac** of the **Mix Shader3** node to **0.250** and connect its output to the **Surface** input socket of the **Material Output** node:

A little trick to tweak the influence of the Add shader node

18. Add a **Frame** (*Shift + A* | **Layout** | **Frame**), box-select all the nodes (except the **Material Output** node) and then press *Ctrl + P* to parent them to the frame; label the frame as **SHADERS**.

19. Select the **SHADERS** frame and go to the **Properties** sidepanel. Expand the **Color** subpanel (right under the **Node** subpanel) by clicking on the little horizontal black arrow, and enable the **Color** checkbox.

20. Click on the color slot and set a light color of your choice (I set it to **RGB 1.000**, which is totally white). Then click on the **+** icon button to the side and in the **Name** slot of the **Add Node Color Preset** pop-up panel, write **Frame**, then click the big **OK** button.

21. Select the **Material Output** node and then *Shift*-select the **Frame** again, then go to the **Color** subpanel and click on the big vertical arrow under the **+** and **–** icon buttons to the side. Click on the **Copy Color** item to copy the color of the **Frame** to the **Material Output** node:

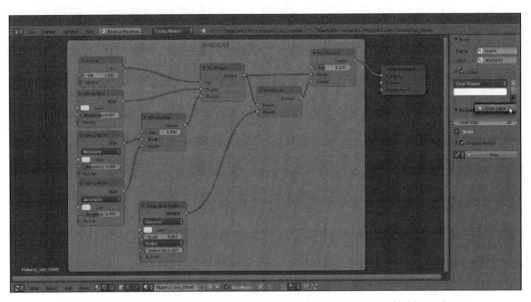

The SHADERS frame with the nodes and the Copy Color tool under the N sidepanel

22. Select any one of the other nodes, for example the **Fresnel** node, enable the **Color** checkbox and set a new color of your choice (for these nodes, I set it to **R 1.000, G 0.819, B 0.617**, which is a light brown).

23. Click on the **+** icon button to the side and in the **Name** slot of the **Add Node Color Preset** pop-up panel, write **Shaders**, then click the big **OK** button.

24. Now box-select all the other nodes inside the frame and click on the **Copy Color** item to copy the color from the **Fresnel** node to all the other selected nodes at once:

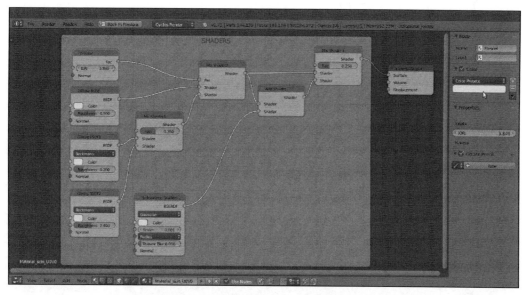

Copying the label color from one node to all the other selected nodes

At this point we have completed the basic shader for the skin; what we have to do now is to add the textures we painted in both *Chapter 10, Creating the Textures*, and *Chapter 11, Refining the Textures*.

So:

25. Put the mouse pointer into the **Node Editor** window and add an **Image Texture** node (*Shift + A | **Texture** | **Image Texture***); label it as **COL** and then use *Shift + D* to duplicate it; move the duplicated one down and change its label to **SCALES**.

    As you label the newly added nodes, also assign colors to them to make them more easily readable inside the **Node Editor** window, and save these colors as presets as we did at step 20.

26. Click on the **Open** button of the **COL** node and browse to the `textures` folder. There, load the image `U0V0_col.png`.

27. Click on the **Open** button of the **SCALES** node and browse to the `textures` folder. There, load the image `U0V0_scales.png`; set the **Color Space** to **Non-Color Data**.

28. Add a **MixRGB** node (*Shift + A | **Color** | **MixRGB***) and label it as **Scales_Col**; connect the **Color** output of the **COL** node to the **Color1** input socket of the **Scales_Col** node and the **Color** output of the **SCALES** node to its **Color2** input socket. Set the **Fac** to **1.000** and the **Blend Type** to **Divide**.

29. Connect the output of the **Scales_Col** node to the **Color** input socket of the **Diffuse BSDF** shader node inside the **SHADERS** frame.

    The result so far is visible in the real-time rendered preview to the right:

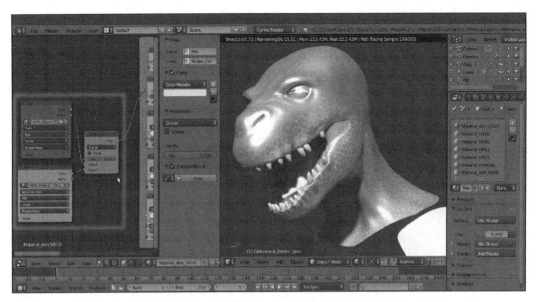

The rendered result of the two combined image texture nodes

As you can see, the glossy component is strong in this one! We must lessen the effect, to obtain a more natural look.

30. Add a new **MixRGB** node (*Shift + A* | **Color** | **MixRGB**) and label it as **Col_Spec**; set the **Color2** to **R 0.474, G 0.642, B 0.683**, then also connect the output of the **Scales_Col** node to the **Color1** input socket of the **Col_Spec** node.

31. Set the **Fac** value to **0.150** and the **Blend Type** to **Add**, then connect its output to the **Color** input sockets of both the **Glossy BSDF1** and **Glossy BSDF2** nodes:

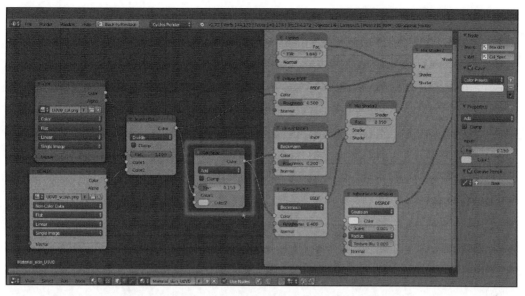

Varying the textures color output for the glossy component

32. Press *Shift + D* to duplicate the **Col_Spec** node and label the duplicate as **Col_SSS**; set the **Fac** value to **1.000** and the **Color2** to **R 0.439**, **G 0.216**, **B 0.141**. Connect the **Color** output of the **Scales_Col** node to the **Color1** input socket of the **Col_SSS** node and the output of this latter node to the **Color** input socket of the **Subsurface Scattering** node; increase its **Texture Blur** to the maximum value.

33. *Shift*-select the **Col_Spec** and the **Col_SSS** nodes and then also the **SHADERS** frame, and press *Ctrl + P* to parent them:

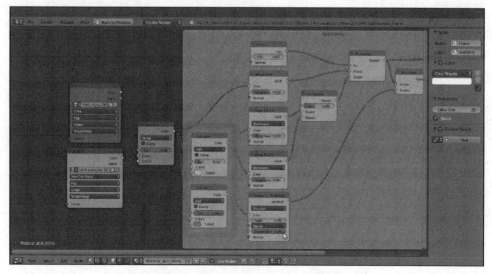

Varying the textures color output also for the SSS node

The new result looks a lot better:

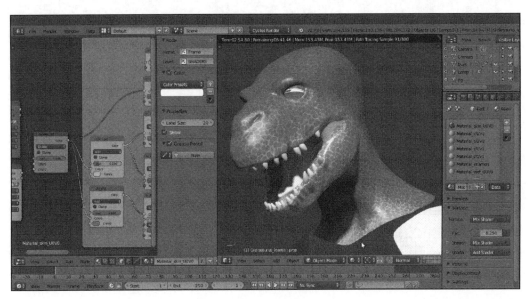

A better result

34. Add an **Attribute** node (*Shift + A* | **Input** | **Attribute**) and label it as **Attribute_UV1**. Connect its **Vector** output to the **Vector** input sockets of the **COL** and **SCALES** nodes and in the name field type **UVMap**:

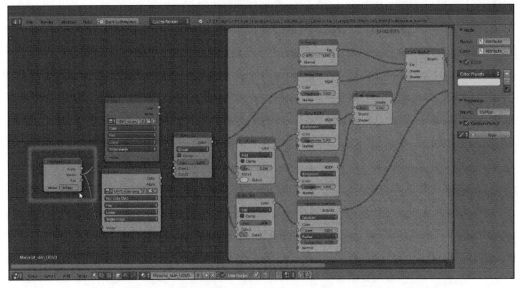

Adding the Attribute node to establish the UV coordinates layer to be used

By the way, the glossy component is still a little unnatural.

35. Add a new **Image Texture** node (*Shift + A* | **Texture** | **Image Texture**) and label it as **VCOL**. Click on the **Open** button, browse to the texture folder and load the image vcol.png.

36. Press *Shift + D* to duplicate the **Attribute** node, change the label to **Attribute_UV2**, and change the **Name** field to **UVMap_norm**. Connect its **Vector** output to the **Vector** input of the **VCOL** node.

37. Add a **Math** node (*Shift + A* | **Converter** | **Math**) and a **MixRGB** node (*Shift + A* | **Color** | **MixRGB**); connect the **Color** output of the **VCOL** node to the first **Value** input socket of the **Math** node; label this one as **Spec_soften** and set the second **Value** to **0.007**. Connect its **Value** output to the **Color1** input socket of the **MixRGB** node, which is now labeled as **Mix_Spec**.

38. Connect the **Color** output of the **Mix_Spec** node to the **Roughness** input socket of the **Glossy BSDF1** node:

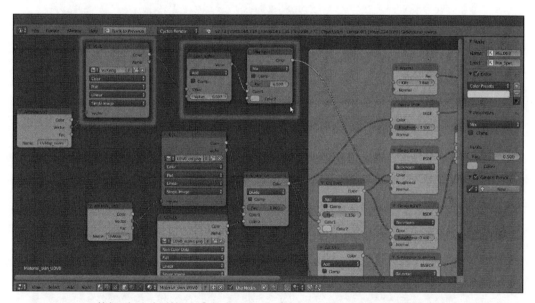

Using the baked Vertex Color image to "soften" the character's skin specularity

The specularity is now a bit more realistic:

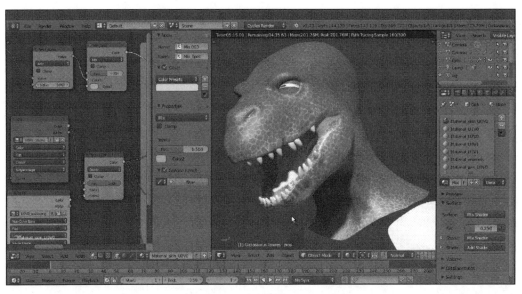

And the rendered result of this operation

Anyway, it's still missing the contribution of the bump effect.

39. Add a **Bump** node (*Shift + A* | **Vector** | **Bump**); connect the output of the **SCALES** node to the **Height** input socket of the **Bump** node and the **Normal** output of this latter node to the **Normal** input socket of the **Diffuse BSDF**, **Glossy BSDF1**, **Glossy BSDF2**, and **Subsurface Scattering** nodes. Set the **Strength** of the **Bump** node to **0.500**:

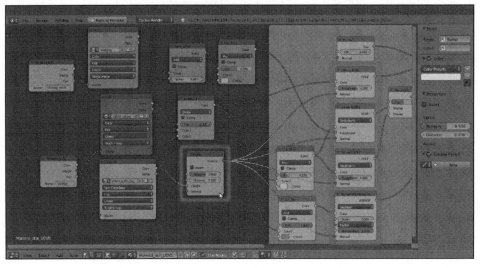

Adding the bump pattern to the shaders

Now we start to see something!

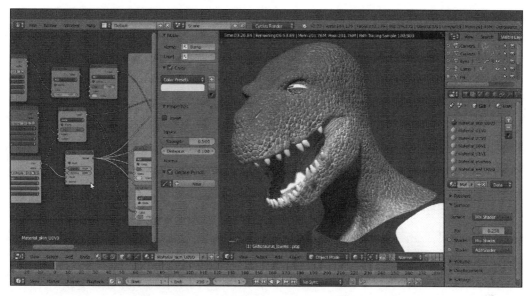

The bump effect in the rendered preview

By the way, the bump pattern is too even and, therefore, unrealistic; we must therefore *break* it in some way.

40. Add a **Noise Texture** node (*Shift + A* | **Texture** | **Noise Texture**) and a **Texture Coordinate** node (*Shift + A* | **Input** | **Texture Coordinate**). Connect the **Object** output of the **Texture Coordinate** node to the **Vector** input socket of the **Noise Texture** node, then set the **Scale** of the texture to **50.000**.

41. Add a **Math** node (*Shift + A* | **Converter** | **Math**) and a **MixRGB** node (*Shift + A* | **Color** | **MixRGB**). Connect the **Color** output of the **SCALES** node to the **Color1** input socket of the **MixRGB** node, and the **Color** output of the **Noise Texture** to the **Color2** input socket.

42. Set the **MixRGB** blend type to **Add**, the **Fac** value to **1.000** and label it as **Scales_Noise**. To see the effect, connect its **Color** output to the **Height** input socket of the **Bump** node (but this is going to change very soon, so it's not mandatory at this step):

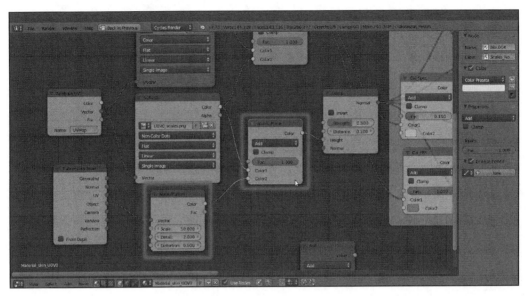

Adding some noise to the bump pattern part 1

43. Select the **Math** node and move it on the link connecting the **Noise Texture** node with the **Scales_Noise** node to paste it in between them: set the **Operation** to **Multiply**, the second **Value** to **1.000**, and label it as **Multiply_Noise**.

44. Press *Shift + D* to duplicate the **Multiply_Noise** node, change the label to **Multiply_Scales** and the second **Value** to **4.000**; paste it between the **SCALES** node and the **Scales_Noise** node.

45. Add an **RGB to BW** node (*Shift + A* | **Converter** | **RGB to BW**) and paste it between the **Noise Texture** node and the **Multiply_Noise** one:

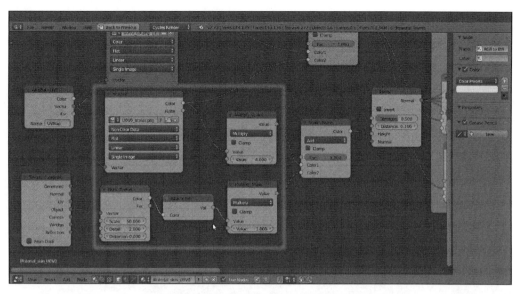

Adding some noise to the bump pattern part 2

46. Press *Shift + D* to duplicate the **Multiply_Scales** node and change the duplicate label to **Multiply_Bump**; connect the output of the **Multiply_Scales** to the first **Value** input socket of the **Multiply_Bump** node and the output of the **Scales_Noise** node to the second **Value** input socket. Connect the output of the **Multiply_Bump** node to the **Height** input socket of the **Bump** node:

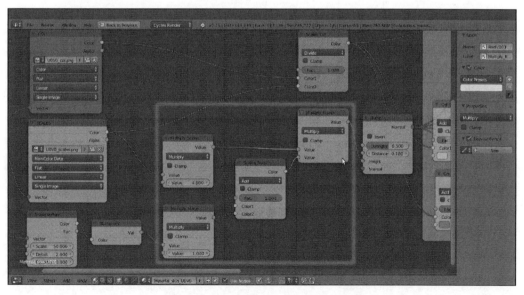

Adding some noise to the bump pattern part 3

47. Add a **MixRGB** node (*Shift + A* | **Color** | **MixRGB**) and paste it between the **VCOL** node and the **Spec_soften** node; label it as **Multiply_Spec**, set the **Blend Type** to **Multiply** and the **Fac** value to **0.850**; connect the output of the **Multiply_Bump** node to the **Color2** input socket of the **Multiply_Spec** node:

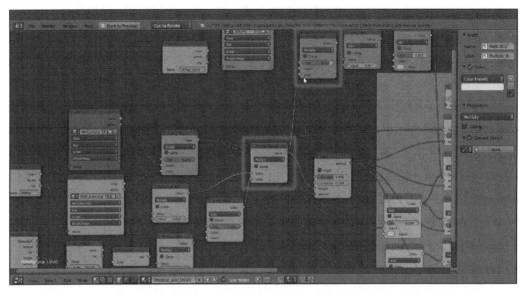

Modulating the specularity with the aid of the bump pattern output

The overall bump effect is almost completed:

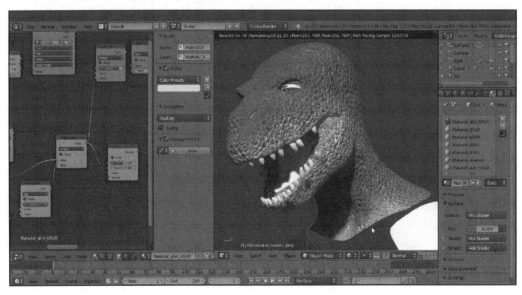

The new Rendered bump effect

What is still missing now is the normal map we obtained from the sculpted **Gidiosaurus** mesh in *Chapter 11, Refining the Textures*.

48. Add a new **Image Texture** node (*Shift + A* | **Texture** | **Image Texture**) and a **Normal Map** node (*Shift + A* | **Vector** | **Normal Map**). Label the **Image Texture** node as **NORMALS**, then connect the **Vector** output of the **Attribute_UV2** node to the **Vector** input socket of the **NORMALS** node.

49. Connect the **Color** output of the **NORMALS** node to the **Color** input socket of the **Normal Map** node, then click on the **Open** button on the **NORMALS** node, browse to the `textures` folder and load the image `norm.png`. Set the **Color Space** of the **NORMALS** node to **Non-Color Data** and click on the empty slot in the **Normal Map** node to select the **UVMap_norm** coordinates layer.

50. Add a **Vector Math** node (*Shift + A* | **Converter** | **Vector Math**), label it as **Average_Normals** and paste it right after the **Bump** node; connect the output of the **Normal Map** node to the second **Value** input socket of the **Average_Normals** node.

51. Set the **Operation** of the **Average_Normals** node to **Average** and connect its **Vector** output to the **Vector** input sockets of the **Diffuse BSDF**, **Glossy BSDF1**, **Glossy BSDF2**, and **Subsurface Scattering** nodes.

52. Set the **Strength** of the **Normal Map** to **2.000**:

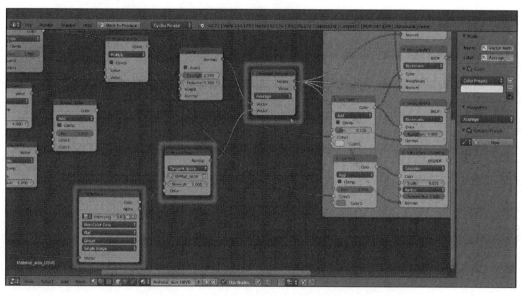

Adding the normal map output to the bump pattern

Finally we have completed the first skin material!

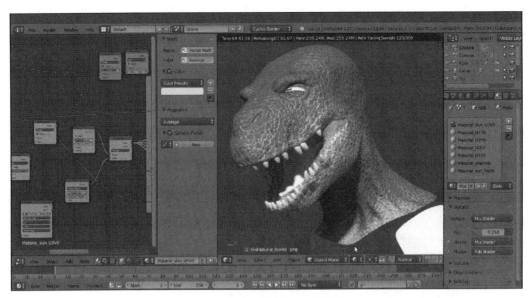

The completed Material_skin_UOVO

53. Save the file as `Gidiosaurus_skin_Cycles.blend`.

How it works...

This material can at first glance appear a bit complex, but actually the design behind it is quite simple as you can see in the following screenshot, where each component has been visually grouped by colors and frames (open the provided `Gidiosaurus_skin_Cycles_01.blend` file to have a better look):

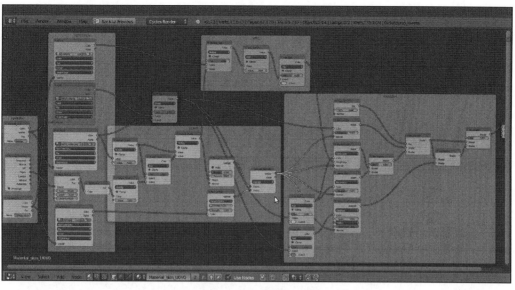

The total skin material network

▸ From step 1 to step 18 we built the **SHADERS** part of the material, that is, the combination of the diffuse with the glossy component and the addition of the subsurface scattering effect.

▸ Note that the glossy component (the *specularity*) is obtained by mixing **two** glossy shaders with different roughness values; by setting the factor value of the **Mix Shader1** node to **0.350**, we give prevalence to the **Glossy BSDF1** node effect, which is to the node connected to the first top **Shader** input socket.

▸ Also, we added the subsurface scattering effect by the **Add Shader** node, and to further tweak the blending of the effect with the rest of the shader, we added the **Mix Shader3** node, to give prevalence to the output of the **Mix Shader2** node (that is the output of the diffuse plus the glossy components).

▸ From step 19 to step 24 we saw some not mandatory but useful tips for assigning colors to the nodes, in order to visually distinguish and/or group them and make the whole material network more easily readable.

▸ At step 25 we started to add the textures, first the diffuse color one and then the grayscale scales image that we used here to add details to the coloration (and later for the bump effect). By mixing the scales with the diffuse color through the **MixRGB** node set to a **Divide** blend type, we automatically obtained a scales pattern on the skin itself.

▸ From step 30 to step 33 we tweaked the diffuse color map to also affect the glossy and the subsurface scattering components, but with different hues.

- Note that at step 34 we used an **Attribute** node to set the UV coordinates layer to be used for the mapping of the textures. It would have been unnecessary in this case, with the **UVMap** coordinates layer being the first one and therefore the default one. Cycles, in fact, in the case of image textures, automatically uses any existing UV coordinates layer. But, because later we also used a different UV coordinates layer, it was better to specify it.

- From step 35 to step 38 we improved the glossiness effect of the skin, by using the output of the `vcol.png` image we had previously baked and tweaked through the nodes inside the **SPEC** frame.

- From step 39 to step 47 we built the **BUMP** effect, by using the output of the **SCALES** image texture added through a **MixRGB** node to the output of a procedural **Noise Texture**. The **RGB to BW** node simply converts the colored output of the procedural noise to a grayscale output (and if you think we could have used the **Fac** output instead, well, it's not the same thing), and the **Multiply_Scales** and **Multiply_Noise** nodes set the strength of the outputs before the adding process. Through the **Multiply_Bump** node we also added the grayscale output of the combined bump to the glossy component.

- From step 48 to step 52 we also added the effect of the normal map we baked from the sculpted high resolution **Gidiosaurus** mesh to the bump pattern. The normal map is averaged, through the **Vector Math** node, with the bump output. Because of this averaging, the strength value of the normal map had to be set to double (**2.000**) to have full effect.

There's more...

Still focusing on the character's **head**, there is a material we can obtain from the skin material with some modification, the material for the wet parts of the character's skin (inner **eyelids**, **tongue**, inner **nostrils**).

Going on from the previously saved file:

1. If you think this is the case, especially if your computer (like mine) isn't very powerful, temporarily disable the **Rendered** preview by moving the mouse cursor inside the 3D viewport and pressing *Shift + Z*.

2. In the **Material** window, click on the `Material_wet_U0V0` material to select it.

3. Put the mouse pointer inside the **Node Editor** window, select the default two nodes already assigned to the material and delete them by pressing the *X* key.

4. Now, in the **Material** window, re-select the `Material_skin_U0V0`; put the mouse in the **Node Editor** window, press *A* twice to select everything, and press *Ctrl + C*.

5. Re-select the `Material_wet_U0V0`, put the mouse pointer inside the empty **Node Editor** window and press *Ctrl + V* to paste the copied material nodes.

Now we have copied the nodes of the skin material to the material assigned to the parts that need to appear wet; it's enough now to tweak this material a bit to modify the bump pattern and the glossiness:

6. In the **Node Editor**, zoom to the **Noise Texture** node inside the **BUMP** frame; left-click on it to select it and then press the *X* key to delete it.

7. Press *Shift + A* and add a **Voronoi Texture** node (*Shift + A* | **Texture** | **Voronoi Texture**); left-click on the node and, by keeping the mouse button pressed, move the node a little bit on the frame, so it should automatically be parented to it.

8. Connect the **Object** output of the **Texture Coordinate** node to the **Vector** input socket of the **Voronoi Texture** node and the **Color** output of this latter node to the **RGB to BW** node input socket; set the **Voronoi Scale** to **200.000**.

9. Add an **Invert** node (*Shift + A* | **Color** | **Invert**) and paste it between the **Voronoi Texture** and the **RGB to BW** nodes:

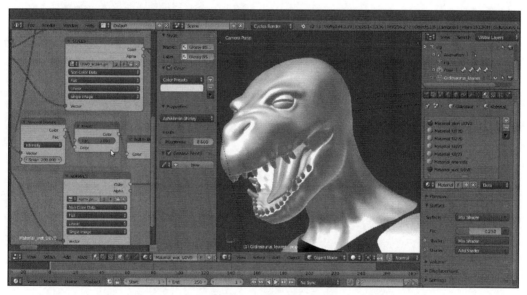

The different texture nodes of the "Material_wet_U0V0"

10. Scroll the **Node Editor** window a bit to the right to find the **Multiply_Noise** node: change the label to **Multiply_Voronoi** and the second **Value** to **0.025**.

11. Find the **Scales_Col** node and change **Blend Type** from **Divide** to **Multiply**.

12. Now go to the **SHADERS** frame; change the **IOR** value of the **Fresnel** node to **15.000** and connect its output to the **Fac** input socket of the **Mix Shader1** node; change the **Distribution** of both the **Glossy BSDF1** and **Glossy BSDF2** nodes to **Ashikhmin-Shirley** and set the **Roughness** of the **Glossy BSDF2** node to **0.600**.

We substituted the **Noise Texture** node with a **Voronoi Texture** node to give a kind of organic look to the surface of the **tongue** of the creature.

In the following screenshot, we can see the result of the wet material; note that for the occasion I opened the mouth wide, to make the inside more visible:

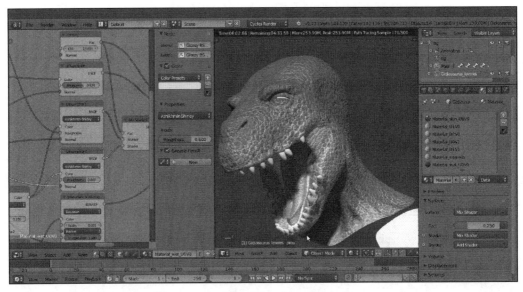

The rendered wet material

One more material we are going to create in this section of the recipe is the **Material_enamels** for **teeth** and **talons**; in this case, we just need mostly the **SHADERS** frame's nodes with the single contribution of the color image texture `U0V0_col.png`, here using the **UVMap2** coordinates layer to avoid having to create **5** different materials for the **talons** alone (originally distributed in different tiles). By the way, nothing is stopping you from creating several talon materials, if you prefer.

13. Again, select, copy and paste the skin material to the enamels material slot through the **Node Editor** window, as we have already done in steps 3, 4 and 5.

14. This time, just delete the unnecessary nodes, in short keeping only the **Attribute** node, the **COL** node and the **SHADERS** frame with its parented nodes.

15. Change the UV coordinates layer in the **Name** slot of the **Attribute** node to **UVMap2** (and the label to **Attribute_UV3**). Lower the **Roughness** value of the **Diffuse BSDF** node to **0.000**.

16. Go to the **SHADERS** frame; select and delete the **Col_Spec** and **Col_SSS** nodes, then connect the **Color** output of the **COL** node also to the **Color** input socket of the **Subsurface Scattering** node.

17. Select and delete the **Glossy BSDF1** and the **Glossy BSDF2** nodes.

18. Add 2 **Anisotropic BSDF** shader nodes (*Shift + A* | **Shader** | **Anisotropic BSDF**), a **Tangent** node (*Shift + A* | **Input** | **Tangent**) and detach the **Add Shader** node from the **Mix Shader3** node.

19. Label the two **Anisotropic BSDF** shader nodes as **Anisotropic BSDF1** and **Anisotropic BSDF2** and connect them to the two **Shader** input sockets of the **Add Shader** node. Connect the output of the **Tangent** node to the **Tangent** input sockets of the two **Anisotropic** shader nodes.

20. Set the **Tangent** of the **Tangent** node to **Z**. Set the **Anisotropy** of both the **Anisotropic** nodes to **0.500**, the **Roughness** of the **Anisotropic BSDF1** node to **0.500** and the **Roughness** of the **Anisotropic BSDF2** node to **0.200**.

21. Connect the **Add Shader** output to both the second **Shader** input sockets of the **Mix Shader1** and **Mix Shader2** nodes.

22. Set the **IOR** value of the **Fresnel** node to **1.540** and connect the **Fresnel** output to the **Fac** input sockets of the **Mix Shader1**, **Mix Shader2**, and **Mix Shader3** nodes.

23. Connect the output of the **Diffuse BSDF** shader node to the first **Shader** input socket of the **Mix Shader1** node, then connect the output of the **Mix Shader1** node to the first **Shader** input socket of the **Mix Shader2** node.

24. Connect the output of the **Subsurface Scattering** node to the second **Shader** input socket of the **Mix Shader3** node.

25. In the **Subsurface Scattering** node, change the **Scale** to **0.020** and the **Radius** to **R 1.000, G 0.400, B 0.100**.

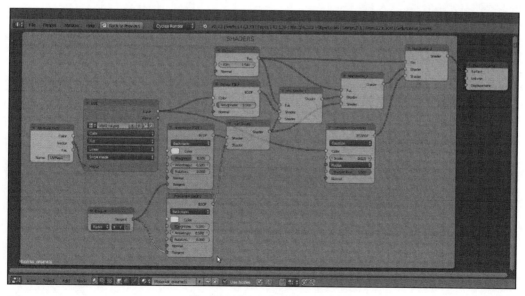

The "Material_enamels" network

26. Save the file.

Thanks to the two **Anisotropic** shaders with their different roughness values, we obtained a nice specularity effect along the length of the **teeth** (and therefore also of the **talons**):

The rendered preview of the teeth (and talons) shader

See also

▶ Shameless self-promotion—one other cookbook, published by Packt Publishing, explaining the logic behind Cycles materials and textures and with several material recipes (https://www.packtpub.com/hardware-and-creative/blender-cycles-materials-and-textures-cookbook-third-edition)

▶ The online documentation (http://wiki.blender.org/index.php/Doc:2.6/Manual/Render/Cycles/Nodes)

Making a node group of the skin shader to reuse it

Once we are satisfied with the reptile skin shader created for the character's **head**, we can copy it to the other parts of the **body**, that is to the other material slots, and then apply the necessary modifications. Those, in this case, just consist of different color and scales image textures.

This means that all the other shader parts can be reused as they are. In this recipe, in fact, we are going to make a node group of these parts so as to easily re-use the shader for the other materials slots.

Getting ready

Just start Blender and re-open the previously saved Gidiosaurus_skin_Cycles_01. blend file.

How to do it...

Let's start to create our skin node group:

1. In the **Material** window, select the slot of the Material_skin_U0V0.

2. Put the mouse pointer in the **Node Editor** window, press the B key and left-click to box-select all the nodes with their respective frames. Then, press the *Shift* key and right-click (twice for each one) to deselect the **Attribute_UV1** node, the **MAPPING** frame, the **COL** node, the **SCALES** node, the **TEXTURES** frame, and the **Material Output** node:

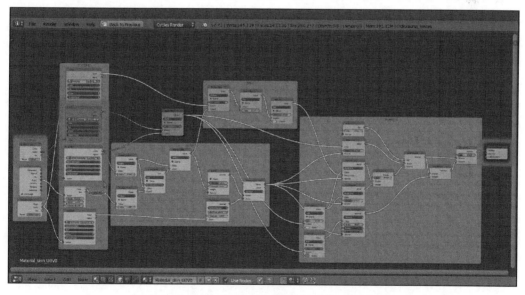

The box-selected nodes and the highlighted deselected ones

3. Press *Ctrl + G* to make a node group of the selected nodes; automatically you are inside the group in **Edit Mode**:

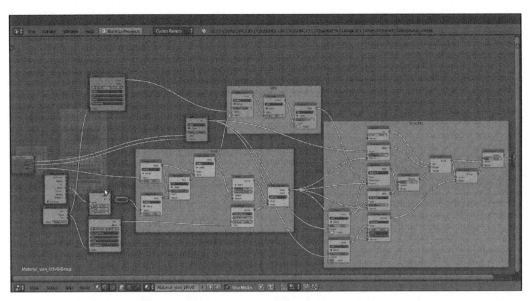

Inside the node group in Edit Mode

4. Click on the **Group Input** node to select it and zoom in on it, then press *N* to call the **Properties** sidepanel. Connect the **Color2** output socket to the first **Value** input socket of the **Multiply_Scales** node, replacing the connection coming from the **Value** output.

5. Go to the **Properties** sidepanel and in the **Interface** subpanel, click on the **Value** item inside the little **Inputs** window; then go down to the **Name** slot and click on the **X** icon button to delete the socket from the **Group Input** node:

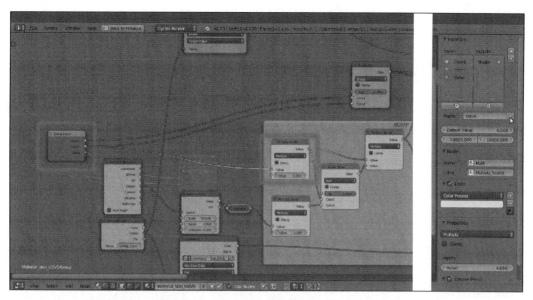

Tweaking the node group input socket connections

6. Still in the **Name** slot in the **Interface** subpanel, select the **Color1** item and rename it **Color_Diff**. Select the **Color2** item and rename it **Color_Scales**:

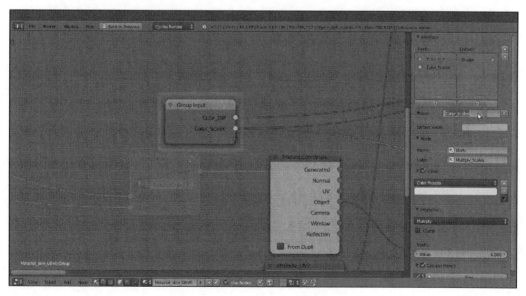

Renaming the node group input sockets

7. Press *Tab* to exit out of **Edit Mode** and close the node group; rename it **Gidiosaurus_skin** and give it a bright yellow color:

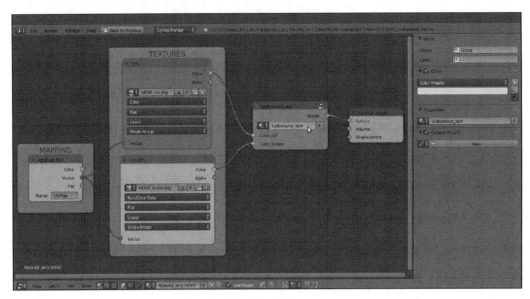

The "Gidiosaurus_skin" node group

8. Now select everything by pressing the *A* key twice and then press *Ctrl + C*.

9. In the **Material** window, select the `Material_U1V0`, then click on the **Use Nodes** button in the **Surface** subpanel.

10. Put the mouse pointer in the **Node Editor** window and delete the already selected default nodes (the **Diffuse BSDF** connected to the **Material Output** nodes), then press *Ctrl + V* to paste all the copied nodes inside the window.

11. Zoom on the **COL** and **SCALES** nodes. Click on the numbered button to the right side of the texture name to make them single users, then click on the folder icon buttons to browse to the `textures` folder and load the proper images according to the material name, that is, the `U1V0_col.png` and `U1V0_scales.png` image textures.

12. Rename the material as `Material_skin_U1V0`:

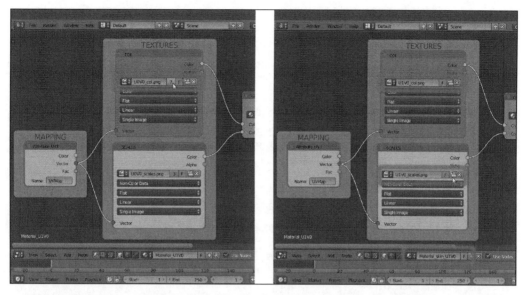

Making the copied textures single users and loading the right image textures for the "Material_skin_U1V0"

13. Repeat step 8 to step 12 for the other remaining **3** material slots and then save the file as `Gidiosaurus_skin_Cycles_02.blend`.

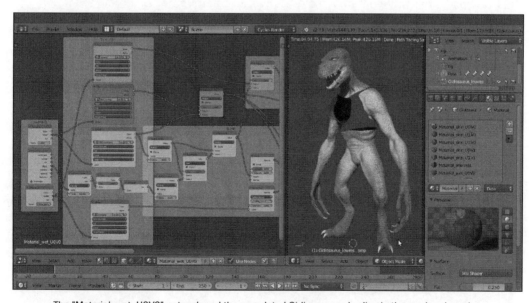

The "Material_wet_U0V0" network and the completed Gidiosaurus shading in the rendered preview

How it works...

Of course, it wasn't mandatory to make a group of the skin shader to reuse it for the other material slots; we could just have selected, copied and pasted all the nodes and frames as they were at the end of the previous recipe.

The (quite big) advantage in having a node group instanced in different materials is that if you need to change something in the internal network, you don't have to repeat the modifications in the node group of each material. It's enough to do it in **Edit Mode** in one of the instances, and all the internal modifications will be reflected in all the instances of the node group used by the other materials.

Building the eyes' shaders in Cycles

The character's **eyes** are made up of two **UV Spheres**, the **Corneas** and the **Eyes** objects: the bigger **Corneas** one enveloping a smaller **Eyes** sphere, which in turn is made up of **three** parts: the **eyeballs**, the **irises**, and the **pupils**.

The **Corneas** sphere was first painted with a totally black **Vertex Color** layer, then painted with a white color only to the vertices corresponding to the front crystalline lens.

The **Eyes** sphere has **three** different materials assigned to the **three** different parts:

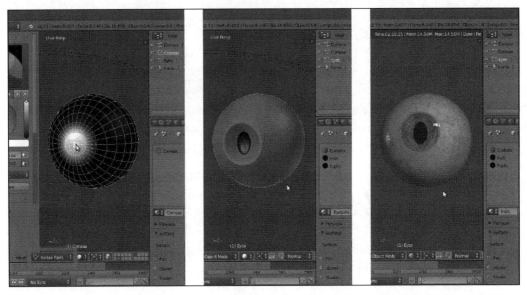

The Corneas object in Vertex Paint mode, the Eyes object with its three materials and the Rendered preview of the textured objects together

Getting ready

Start Blender and open the `Gidiosaurus_skin_Cycle_02.blend` file; save it as `Gidiosaurus_shaders_Cycles.blend`.

1. Enable only the **6th** and the **12th** scene layer, in order to have visible only the **Corneas**, the **Eyes** and the **Lamp** objects (actually the **Camera** is also on the **6th** scene layer, but it's hidden and at the moment we don't need it).

2. Zoom the 3D view onto the **Corneas** and **Eyes** objects, and press _Shift + Z_ to start the **Rendered** preview.

3. In the **Outliner**, disable the _Restrict view-port visibility_ button of the **Eyes** object to hide it.

4. Select the **Corneas** object and go to the **Material** window.

How to do it...

So, let's start with the **Corneas** material, first:

1. In the **Material** window, click on the **New** button in the **Surface** subpanel. Rename the material as `Corneas`.

2. In the **Material** window, switch the **Diffuse BSDF** shader node with a **Mix Shader** node (label it as **Mix Shader_1**). In the first **Shader** slot, select a **Diffuse BSDF** shader node and in the second one select a **Glossy BSDF** shader (label it as **Glossy BSDF1**).

3. Go to the **Node Editor** window and set the **Roughness** of the **Glossy BSDF1** shader to **0.150**, the **Color** to pure white and the **Distribution** to **Sharp**.

4. Select the **Mix Shader_1** node and press _Shift + D_ to duplicate it. Label the duplicate as **Mix Shader_2**, then add a **Subsurface Scattering** node (_Shift + A_ | **Shader** | **Subsurface Scattering**). Connect the output of the **Mix Shader_1** node to the first **Shader** input socket of the **Mix Shader_2** node and the output of the **Subsurface Scattering** shader node to the second **Shader** input socket.

5. Change the **Subsurface Scattering** falloff from **Cubic** to **Gaussian**, set the **Scale** to **0.001** and the **Radius** to **R 9.436, G 3.348, B 1.790**.

6. Add a **Fresnel** node (*Shift + A* | **Input** | **Fresnel**) and connect its output to the **Fac** input socket of the **Mix Shader_2** node; set the **IOR** to **1.340**:

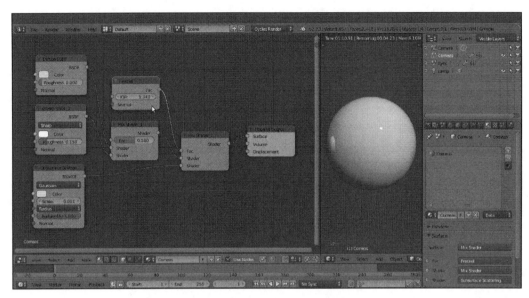

The basic starting "Corneas" shader

7. Add a new **Mix Shader** node (*Shift + A* | **Shader** | **Mix Shader**), label it as **Mix Shader_3** and paste it between the **Mix Shader_2** and the **Material Output** node.

8. Add a new **Mix Shader** node (*Shift + A* | **Shader** | **Mix Shader**), label it as **Mix Shader_4** and connect its output to the second **Shader** input socket of the **Mix Shader_3** node.

9. Add a **Transparent BSDF** shader (*Shift + A* | **Shader** | **Transparent BSDF**) and connect it to the first **Shader** input socket of the **Mix Shader_4** node.

10. Select and press *Shift + D* to duplicate the **Glossy BSDF1** node; label the duplicate as **Glossy BSDF2** and connect its output to the second **Shader** input socket of the **Mix Shader_4** node:

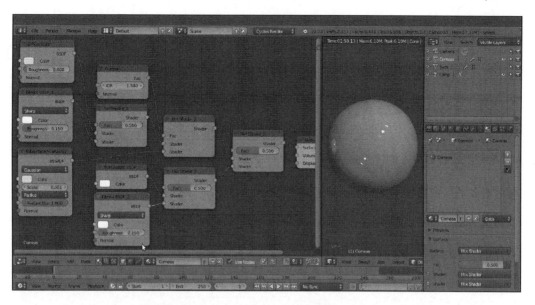

The "Corneas" shader with the added transparency nodes

11. Add a **Layer Weight** node (*Shift + A* | **Input** | **Layer Weight**) and a **Math** node (*Shift + A* | **Converter** | **Math**); set the **Blend** factor of the **Layer Weight** to **0.300** and connect its **Facing** output to the first **Value** input socket of the **Math** node, then set the second **Value** to **0.100** and check the **Clamp** item.

12. Connect the **Math** (labeled as **Add**) output to the **Fac** input sockets of the **Mix Shader_1** and **Mix Shader_4** nodes.

13. Add an **Attribute** node (*Shift + A* | **Input** | **Attribute**) and a **ColorRamp** node (*Shift + A* | **Converter** | **ColorRamp**). In the **Name** slot of the **Attribute** node, type **Col**, then connect its **Color** output to the **Fac** input socket of the **ColorRamp** node.

14. In the **ColorRamp** node, set the **Interpolation** to **B-Spline** and move the white color stop to position **0.100**. Connect its **Color** output to the **Fac** input socket of the **Mix Shader_3** node.

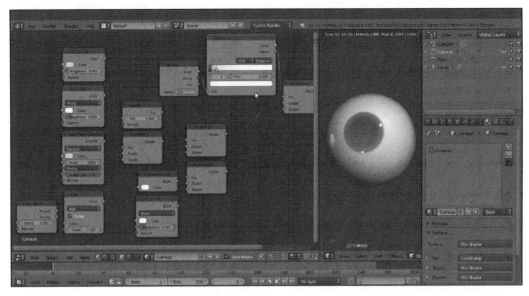

The "Corneas" shader with the transparency area located by the Vertex Color layer

15. Add two **Image Textures** nodes (*Shift + A | Texture | Image Texture*) and label them respectively as **COL** and **BUMP**.

16. Add an **Attribute** node (*Shift + A | Input | Attribute*); in the **Name** slot type **UVMap.001** and connect its **Vector** output to the **Vector** input sockets of the two image texture nodes.

17. Add an **RGB** node (*Shift + A | Input | RGB*), a **MixRGB** node (*Shift + A | Input | MixRGB*) and a **Hue Saturation Value** node (*Shift + A | Input | Hue/Saturation*).

18. Click on the **Open** button of the **COL** node to browse to the `textures` folder and load the image `eyeball_col.jpg`.

19. Connect the **Color** output of the **COL** node to the **Color2** input socket of the **MixRGB** node and the output of the **RGB** node to the **Color1** input socket; set the **Blend Type** to **Burn** and the **Fac** value to **0.800**.

20. Connect the **Color** output of the **MixRGB** node to the **Color** input socket of the **Hue Saturation Value** node, and the output of this latter node to the **Color** input sockets of the **Diffuse BSDF** and **Subsurface Scattering** nodes.

21. Set the **RGB** node color to **R 0.800, G 0.466, B 0.000**; set the **Saturation** value of the **Hue Saturation Value** node to **0.900**.

22. Click on the **Open** button of the **BUMP** node to browse to the `textures` folder and load the image `eyeball_bump.jpg`; set **Color Space** to **Non-Color Data**.

23. Add a **Bump** node (*Shift + A* | **Vector** | **Bump**) and connect the **Color** output of the **BUMP** node to the **Height** input socket of the **Bump** node. Connect the **Normal** output of this latter node to the **Normal** input sockets of the **Diffuse BSDF**, **Glossy BSDF1**, and **Subsurface Scattering** nodes, and set the **Strength** to **0.050**.

24. If you wish, add frames and colors to the different components to make the shader more easily readable:

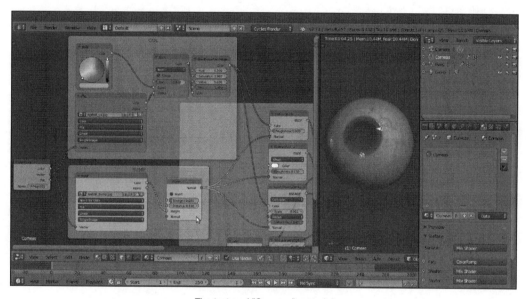

The textured "Corneas" material

Now let's quickly see the materials for the **Eyes** object:

▶ As you can see in the following screenshot, the `Eyeballs` material is essentially the same as we just made for the **Corneas** except for the transparent part; this material, by the way, is obsolete because it's hidden behind the **Corneas'** opaque surface, so can be safely omitted (but I left it in place in case you want to try the totally transparent **Cornea**):

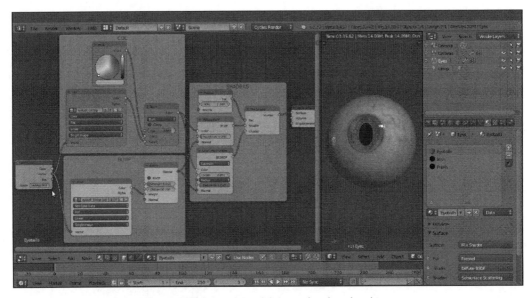

The "Eyeballs" material and the completed rendered eye

▶ The `Irises` material follows the same scheme; the only differences are in the fact that it uses different image textures (`iris_col.jpg` and `iris_bump.jpg`) and that a contrasted (by a **ColorRamp** node) version of the bump image is used as a factor for the mixing of an **Emission** shader; note that the color map is also connected to this **Emission** shader:

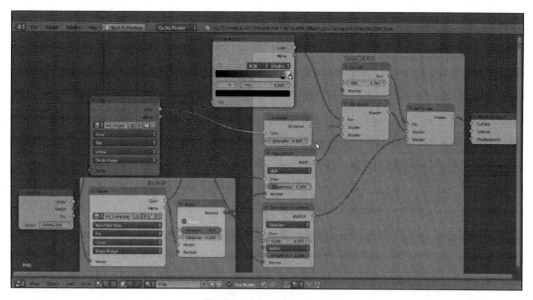

The "Irises" material network

▸ The Pupils are a simple, basic, black diffuse material.

To have a look at these materials, open the `Gidiosaurus_shaders_Cycles.blend` file and select the **Corneas** and **Eyes** objects in the **Outliner**.

How it works...

These shaders are quite simple; the more complex one is the shader for the **Corneas**, essentially because it's made up of **two** materials, one with a slight bump effect and one totally smooth, mixed on the ground of the black and white **Vertex Color** layer that takes care also of the distribution of the transparent and opaque materials on the **Corneas** object itself.

If you are wondering why we didn't use the `Eyeball` material on the underlying **Eyes** sphere, leaving the **Corneas** object totally transparent, the reason is simple: in Cycles, to have a material transparent but also reflecting the environment, you need to use a **Transparent** shader mixed with a **Glass** or a **Glossy** shader node, that inevitably will make whatever material is behind appear darker; sometimes this can look right, in this case I preferred to use a different approach.

 Note that the transparent part in front of the iris of the cornea, to be anatomically correct, should be a convex, bulging half sphere; instead, we modeled the cornea as a simple spherical sheath around the eyeball to avoid complications with the open/closed movements of the eyelids.

Building the armor shaders in Cycles

The last thing to do, for this chapter, is to create the shaders for the **Armor** object, made up of metallic **plates** and leather **tiers**.

Getting ready

Continuing from the previously saved blend file:

1. Enable the **6th** and the **13th** scene layer and select the **Armor** object in the **Outliner**.

2. Put the mouse pointer in the 3D viewport and press the *0* key on the numpad to go into **Camera** view; fit the window into the field of view.

3. Go to the **Material** window and press the **+** icon button to the right side to add **four** empty material slots to the **armor**. Select the first material slot and click on the **New** button in the **Surface** subpanel, and rename the material Armor_U0V0.

4. Select the **second** material slot, click on the **New** button and rename the material as Armor_U1V0; repeat for the **third** slot and rename the material as Leather and repeat also for the **fourth** slot and rename the material Armor_rivets.

5. Switch the **Node Editor** window temporarily with a **UV/Image Editor** window, then press *Tab* to go into **Edit Mode**; go to the **UV Maps** subpanel under the **Object Data** window to be sure you have the **UVMap** coordinates layer (the first one) as the active one, then enable the *Keep UV and edit mode mesh selection in sync* button on the **UV/Image Editor** toolbar.

6. In the **Node Editor** window, box-select the UV islands of the **U1V0** tile, then in the **Material** window, select the Armor_U1V0 material and click on the **Assign** button.

7. Still in **Edit Mode**, select all the tiers vertices and then select the Leather material, click on the **Assign** button; repeat the operation by selecting all the rivets and assigning them to the Armor_rivets material.

8. Disable the *Keep UV and edit mode mesh selection in sync* button on the **UV/Image Editor** toolbar, go out of **Edit Mode** and switch the **UV/Image Editor** window back to the **Node Editor** window.

9. Put the mouse pointer inside the 3D viewport and press *Shift + Z* to start the **Rendered** preview.

How to do it...

We are first going to create the shader for the metal **plates**:

1. In the **Material** window, select the `Armor_U0V0` material slot.

2. Go to the **Node Editor** window and switch the **Diffuse BSDF** shader node with a **Mix Shader** node; in the first **Shader** slot, select a **Diffuse BSDF** shader node and in the second one, select an **Anisotropic BSDF** shader.

3. Go to the **Node Editor** window and set the **Roughness** of the **Diffuse BSDF** shader to **0.300** and the **Anisotropy** of the **Anisotropic BSDF** shader to **0.300**.

4. Add a **Fresnel** node (_Shift + A_ | **Input** | **Fresnel**) and connect its output to the **Fac** input socket of the **Mix Shader** node; set the **IOR** to **100.000**.

5. Add a **Tangent** node (_Shift + A_ | **Input** | **Tangent**) and connect its output to the **Tangent** input socket of the **Anisotropic BSDF** shader node; set the **Tangent** to **Z**.

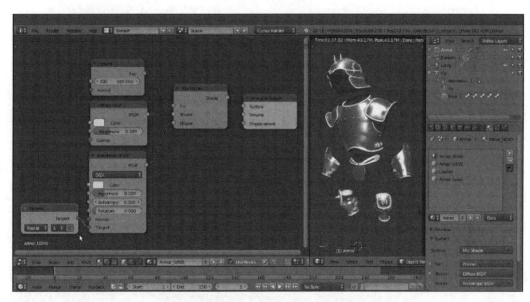

Starting to build the metal shader for the armor

6. Add a **Frame** (_Shift + A_ | **Layout** | **Frame**) and parent the nodes, except the **Material Output**, to it, then label it as **SHADERS**.

7. Add three **Image Textures** nodes (_Shift + A_ | **Texture** | **Image Texture**) and a **Voronoi Texture** node (_Shift + A_ | **Texture** | **Voronoi Texture**), then add two **Attribute** nodes (_Shift + A_ | **Input** | **Attribute**) and a **Texture Coordinate** node (_Shift + A_ | **Input** | **Texture Coordinate**).

8. Label the **Attribute** nodes as **Attribute_UV1** and **Attribute_UV2**. Label the **Image Texture** nodes as **COL_iron**, **NORMALS_iron**, and **VCOL_iron**.

9. Connect the **Vector** output of the **Attribute_UV1** node to the **Vector** input socket of the **COL_iron** node. Connect the **Vector** output of the **Attribute_UV2** to the **Vector** input sockets of both the **VCOL_iron** and **NORMALS_iron** nodes. Connect the **Object** output of the **Texture Coordinate** node to the **Vector** input socket of the **Voronoi Texture** node.

10. Click on the **Open** button of the **VCOL_iron** node, browse to the `textures` folder and load the image `vcol2.png`. Set the **Color Space** to **Non-Color Data**. Connect its **Color** output to the **Roughness** input socket of the **Anisotropic BSDF** shader node.

11. Click on the **Open** button of the **COL_iron** node, browse to the `textures` folder and load the image `iron_U0V0.png`. Connect its **Color** output to the **Color** input sockets of the **Diffuse BSDF** and **Anisotropic BSDF** shader nodes.

12. Click on the **Open** button of the **NORMALS_iron** node, browse to the `textures` folder and load the image `norm2.png`. Set the **Color Space** to **Non-Color Data**.

13. Set the **Scale** of the **Voronoi Texture** to **15.000**:

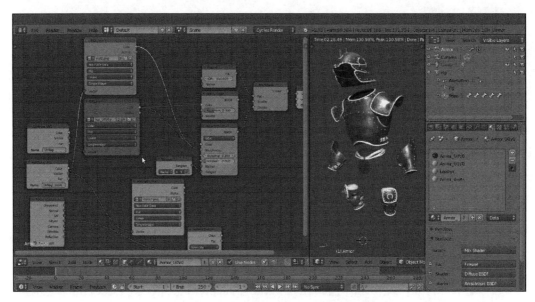

Adding the textures to the "Armor_U0V0" material

14. Add a **ColorRamp** node (*Shift + A* | **Converter** | **ColorRamp**) and a **Math** node (*Shift + A* | **Converter** | **Math**). Paste the **ColorRamp** node right after the **VCOL** node, and the **Math** node right after the **ColorRamp**.

15. Label the **ColorRamp** as **ColorRamp_Vcol** and set the **Interpolation** to **B-Spline**, then move the black color stop to position **0.245** and the white color stop to position **0.755**.

16. Label the **Math** node as **Spec_soften** and set the second **Value** to **0.100**.

17. Add a **MixRGB** node (*Shift + A* | **Color** | **MixRGB**) and label it as **Difference_Col_iron**; set the **Blend Type** to **Difference** and the **Fac** value to **0.300**.

18. Connect the **Color** output of the **COL** node to the **Color1** input socket and the **Color** output of the **ColorRamp_Vcol** node to the **Color2** input socket. Connect the **Color** output of the **Difference_Col_iron** node to the **Color** input sockets of the **Diffuse BSDF** and the **Anisotropic BSDF** shader nodes, replacing the old connections.

19. Add a **Normal Map** node (*Shift + A* | **Vector** | **Normal Map**), a **Bump** node (*Shift + A* | **Vector** | **Bump**), and a **Vector Math** node (*Shift + A* | **Converter** | **Vector Math**).

20. Connect the **Color** output of the **NORMALS_iron** node to the **Color** input socket of the **Normal Map** node; click on the empty slot (*UV Map for tangent space maps*) on this latter node to select the **UVMap_norm** item.

21. Connect the **Normal** output of the **Normal Map** node to the first **Vector** input socket of the **Vector Math** node; label this latter as **Average_Normals** and set the **Operation** to **Average**, then connect its **Vector** output to the **Normal** input sockets of the **Diffuse BSDF** and **Anisotropic BSDF** shader nodes.

22. Add a **MixRGB** node (*Shift + A* | **Color** | **MixRGB**), label it as **Add_Bump**, set the **Blend Type** to **Add** and the **Fac** value to **1.000**. Connect the **Color** output of the **COL** node to the **Color1** input socket of the **Add_Bump** node also, and the **Color** output of the **Voronoi Texture** node to the **Color2** input socket.

23. Connect the **Color** output of the **Add_Bump** node to the **Height** input socket of the **Bump** node, and the **Normal** output of this latter node to the second **Vector** input socket of the **Average_Normals** node. Set the **Strength** of the **Bump** node to **1.000**.

24. Add two **Math** nodes (*Shift + A* | **Converter** | **Math**), label them respectively as **Bump_strength1** and **Bump_strength2**; set the **Operation** to **Multiply** for both, then paste the **Bump_strength1** node between the **COL_iron** and the **Add_Bump** nodes and set the second **Value** to **0.020**. Paste the **Bump_strength2** node between the **Voronoi_Texture** and the **Add_Bump** nodes, and set the second **Value** to **0.010**.

25. Add frames to highlight the different components:

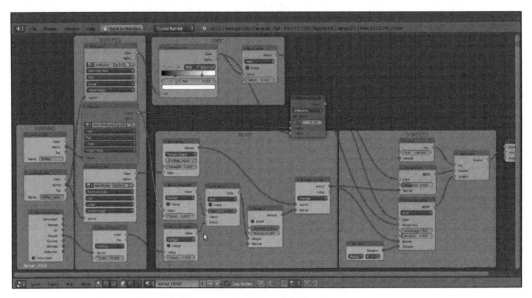

The completed "Armor_UOVO" material

The first **Armor** shader is ready! Now it's very easy to obtain the others:

26. Press *A* twice to select all the nodes, then press *Ctrl + C* to copy them.

27. In the **Material** window, select the `Armor_U1V0` material slot and in the **Node Editor** window, delete the default **Diffuse** and **Material Output** nodes; then press *Ctrl + V* to paste the nodes copied from the other material.

28. Zoom to the **COL** node and click on the numbered button to the right side of the texture name slot to make it single user, then click on the folder icon button to browse to the `texture` folder and load the image `iron_U1V0.png`.

29. Reselect the `Armor_U0V0` material slot and repeat the step 26 and 27, this time pasting the nodes inside the `Armor_rivets` material slot:

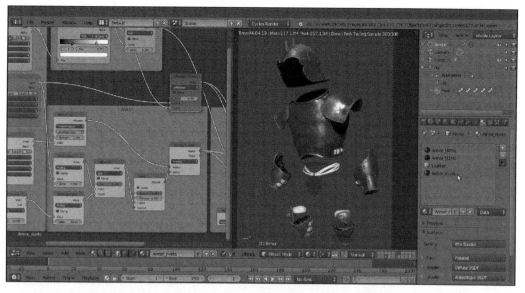

The "Armor_rivets" material and the rendered completed armor

30. Save the file.

How it works...

The construction of the metallic **armor plates** material follows basically the same scheme we used for the other materials:

▸ First the shaders were produced, where the metallic look is mainly due to the **Anisotropic BSDF** shader mixed with the diffuse component with a quite high **IOR** value (metals can often have values from **20.000** to **200.000**; we used a midway value of **100.000**).

▸ The shininess of the metallic surface has been modulated through the output of the vcol2.png image, a **Dirty Vertex Color** layer we had previously baked to an image.

- ▶ The color of the **Armor** surface has been modulated as well through a **Difference** node with the same `vcol2.png` image.

- ▶ The bump pattern works by first adding the **Voronoi** and the **color map** output and then averaging the result with the **normal map** output.

There's more...

The last material created for our character is a very simple leather material made mainly from the output of a **Voronoi Texture** node, contrasted, inverted, and used as bump pattern:

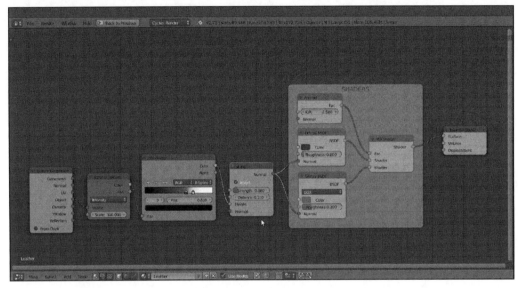

The simple "Leather" material

This completes the creation of the **Gidiosaurus** shaders in **Cycles**:

The completed Gidiosaurus character in Cycles

Of course, reflecting materials, for example, the metallic **armor** surface or the **corneas** (but to some extent also the reptile **skin**), need something to reflect to show them at their best; we'll see this in the last chapter of this cookbook.

In the next chapter, which is the penultimate chapter, we'll see the creation of the same materials in **Blender Internal**.

13

Creating the Materials in Blender Internal

In this chapter, we will cover the following recipes:

- ▶ Building the reptile skin shaders in Blender Internal
- ▶ Building the eyes' shaders in Blender Internal
- ▶ Building the armor shaders in Blender Internal

Introduction

In this chapter we'll see how to set up the materials for the **Gidiosaurus** and the **Armor** in the **Blender Render** engine; in fact, although not exactly of the same quality as in **Cycles**, it is also possible to obtain quite similar shader results in **Blender Internal**:

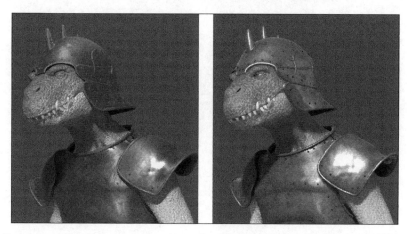

Comparison of the Gidiosaurus character rendered in Cycles (left) and Blender Internal (right)

If you are wondering why we should re-do in the **Blender Render** engine, which is quite old and no longer developed and/or supported, the same thing we have already done in **Cycles**, there are several possible reasons: for example, no doubt **Cycles** is superior in quality but, compared with the scanline **BI**, its rendering is (and, being a path-tracer, always will be) slower; even with the aid of a render-farm, rendering times are still a *money* issue in the production of animations.

The previous screenshot shows, for comparison, only the top parts of two full shot renderings of the **Gidiosaurus** character: the **Cycles** rendering to the left took around **1** hour and **20** minutes (**1920 × 1080** resolution CPU rendering with *Intel Core 2 Duo T6670 2.20 GHz* and **4** GB of RAM, in Ubuntu 12.04 64-bit); the **Blender Internal** rendering to the right took only **26** minutes.

One other reason is that **Cycles'** normals baking capabilities are still not as good as in **Blender Internal** (at the moment, it bakes only the real geometry, contrary to **Blender Internal**, which can also bake the bump output of textures to normal maps), or that it's not as flexible for **Non-Photorealistic Rendering** (**NPR**) as the **Blender Render** engine.

Just a quick note: normally, materials under the **Blender Render** engine are created directly in the slots inside the **Material** window, often switching to the **Texture** window and back; in the following screenshot, you can see the **Rendered** preview of a generic Red *mono* material assigned to a **UV Sphere**:

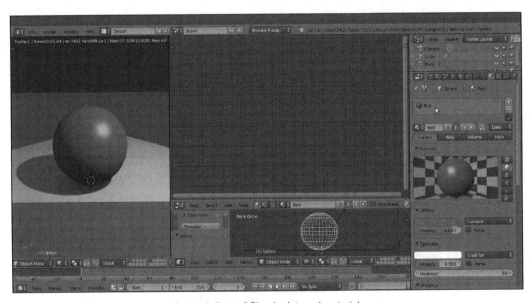

A generic "mono" Blender Internal material

But, it's also possible to use node materials in **Blender Internal**, created and connected inside the **Node Editor** window; basically, let's say that *two or more materials can be mixed through nodes* to obtain more advanced results. In the following screenshot, for example, the mono Red material is mixed with a mono Green material through the output of a **Voronoi** texture connected to the **Fac** input socket of a **MixRGB** node:

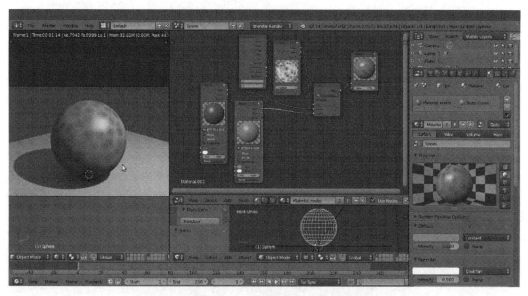

Two mono materials mixed in the Node Editor window

This is the way we are going to create the **Blender Internal** shaders.

Building the reptile skin shaders in Blender Internal

Because we want to keep the materials we already created for **Cycles** in the same blend file (and the reason will be clear in the next chapter), before we start with the creation of the **Blender Internal** shaders, we must prepare the file a bit.

Getting ready

The first thing to do is to open the last saved blend file, add **Frames** to each material in the **Node Editor** window, and label them with the material name followed by the suffix **_Cycles**; this is to later distinguish them from the material we will build for **BI**.

Therefore:

1. Start Blender and load the `Gidiosaurus_shaders_Cycles.blend` file.

2. In the **Outliner**, select the **Gidiosaurus_lowres** mesh, go to the **Material** window and click on the `Material_skin_UOVO` slot; put the mouse pointer inside the **Node Editor** window and press *Shift + A* to add a **Frame** (*Shift + A* | **Layout** | **Frame**).

3. Press *A* to select all the nodes (the added **Frame**, already selected, becomes the active one) and then press *Ctrl + P* to parent them to the active **Frame**.

4. Select only the **Frame** and press *N* to call the **Properties** sidepanel; in the **Label** slot under the **Name** subpanel, type **Material_skin_UOVO_Cycles**, then go down to the **Properties** subpanel and increase the **Label Size** to **40**.

5. Repeat the procedure for all the Cycles' **Gidiosaurus_lowres** materials, for the **Eyes** and **Corneas** and for the **Armor** materials.

   So, for example, the `Material_skin_UOVO`, in the **Node Editor** window, becomes this:

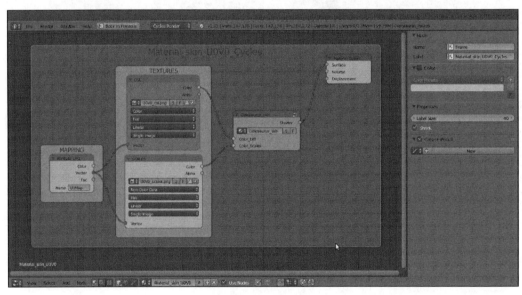

A "framed" Cycles material

Also, the `Material_wet_U0V0`, becomes this:

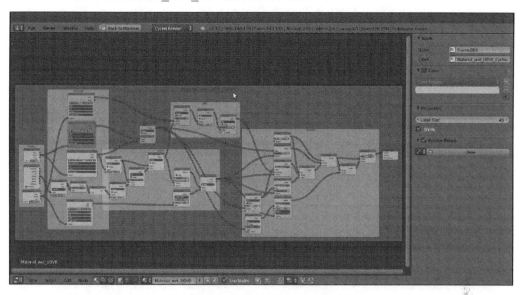

Another "framed" Cycles material

Note that the name of the material is the same as before, the only difference is that a **Frame** labeled with the **_Cycles** suffix has been added in the **Node Editor** window to visually group all the Cycles' nodes that are a constituent of the shader.

6. Now go to the *Scene data block* button on the main top header; left-click on it and rename the **Scene** label as **Cycles**:

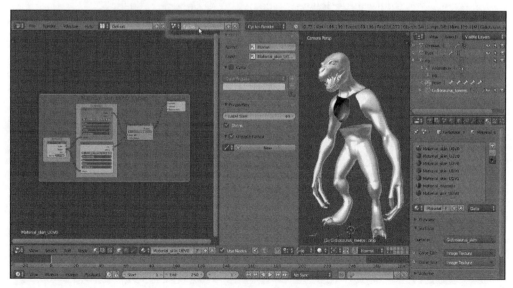

Renaming the Scene label

7. Click on the **+** icon button to the right of the datablock name; in the pop-up little **New Scene** panel, select the **Link Objects** item:

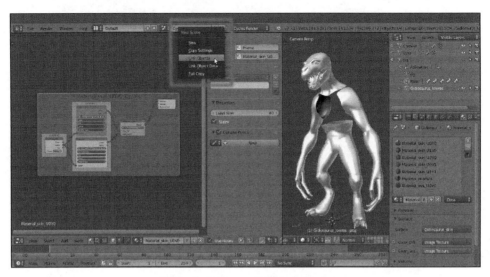

Adding a new scene with linked objects

At this point we have created a new scene (automatically labeled as **Cycles.001**) that is sharing the same objects of the other (**Cycles**) scene (be aware of this: the objects in one scene are not a copy of the others, *they are the same objects shared/linked between the two scenes*); you can say which objects are actually linked from one scene to another, by their blue pivot point (for example, look at the highlighted pivot point of the **Gidiosaurus_lowres** object in the following screenshot):

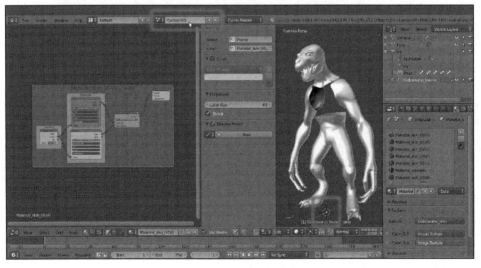

A new scene with linked objects

The advantages of creating new scenes with linked objects are obvious: we can have totally different rendering engines, or different worlds or lamps, in the different scenes and use the same objects and meshes data; so, for example, any modification to a linked object in one scene will automatically be transferred to the other scenes.

Furthermore, avoid duplicating the objects for each scene; this will help to keep a small file size.

8. Rename the scene from **Cycles.001** to **BI**, then move to the *Engine to use for rendering* button a bit to the right and switch from **Cycles Render** to **Blender Render**.

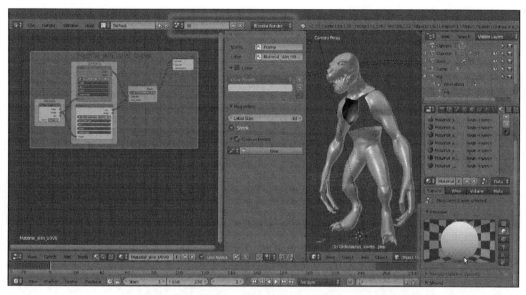

Switching to the Blender Render engine and the "empty material" preview

 Note that the **Preview** subpanel of the **Material** window shows an *empty material*, to point out that under the current **Blender Render** engine, the material slot, although filled with the **Cycles** material, doesn't have anything to render yet.

9. In the **Outliner**, select the **Lamp** (be sure to have enabled both the **11th** and the **6th** scene layers); go to the **Object Data** window, set the energy to **14.000** and the color to **R 1.000, G 1.000, B 0.650**; under the **Shadow** subpanel, enable the **Buffer Shadow** item, **Filter Type** to **Gauss**, **Soft** = **12.000**, **Size** = **4000**, and **Samples** = **16**. Set **Clip Start** = **9.000** and **Clip End** = **19.000**.

10. Go to the **World** window and enable the **Ambient Occlusion** by checking the item in the subpanel of the same name; leave the **Blend Mode** to **Add** and set the **Factor** to **0.35**.

11. Go further down to the **Gather** subpanel and click on the **Approximate** button: check the **Pixel Cache** item and then check also the **Falloff** checkbox under the **Attenuation** item; set the **Strength** to **0.900**.

12. Enable the **Indirect Lighting** item just above and set the **Factor** to **0.65**.

    These **World** settings are to obtain a sort of **Global Illumination** effect in the **Blender Render** engine; to learn more, have a look at http://www.blender.org/manual/render/blender_render/world/index.html.

13. Save the file as Gidiosaurus_shaders_Blender_Internal.blend.

How to do it...

Let's start with the first top **Gidiosaurus** skin material, so:

1. Be sure to have the **Gidiosaurus_lowres** object selected and, back in the **Material** window, click on the Material_skin_U0V0 slot.

2. Put the mouse pointer inside the **Node Editor** window and press *Shift + A* (*Shift + A* | **Input** | **Material**) to add a **Material** node to the window; then press again *Shift + A* and add an **Output** node (*Shift + A* | **Output** | **Output**):

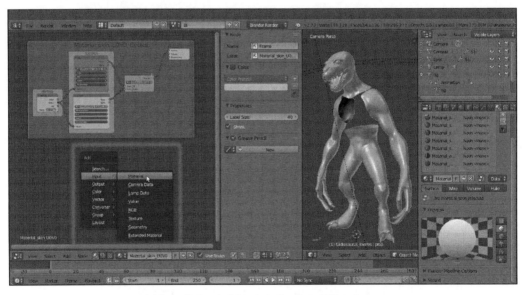

Adding a first material node in the Node Editor window

3. Connect the **Color** output of the **Material** node to the **Color** input socket of the **Output** node:

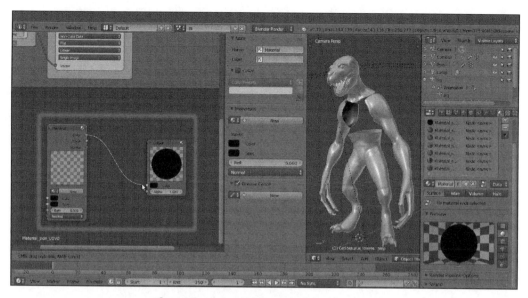

Connecting the material node to the output node

4. Now click on the **New** button on the **Material** node to create a new default **Blender Internal** material:

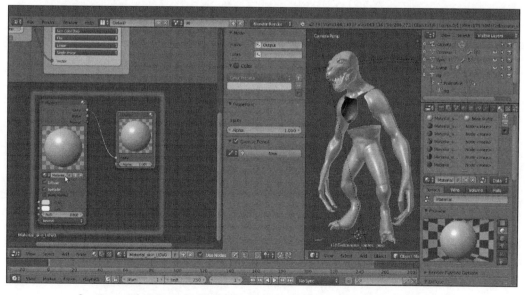

Creating a default "mono" material by clicking on the New button in the material node

5. In the **Properties** sidepanel of the **Node Editor** window (*N* key to call it) label the **Material** node as **COL** and assign a color.

   If you look now at the **Material** window, close to the right side of the material datablock (the name of the material), there is an already enabled and squared button with the symbol of the nodes.

   In our case, that button is already enabled because we are already using material nodes; because it's enabled, a second material datablock slot has appeared just further down: that's the datablock slot for any node selected inside the **Node Editor** window and that is part of a material node.

   The purpose of this second datablock slot is to let us know which material is the selected one and we are therefore going to edit it by tweaking all the values in the subpanels below.

6. Go to the **Material** window to find the second material name slot: rename the material selected in the **Node Editor** window as `Material_UOVO_Col`; you can do the same thing by clicking on the name datablock on the **COL** node interface.

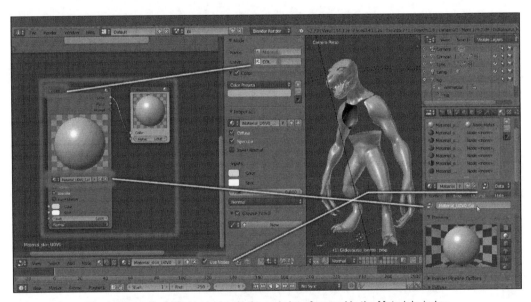

The corresponding datablock slots in the node interface and in the Material window

7. In the **Node Editor** window, or in the *N* **Properties** sidepanel, deselect the **Specular** item.

8. Go to the top of the **Material** window and click on the pin icon to the left of the contest; by doing this only the selected material is shown in the window.

9. Go to the **Diffuse** sidepanel and click on the **Diffuse Shader Model** button to select the **Oren-Nayar** item; then go down to the **Shading** subpanel and enable the **Cubic Interpolation** item:

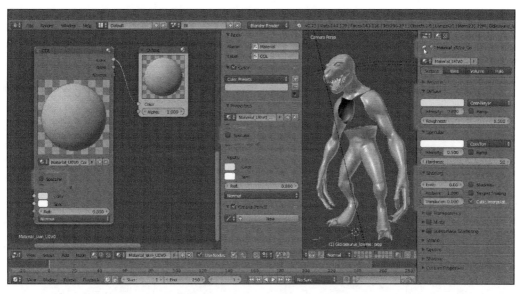

The Specular item to be disabled in the Node Editor window and the shader's parameters to be tweaked in the Material window

10. At this point, press *Shift + B* to draw a box around the character's head in the **Camera** view and then zoom to it. If your computer is powerful enough to allow you to work without slowing down, put the mouse pointer inside the 3D viewport and press *Shift + Z* to start the **Rendered** preview; in any case, you can easily enable or disable the preview every time you need it:

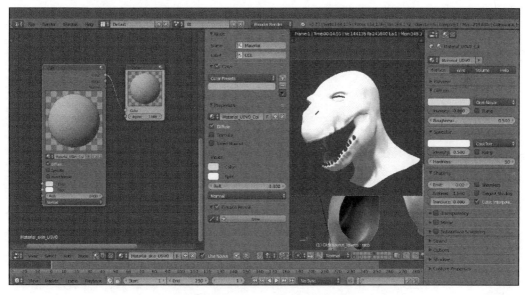

Cropping and starting the rendered preview

11. Click on the **Texture** window icon at the top right of the main **Properties** panel, just above the contest, be sure to have the **first** top texture slot selected and click on the **New** button to automatically load a default **Image or Movie** texture panel:

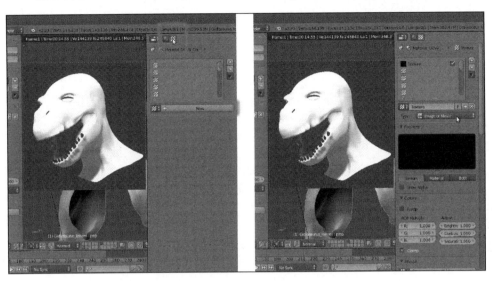

Adding a first texture slot to the material

12. Collapse the **Preview** and the **Colors** subpanels, which at this moment we don't need, and click on the double little arrows to the left side of the **New/Open** buttons in the **Image** subpanel (remember that we have already loaded inside the blend file all the image textures we need, because of the **Cycles** shaders!): in the pop-up menu, select the U0V0_col.png item:

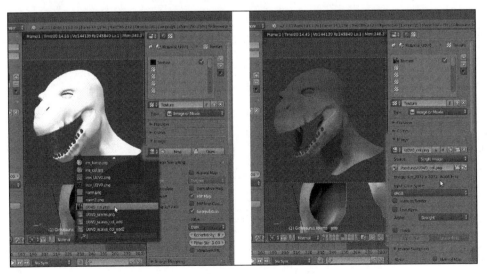

Selecting the right image texture from the drop-down list

13. Go further down to find the **Mapping** subpanel: be sure to have the **Coordinates** set to **UV**, the **Projection** to **Flat** (default settings) and click on the **Map** empty slot to select the **UVMap** item.

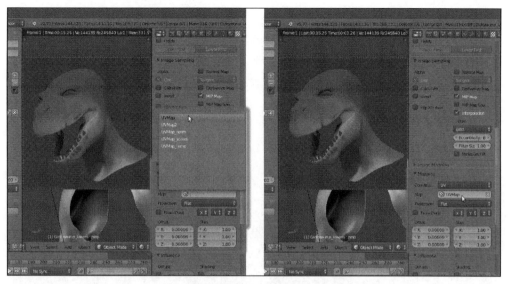

Selecting the right UV coordinates mapping

14. Go even further down to find the **Influence** subpanel: be sure that the diffuse **Color** channel is the one enabled and that the slider is set to **1.000** (again, default settings):

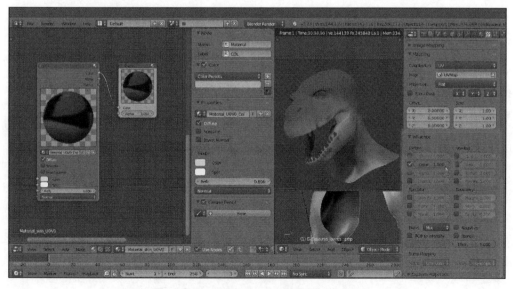

The Influence settings subpanel for the texture

15. Scroll back to the top of the **Texture** window and click on the *Unique datablock ID name* slot, where the generic **Texture** name is written; rename it as U0V0 (as you can see in the following screenshot, this is the name that also appears in the textures list window):

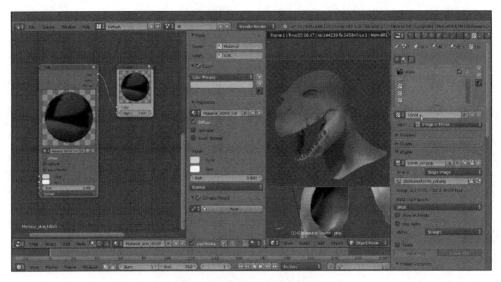

Renaming the texture datablock

16. Now click on the empty **second** slot: again, click on the **New** button, click on the double arrows and this time load the image U0V0_scales.png.

17. In the *Unique datablock ID name* slot, rename it as U0V0_scales_col_add1.

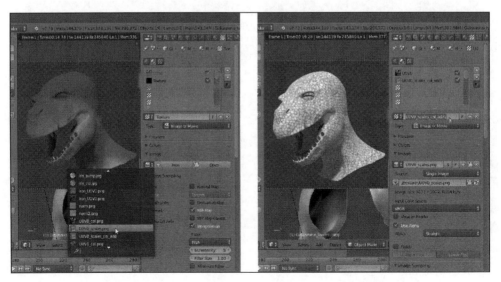

Adding a new texture slot, loading a new image texture and renaming it accordingly

Note that as we load the U0V0_scales.png image in the **second** texture slot, the **Rendered** preview changes to show the grayscale image mapped on the model; this is because, by default, the **Influence** of any new added texture is set to the **Color** channel with a value **1.000** and **Blend Type** to **Mix**.

18. In the **Input Color Space** slot under the **Image** subpanel, change the default **sRGB** to **Non-Color**; then, scroll down to the **Mapping** panel to set the **UVMap** coordinates item and then go to the **Influence** subpanel: leave the **Color** channel enabled but move the slider to the lower value of **0.350**, then change the **Blend Type** to **Linear Light** (for the **Blender Internal** materials, the **Blend Type** works as the layer system of a 2D image editor such as **Photoshop** or **Gimp**); enable the **RGB to Intensity** item and change the pink color to **R 0.130, G 0.051, B 0.030**.

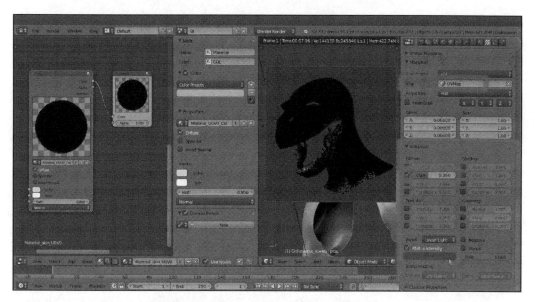

Tweaking the Influence settings for the second texture

19. Go up to expand the **Colors** subpanel: set the **Brightness** and the **Contrast** to **0.500**, to make the texture less bright and less contrasted. Go down to the **Image Sampling** subpanel and set the **Filter Size** to **3.00**, to blur the image (values beyond **1.00** start to blur the image more and more):

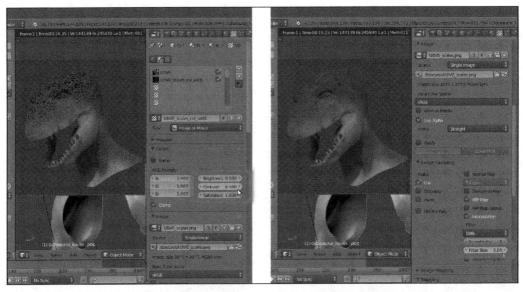

Modifying the appearance of the second image texture

20. Select the **third** empty texture slot and repeat the procedure, again loading the U0V0_scales.png image; in the *Unique datablock ID name* slot, rename it as U0V0_scales_col_add2.

21. Scroll down to the **Mapping** panel to set the **UVMap** coordinates item and then in the **Influence** subpanel, leave the **Color** channel enabled at value **1.000** but change the **Blend Type** to **Subtract**. Set the **Brightness** to **0.100** and the **Contrast** to **1.500**. Again, set the **Filter Size** to **3.00**.

22. Select the **fourth** texture slot, load again the U0V0_scales.png image, rename it U0V0_scales_col, set the **UVMap** coordinates layer, **Color** = **1.000** and **Blend Type** = **Divide**:

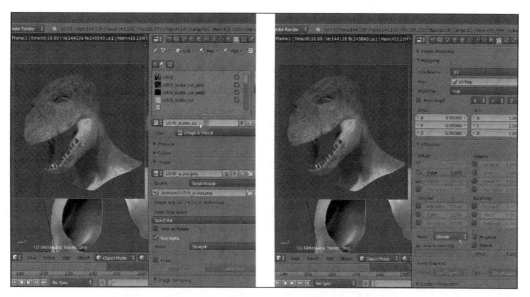

Adding more texture slots with different settings

23. Select the **fifth** texture slot, load the `vcol.png` image again, rename it `vcol`, set the **UVMap_norm** coordinates layer, **Color = 0.800** and **Blend Type = Screen**:

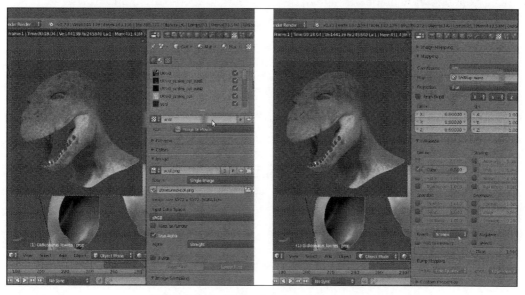

Adding the baked Vertex Color image texture as well

At this point we have completed the **first** component of the skin shader, that is, the **diffuse color** component; in the following *F12* render you can see the final result:

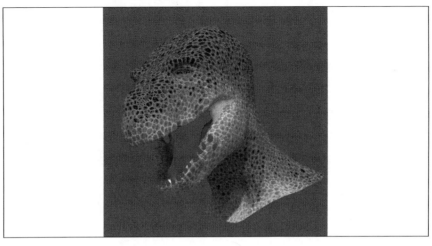

The completed diffuse color component of the Blender Internal skin material

Note that this *F12* render result is quite different from the **Rendered** real-time preview; this is probably due to the complexity of using several textures inside a node material system with the (sadly) bad real-time viewport performances of Blender.

 Also note that the only parts of the **Gidiosaurus** mesh that appear in the rendered image are actually the parts we assigned a **Blender Internal** material to; in fact, the **teeth** and the **tongue** are rendered as blank shapes (even working as a mask).

Now, we can carry on with building the second component of the shader, the **glossy** component.

24. Put the mouse pointer inside the **Node Editor** window and add a new **Material** node (*Shift + A* | **Input** | **Material**); label it as **SPEC** and then click on the **New** button to create a new material: rename it `Material_U0V0_Spec`.

25. Go to the **Material** window; in the **Diffuse** sidepanel, change the shader model to **Oren-Nayar**, then change the color to a deep blue **R 0.020, G 0.051, B 0.089**.

26. Enable the **Ramp** item: in the slider, switch the positions of the two color stops (that is: white color stop to position **0.000** and black color stop to position **1.000**), then select the white color stop; put the mouse on the deep blue color slot of the **Diffuse** subpanel and press *Ctrl + C* to copy it; put the mouse pointer on the color slot of the selected color stop and press *Ctrl + V* to paste the deep blue color.

27. Click on the **Diffuse Ramp Input** button at the bottom of the subpanel to select the **Normal** item and on the **Diffuse Ramp Blend** button to the right to select the **Multiply** item:

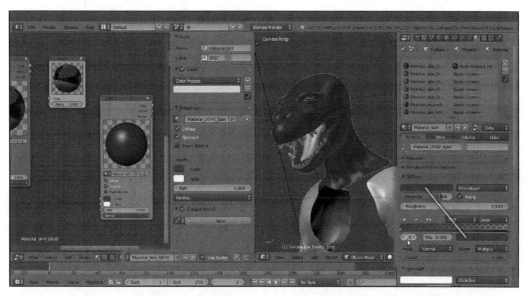

The "Material_UOVO_Spec", to be used inside the "Material_skin_UOVO" node material

28. Scroll down to the **Specular** subpanel: change the color to a light blue **R 0.474, G 0.642, B 0.683**; set the **Intensity** to **0.600** and the **Hardness** to **10**.

29. Enable the **Ramp** item: select the white color stop and change the color to **R 0.761, G 1.000, B 0.708**, then set the **Diffuse Ramp Input** button to **Normal** and the **Diffuse Ramp Blend** to **Color**.

30. Go to the **Shading** subpanel and enable the **Cubic Interpolation** item:

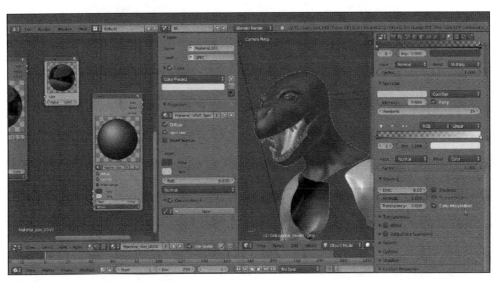

Setting the parameters of the specularity component

31. Go to the **Textures** window; select the top **first** empty texture slot and click on the **New** button. Load the image `vcol.png`, rename the ID datablock as `vcol_light` and go to the **Colors** subpanel: set the **Brightness** to **1.150** and the **Contrast** to **0.850**. Go down to the **Mapping** subpanel and set the **UVMap_norm** coordinates layer, then in the **Influence** subpanel disable the diffuse **Color** channel and enable both the **Intensity** and the **Hardness** channels under **Specular**; set the **Blend Type** to **Value**:

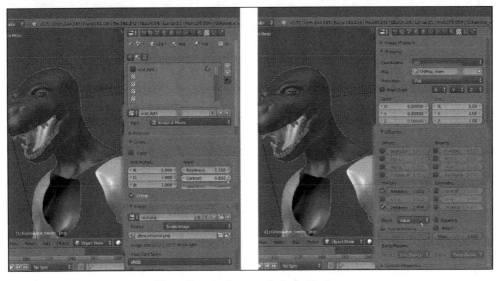

The settings for the specularity first texture

32. Go to the **second** slot and load the image UOVO_scales.png; rename it as UOVO_scales_hardness, in the **Mapping** subpanel, set the **UVMap** coordinates layer, in the **Influence** subpanel disable the diffuse **Color** and enable the **Hardness** channel under **Specular** to **0.125**. In the **Image Sampling** subpanel set the **Filter Size** to **5.00**.

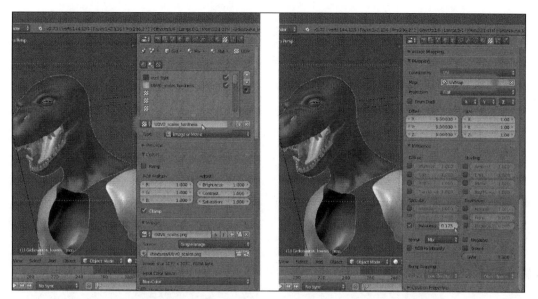

Re-using the "UOVO_scales.png" image texture for the specularity hardness

33. In the **third** slot load the image Ice_Lake_Ref.hdr, a free high dynamic range image licensed under the Creative Commons Attribution-Noncommercial-Share Alike 3.0 License from the **sIBL Archive** (http://www.hdrlabs.com/sibl/archive.html); there is a reason we are now using the **hdr** image, and it's explained in the *How it works...* section.

34. Rename the image ID datablock as `env_refl_skin` and in the **Colors** subpanel, set the **Brightness** to **1.200** and the **Contrast** to **1.500**; go to the **Mapping** subpanel and set the **Texture Coordinates** to **Reflection**. Down in the **Influence** subpanel, enable both the **Intensity** channel under **Diffuse** and **Specular** and set their sliders to **0.500**; enable also, the **Color** channel under **Specular** and set the sliders of both the **Color** channels to **0.500** as well. Set the **Blend Type** to **Screen**, enable the **RGB to Intensity** item and set the color to the same deep blue of the diffuse color (**R 0.020, G 0.051, B 0.089**):

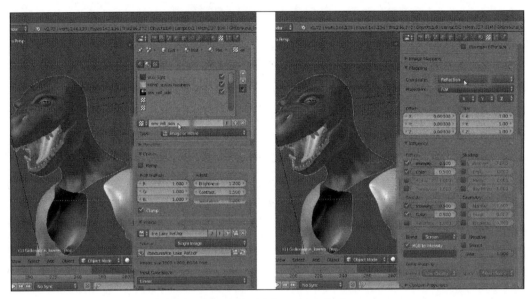

Using the environment hdr image as reflection map

If you want to see the effect of the single components in the **Rendered** preview as we build the shader, just temporarily disconnect the **COL** node link to the **Output** node and replace it with the **Color** output of the **SPEC** node (in this case):

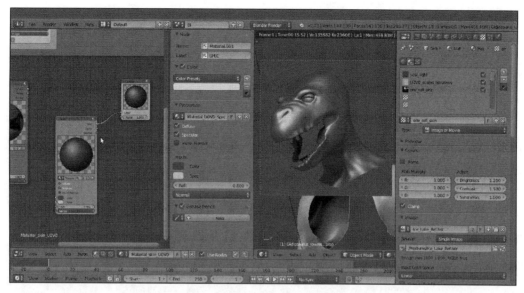

Testing the specularity component material in the rendered preview

35. At this point, add a **MixRGB** node (*Shift + A* | **Color** | **MixRGB**) and move it on the link connecting the **COL** node to the **Output** node, to automatically paste it between them; then connect the **Color** output of the **SPEC** node to the **Color2** input socket of the **MixRGB** node, set the **Blend Type** of this latter node to **Add** and its **Fac** value to **1.000**:

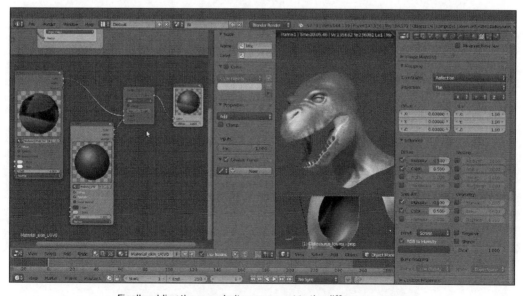

Finally adding the specularity component to the diffuse component

36. Add a **RGB Curves** node (*Shift + A* | **Color** | **RGB Curves**) and a **ColorRamp** node (*Shift + A* | **Converter** | **ColorRamp**); paste the **RGB Curves** node between the **SPEC** and the **MixRGB** node, then connect the **Color** output of the **SPEC** node also to the **ColorRamp** input socket:

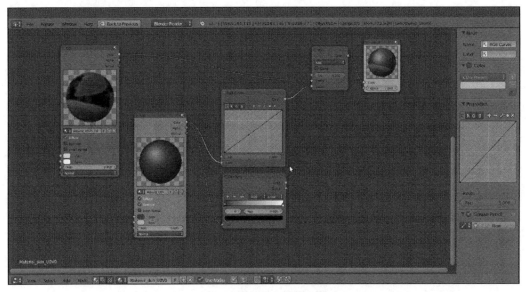

Adding new nodes

37. Press *Shift + D* to duplicate the **MixRGB** node, change the **Blend Type** of the duplicate to **Multiply** and paste it between the **RGB Curves** and the first **Add-MixRGB** nodes: set the **Fac** value to **0.500**. Connect the **Color** output of the **ColorRamp** node to the **Color2** input socket of the **Multiply-MixRGB** node.

38. Press *Shift + D* to duplicate the **Multiply-MixRGB** node and paste the duplicate between the first **Multiply-MixRGB** node and the **Add-MixRGB** node. Set the **Fac** value of the last **Multiply-MixRGB** node to **0.600** and the **Color2** to **R 0.347, G 0.462, B 0.386**.

39. Go to the **RGB Curves** node and left-click inside the interface window to add a point; set its coordinates to **X = 0.38636** and **Y = 0.36875**. Add a second point and set its coordinates to **X = 0.64545** and **Y = 0.84375**.

40. Go to the **ColorRamp** node and set the **Interpolation** to **B-Spline**, then move the black color stop to position **0.195** and the white color stop to position **0.800**:

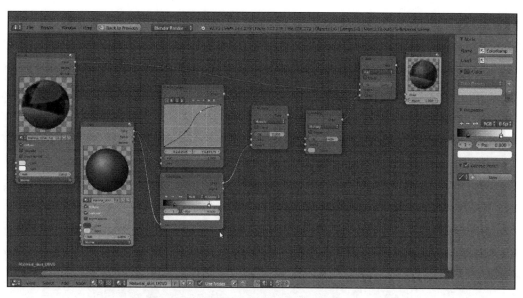

Tweaking the specularity component through the new nodes

41. Add a **Geometry** node (*Shift + A* | **Input** | **Geometry**), a **Vector Math** node (*Shift +
A* | **Converter** | **Vector Math**), a **Math** node (*Shift + A* | **Converter** | **Math**), and a
ColorRamp node (*Shift + A* | **Converter** | **ColorRamp**).

42. Add a **Frame** (*Shift + A* | **Layout** | **Frame**), label it as **FAKE_FRESNEL** and parent the
last **four** added nodes to it.

43. Set the **Operation** of the **Vector Math** node to **Dot Product**, then connect the **View**
output of the **Geometry** node to the first **Vector** input socket of the **Vector Math**
node, and the **Normal** output of the **Geometry** node to the second **Vector** input
socket of the **Vector Math** node.

44. Connect the **Value** output of the **Dot Product** node to the first **Value** input socket
of the **Math** node; set the **Operation** of this latter node to **Multiply** and the second
Value to **0.100**.

45. Connect the output of the **Math** node to the **Fac** input socket of the **ColorRamp**
node; set the **Interpolation** of this latter node to **B-Spline**, then move the black color
stop to position **0.150** and the white color stop to position **0.000**.

46. Connect the **Color** output of the **ColorRamp** node to the **Fac** input socket of the **Add-MixRGB** node:

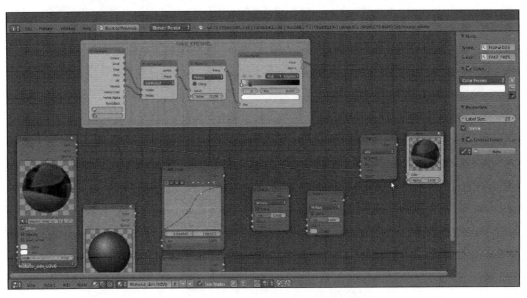

Adding the output of a fake Fresnel as factor for the blending of the two components

Let's do a *F12* rendering to see the result so far:

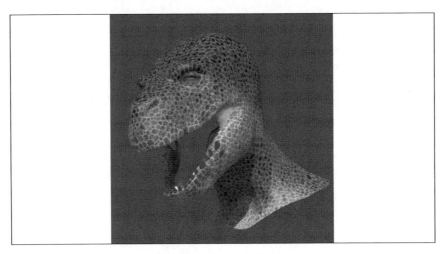

The F12 rendered result so far

47. Now, select the **COL** material node and press *Shift + D* to duplicate it. Label the duplicated one as **SSS**, then through the **Node Editor** window, enable the **Specular** item. Click on the **2** icon button to the right side of the material name datablock to make it single user and rename the new copy of the material as Material_U0V0_SSS.

48. Go to the **Material** window and change the **Diffuse Shader Model** to **Minnaert** and the **Diffuse** color to **R 0.439, G 0.216, B 0.141**. Move down to the **Specular** subpanel and change the color to the same **R 0.439, G 0.216, B 0.141** brownish hue (copy and paste), then set the **Intensity** to **0.600** and the **Hardness** to **12**.

49. Go down to the **Subsurface Scattering** subpanel and enable it by checking the checkbox: set the **IOR** value to **3.840**, the **Scale** to **0.001**, copy and paste the brownish color also in the scattering color slot, set the **Color** slider to **0.000** and the **Texture** slider to **1.000**. Set the **RGB Radius: R 9.436, G 3.348, B 1.790**.

50. Go to the **Texture** window and set to **0.300** the **Color** channel sliders of the U0V0, U0V0_scales_col_add2, and U0V0_scales_col texture slots, then set to **0.117** the **Color** channel slider of the U0V0_scales_col_add1 texture slot.

51. Select the last vcol texture slot and click on the **X** icon (*Unlink datablock*) button to clear it; click on the double little arrows to the left side of the **New** button and select the vcol_light item from the pop-up menu. Set the **Mapping** to **UVMap_norm**, and under the **Influence** subpanel, the **Color** of **Diffuse** to **0.267** and the **Blend Type** to **Screen**.

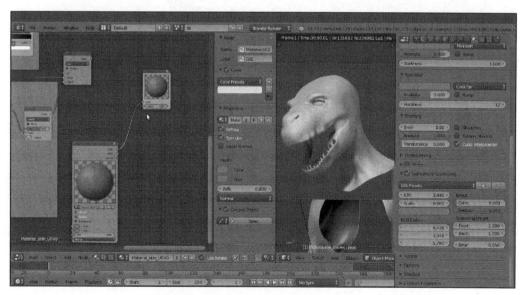

Testing the output of the SSS component material

52. Add a new **MixRGB** node (*Shift + A* | **Color** | **MixRGB**), paste it between the **Add-MixRGB** and the **Output** node and set the **Fac** value to **0.250**.

53. Press *Shift + D* to duplicate this **Mix-MixRGB** node; change the **Blend Type** of the duplicated one to **Screen**, set the **Fac** value to **1.000** and connect the output of the **Add-MixRGB** also to the **Color1** input socket of the **Screen-MixRGB** node; connect the output of the **SSS** node to the **Color2** input socket of the **Screen-MixRGB** node.

54. Connect the output of the **Screen-MixRGB** node to the **Color2** input socket of the first **Mix-MixRGB** node.

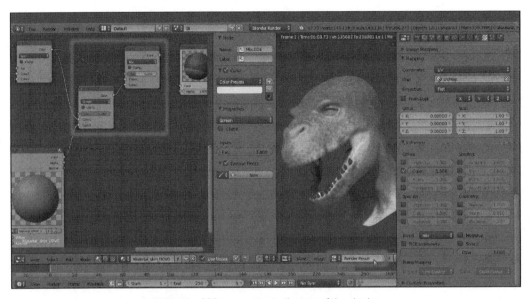

Adding the SSS component to the rest of the shader

55. Add a new **Material** node (*Shift + A* | **Input** | **Material**) and click on the **New** button to create a new material; label the node as **Scales_bump** and rename the material as `Material_U0V0_Scales_bump`.

56. In the **Material** window set the **Diffuse Shader Model** to **Oren-Nayar** and the **Specular Shader Model** to **Blinn**, **Intensity** = **0.100** and **Hardness** = 5. In the **Shading** subpanel enable the **Cubic Interpolation** item.

57. Go to the **Texture** window and in the **first** slot load the `U0V0_scales.png` image; rename the ID datablock as `U0V0_scales_bump1`. In the **Image Sampling** subpanel set the **Filter Size** to **5.00**, the **Mapping** to **UVMap** and in the **Influence** subpanel disable the **Color** channel and enable the **Normal** channel under **Geometry**: set the slider to **0.100** and go to the bottom to click on the **Bump Method** slot and select **Best Quality**:

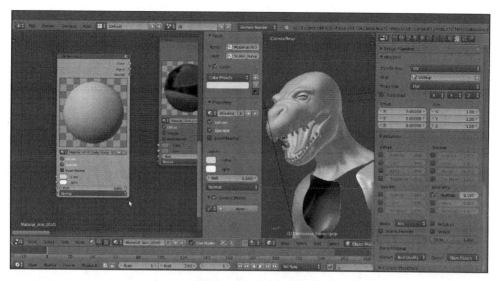

The bump material node

58. Go back to the top of the panel and click on the big black arrow to the right of the texture window; select the **Copy Texture Slot Settings** item.

59. Select the empty **second** texture slot and click on **New** to add a generic texture, then click again on the black arrow to select the **Paste Texture Slot Settings** item.

60. In the *ID datablock* slot, click on the **2** icon button to make it single user and rename it U0V0_scales_bump2.

61. Go down to the **Image Sampling** subpanel and set the **Filter Size** to **1.00**, then go down to the **Influence** subpanel and set the **Normal** slider to **0.200**.

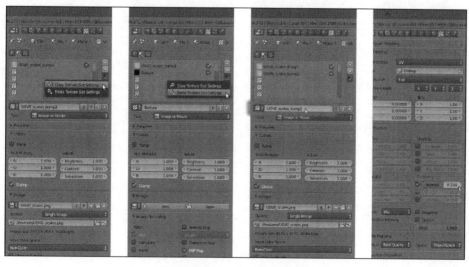

Copying and pasting a texture slot

62. Press *Shift + D* to duplicate the node; make the material of the duplicated one single user and rename it as `Material_Clouds_noise`, then label the node as **Clouds_noise**.

63. In the **Texture** window, delete (unlink) `U0V0_scales_bump1` and `U0V0_scales_bump2`, and then select the **first** slot and click on the **New** button: change the automatic `Texture.001` ID datablock name with `Clouds_noise`, click on the **Type** button and in the pop-up menu select the **Clouds** item.

64. In the **Colors** subpanel set the **Brightness** to **0.500** and the **Contrast** to **1.500**, in the **Mapping** subpanel set the **UVMap_scales** coordinates layer, in the **Clouds** subpanel switch from **Grayscale** to **Color**, set the **Size** to **0.20**, the **Depth** to **0.3** and the **Nabla** to **0.05**.

65. In the **Influence** subpanel disable the **Color** channel and enable the **Normal** channel under **Geometry**: set the slider to **0.250** and go to the bottom to click on the **Bump Method** slot and select **Best Quality**:

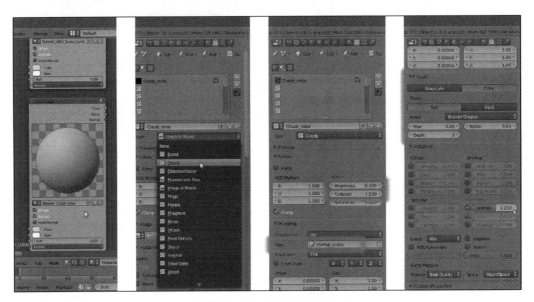

The second bump material node

66. Press *Shift + D* to duplicate the **Scales_bump** node; make the material of the duplicated one single user and rename it as `Material_Normal_map`, then label the node as **Normal_map** as well.

67. In the **Texture** window, delete (unlink) the `U0V0_scales_bump1` and `U0V0_scales_bump2`; select the **first** slot and click on the **New** button: change the automatic `Texture.001` ID datablock name to `normal` and then load the `norm.png` image.

68. In the **Mapping** subpanel set the **UVMap_norm** coordinates layer, then go to the **Image Sampling** subpanel and enable the **Normal Map** item; go to the **Influence** subpanel, disable the **Color** channel and enable the **Normal** channel: set the slider to **1.000** (higher values don't have an effect with normal maps in **Blender Internal**).

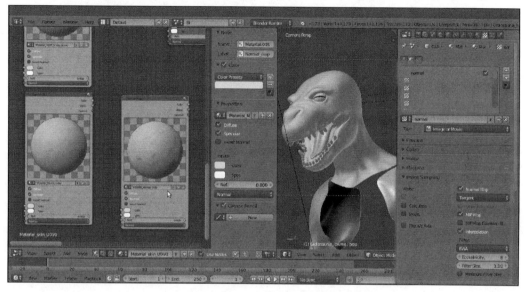

The normal map material node

69. Add a **Vector Math** node (*Shift + A* | **Converter** | **Vector Math**) and connect the **Normal** (blue) output of the **Scales_bump** node to the first **Vector** input socket of the **Vector Math** node, and the **Normal** output of the **Clouds_noise** node to the second **Vector** input socket.

70. Press *Shift + D* to duplicate the **Vector Math** node, set the **Operation** of the duplicate to **Average** and connect the **Vector** output of the **Add-Vector Math** node to the first **Vector** input socket of the **Average-Vector Math** node, and the **Normal** output of the **Normal_map** node to the second **Vector** input socket.

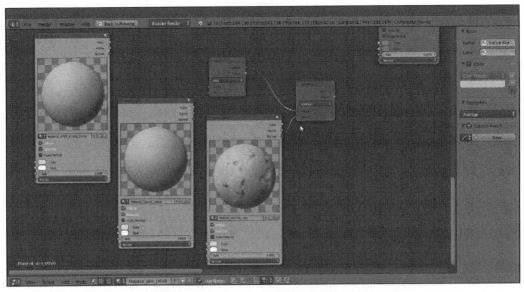

Connecting the outputs of the three bump nodes

71. Connect the **Vector** output of the **Average-Vector Math** node to the **Normal** input sockets of the **COL, SPEC,** and **SSS** material nodes.

72. Add frames everywhere to make things clear but especially to visually group and separate the nodes of the **Blender Internal** material from the **Cycles** ones.

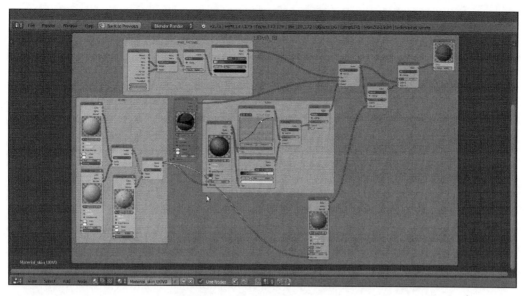

The completed "UOVO_BI" node material

73. Save the file.

How it works...

You have probably noticed that a few of the nodes we can find in the **Cycles** material system are also available for the material nodes in **Blender Internal**; sadly, some are still missing (and probably forever will be), as, for example, a **Fresnel** node that, in fact, we had to approximate with a combination of other different nodes.

Anyway, although not all the same nodes are at our disposal, we had enough of them to try to obtain a result as close as possible as the result we obtained in the **Cycles** material (in the previous *Chapter 12, Creating the Materials in Cycles*).

One thing you should absolutely keep in mind when loading the textures into the material nodes in **Blender Internal** is their order in the texture stack. This is important and must be taken into consideration according to the result we need, because a texture can totally overwrite the texture in the above slot (with the default **Mix** blend type) but can also be added, subtracted, multiplied, divided, and so on; the textures stack works the same as the layer stack system of a 2D graphic editor (**Gimp**, for instance), with the order from the top to the bottom and the different blending options (the **Blend Type** items).

Having said that, let's see the steps:

- From step 1 to step 9 we created a basic **Blender Internal** material node by using both the **Node Editor** and the **Material** window.

- From step 10 to step 23 we assigned the proper textures to the basic material node that becomes, in this case, the `Material_U0V0_Col`, the basic **diffuse color** component of the shader.

  These steps have been described in the most detailed way possible because they are the same steps for all the textures added to the materials; of course, the values and the settings can be different, but basically:

  - We add a texture (image or procedural)
  - We set a mapping orientation
  - We set the influence value on the selected channel (also more than one at a time)
  - Because the same texture can be used (with different settings) more than once, we always rename the *Unique datablock ID* name to make them easily recognizable in the pop-up menu list.

- The **Filter Size** value in the **Image Sampling** subpanel is really useful for blurring an image texture: a value of **1.00** is the default sharpness, while a higher value makes the image more and more blurred.

- From step 24 to step 30 we created the **glossy/specular** `Material_U0V0_Spec` node.

- From step 31 to step 34 we added the textures to the `Material_U0V0_Spec` material. This material should represent the **glossy/specular/mirror** component of the shader, that is probably the most important thing for obtaining a correct visual result; in **Cycles** the **Glossy BSDF** shader node provides the result perfectly, while in **Blender Internal**, we have two options: one, by enabling the (slow and imperfect) internal ray-tracing **Mirror** item, or by faking it. We faked it by setting an image (the same **hdr** we'll use in the next chapter in the **World** both for **Cycles** and **BI**) on the **Reflection** channel of the shader, hence giving the impression of an environment (slightly) mirrored by the character's skin.

- At step 35 we added together the outputs of the **COL** and of the **SPEC** nodes.

- From step 36 to step 40 we tweaked the output of the **SPEC** nodes to obtain a more realistic output/distribution of the glossiness on the mesh's surface, trying to mimic, as much as possible, the glossy output of the **Cycles** shader version.

- From step 41 to step 46 we built a fake **Fresnel** to work as a factor for the blending of the **glossy** and the **diffuse** components; this works by calculating the dot product of the vectors of the point of view and the mesh's normals. Be aware that it isn't actually working as the real **Fresnel** node that you find in **Cycles**, and that it has several limitations. By varying the second **Value** of the **Math** node and/or the black color stop position of the **ColorRamp** node, we can obtain several nice effects in some way visually similar to the real output. If you are wondering why we don't use the output of a **BI** material with a **Fresnel** diffuse shader model, sadly it doesn't seem to work correctly (actually, it doesn't seem to work at all).

- From step 47 to step 51 we built the **SSS** material node by duplicating the **COL** node, making a new copy of the material and renaming it as `Material_U0V0_SSS`, then enabling **Subsurface Scattering** and modifying the influence values of the textures; the values of the subsurface scattering (**IOR**, **Scale**, **RGB Radius**), instead, were borrowed from the **Cycles** version of the shader.

- From step 52 to step 54 we added the output of the **SSS** node to the rest of the shader by using a **Blend Type** set to **Screen** plus a **Mix** one set to a low **Fac** value; basically, the exact copy of what we did in **Cycles**.

- From step 55 to step 71 we created the **bump pattern**, divided into **three** different material nodes to give us more flexibility in adding and averaging them together in a way that is as similar as possible to **Cycles**:

The F12 rendered final result in Blender Internal

There's more...

The other missing shaders for the **Gidiosaurus** skin are solved in exactly the same way we used in the previous chapter for the other **Cycles** skin shaders: by selecting the entire **BI** frame with all the parented nodes and pressing *Ctrl + C* to copy them, then selecting the different material slots and pressing *Ctrl + V* to paste everything; in **Blender Internal**, we have to make the single materials inside the nodes single user one by one and then substitute the textures according to the **UDIM** tile the material corresponds to (U1V0_col.png, U1V0_scales.png, U2V0_col.png, and so on).

So, in the end, each material will have *two sets of nodes*, one for the **Cycles** shader and one for the **Blender Internal** shader, and each one works under the respective render engine; this will be useful, as we'll see in the next chapter, for the rendering stage.

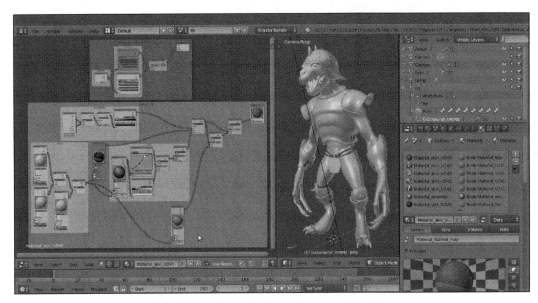

Two different sets of nodes for the same material

See also

- http://www.blender.org/manual/render/blender_render/materials/index.html
- http://www.blender.org/manual/render/blender_render/textures/index.html

Building the eyes' shaders in Blender Internal

We'll now see how to make the shaders for the **Gidiosaurus's eyes**; they are composed of two objects, the **Corneas** and the **Eyes** objects, so let's start with the first one.

Getting ready

Enable the **6th** and the **12th** scene layers and select the **Corneas** object; in the **Outliner**, disable the **Eyes** object's visibility in the viewport to hide it, put the mouse pointer inside the **Camera** view, zoom to one of the **eyeballs** and then start the **Rendered** preview.

How to do it...

Let's start to create the `Corneas` material:

1. Put the mouse pointer in the **Node Editor** window and add: a **Material** node (*Shift + A* | **Input** | **Material**), a **Geometry** node (*Shift + A* | **Input** | **Geometry**), a **MixRGB** node (*Shift + A* | **Color** | **MixRGB**) and an **Output** node (*Shift + A* | **Output** | **Output**).

2. Connect the **Color** output of the **Material** node to the **Color** input socket of the **Output** node, then click on the **New** button on the **Material** node to create a new material and rename it `Cornea_bump`.

3. In the **Material** window, expand the **Render Pipeline Options** subpanel and enable the **Transparency** item; in the **Diffuse** subpanel set the shader model to **Oren-Nayar** and the color to a bright orange = **R 0.930, G 0.386, B 0.082**. In the **Specular** subpanel set the shader model to **WardIso** and the **Slope** to **0.070**. In the **Shading** subpanel enable the **Cubic Interpolation** item.

4. Go down to expand the **Transparency** subpanel; set the **Fresnel** value to **1.380** and the **Blend** to **1.700**.

5. Go further down to enable the **Mirror** item in the subpanel with the same name, set the **Reflectivity** to **0.200**, the **Fresnel** to **1.380** and the **Blend** to **1.500**.

6. Go to the **Texture** window and in the **first** slot load the image `eyeball_col.jpg`, rename the ID datablock as `eyeball_col` and set the **UVMap.001** as the coordinates layer; in the **Influence** subpanel set the diffuse **Color** channel to **0.200** and the specular **Color** channel to **0.200** as well, set the **Blend Type** to **Color**.

7. In the **second** texture slot load the image eyeball_bump.jpg, rename the ID datablock as Eyeball_bump, set **UVMap.001** as the coordinates layer and disable the **Color** channel to enable the **Normal** one at **0.007**; set the **Bump Method** to **Best Quality**:

The "Corneas" material nodes

8. Paste the **MixRGB** node between the **Material** and the **Output** nodes; then, connect the **Vertex Color** output of the **Geometry** node to the **Fac** input socket of the **MixRGB** node. Click on the last empty field at the bottom of the **Geometry** node to select the **Col** item from the pop-up list (it's the name of the **Vertex Color** layer that has been created, and mentioned, at the beginning of the *Building the eyes' shaders in Cycles* recipe in *Chapter 12, Creating the Materials in Cycles*).

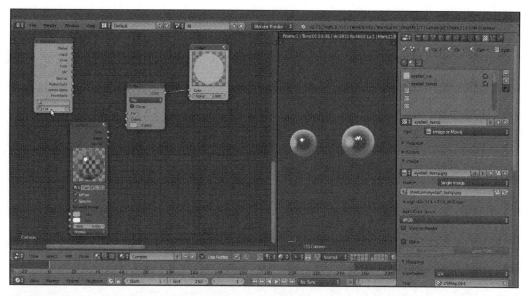

The gray color of the Color2 socket of the MixRGB node showing in the rendered preview at the location established by the Vertex Color layer output used as factor

In the preceding screenshot, the effect of the **Vertex Color** layer is visible: the two gray dots on the eyeballs are actually the crystalline lens areas filled, only at the moment, with the gray color of the empty **Color2** input socket of the **MixRGB** node.

9. Press *Shift + D* to duplicate the **Material** node, click on the **2** icon button to the right side of the name datablock of the duplicated node to make the material single user, rename the new material, simply, `Cornea` and, in the **Texture** window, select the **second** slot texture, `eyeball_bump`, to click on the **X** icon button and delete it.

10. Connect the **Color** output of the second **Material** node to the **Color2** input socket of the **MixRGB** node.

The completed "Corneas" material

Now, go to the **Outliner** and enable the **Eyes** object visibility in the viewport to show it:

11. With the **Corneas** object still selected, put the mouse pointer on the first **Material** node in the **Node Editor** window and press *Ctrl + C* to copy it.

12. Select the **Eyes** object and, in the **Material** window, select the Eyeballs material slot; put the mouse pointer in the **Node Editor** window and press *Ctrl + V* to paste the material node we copied before.

13. Click on the **2** icon button to make the material single user and rename it Eyes. Add an **Output** node (*Shift + A | Output | Output*) and connect the **Color** output of the **Eyes** material node to the **Color** input socket of the **Output** node.

14. Go to the **Material** window and disable the **Transparency** item in the **Render Pipeline Options** subpanel; go to the **Mirror** subpanel and disable it.

15. Enable the **Subsurface Scattering** subpanel: set the **IOR** to **1.340**, the **Scale** to **0.001**, the scattering color to the orange **R 0.930, G 0.386, B 0.082** and the **RGB Radius** to the **R 9.436, G 3.348, B 1.790** values.

The "Eyeballs" material SSS settings

16. Go to the **Texture** window; select the `eyeball_col` texture and set the diffuse **Color** to **0.855**, disable the specular **Color** channel and set the **Blend Type** to **Linear Light**; select the `eyeball_bump` texture and set the **Normal** channel slider to **0.005**.

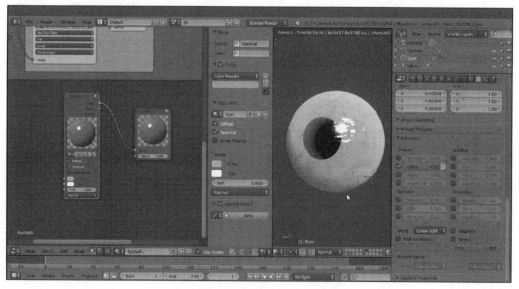

The "Eyeballs" material texture settings

Now let's see the **iris**:

17. Box-select both the `Eyes` material node and the connected **Output** node and press *Ctrl + C* to copy them; go to the **Material** window and select the `Irises` material slot, then put the mouse pointer in the **Node Editor** window and press *Ctrl + V* to paste them.

18. Make the duplicated node's material single user and rename it `Iris`; change the **Diffuse** subpanel color to **R 0.429**, **G 0.153**, **B 0.000**, then go to the **Shading** subpanel and set the **Emit** value to **0.07**. Go to the **Subsurface Scattering** subpanel and change the scattering color to **R 0.220**, **G 0.033**, **B 0.032**.

19. Go to the **Texture** window and delete (unlink) the two texture slots. In the **first** slot, load the image `iris_col.jpg`, rename the ID datablock `iris_col`, and set **UVMap.001** as the UV coordinates layer. In the **second** slot, load the image `iris_bump.jpg`, rename as `iris_bump`, set **UVMap.001** as the UV coordinates layer and in the **Influence** subpanel disable the **Color** channel and enable the specular **Intensity** and **Hardness** channels with value **1.000**, then enable also the **Normal** channel with value **1.000**. Set the **Bump Method** to **Best Quality**.

20. In the **third** texture slot, load again the `iris_bump.jpg` image; rename the ID datablock as `iris_ST`. In the **Image Sampling** subpanel, under **Alpha**, disable the **Use** item and enable the **Calculate** item. Set the **UVMap.001** coordinates layer and in the **Influence** subpanel disable the **Color** channel and enable only the **Stencil** item at the bottom:

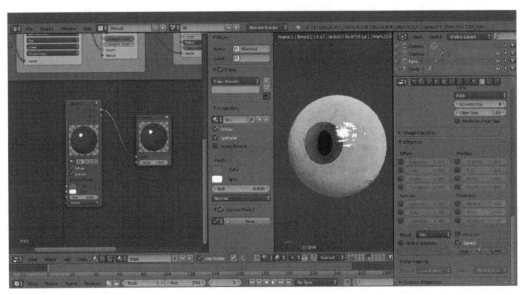

The "Irises" material and the Stencil item

21. In the **fourth** texture slot, load the `iris_col.jpg` image, rename the ID datablock as `iris_emit`. Set the **UVMap.001** coordinates layer and in the **Influence** subpanel disable the **Color** channel and enable the **Emit** channel at value **1.000**.

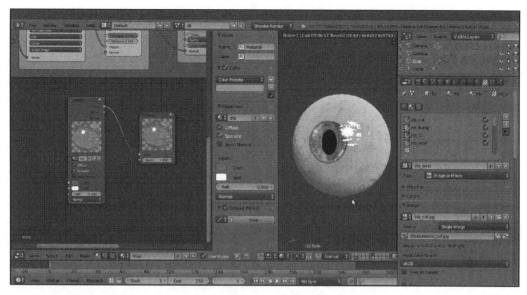

The "Irises" material emitting (fake) light

Regarding the `Pupils` material, it's a simple basic material with pure black as **Diffuse** color and the **Intensity** slider under the **Specular** subpanel set to **0.000** to be totally matte.

22. Save the file.

How it works...

For the **Corneas** object: we created two copies of the same transparent material, but then we removed the bump from one of them, because usually a **cornea** has bumps due to the veins on the **eyeball** but not on the **crystalline lens**, that is smooth; the two materials are mixed, exactly as in the **Cycles** version, through the output of the **Col Vertex Color** layer.

Regarding the `Irises` material: the `iris_ST` texture, set as a **stencil map**, works as a mask for the following texture to appear through its black areas.

Although it could have been solved by simply leaving a blank material slot, I assigned a black matte material to the **pupils**; I preferred to assign a material anyway, to avoid possible issues in the following stages such as, for example, in the rendering of the character against an alpha backdrop, of the separated passes and in the compositing.

Note that the `Corneas` is the only material where I enabled the ray-tracing mirror, which in the character's **skin** and in the **armor** are instead faked, to obtain faster rendering times (the **eyes** are really a small surface to be rendered).

Building the armor shaders in Blender Internal

We arrive finally at making the **Armor** shaders under the **Blender Internal** engine; we have **four** materials, here: the two **UDIM** plate shaders, the rivets shaders and the leather material for the tiers.

Getting ready

Enable the **6th** and the **13th** scene layers and select the **Armor** object; if your computer is powerful enough, use the **Rendered** preview while you are working.

How to do it...

Let's start with the first **UDIM** tile material creation, the main **armor** plates:

1. Put the mouse pointer in the **Node Editor** window and add a **Material** node (*Shift + A* | **Input** | **Material**), a **MixRGB** node (*Shift + A* | **Color** | **MixRGB**) and an **Output** node (*Shift + A* | **Output** | **Output**). In the *N* **Properties** sidepanel, label the **Material** node as **COL**.

2. Connect the **Color** output of the **COL** node to the **Color** input socket of the **Output** node, then click on the **New** button on the **Material** node to create a new material and rename it `Armor_U0V0_col`; in the **Node Editor** window, disable the **Specular** item.

3. Go to the **Material** window and find the **Diffuse** subpanel; change the shader model to **Oren-Nayar**, set the color to **R 0.817, G 0.879, B 1.000** and the **Roughness** value to **0.313**.

4. Go down to the **Specular** subpanel: set the shader model to **WardIso**, the **Intensity** to **1.000**, the **Slope** to **0.270**, and the color to **R 0.381, G 0.527, B 0.497**. In the **Shading** subpanel enable the **Cubic Interpolation** item.

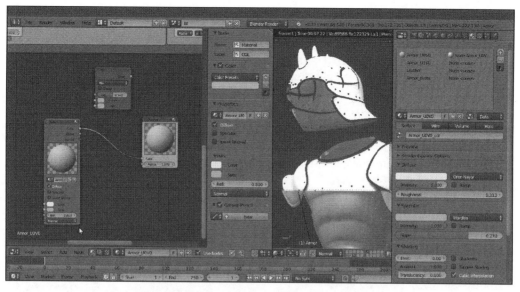

Starting the "Armor_U0V0" material in Blender Internal

5. Go to the **Texture** window and in the **first** texture slot, load the image iron_U0V0. png; rename the ID datablock as iron_U0V0 and set the **UVMap** coordinates layer, then go to the **Influence** subpanel and enable the diffuse **Intensity** channel at value **1.000**, leave the **Color** channel as it is and change the **Blend Type** to **Multiply**:

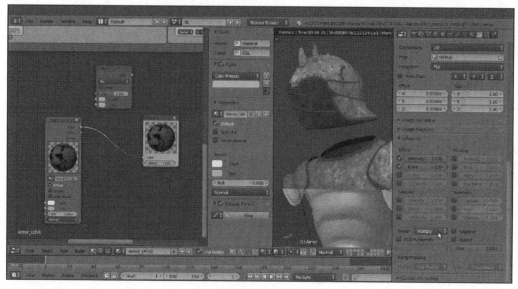

Adding the first texture image

6. In the **second** texture slot, load the image vcol2.png, rename the ID datablock as vcol2 and set the **UVMap_norm** UV coordinates layer; go to the **Colors** subpanel, enable the **Ramp** item and set the **Interpolation** to **B-Spline**, then move the black color stop to position **0.245** and the white color stop to position **0.755**. In the **Image Sampling** subpanel set the **Filter Size** to **1.10** and in the **Influence** subpanel enable the diffuse **Intensity** channel at value **0.500**, the diffuse **Color** channel at **0.300**, set the **Blend Type** to **Difference** and enable the **Negative** item.

7. In the **third** texture slot, load the image Ice_Lake_Ref.hdr and rename the ID datablock as env_refl_armor. Set the **Mapping** coordinates to **Reflection** and, in the **Image Sampling** subpanel, the **Filter Size** to **6.00**; in the **Colors** subpanel set the **Brightness** to **1.800** and the **Contrast** to **2.000**, then move to the **Influence** subpanel and set both the diffuse **Intensity** and **Color** channels to **0.600** and the **Blend Type** to **Multiply**:

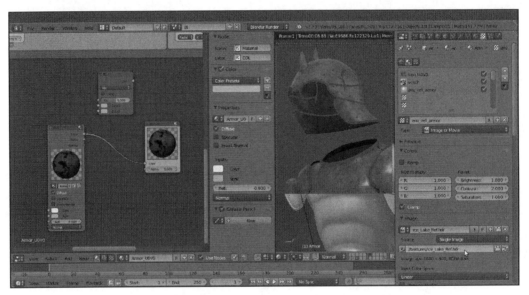

Adding the hdr image as reflection map

8. Go to the **Node Editor** window and press *Shift + D* to duplicate the **COL** node; label the duplicate as **SPEC1**, then make the material single user and rename it Armor_U0V0_spec1; disable the **Diffuse** item on the node interface and enable back, the **Specular** one.

9. Go to the **Texture** window; select the first iron_U0V0 texture slot and go straight to the **Influence** subpanel: disable the diffuse **Intensity** and **Color** channels and enable the specular **Intensity**, **Color** and **Hardness** channels at **1.000**. Set the **Blend Type** to **Mix**.

10. Select the **second** `vcol2` texture slot, disable the diffuse **Intensity** and **Color** channels and enable the specular **Intensity** channel at **0.300**.

11. Select the **third** `env_refl_armor` texture slot, disable the diffuse **Intensity** and **Color** channels and enable the specular **Intensity** and **Color** channels at **0.500**.

12. Press *Shift + D* to duplicate the **SPEC1** node and label the duplicated one as **SPEC2**: make the material single user and rename it as `Armor_U0V0_spec2`. In the **Material** window go to the **Specular** subpanel and set the **Slope** to the maximum = **0.400**.

13. Now, connect the **Color** output of the **SPEC1** material node to the **Color1** input socket of the **MixRGB** node and the **Color** output of the **SPEC2** node to the **Color2** input socket; set the **Blend Type** of the **MixRGB** node to **Add** and the **Fac** value to **0.900**.

14. Press *Shift + D* to duplicate the **MixRGB** node and connect the output of the first **MixRGB** node to the **Color1** input socket of the duplicated **MixRGB** node, and the **Color** output of the **COL** node to the **Color2** input socket; set the **Fac** value of the second **MixRGB** node to **1.000** and connect its output to the **Color** input socket of the **Output** node.

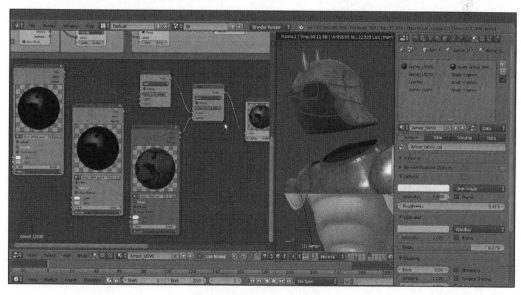

Adding the specular component

15. Add a **Math** node (*Shift + A* | **Converter** | **Math**) and paste it between the two **MixRGB** nodes; set the **Operation** to **Multiply** and the second **Value** to **2.000**.

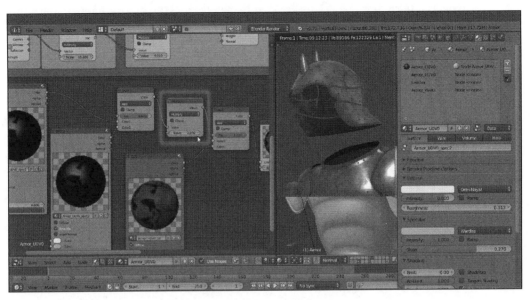

Enhancing the specularity

16. Add a **Material** node (*Shift + A* | **Input** | **Material**) and label it as **BUMP**; create a new material and rename it as `Armor_U0V0_normals`; in the **Shading** subpanel enable the **Cubic Interpolation** item.

17. Go to the **Texture** window and in the **first** texture slot, load the image `norm2.png`, rename the ID datablock as `norm2` and in the **Image Sampling** subpanel enable the **Normal Map** item; in the **Mapping** subpanel set the **UVMap_norm** coordinates layer and in the **Influence** subpanel disable the **Color** channel and enable the **Normal** one at **0.500**.

18. In the **second** texture slot, load the image `iron_U0V0.png`, mapping to **UVMap** layer and **Influence** to **Normal** at **0.010**; set the **Bump Method** to **Best Quality**.

19. Go to the **Node Editor** window and connect the **Normal** output of the **BUMP** node to the **Normal** input sockets of the **SPEC1**, **SPEC2**, and **COL** nodes.

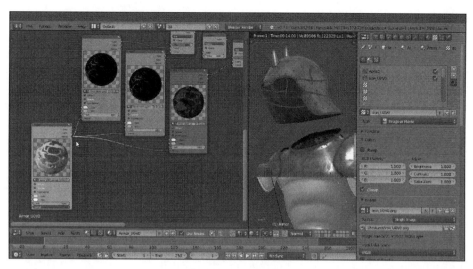

Adding the bump pattern

20. Box-select and press *Ctrl + C* to copy all these nodes, go to the **Material** window to select the `Armor_U1V0` material slot and, back in the **Node Editor** window, paste the copied nodes: then make the materials inside the nodes as single users, rename them accordingly and go to the **Texture** window to substitute the `iron_U0V0.png` image with the `iron_U1V0.png` image.

21. Copy and paste again, the nodes for the `Armor_rivets` material slot, but don't substitute the texture image: instead, simply delete the **BUMP** node, which wouldn't be of any use in such small parts.

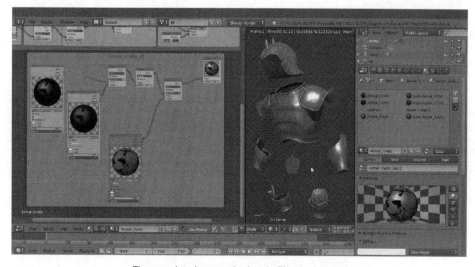

The completed armor shaders in Blender Internal

22. Save the file.

How it works...

These shaders work, and have been built, exactly the same way as for the **Gidiosaurus' skin** and **eyes**; the only thing worth noting here is the order of the normal map and of the texture used for the bump pattern: in fact, to work together, in **Blender Internal**, the normal map must be placed higher in the texture stack, otherwise it will overwrite the effect of the bump map.

There's more...

The `Leather` material is a simple basic **Oren-Nayar** diffuse shader with the usual **WardIso** specular shader model, provided with a bump effect obtained through a **Voronoi** procedural texture with default values, except for the **Size**.

Note that the **Voronoi** texture influences the **Color** channel with the **Multiply** blend type and the **Normal** channel with a **negative** low value to obtain an actual bulging out pattern, instead of a concave one; negative values, in fact, reverse the *direction* of the bump.

The size of the procedural texture along the three axes is also further tweaked in the **Mapping** subpanel, scaling the three axes differently to resemble the dimensions of the **Texture Space** (basically the mesh bounding box, than can be made visible through the subpanel of the same name in the **Object Data** window), in order to avoid stretching along the mesh.

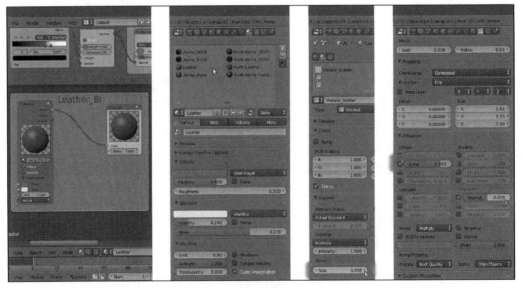

The "Leather" material in Blender Internal

Note also that in all these **Blender Internal** materials, simple mono materials (as for example the `Leather BI` material shown here earlier) are loaded inside a **Material** node and then connected to an **Output** node in the **Node Editor** window even if this wouldn't be necessary for the material itself to work: but, to let the **Blender Internal** and the **Cycles** render engines work together (through the compositor, as we'll see in the next chapter), it is mandatory to have all the shaders as nodes.

14
Lighting, Rendering, and a Little Bit of Compositing

In this chapter, we will cover the following recipes:

- ▶ Setting the library and the 3D scene layout
- ▶ Setting image based lighting (IBL)
- ▶ Setting a three-point lighting rig in Blender Internal
- ▶ Rendering an OpenGL playblast of the animation
- ▶ Obtaining a noise-free and faster rendering in Cycles
- ▶ Compositing the render layers

Introduction

In this last chapter, we are going to see recipes about the more common stages needed to render the complete final animation: lighting techniques in both the render engines, fast rendering previews, rendering settings, and the integrated compositing.

But first, let's see the necessary preparation of the 3D scene layout.

Setting the library and the 3D scene layout

In this recipe, we are going to prepare a little both the file to be used as the library and the *hero* blend file, which is the file that will output the final rendered animation.

Getting ready

Start Blender and load the `Gidiosaurus_shaders_Blender_Internal.blend` file:

1. Go to the **Object Modifiers** window and check that the **Armature** modifiers are correctly enabled for *all the objects* (that is, the **Armature** modifiers must be enabled both for the rendering and for the 3D viewport visibility), then save the file.

2. Press *Ctrl + N* and click on the **Reload Start-Up File** pop-up panel to confirm a new brand file: immediately save it as `Gidiosaurus_3D_layout.blend`.

 Saving the file at this point is necessary to automatically have a *relative path* for all the assets we are going to link.

How to do it...

Let's load the assets as links in the file:

1. Select and delete (*X* key) the default **Cube** primitive in the middle of the 3D scene, then *Shift*-select both the **Camera** and the **Lamp** and move them (*M* key) to the **6th** scene layer.

2. Still in the **1st** scene layer, click on the **File** item in the top main header and then navigate to select the **Link** item; or else, just press the *Ctrl + Alt + O* keys shortcut.

   In the blend files provided with this cookbook, I moved a copy of the `Gidiosaurus_shaders_Blender_Internal.blend` file to the `4886OS_14_blendfiles` folder, to simplify the process, but anyway:

3. Browse to the folder where the `Gidiosaurus_shaders_Blender_Internal.blend` file is saved; click on it and browse further to click on the **Group** item/folder, then select the **Gidiosaurus** item and click on the top right **Link from Library** button.

   The linked **Gidiosaurus** character appears at the **3D Cursor** position, in our case in the middle of the scene:

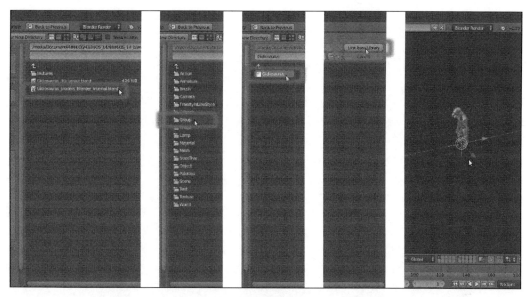

Linking the Gidiosaurus group

4. Zoom to the **Gidiosaurus** object and press *Ctrl + Alt + P* to make a proxy; in the pop-up menu panel that appears, select the proxified **rig** item, then *Shift*-enable the **11th** scene layer and move the **rig** on that scene layer (*M* key):

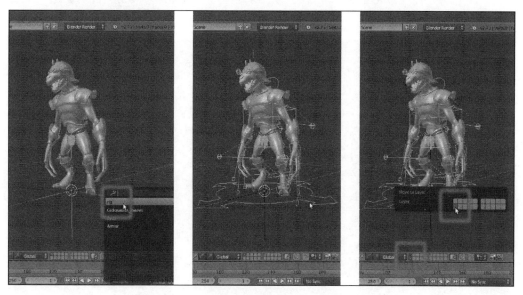

Making a proxy of the rig and moving it to the 11th scene layer

5. Click on the *Screen datablock* button on the top main header to switch from the **Default** screen layout to the **Animation** screen layout:

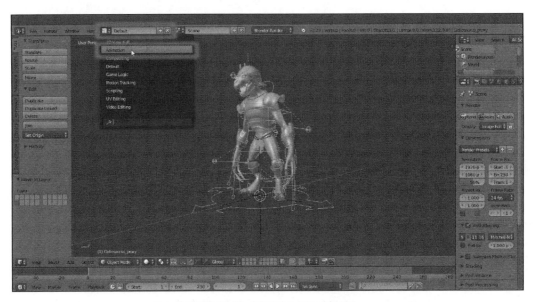

Switching to the Animation screen layout

6. Click on the **Mode** button in the **Dope Sheet** toolbar and switch from the **Dope Sheet** window to the **Action Editor** window:

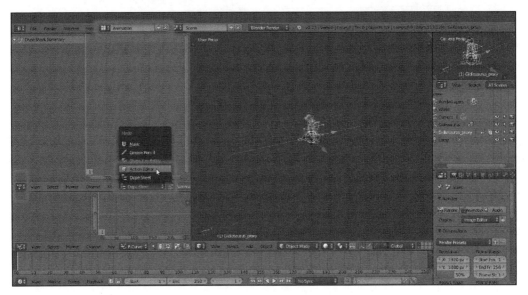

Switching to the Action Editor window

7. Click on the **File** item in the top main header and then navigate to select the **Link** item, or just press the *Ctrl + Alt + O* keys shortcut; the screen opens automatically at the last location we previously browsed to.

8. Click on the two dots above the **Gidiosaurus** item to navigate backward (to go up one level) and click on the **Action** item/folder to select the **Gidiosaurus_walkcycle** item; then click as before on the **Link from Library** button:

Browsing to the Action folder directory

9. Scroll a bit to the left of the **Action Editor** window's toolbar to reveal the **New** button; click on the double arrows to the left side of the **New** button to select the **LF Gidiosaurus_walkcycle** item from the pop-up menu.

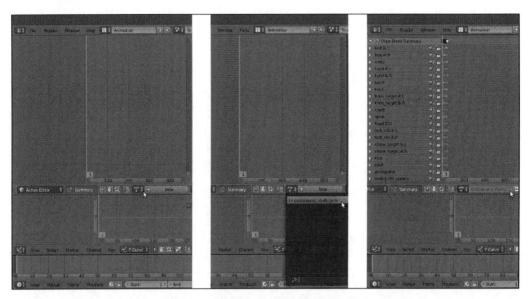

Loading the linked action in the Action Editor window

10. Go back to the **Default** screen and click on the **Play Animation** button in the **Timeline** toolbar.

Depending on the power of your system, you will see the animated character start to move, more or less fluidly, in the 3D viewport; the frame-rate (number of frames per second) played by Blender in real-time is shown in red at the top left corner of the 3D view-port:

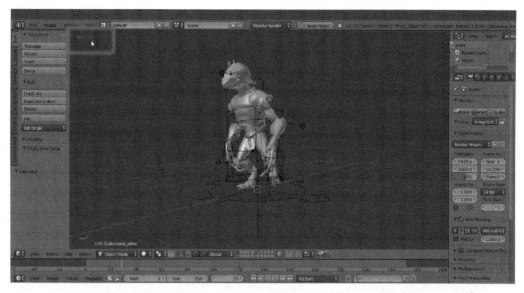

The 3D view-port showing the animation and the frame-rate at the top left corner

It should be around **24** frames per second; in my case, it barely arrives at **0.70** to **0.80**... so an arrangement must be found to show a faster and natural-looking movement.

11. Go to the **Scene** window and enable the **Simplify** subpanel: set the **Subdivision** level to **0**.

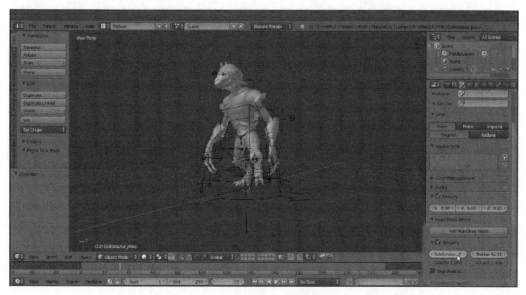

The Simplify subpanel under the Scene window in the main Properties panel

Without subdivision levels, even on my old laptop the real-time frame-rate is now **24** frames per second.

12. Go to the **Render** window and, in the **Dimensions** subpanel, under **Frame Range**, set the **End Frame** to **40**; under **Resolution** switch the **X** and **Y** values, that is **X** = **1080** px and **Y** = **1920** px.

13. Go to the **Outliner** and click on the **Display Mode** button to switch from **All Scenes** to **Visible Layers**. Then *Shift*-enable the **6th** scene layer and select the **Lamp**.

14. Go to the **Object Data** window and, in the **Lamp** subpanel, change the lamp type from **Point** to **Spot**; set the color to **R 1.000, G 1.000, B 0.650** and the **Energy** to **14.000**.

15. Put the mouse pointer in the 3D viewport and press *N* to call the side **Properties** panel; go to the top **Transform** subpanel and set **Location** as **X = 6.059204, Y = -9.912249, Z = 7.546275** and **Rotation** as **X = 55.789°, Y = 0°, Z = 30.562°**.

16. Back in the **Object Data** window, go down to the **Shadow** subpanel and switch from **Ray Shadow** to **Buffer Shadow**; under **Filter Type** set the **Shadow Filter Type** to **Gauss**, the **Soft** to **12.000**, the **Size** to **4000** and the **Samples** to **16**. Set the **Clip Start** value to **9.000** and the **Clip End** value to **19.000**.

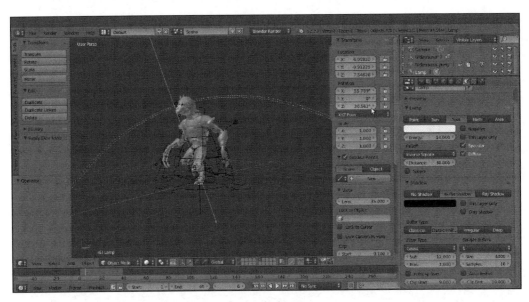

Setting the Lamp

17. Select the **Camera** and in the **Object Data** window set the **Focal Length** under **Lens** to **60.00**; in the **Transform** subpanel under the *N* side **Properties** panel input these values: **Location** as **X = 5.095385, Y = -6.777483, Z = 1.021429** and the **Rotation** as **X = 91.168°, Y = 0°, Z = 37.526°**. Put the mouse pointer in the 3D viewport and press the *O* numpad key to go in **Camera** view:

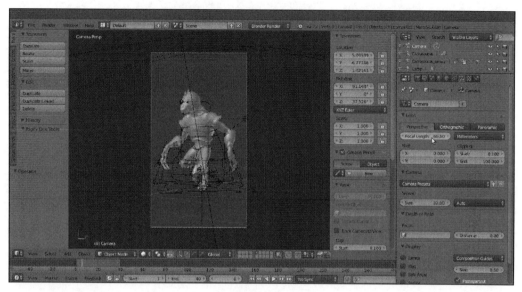

Setting the Camera

18. Now click on the **Scene** datablock button on the top main header and rename it **BI** (**Blender Internal**). Click on the **+** icon button to the right and from the **New Scene** pop-up menu select the **Link Objects** item.

19. Change the **BI.001** name of the new scene in **Cycles** and click on the *Engine* button to the right to switch to the **Cycles Render** engine:

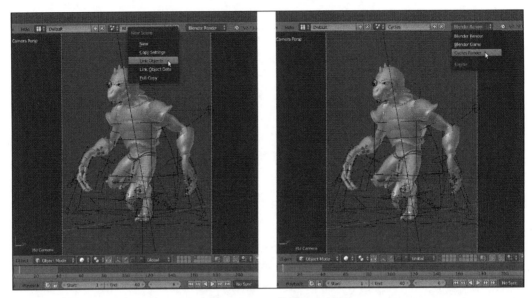

Adding a new scene with linked objects

20. Go to the **Outliner** and select the **Lamp**; go to the **Object Data** window and, in the **Nodes** subpanel, click on the **Use Nodes** button and then set the **Strength** to **10000.000**. Go to the **Lamp** subpanel and set the **Size** to **0.500** and enable the **Multiple Importance** item.

21. Save the file.

How it works...

A scheme of what we made in this recipe is: we prepared a blend file that *links* both the **character** and the **action**; this means that *neither* of them is *local* to the file and they cannot be directly edited in this file. Moreover, the character, in its library file, links the textures that are contained in the `textures` folder (which is at the same level as the blend files).

The **Simplify** subpanel in the **Scene** window allows us to *globally* modify some of the settings that can usually slow a workflow, such as the **subdivision** levels, the number of **particles**, the quality of **ambient occlusion** and **subsurface scattering**, and the **shadows** samples; through this panel they can be temporarily lowered or even disabled to have faster and more responsive previews of the rendering and the animation. Just remember that the **Simplify** subpanel also affects the rendering, so you have to disable it before starting the final rendering task.

See also

- ▶ http://www.blender.org/manual/data_system/introduction.html#copying-and-linking-objects-between-scenes
- ▶ http://www.blender.org/manual/data_system/scenes.html
- ▶ http://www.blender.org/manual/data_system/linked_libraries.html

Setting image based lighting (IBL)

The **image based lighting** technique is almost essential in computer graphics nowadays; as the name itself says, it's a technique to light a scene based on the pixel color information of an image, usually an **hdr** image (**High Dynamic Range** image); other image formats can also work, although not so well.

In Blender it's possible to obtain **IBL** both in **BI** and in **Cycles**, although with different modalities.

Getting ready

Start Blender and load the previously saved Gidiosaurus_3D_layout.blend file; save it as Gidiosaurus_IBL.blend.

How to do it...

We can divide this recipe into two parts: **IBL** in **Cycles** and in **Blender Internal**.

Image based lighting in Cycles

Let's start with the **Cycles Render** engine:

1. First, split the 3D window vertically into two windows, then change the upper one into a **Node Editor** window. In the toolbar, click on the **World** icon button to the right side of the **Object** icon button (selected by default; it's the one enabled for building the objects' shaders). Check the **Use Nodes** checkbox (or, click on the **Use Nodes** button inside the **Surface** subpanel in the **World** window); a **Background** node connected to a **World Output** node will appear in the **Node Editor** window.

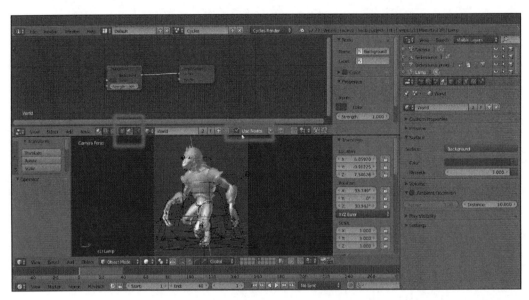

Enabling the World nodes in the Node Editor window

2. Click on the dotted button to the right side of the **Color** slot in the **Surface** subpanel under the **World** window, to call the pop-up menu and select an **Environment Texture** node, which is automatically added and correctly connected to the **Color** input socket of the **Environment** node; then, click on the double arrows to the left side of the **Open** button (both in the **Node Editor** or in the **World** window) and select the L Ice_Lake_Ref.hdr item.

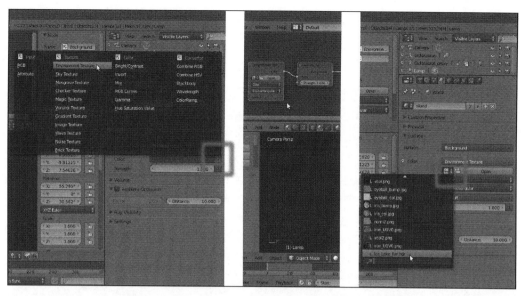

Adding an Environment node to the World and loading the hdr image

3. In the **World** window or in the **Node Editor** window, set the **Color Space** to **Non-Color Data**.

4. In order to gain some feedback, start the **Rendered** preview in the bottom **Camera** view, then go back to the **Node Editor** and add a **Texture Coordinate** node (*Shift + A* | **Input** | **Texture Coordinate**) and a **Mapping** node (*Shift + A* | **Vector** | **Mapping**).

5. Connect the **Generated** output of the **Texture Coordinate** node to the **Vector** input socket of the **Mapping** node and the output of this latter node to the **Vector** input socket of the **Environment Texture** node; set the **Rotation Z** value of the **Mapping** node to **-235**.

Rotating the hdr image to match the position of the Lamp

6. Now add a **Math** node (*Shift* + *A* | **Converter** | **Math**) and a **MixRGB** node (*Shift* + *A* | **Color** | **MixRGB**); connect the **Color** output of the **Environment Texture** node to the first **Value** input socket of the **Math** node, set the **Operation** of this latter node to **Multiply** and the second **Value** to **10.000**.

7. Connect the output of the **Multiply-Math** node to the **Color1** input socket of the **MixRGB** node and set the **Color2** to pure white; connect the Color output of the **MixRGB** node to the **Strength** input socket of the **Background** node:

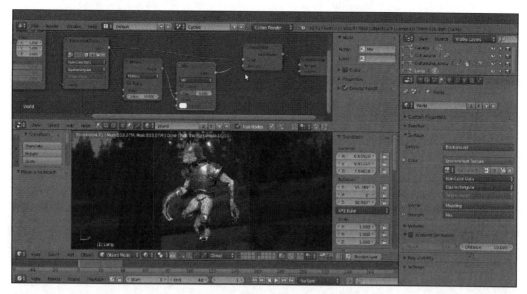

Adding nodes to the World

8. Press *Shift + D* to duplicate both the **Math** and the **MixRGB** nodes: paste the duplicated **MixRGB** node between the first **MixRGB** and the **Background** nodes; set the **Operation** of the duplicated **Math** node to **Add**.

9. Add a **Light Path** node (*Shift + A* | **Input** | **Light Path**); connect its **Is Camera Ray** output to the first **Value** input socket of the duplicated **Add-Math** node and the **Is Glossy Ray** output to the second **Value** input socket; connect the **Value** output of the **Add-Math** node to the **Fac** input socket of the second **MixRGB** node and enable the **Clamp** item:

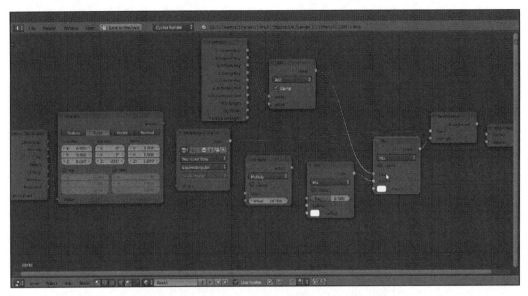

The completed IBL World setup for the Cycles render engine

10. Go to the **Settings** subpanel and enable the **Multiple Importance** item, then click on the *World datablock* to change the name in **World_Cycles**.

11. Go to the **Render** window and in the **Film** subpanel enable the **Transparent** item.

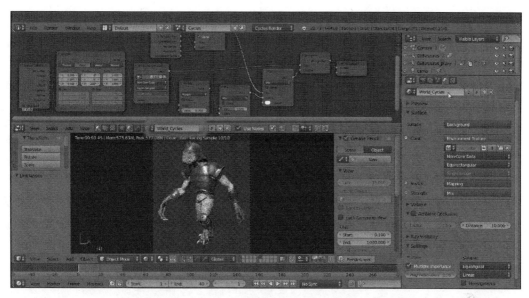

Renaming the World and some more settings in the main window

12. Save the file.

Image based lighting in Blender Internal

Now let's see the same thing in **Blender Internal**:

1. Click on the *Scene datablock* button in the top main header to switch from **Cycles** to **BI**.

2. In the **World** window to the right, click on the **2** icon button to the right side of the **World** name datablock to make it single user, then rename it **World_BI**.

3. Go directly to the **Texture** window: click on the **New** button, then click on the double arrows to the side of the image datablock to select the `L Ice_Lake_Refl.hdr` item from the pop-up menu:

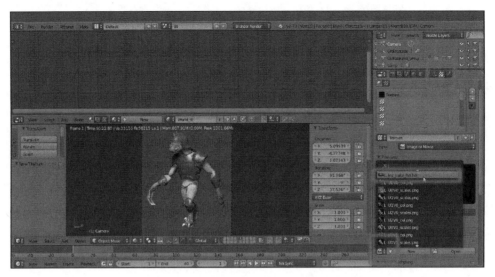

Selecting the hdr image in the Blender Internal World

4. Rename the *ID name datablock* to **Ice_Lake_Refl**, then go down to the **Mapping** subpanel and click on the **Coordinates** slot to select the **Equirectangular** item; set the **Offset** to **X = 0.80500** and then go further down to the **Influence** panel and enable the **Horizon** item.

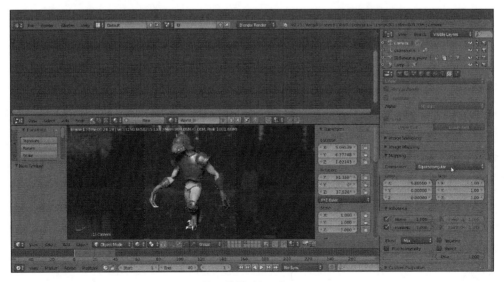

First BI World settings

5. Back in the **World** window, in the **World** subpanel enable the **Real Sky** item.

6. Enable the **Environment Lighting** subpanel and click on the **Environment Color** button to select the **Sky Texture** item.

7. In the **Gather** subpanel, enable the **Approximate** method, the **Pixel Cache** item, the **Falloff** item and set the **Strength** value of this latter item to **0.900**.

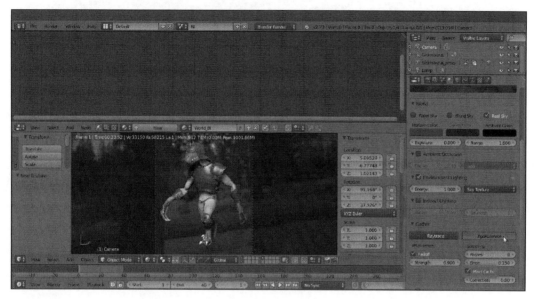

More BI World settings

8. Go to the **Render** window and in the **Shading** subpanel click on the **Alpha Mode** slot to switch from the **Sky** to the **Transparent** item:

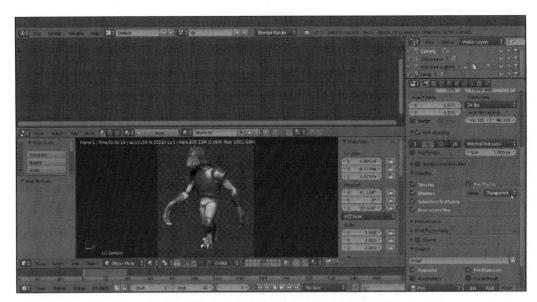

Enabling the transparent background for the rendering

9. Save the file.

How it works...

In **Cycles**: at steps 6 and 7 we added nodes to increase the source light intensity of the **hdr** image; because this also increased the contrast of the image, at steps 8 and 9 we made it less contrasted again but kept the same light intensity, thanks to the **Light Path** node. The light rays shoot from the **Camera** position and directly hit a surface (**Is Camera Ray**) or any glossy surface (**Is Glossy Ray**) and have value = **1.000**, hence corresponding to the **Color2** socket of the second **MixRGB** node, therefore giving a pure white (**1.000**) value to the **Background** node's **Strength**; any other ray (transmitted, shadows, reflected, transparent, and so on) has the high contrast **Strength** values we established at steps 6 and 7.

We used the **Mapping** node for the sole reason of matching (visually and thanks to the **World Background** item enabled in the **Display** subpanel under the *N* side **Properties** panel) the source light direction of the image with the position of the **Lamp** in the 3D scene: that's why we rotated the **hdr** image to negative **235** degrees on the *z* (vertical) axis.

In **Blender Internal**: we can't rotate the image, so instead we offset it on the *x* axis to (almost perfectly) match the position it has in **Cycles**.

The **Approximate** gathering method is the one developed during the production of the short open movie *Big Buck Bunny* (`https://peach.blender.org/`) to have faster rendering and absence of noise in **Ambient Occlusion**, inevitable with the default **Raytrace** method (that still remains the more accurate, by the way).

Note that, in both the render engines, we didn't load a brand new `Ice_Lake_Ref.hdr` image from the `textures` folder, but we instead used the linked one coming from the materials of the character, as indicated by the `L` in front of the name and by the name itself and all the settings grayed in the image datablock subpanel.

See also

The free **sIBL** addon currently, only works with **Cycles** materials but it can read the `.ibl` file provided with the free **hdr** images at the **sIBL Archive** (link provided further) and therefore, in one click, it can create the complete nodes setup to provide image based lighting in Blender.

- ▸ The official documentation about the addon (`http://wiki.blender.org/index.php/Extensions:2.6/Py/Scripts/Import-Export/sIBL_GUI`)
- ▸ An updated and bug-fixed version of the addon (`https://raw.github.com/varkenvarken/blenderaddons/master/sibl.py`)
- ▸ The sIBL archive (`http://www.hdrlabs.com/sibl/archive.html`)
- ▸ Official documentation about the **World** in Blender:

  - ❏ `http://www.blender.org/manual/render/cycles/world.html`
  - ❏ `http://www.blender.org/manual/render/blender_render/world/index.html`

Setting a three-point lighting rig in Blender Internal

Thanks to the global illumination, a path-tracer like **Cycles** doesn't necessarily need big lighting setups; in fact, in the recipes we made, we only used one single **Spot** lamp in addition to the **IBL** and the results have been quite good anyway.

In **Blender Internal**, instead, a minimum arrangement of lamps must be done to obtain satisfying results, even with the aid of the **World** settings we have previously seen.

In this recipe, we are therefore going to see a classic *movie* three-point lighting rig, an industry standard. The effect of the main **key light** is enhanced by the other two lamps: the **fill light**, to brighten (and color) the shadow areas on the subject, and the **backlight**, to create a light rim on the subject edges thus making it stand out against the background.

Getting ready

Start Blender and load the previously saved `Gidiosaurus_IBL.blend` file; if necessary, switch to the **Blender Render** engine by the *Engine to use for rendering* button in the top main header.

1. Put the mouse pointer inside the **Camera** view and press the numpad 7 key to go in **Top** view, then press numpad 5 to switch from **Perspective** to **Ortho** view.

2. Press *Shift + C* to put the **3D Cursor** at the center of the scene and then go to the **Outliner** to select the **Gidiosaurus** item: press the numpad period (.) key to center and zoom the view on the selected object:

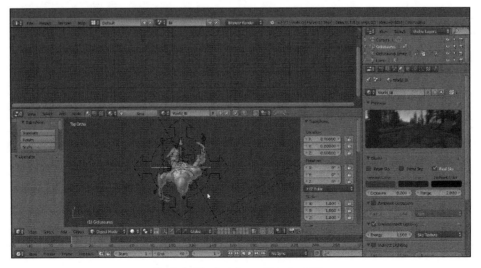

Centering the top view on the character

3. Press *Ctrl + Spacebar* to disable the widget and scroll the mouse wheel to zoom backward and show the **Spot** lamp, then press the dot (.) key to switch the **Pivot Point** from **Median Point** (or whatever else) to **3D Cursor**.

4. Select the **Lamp**, then go to the **Object Data** window.

5. Remember to go to the **Scene** window and disable the **Simplify** subpanel!

6. Save the file as Gidiosaurus_lighting.blend.

Don't take into consideration the **Node Editor** window at the top showing the **Lamp** nodes under **Cycles**; the settings to look for are those inside the main **Properties** panel to the right:

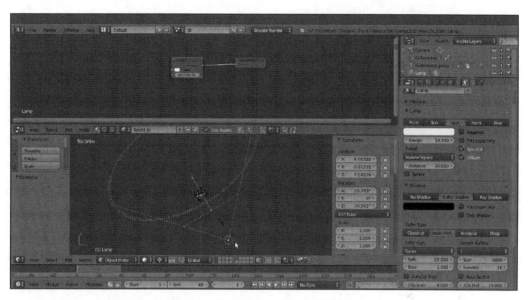

These are the settings you are looking for...

How to do it...

Let's go with the settings of the lights:

1. In the **Outliner**, rename the **Lamp** item as **Light_key**.

2. Press *Shift + D* to duplicate the **Key_light** lamp, press *R* and, while still in **Top** view, rotate the duplicated lamp approximately **-145** degrees, then go in **Side** view (numpad *3* key) and rotate it around **15** degrees: in the **Outliner**, rename it as **Light_back**.

3. In the **Object Data** window, set the color to a light blue = **R 0.700, G 0.900, B 1.000** and the **Energy** to **5.000**:

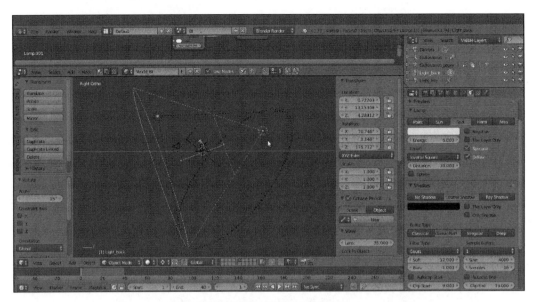

Positioning the Light_back lamp

4. Go back in **Top** view (numpad *7* key) and re-select the **Light_key** lamp, press *Shift + D* and rotate the duplicate by **100** degrees; in the **Outliner**, rename it as **Light_fill**. Go in **Front** view (numpad *1* key) and rotate it around **-25** degrees.

5. In the **Object Data** window, set the color to a lighter blue = **R 0.500, G 0.800, B 1.000** and the **Energy** to **2.000**:

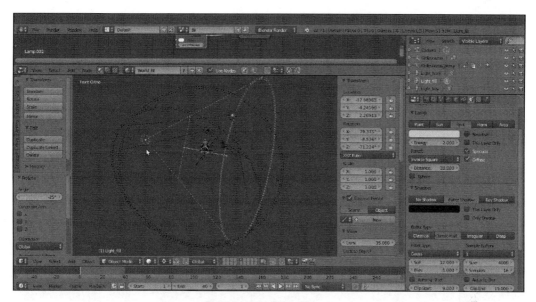

Positioning the Light_fill lamp

6. Go to the **Object** window and in the **Display** subpanel enable the **Name** item for the three lamps; then, back to the **Object Data** window and in the **Spot Shape** subpanel, enable the **Show Cone** item for each one:

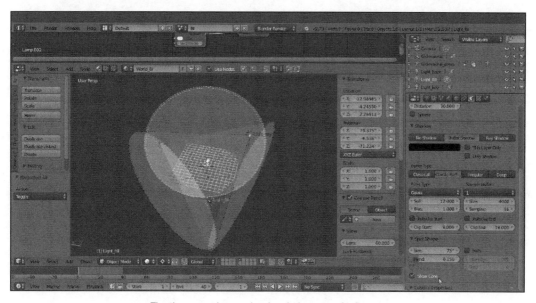

The three spot lamps showing their cones of influence

7.   In the **Outliner**, disable the 3D viewport visibility of the **Light_back** and **Light_fill** lamps by clicking on the respective eye icon, then go in **Side Ortho** view and select the **Light_key** lamp.

8.   Go to the **Spot Shape** subpanel again and lower the **Size** value from the default **75°** to **30°** (or the smallest possible value that still comprehends the whole character):

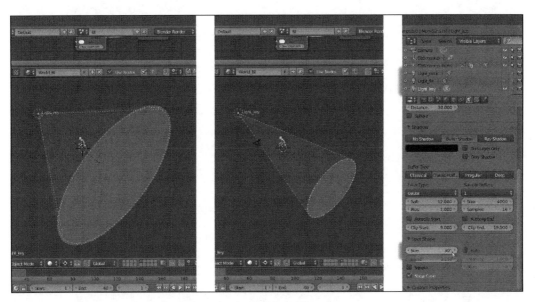

Lowering the spot lamp size value

9.   Repeat steps 7 and 8 for the other two lamps as well, then *Shift*-select all the three lamps and move them upward (on the z axis) a bit, just to better center the light cones' centers on the position of the feet of the character.

10. Save the file.

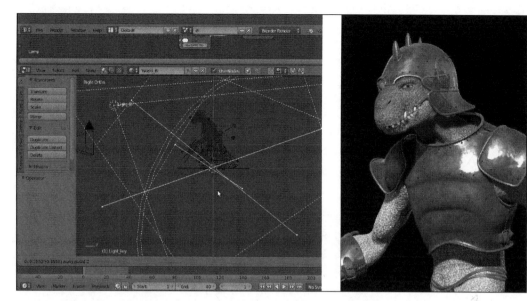

The final result of the three-point lighting rig

How it works...

A classic three-point lighting rig can in some way compensate for the lack of real global illumination in **Blender Internal**, although to obtain really good results, three lamps are usually not enough; in any case, the lighting rig of this recipe can be used as a base for even more complex setups.

When using more than one lamp in **Blender Internal**, we should always be sure that the shadows are enabled for all of them, unless we want particular effects; in fact, a back lamp with disabled shadows can easily *shine* through the model and also illuminate parts that shouldn't be in light, giving unrealistic results.

To calculate the buffered shadows, **Spot** lamps take into consideration everything inside their cone from the **Clip Start** to the **Clip End** values; this is why we lowered the **Size** values of the cones as much as possible.

One other crucial factor that can slow the calculation and the rendering times is, obviously, the size of these buffers, which we set to **4000** for each one of the three lamps; quite big, but because we set the cones that large enough to just comprehend the shape of their target object. This means we could use big shadow buffers, to obtain more details in the shadows if needed.

We do all of this, even though the **Gidiosaurus** was the only object to be rendered in the scene.

See also

▶   http://www.blender.org/manual/render/blender_render/lighting/index.html

Rendering an OpenGL playblast of the animation

Playblast is a term used by a famous commercial package to indicate the preview of the animation in true speed; although I've heard only very few people using it in relation to Blender, I thought it might be a good way to indicate the fast OpenGL preview rendering obtained for checking the animated action.

Getting ready

Start Blender and load the Gidiosaurus_lighting.blend file.

1. In the **Outliner**, select the **Light_key** lamp item and go to the **Object Data** window, under the **Spot Shape** subpanel, to disable the **Show Cone** item.

2. Repeat the procedure for the **Light_back** and **Light_fill** lamps, then disable their visibility in the 3D viewport by clicking on the respective eye icon.

3. Disable the visibility in the viewport for the **Gidiosaurus_proxy** item (the linked and proxified rig) also and/or disable the **11th** scene layer.

4. Save the file as Gidiosaurus_playblast.blend.

How to do it...

Here are the steps to begin with the OpenGL rendering:

1. Put the mouse pointer inside the 3D viewport and press the numpad *0* key to go in **Camera** view; press the *Z* key to go in **Solid** viewport shading mode, then scroll the mouse wheel to zoom the **Camera** view inside the window:

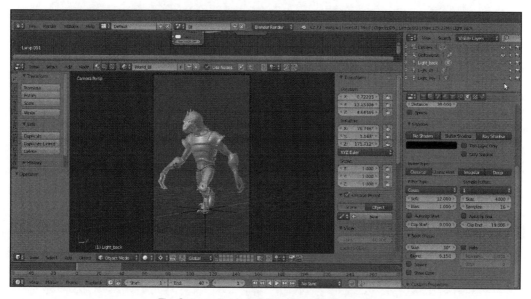

The Camera view in Solid viewport shading mode

2. Go to the **Render** window and to the **Dimensions** subpanel; check for the **X** and **Y** sizes of the rendering under **Resolution**, specified in pixels, and move the *Percentage scale for render resolution* slider, usually set to **50%**, to **100%**.

3. Go down to the **Output** subpanel and click on the folder icon button to the end of the path slot; browse to the location you want to save your rendering, then type in the first line of the path to the folder you want to create at that location, followed by the slash (/) and press *Enter*.

4. A pop-up will ask you to confirm the creation of the new directory; confirm and then type a generic frame name in the second line, go to the left side vertical bar to be sure that the bottom **Relative Path** item is enabled and finally click on the **Accept** button at the top left of the screen.

   I used **playblast** for the folder and **plbst** for the frame name respectively.

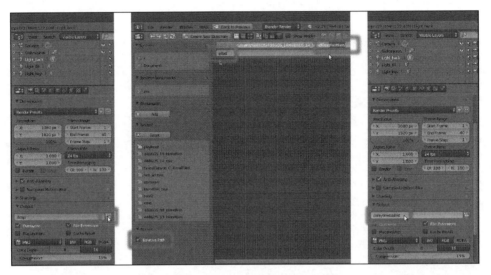

The new directory and the rendered frames name

5. Save the file, then go to the **Camera** view toolbar and click on the last *ciak* icon button to the left to start the OpenGL playblast:

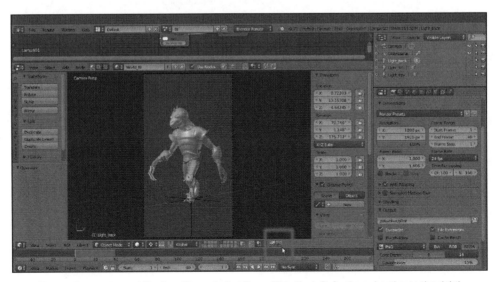

The two buttons to start the OpenGL rendering (for a still to the left, for the animation to the right)

How it works...

In our example, the OpenGL playblast rendered single `.png` images with an alpha background because, as you can see in the **Render** window visible in the previous screenshot, these are the settings of the **Output** subpanel. Be aware that the resolution, the format and the path where the playblast frames are saved, always depend on the settings in the **Render** window, the same settings that will be used for the final real rendering (but of course the resolution of the playblast can be easily and temporarily be made smaller with the slider of the percentage scale).

There's more...

Once we have rendered all the frames, we can use an external player to see them in sequence (in **Ubuntu**, I use the free player **DJV Imaging**, `http://djv.sourceforge.net`) or, just quickly build a movie through the **Blender Sequencer**:

1. Go to the *Screen datablock* button on the top main header and click it to switch to the **Video Editing** screen:

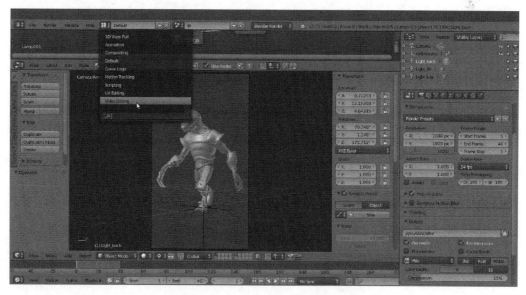

Switching to the Video Editing screen layout

2. Put the mouse pointer in the **Video Sequence Editor** window at the bottom and press *Shift + A*; from the pop-up menu select the **Image** item (*Add an image or image sequence to the sequencer*), then browse to the `playblast` folder location, click on it and once inside, press the *A* key to select all the contained frames, then press *Enter* to confirm. The frames are added to the **Video Sequence Editor** window as a single strip and the current frame appears in the preview window:

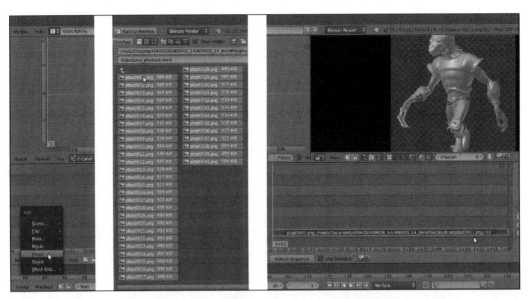

Loading the rendered frames in the Video Sequence Editor

3. Go back to the **Default** screen and to the **Render** window under the main **Properties** panel. In the **Output** subpanel, where you can change the path to save the movie in a different location (or also leave it as it is), click on the **File Format** button to select a **Movie** format, for example, **AVI JPEG**. Choose **BW** or **RGB** and the **Quality** compression ratio (but the default **90%** is usually OK); then go to the **Post Processing** subpanel and ensure that the **Sequencer** item is enabled:

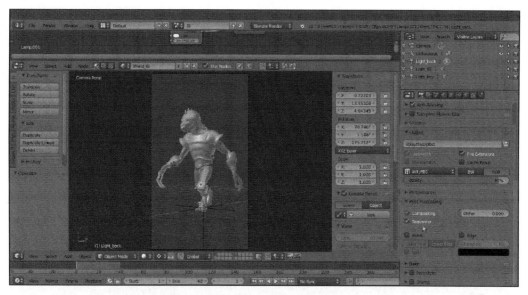

The Output and the Post Processing subpanels inside the Render window

4. Go to the top of the **Render** window and click on the **Animation** button; remember that Blender uses two different buttons to start the rendering of a still image or of an animation, both for the final rendering and for the 3D viewport toolbar OpenGL preview we have seen in the *How to do it...* section.

The rendering starts and the **Sequencer** processes all the `.png` images outputted by the playblast, transforming them into a single compressed `.avi` movie then saved in the same directory as the frames.

The process is visible in the **UV/Image Editor** window that replaced the **Camera** view, indicated in the toolbar by the **Render Result** label on the image datablock to the left (because the **Image Editor** item is the one selected in the **Display** slot under the **Render** subpanel) and by the **Sequence** label visible in the **Layer** slot to the right:

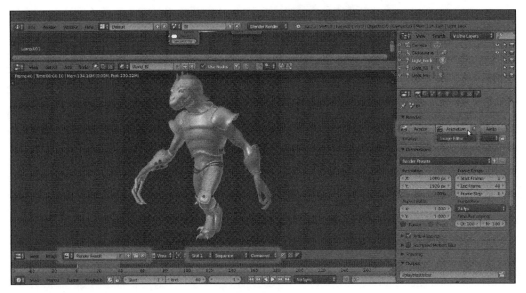

The Render Result window

See also

▶ http://www.blender.org/manual/render/display.html

▶ http://www.blender.org/manual/render/output/video.html

▶ http://www.blender.org/manual/render/output.html

Obtaining a noise-free and faster rendering in Cycles

The **Cycles Render** engine can be very slow compared to **Blender Internal**; by the way, some of the rendering settings can be tweaked to make it work faster; the goal here is to avoid fireflies and noise, usually due to low samples and a light source that is too bright.

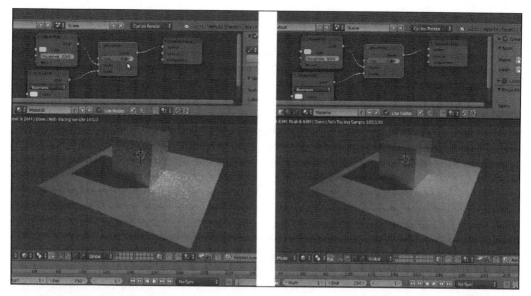

Rendered previews of an example scene, showing a cube on a plane with and without noise and fireflies

Getting ready

Start Blender and load the `Gidiosaurus_playblast.blend` file.

1. Click on the *Scene datablock* button in the top main header to switch from **BI** to **Cycles**.

2. Go to the **Outliner** and enable the visibility of the **Light_key** lamp in the viewport by clicking on the grayed eye icon.

3. Put the mouse pointer inside the **Camera** view and press *Shift + B* to draw a box around the character's head, then zoom to it.

4. Save the file as `Gidiosaurus_render.blend` and press *Shift + Z* to start the **Rendered** preview.

How to do it...

If you have a capable graphic card supporting **GPU** (go to the last *See also* section for the link to a list of supported **GPU** graphic cards for **Cycles**), the next thing to do is:

1. Call the **User Preferences** panel (*Ctrl + Alt +U*) and go to the **System** tab; on the bottom left there is the **Compute Device** item and the slot you can click on to select the device for the rendering: if you have a graphic card that supports this feature, set the GPU instead of the default CPU, and to make this permanent, click on the **Save User Settings** button, or press *Ctrl + U*, and close the panel.

2. Go to the **Render** window under the main **Properties** panel and, in the top **Render** subpanel it is now possible to select the **GPU** item as a rendering device, but only if your graphic card supports **CUDA**.

   This will boost your rendering speed several times, making it possible to significantly increase the rendering samples in the **Sampling** subpanel to reduce or even avoid the noise and keep good rendering times. Using the **GPU**, it's also possible to increase the size of the **X** and **Y Tiles** in the **Performance** subpanel (two or three times the default size is **64**).

   But, not everyone has a **GPU** graphic card yet, and there are also cases where you have to mandatorily use the **CPU** instead (for example, for very big scenes with a lot of geometry that doesn't fit inside the somewhat limited **RAM** of a graphic card).

   In such cases, there are things you can do to try to obtain faster and better quality render results:

3. Select the **Light_key** lamp and in the **Node Editor** window add a **Light_Falloff** node (*Shift + A | Color | Light Falloff*); connect its **Linear** output to the **Strength** input socket of the **Emission** node, set the **Strength** to **1000.000** and the **Smooth** value to **1.000**.

4. Click on the color box of the **Emission** node and change the color to **R 0.800, G 0.800, B 0.650**.

5. Go to the **Render** window and in the **Sampling** subpanel set the **Samples** to **200** or a higher value both for **Render** and **Preview**, to reduce the noise as much as possible.

6. Set the **Clamp Direct** and the **Clamp Indirect** values to **3.00** or **4.00** or even higher (they are set to **0.00** by default); when possible, it is better to leave the **Clamp Direct** item at **0.00** or use values higher then **2.00**, otherwise you could get weird effects in the texturing.

7. In the **Light Path** subpanel, disable both the **Reflective Caustics** and the **Refractive Caustics** items (unless you really need to have caustics in your render) and set the **Filter Glossy** value to **4.00 – 6.00**.

8. In some cases, it won't be possible to totally eliminate the noise or the fireflies; but, because we are going to render an animation, that is several frames in sequence, at least we can make the noise less noticeable and more *natural* looking: go back to the **Sampling** subpanel and click on the **Seed** slot to type #frame. This creates an automated driver that takes the seed value from the current frame number, in order to have different noise at every frame.

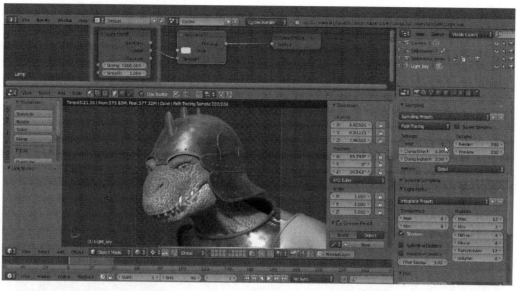

The Light Falloff node for the Lamps, the Seed driver for the noise, the Caustics items and the Filter Glossy value

See also

▸ http://www.blender.org/manual/render/cycles/reducing_noise.html

▸ http://www.blender.org/manual/render/cycles/settings/index.html

▸ http://www.blender.org/manual/render/cycles/gpu_rendering.html

▸ http://www.blender.org/manual/render/workflows/animations.html

▸ http://www.blender.org/manual/render/blender_render/performance.html

▸ A list of supported GPU graphic cards for Cycles can be found at https://developer.nvidia.com/cuda-gpus

Compositing the render layers

We have seen that the rendering in the **Cycles Render** engine is quite slow but of very good quality, while the scanline **Blender Render** engine is faster but with a lower quality.

Thanks to the Blender integrated **Compositor** and to the **render layers**, it is possible to mix separated and different passes of both the renderers, obtaining a compromise between quality and speed, for example, by over-imposing the **glossy pass** obtained in **Cycles** on the **diffuse pass** obtained in **BI**, and so on.

Getting ready

To mix different passes obtained from the two render engines, we must first apply some modification to the materials of the library file:

1. Start Blender and load the Gidiosaurus_shaders_Blender_Internal.blend file, which is the file we used as library for the proxified character and the walkcycle action.

2. In the **Outliner** select the **Gidiosaurus_lowres** item, be sure to be in the **BI** scene and go to the **Material** window; select the first material slot, that is the Material_skin_UOVO slot, and in the **Node Editor** window select the **SPEC** material node:

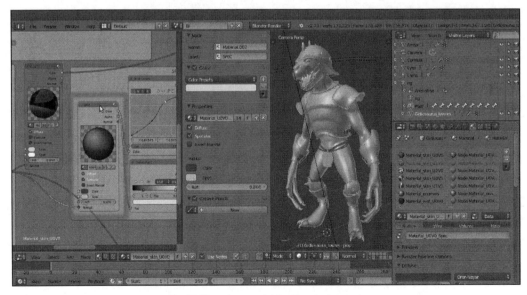

The SPEC node material for Blender Internal

3. Go to the **Texture** window and click on the *Enable/Disable each texture* checkbox at the right side of the **env_refl_skin** texture slot to disable it:

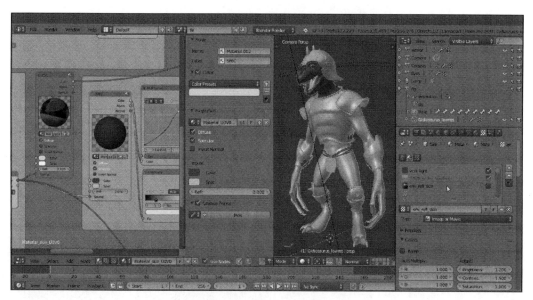

The disabled "env_refl_skin" texture slot

4. Go back to the **Node Editor** window and select the **COL** node (this seems to be important, because of a bug in the **Blender Internal** working method with linked material nodes and the **despgraph** that doesn't update the materials and, therefore, doesn't render the diffuse color correctly).

5. Select the second `Material_skin_U1V0` slot, go to the **Node Editor**, select the **SPEC** material node, disable the `env_refl_skin` texture slot, select the **COL** material node, then go to the third `Material_skin_U2V0` slot, and so on: repeat for all the materials of the **Gidiosaurus** and of the **Armor** objects (for the **Armor** disable the `env_refl_armor` slots on both the **SPEC1** and **SPEC2** material nodes; **Eyes** and **Corneas** have the real ray-tracing mirror enabled and don't need any textures disabled).

    Remember to leave the **COL** material nodes as the selected ones in the **Node Editor** window, or the diffuse color won't show in the rendering.

6. Go to the **Object** window and, in the **Relations** subpanel, assign a different **Pass Index** to the objects: assign **1** to the **Gidiosaurus_lowres** object, **2** to the **Armor** object, **3** to the **Eyes**, and **4** to the **Corneas**.

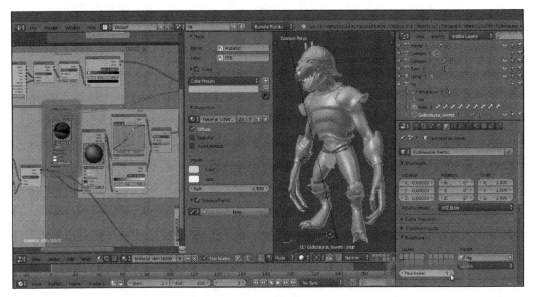

The Pass Index slot

7. Save the file as Gidiosaurus_shaders_library.blend.

    Now, because up to this point we have used the Gidiosaurus_shaders_Blender_Internal.blend file as library source, we must now substitute the file to be rendered the path to the new library source:

8. Open the Gidiosaurus_render.blend file and go to the **Outliner** window: click on the *Type of information to display* button at the top to switch from **Visible Layers** to **Blender File**; expand the panel to find the **//Gidiosaurus_shaders_Blender_Internal.blend** item at the bottom:

The library path in the Outliner

9. Double left-click on the item and rename it as **//Gidiosaurus_shaders_library.blend**, then press *Enter* to confirm and save the file:

The modified library path

10. Press *Ctrl + O | Enter* to re-load the file: now all the assets should be linked from the new library file.

11. Save the file as `Gidiosaurus_compositing.blend`.

How to do it...

At this point we must prepare the passes for the two scenes that will be used later, as elements to be mixed through a third new *compositing* scene:

1. Click on the **+** icon button to the right side of the *Scene datablock* button in the main top header and, in the **New Scene** pop-up menu, select the **New** item: this creates a new **empty** scene; rename it **comp**.

2. Click on the *Screen datablock* button to the left and switch to the **Compositing** screen, then click again on the *Scene datablock* button and re-select the newly created **comp** scene.

3. Click again on the *Screen datablock* button and go back to the **Default** screen; go to the *Scene datablock* button and select either the **BI** or the **Cycles** scene.

4. From now on, it's enough to select the **Compositing** layout in the *Screen datablock* button to switch automatically to the **comp** scene, and the **Default** layout to go to the **BI** or the **Cycles** scene (depending on the last one selected).

5. Go to the **Default** screen and, if not already loaded, load the **BI** scene; in the main **Properties** panel, go to the **Render Layers** window (the second icon button from the left in the *Type of active data to display and edit* windows row).

6. Double click on the **RenderLayer** name in the first slot at the top of the subpanel to rename it as **BI**. Go down to the **Passes** subpanel, disable the **Z** pass item and enable **Object Index**; then go to the second column and enable the **Shadow** pass but then also click on the *Exclude shadow pass from combined* button to its extreme right side: do the same also for the **Emit**, the **AO** and the **Indirect** passes.

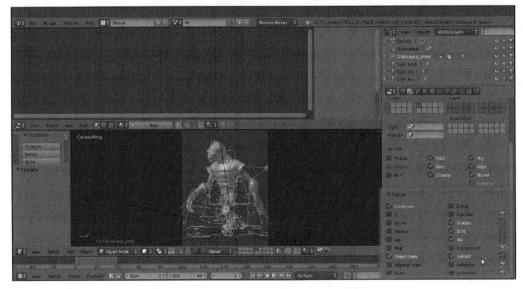

The Passes setting for the Blender Render scene

7. Click again on the *Scene datablock* button in the top main header and switch to the **Cycles** scene.

8. Double click on the **RenderLayer** name in the first slot at the top of the subpanel to rename it as **Cycles**, then disable the **Combined** and the **Z** passes, leave the already enabled **Shadow** pass as it is and enable also the **Glossy Direct**, **Indirect** and **Color** passes:

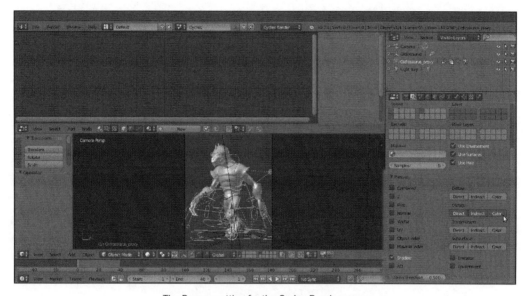

The Passes setting for the Cycles Render scene

9. Now click on the *Screen datablock* button and switch to the **Compositing** screen.

10. In the **Node Editor** window toolbar, go to the *Node tree type to display and edit* row, click on the *Compositing nodes* button (the middle one) and then enable the **Use Nodes** checkbox:

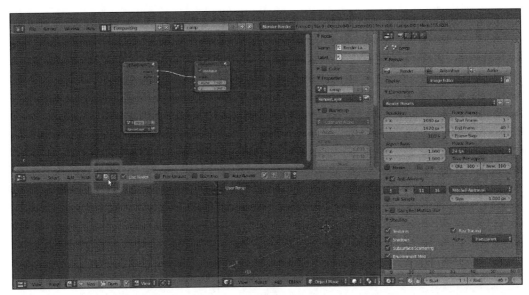

The Compositing nodes button

Two compositing nodes are automatically added in the **Node Editor** window: a **RenderLayers** node connected to a **Composite** node.

11. Click on the double arrows to the side of the *Scene datablock* on the **RenderLayers** node to switch from the **comp** scene to the **BI** scene, and, if necessary, in the bottom **Layer** button, select the name of the respective render layer (that we labeled as **BI** again; it shouldn't be necessary to select it, by the way, because it's the only render layer in the scene).

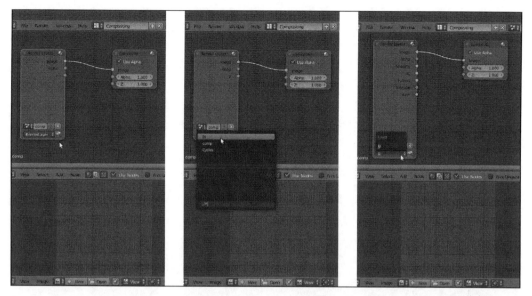

The render layer selector in the RenderLayers node and the output sockets to the Composite node

12. Press *Shift + D* to duplicate the **RenderLayers** node and repeat the procedure in the duplicated one, this time selecting the **Cycles** scene datablock and render layer:

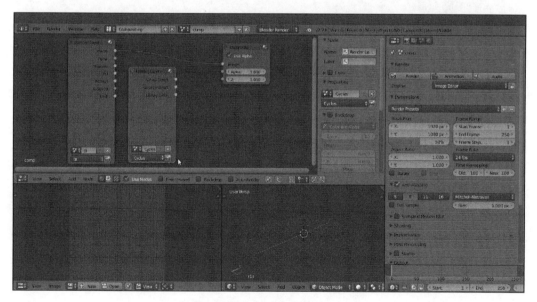

The duplicated RenderLayers node

13. Put the mouse pointer inside the **Node Editor** window and press *Shift + A* to add a **Viewer** node (*Shift + A* | **Output** | **Viewer**); connect the **Image** output of the **BI RenderLayers** node also to the **Image** input socket of the **Viewer** node.

14. Move down and switch the **3D View** window with another **UV/Image Editor** window.

15. In the left image editor window, click on the double arrows to the left of the image datablock (*Browse Image to be linked*) and from the pop-up menu select the **Viewer Node** item.

16. In the right image editor window, instead, select the **Render Result** item.

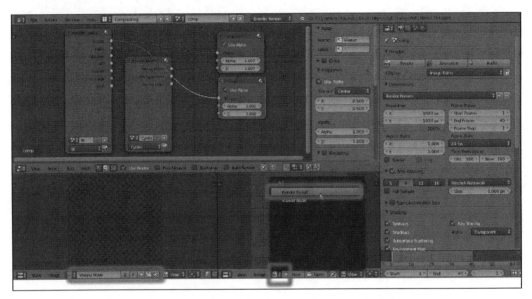

The Viewer node and the Viewer Node and Render Result windows

17. At this point, press *F12* or click on the **Render** button inside the main **Properties** panel to start the rendering.

    When the rendering is done, only the **BI** render is visible in the two bottom editor windows, because at the moment it's the only **RenderLayers** node connected to the **Viewer** and to the **Composite** nodes.

18. Connect the **Glossy Direct** output of the **Cycles RenderLayers** node to the **Image** input socket of the **Viewer** node to see the single *specularity* pass in the left **UV/ Image Editor**.

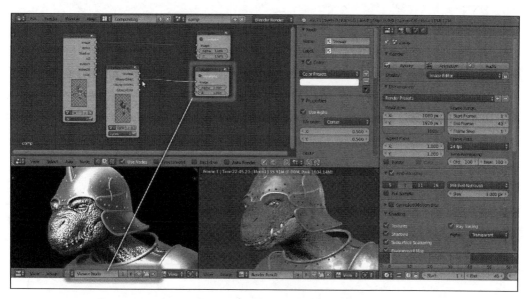

The Glossy Direct pass visualized in the Viewer Node window

In fact, we could also add more than one **Viewer** node to the **Node Editor** window and use them to visualize the different passes of **RenderLayers**, by connecting each pass output to each **Viewer** node; the last selected **Viewer** node will be the one visualized in the **Viewer Node** bottom window.

19. Enable the **Auto Render** item at the extreme right side on the **Node Editor** window toolbar, add a **Mix** node (*Shift + A | Color | Mix*) and paste it between the **Image** output of the **BI RenderLayers** node and the **Image** input socket of the **Composite** node; change the **Blend Type** to **Add** and then connect the **Glossy Direct** output of the **Cycles RenderLayers** node to its second **Image** input socket. Set the **Fac** value to **0.050** and label it as **Add_GLOSSY_01**.

20. If you want, also connect the output of the **Add_GLOSSY_01** node to the
Viewer node.

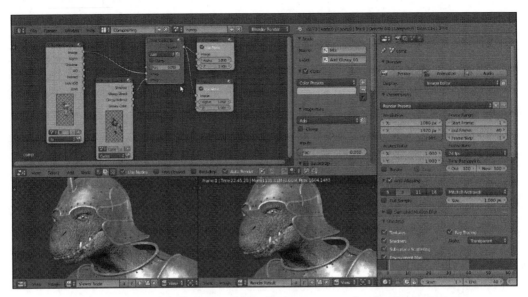

The Glossy pass, rendered in Cycles, added to the Image pass rendered in Blender Internal;
note that now the armor looks too lightened

21. Press *Shift + D* to duplicate the **Add_GLOSSY_01** node, label it as **Add_GLOSSY_02**
and paste it between the **Add_GLOSSY_01** and the **Composite** nodes; connect the
Glossy_Indirect output of the **Cycles RenderLayers** node to the second **Image** input
socket of the **Add_GLOSSY_02** node.

22. Press *Shift + D* to duplicate the **Add_GLOSSY_01** node again, label it as **Mul_
GLOSSY**, change the **Blend Type** to **Multiply** and set the **Fac** value back to **1.000**;
connect the output of the **Add_GLOSSY_02** node to its first **Image** input socket and
the **Glossy_Direct** output of the **Cycles RenderLayers** node to its second **Image** input
socket. Connect the output of the **Mul_GLOSSY** node to the **Composite** node.

23. Add an **ID Mask** node (*Shift + A* | **Converter** | **ID Mask**), set the **Index** value to **2** and connect the **IndexOB** output of the **BI RenderLayers** node to the **ID value** input socket, then connect the **Alpha** output to the **Fac** input socket of the **Mul_GLOSSY** node; enable the **Anti-Aliasing** item.

24. For the moment, disconnect the **Viewer** node.

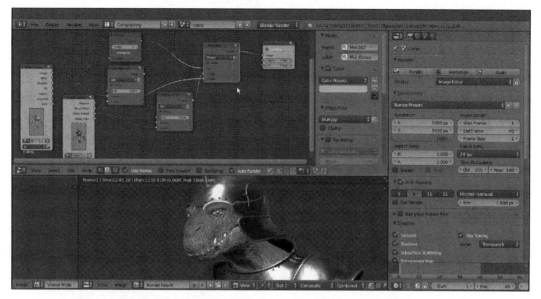

The IndexOB output used as a mask for the addition of the Glossy pass only on the character's skin

25. Press *Shift + D* to duplicate a new **Mix** node, label it as **Mix_GLOSSY** and set the **Blend Type** to **Mix** and the **Fac** value to **0.900**; connect the output of the **Add_GLOSSY_02** node to the first **Image** input socket and the output of the **Mul_GLOSSY** node to the second **Image** input socket.

26. Press *Shift + D* to duplicate another **Mix** node, label it as **Color_GLOSSY** and set the **Blend Type** to **Color** and the **Fac** to **0.050**; connect the output of the **Mix_GLOSSY** node to the first **Image** input socket and the **Glossy_color** output of the **Cycles RenderLayers** node to the second **Image** input socket:

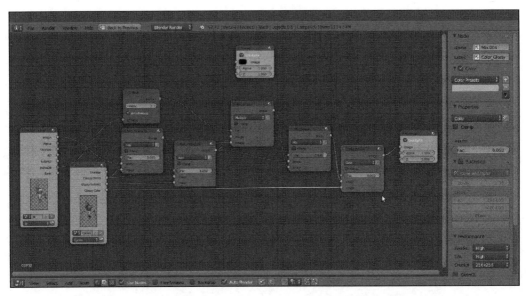

Adding more compositing nodes to re-build the separately rendered Glossy passes

27. Add a new **Mix** node (*Shift + A* | **Color** | **Mix**) right after the **Color_GLOSSY** one, label it as **Mul_AO**, set the **Blend Type** to **Multiply** and connect the **AO** output of the **BI RenderLayers** node to the second **Image** input socket; set the **Fac** to **0.500**.

28. Add a new **Mix** node (*Shift + A* | **Color** | **Mix**), label it as **SHADOWS**, change the **Blend Type** to **Multiply** and set the **Fac** value to **1.000**; connect the **Shadow** output of the **BI RenderLayers** node to its first **Image** input socket and the **Shadow** output of the **Cycles RenderLayers** node to the second **Image** input socket.

29. Press *Shift + D* to duplicate the **Mul_AO** node and label it as **Mul_SHADOWS**; paste it right behind the **Mul_AO** node and set the **Fac** value slider to **1.000**.

30. Connect the output of the **SHADOWS** node to the second **Image** input socket of the **Mul_SHADOWS** node.

31. Add a new **Mix** node (*Shift + A* | **Color** | **Mix**), label it as **Color_SHADOWS** and paste it right behind the **SHADOWS** node; set the **Blend Type** to **Add**, the **Fac** to **0.500** and enable the **Clamp** item: set the color of the second **Image** socket to **R 0.640**, **G 0.780**, **B 1.000**.

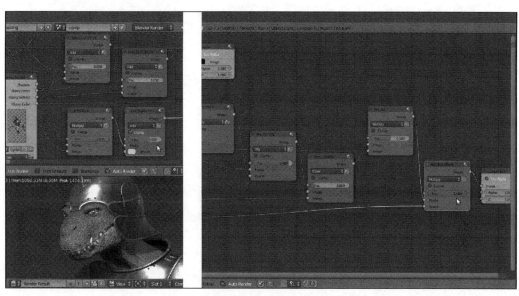

Multiplying and coloring the shadow pass

32. Add a new **Mix** node (*Shift + A* | **Color** | **Mix**) right behind the **Mul_SHADOWS** one, label it as **Add_INDIRECT**; set the **Blend Type** to **Add**, the **Fac** to **0.300** and connect the **Indirect** output of the **BI RenderLayers** to the second **Image** input socket.

33. Repeat the previous step but label the node as **Add EMIT**, set the **Fac** value to **1.000** and connect the **Emit** output of the **BI RenderLayers** node to the second **Image** input socket.

34. Add one more **Mix** node (*Shift + A* | **Color** | **Mix**), label it as **Col_EMIT**, set the **Blend Type** to **Multiply** and paste it behind the **Add_EMIT** node; set the color of the second **Image** socket to **R 1.000**, **G 0.542**, **B 0.073**.

35. Add a new **ID Mask** node (*Shift + A* | **Converter** | **ID Mask**), connect the **IndexOB** output of the **BI RenderLayers** node to the **ID value** socket, set the **Index** value to **3** and connect its **Alpha** output to the **Fac** input socket of the **Col_EMIT** node.

Coloring and adding the eyes

36. Connect the output of the **Col_EMIT** also to the **Image** input socket of the **Viewer** node:

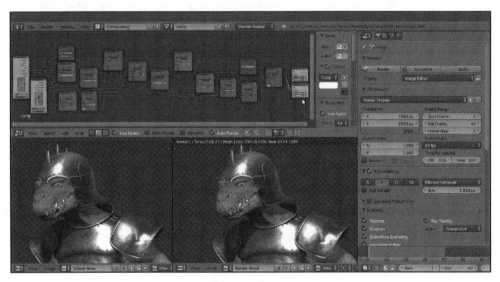

The completed compositing network

37. Save the file.

How it works...

In the *Getting ready* section:

▸ From step 2 to step 5 we disabled the **env_refl_skin** and the **env_refl_armor** texture slots in all the material nodes of the **BI** shaders; in fact, because we are going to add the **Cycles** reflection on the **BI** diffuse, we don't need to fake the environment reflection on the character and on the armor surfaces anymore.

▸ In step 6 we assigned a different **Index Pass** number to each one of the objects; this is useful to later *separate* the objects in the **Compositor** for particular effects (in our case we only needed the armor **Index Pass** number, but it's a good habit to give index passes to all the objects for any eventuality).

▸ At step 7 we saved the file with a new name, and at steps 8 and 9 we changed, in the file to be rendered, the path to the new library file.

In the *How to do it...* section:

▸ From step 1 to step 3 we added a new empty scene, **comp**, to the blend file, linked to the **Compositing** screen layout and to be used for the compositing.

▸ In fact, in the **comp** scene, all the **compositing** nodes are connected together so as to recreate the best possible rendering look of the **Gidiosaurus**, using the different passes from the different **BI** and **Cycles** scenes through the **render layers**.

▸ From step 4 to step 7 we enabled the required passes in the **Render layers** windows of both the **BI** and **Cycles** scenes; note that basically we set an almost complete *only-diffuse* render in **Blender Internal** (besides the **Indirect**, **Ambient Occlusion** and **Emit** passes, subtracted from the total render and separately outputted), while we set the **Glossy** passes in the **Cycles** engine.

▸ From step 8 to step 15 we set up the **RenderLayers** nodes, the **Viewer** and the **Composite** nodes.

The **RenderLayers** node outputs the rendering of a particular scene also delivering the enabled passes for that scene, through the **Render Layer** setup.

The **Compositing** node is the mandatory final output node and must always be connected as the last step of the compositing chain.

The **Viewer** node, instead, is optional but always used anyway to visualize the different steps of the compositing itself.

▸ At step 16 we started the rendering; Blender starts to render the **BI** and the **Cycles** scenes using the settings setup for each scene (and not the settings of the **comp** scene, which are true only for the compositing).

▸ From step 18 to step 34 we mixed the different passes together. Basically, we used the same approach that we have seen in the creation of the shaders, that is, by decomposing the final result into the different components; then, we obtained the diffuse from the **Blender Internal** engine because it's quite fast for that, and the glossy component from the **Cycles** render engine for the same reasons, and then we re-mixed them. The **Subsurface Scattering** pass is actually rendered together at the diffuse component in **BI** and is delivered through the **Combined** (**Image**) pass.

▸ The **Mix_GLOSSY** node added at step 24 is to tweak the strength of the multiplied **Glossy Direct** pass; we couldn't use the **Fac** value, in this case, because it was already used by the **ID Mask** output to *isolate*, thanks to the **Object Index**, the **Armor** from the rest of the render.

▸ With the **Col_SHADOWS** node at step 30 we obtained two goals: first, we set the dark intensity of the shadows to **0.500** and, second, we gave them a bluish coloration.

▸ The emission pass for the eyes has been added to the rendering through the same technique used to multiply the glossy only on the **Armor**, that is, by an **ID Mask** node and the **Object Index**.

See also

▸ http://www.blender.org/manual/render/blender_render/layers.html

▸ http://www.blender.org/manual/render/blender_render/passes.html

▸ http://www.blender.org/manual/render/post_process/layers.html

▸ http://www.blender.org/manual/composite_nodes/index.html

Index

Thank you for buying
Blender 3D Cookbook

About Packt Publishing

Packt, pronounced 'packed', published its first book, *Mastering phpMyAdmin for Effective MySQL Management*, in April 2004, and subsequently continued to specialize in publishing highly focused books on specific technologies and solutions.

Our books and publications share the experiences of your fellow IT professionals in adapting and customizing today's systems, applications, and frameworks. Our solution-based books give you the knowledge and power to customize the software and technologies you're using to get the job done. Packt books are more specific and less general than the IT books you have seen in the past. Our unique business model allows us to bring you more focused information, giving you more of what you need to know, and less of what you don't.

Packt is a modern yet unique publishing company that focuses on producing quality, cutting-edge books for communities of developers, administrators, and newbies alike. For more information, please visit our website at www.packtpub.com.

About Packt Open Source

In 2010, Packt launched two new brands, Packt Open Source and Packt Enterprise, in order to continue its focus on specialization. This book is part of the Packt open source brand, home to books published on software built around open source licenses, and offering information to anybody from advanced developers to budding web designers. The Open Source brand also runs Packt's open source Royalty Scheme, by which Packt gives a royalty to each open source project about whose software a book is sold.

Writing for Packt

We welcome all inquiries from people who are interested in authoring. Book proposals should be sent to author@packtpub.com. If your book idea is still at an early stage and you would like to discuss it first before writing a formal book proposal, then please contact us; one of our commissioning editors will get in touch with you.

We're not just looking for published authors; if you have strong technical skills but no writing experience, our experienced editors can help you develop a writing career, or simply get some additional reward for your expertise.

Blender 2.6 Cycles: Materials and Textures Cookbook

ISBN: 978-1-78216-130-1   Paperback: 280 pages

Over 40 recipes to help you create stunning materials and textures using the Cycles rendering engine with Blender

1. Create naturalistic materials and textures - such as rock, snow, and ice - using Cycles.

2. Learn Cycle's node-based material system.

3. Get to grips with the powerful Cycles rendering engine.

Blender 3D Basics Beginner's Guide
Second Edition

ISBN: 978-1-78398-490-9   Paperback: 526 pages

A quick and easy-to-use guide to create 3D modeling and animation using Blender 2.7

1. Explore Blender's unique user interface and unlock Blender's powerful suite of modeling and animation tools.

2. Learn how to use Blender, and also the principles that make animation, lighting, and camera work come alive.

3. Start with the basics and build your skills through a coordinated series of projects to create a complex world.

Please check **www.PacktPub.com** for information on our titles

Blender Cycles: Materials and Textures Cookbook
Third Edition

ISBN: 978-1-78439-993-1   Paperback: 400 pages

Over 40 practical recipes to create stunning materials and textures using the Cycles rendering engine with Blender

1. Create realistic material shaders by understanding the fundamentals of material creation in Cycles.

2. Quickly make impressive projects production-ready using the Blender rendering engine.

3. Discover step-by-step material recipes with complete diagrams of nodes.

Blender Cycles: Lighting and Rendering Cookbook

ISBN: 978-1-78216-460-9   Paperback: 274 pages

Over 50 recipes to help your master the Lighting and Rendering model using the Blender Cycles engine

1. Get acquainted with the lighting and rendering concepts of the Blender Cycles engine.

2. Learn the concepts behind nodes shader system and get the best out of Cycles in any situation.

3. Packed with illustrations and a lot of tips and tricks to make your scenes come to life.

Please check **www.PacktPub.com** for information on our titles